The Writing on the Wall

Mesopotamian Civilizations

General Editor
Jerrold S. Cooper, *Johns Hopkins University*

Editorial Board

The Writing on the Wall

Studies in the Architectural Context of
Late Assyrian Palace Inscriptions

John Malcolm Russell

Eisenbrauns
Winona Lake, Indiana
1999

Library of Congress Cataloging-in-Publication Data

Russell, John Malcolm.
    The writing on the wall : studies in the architectural context of late
Assyrian palace inscriptions / John Malcolm Russell.
        p.   cm. — (Mesopotamian civilizations ; 9)
    Includes bibliographical references and index.
    ISBN 0-931464-95-1 (alk. paper)
    1. Cuneiform inscriptions, Akkadian.   2. Palaces—Iraq—Assyria.
I. Title. II. Series.
PJ3835.R87   1999
492'.1—dc21
                          99-14100
                          CIP

to Irene Winter

who made this possible

Contents

Acknowledgments

I am grateful to many people for helping to propel this project along. Foremost among these is David Stronach, who invited me to join the University of California, Berkeley excavation at Nineveh in 1989 and 1990, and once there, made sure that we saw every Assyrian site reachable from Mosul. Daily excavation in Sennacherib's palace at Nineveh and two trips to Nimrud allowed me the opportunity to examine the Assyrian palace inscriptions at those sites. I am likewise grateful to Manhal Jabur for showing me his excavations on the Nebi Yunus arsenal. Samuel Paley and Richard Sobolewski shared photographs and notes from the Polish excavations at Nimrud; Sam also helped me identify inscriptions on Assurnasirpal thresholds from my sometimes-indistinct slides.

Much of my "excavation" outside Iraq was conducted in the archives of the Department of Western Asiatic Antiquities at the British Museum. There, John Curtis, Julian Reade, Dominique Collon, and Christopher Walker were very generous with their time and expertise. In New York, Prudence Harper, Kim Benzel, and Cynthia Wilder of the Ancient Near East Department of the Metropolitan Museum assisted me with archives and photographs relating to their Assurnasirpal sculptures.

I am also very grateful to Jerrold Cooper, Pamela Gerardi, Irene Winter, and two anonymous readers, who read preliminary drafts of the manuscript and made countless valuable comments and suggestions. Likewise, to Grant Frame, who checked the Akkadian, and to my students Elizabeth Hendrix and Ellen Belcher, who read the final chapter following a semester of intensive study of Nimrud and Khorsabad in my seminar at Columbia University. Also at Columbia University, I received invaluable assistance from Gregory Schmitz on photographic questions, from Kathleen Davis of Interlibrary Loan, from my research assistants Aimée Bessire and Erhmei Yuan, and from my late friend and colleague Edith Porada, who insisted that "God lives in the details."

Preface

This book has two goals: (1) to serve as a handbook to the architectural context and publication history of Neo-Assyrian palace inscriptions, and (2) to propose by example various types of future studies that might be based on this material. These dual goals result largely from the fact that the book was written in response to a variety of needs and opportunities, over a period of years. It first appeared over a decade ago as a chapter of my dissertation on Sennacherib's "Palace Without Rival" in Nineveh. My goal then was to investigate the locations of inscriptions in the palaces of Sennacherib's predecessors, and then to see how Sennacherib retained or modified their conventions. It seemed that the best way to accomplish this would be, on the one hand, to look at the corpus of inscriptions of each king and pull out the ones from documented palatial contexts, and on the other hand, to examine the excavation reports for the individual palaces in order to determine what inscriptions were found in each.

It soon became clear that assembling the basic information would be no simple matter, in part because palace inscriptions have often been published in composite editions with either minimal or no reference to the provenience of individual exemplars, and in part because most of the palace excavation reports include little specific information on inscriptions. That chapter grew to 160 pages, by which point it was too long and too broad for the dissertation. It did seem to be a potentially useful guide to the original location and publication of a large body of inscriptions, though it raised far more questions than it answered and exposed great lacunae in the publication of the sources. Most of this, however, was not directly relevant to the subject of the dissertation. This "chapter" was therefore radically abridged for the dissertation and further abridged for the published version, with the intention of returning to the original in due course.

The piece sat until 1989, when I spent two seasons excavating in the environs of Sennacherib's palace at Nineveh. During this time I had the opportunity to study many previously excavated unpublished inscriptions in situ and, in particular, a large number of examples in the palaces of Assurnasirpal II at Kalhu and Sennacherib at Nineveh. I decided that this new information could be presented most clearly in the context of the palace inscriptions manuscript.

In 1992, I worked on A. H. Layard's papers in the British Museum and British Library. It soon became clear that there was a treasure trove in Layard's unpublished hand copies of inscriptions from his excavations at Kalhu and Nineveh. While these copies had occasionally been mentioned in the literature, and some of them had been used by Tadmor (1968) and Reade (1985), they had not been the subject of a thorough study, nor had they been fully catalogued. I catalogued the copies and determined that a number of them would add valuable information to the palace inscriptions manuscript, particularly in the chapter on Assurnasirpal II, where the sheer volume of Layard's copies could form the basis for preliminary studies on the distribution of inscription types in the palace. I recognized that the records of the excavation of the Northwest Palace are incomplete and any conclusions I might suggest would therefore be highly provisional, but there seemed little prospect that Assurnasirpal II's inscriptions would be fully published unless we could begin to articulate the types of very important questions that this body of material raises.

Also in 1992, I undertook the completion of this by now rather hybrid manuscript. The last great Assyrian king, Assurbanipal, was still unrepresented, in part because the original manuscript had stopped with Sennacherib and in part because the only substantial body of Assurbanipal palace inscriptions was the epigraphs, or captions, carved on the narrative reliefs. I had long been interested in these epigraphs, but they had recently been the subject of a definitive study by Gerardi (1988), and it seemed that there might be little new to add. One interesting aspect of the epigraphs, however, the clay tablets that contain duplicates of the texts carved on the reliefs, had only been touched on by Gerardi. The relationship between the tablets and the reliefs had not yet been clearly defined, and to do so might throw light on the process by which text becomes image, or image text. Again, this was a substantial digression from the handbook format of the manuscript, but as a further example of the value of studying texts in context, it seemed worth the effort.

The final result should serve a variety of interests and purposes. Embedded in the various studies is the handbook to Assyrian palace inscriptions—their architectural context and publication history—that was my original goal. There is information on a number of unpublished inscriptions and a few short ones are published here for the first time. The book makes a good case for using archival sources alongside original sources in the preparation of inscription editions and studies. And if the book does not definitively demonstrate the processes by which ideas become substance, at least it offers some thoughts on the subject to help keep the ball rolling. This last goal is unquestionably the most important: though this book is not the final word on any of the subjects it addresses, it will serve its purpose if the issues raised in its various studies fuel further work on the relationships between texts and contexts.

Chapter 1

Introduction

Once upon a time, a long time ago, anyone fortunate—or unfortunate—enough to enter the palace of "the king of the world, king of Assyria," would have been surrounded by texts. In the first great Neo-Assyrian palace, the palace of Assurnasirpal II at Kalhu (Nimrud), texts were everywhere. The bull and lion colossi in the major doorways carried texts. The pavement slabs in those doorways, and in every other doorway, carried texts. Every floor slab in every paved room carried a text. And each one of the hundreds of wall slabs, sculptured and plain, carried a text. We can get some intimation of the effect by visiting the Assyrian galleries of the British Museum and the Metropolitan Museum or by walking through the restored remains of the palace at Kalhu (figs. 1 and 2). Even at a glance, it is clear that, whatever else this palace may have been or may have been thought to be, it was also a place to display texts.

Some of the monarchs who succeeded Assurnasirpal also built palaces—Shalmaneser III and Tiglath-pileser III at Kalhu, Sargon II at Dur Sharrukin, Sennacherib and Assurbanipal at Nineveh, among others—and each of these is to a greater or lesser degree also a showplace for texts. Visitors to these palaces would have been surrounded by mysterious texts, mysterious because virtually the only people who could actually read them would have been the court scribes who composed them. Though the content of these texts may have been a mystery, their context was not. There they were—in front, behind, underfoot—waiting to be touched, pondered, perhaps even read. My analogy with the story of Belshazzar (Daniel 5), while historically anachronous—Belshazzar was the son of the last Neo-Babylonian king, and the story would therefore have taken place in Babylon in 539 B.C., 73 years after the fall of Nineveh—is nevertheless suggestive. The writing on the wall in the Assyrian palaces contained important information, including reports of the downfall of kingdoms, but without the help of a scribe, this information would have been as inaccessible to most viewers as was, rather improbably, the Aramaic *mene teqel peres* to Belshazzar's Babylonian-literate "wise" men.

Fig. 1. New York, Metropolitan Museum of Art, view of Assyrian gallery (photo: Metropolitan Museum of Art).

For us today, Assyrian palaces pose mysteries of a different sort. However we may imagine them to have looked, too much of the physical fabric of even the best-preserved palaces has been lost to allow us to say with even the smallest degree of confidence "this *is* the way they looked." Even were we to discover an Assyrian palace miraculously intact in every detail, we still could not say this, since our eyes are not their eyes. What they saw, inside and outside their palaces, was Assyria of the early first millennium B.C., and our eyes can never recapture that sight.

There is no better example of the distance between the Assyrians and ourselves than the palace inscriptions. At first glance, the interpretive balance seems not to be entirely in favor of the Assyrians. In terms of their raw content, Assyrian palace inscriptions have never been more accessible than they are today. In the Assyrian period, in order to see these inscriptions, one first had to get into the palace, for most people probably no small feat. If you then wanted to know what one of these inscriptions said and were not yourself a scribe, you had to find someone who could read it, and people with the required degree of literacy must have been very scarce. Today, by contrast, anyone can pick up a book of Assyrian texts in translation and read them effortlessly, anywhere, at any time. This

Fɪɢ. 2. Kalhu, Northwest Palace of Assurnasirpal II, Room H, view of interior (photo: author).

is a wonderful thing and no one would argue that these texts should be kept deliberately inaccessible today. It is important to keep in mind the obvious, however, which is that they lose a great deal in translation. This is, of course, true in the narrow sense—even a translation from one modern language into another is at best an approximation of the original, since most words and grammatical constructions in one language will not have exact equivalents in another. At least in these cases, though, native speakers of the language being translated can be consulted in order to make the approximation as close as possible. All native Assyrian speakers have been dead for more than 2000 years, and while we believe we understand many Assyrian words, many others remain completely or partially obscure. This is a serious problem, but it is not the main problem.

The main problem also results from translation, but in a broader physical and conceptual sense: translation from the palace of an absolute ruler whose authority derives from his royal predecessors and the gods and who rules by force for economic gain a heterogeneous empire centered on Assyria in the early first millennium B.C. to the pages of a printed book in the democratic secular multinational capitalistic Eurocentric late second millennium A.D. On the pages of a printed book, many Assyrian texts could pass for what we call "history," and the

Fig. 3. Nineveh, Southwest Palace of Sennacherib, Room I, Door *e*, inscribed threshold of Sennacherib, width 211 cm (photo: author).

unwary may assume that the impulse behind the creation of these texts is similar to the impulses behind the writing of modern works of history. This may well be, but the burden of proof is on us, for it is too often forgotten that every Assyrian "historical" inscription was intended to function in a very specific context. This context—whether engraved in stone at the palace doorway, inscribed on a terracotta cylinder buried in the middle of the palace wall, or read aloud—may influence its content and will surely influence the way it is perceived (figs. 3 and 4).

In trying to guess the meanings of uncertain words, we rely heavily on their context. The primary value of the two multi-volume Assyrian dictionaries is not that they tell us what words mean but rather that they show us their contexts. The problem is that, through no fault of their own, they do not enable us to see these contexts sufficiently in context. Meaning is the interface between the physical world and the realm of imagination. In attempting to determine the meaning of an Assyrian palace inscription, we are faced with two general challenges: (1) reconstructing its physical context and (2) experiencing the thought patterns of those who wrote it and those who perceived it. We will probably never be able fully to meet either of these challenges, but we can go as far as we can and hope that it is far enough, hope that the inevitable deficiencies in our

FIG. 4. Nineveh, Southwest Palace of Sennacherib, inscribed cylinder of Sennacherib ("Rassam Cylinder"), baked clay. British Museum, WA 22503 (photo: Trustees of the British Museum).

results will be a matter only of resonance, not fundamental misunderstanding. This book addresses the former challenge, the reconstruction of context, in the conviction that we cannot hope to imagine the impact of a palace inscription without first imagining its physical setting. Unless we try to place our eyes exactly where the Assyrians placed theirs, we cannot hope to begin to see what they saw.

An example will serve both to define the problem and to suggest the possible rewards of a contextual approach. Chapter 4 focuses on a single short text of Adad-nirari III (810–783 B.C.), an extended genealogy, three exemplars of which were found on stone slabs at Kalhu. It is, by Assyriological standards, well published. Cuneiform copies are found in Layard (1851), Rawlinson (1861), and Delitzsch (1912), a transliteration and translation in Schrader (1889) and Grayson (1996), and bibliographies in Borger (1967) and Schramm (1973). Only Layard's publication, however, gives the exact provenience of these inscriptions—pavement slabs in Doors *a* and *b* in Plan IV—and to interpret this reference, one must know that Plan IV is published in Layard (1849a). Plan IV turns out to be a group of rooms that Layard called the "upper chambers," apparently part of a secondary throne room in a palace of Adad-nirari III. The architecture of these rooms and some further rooms associated with them excavated by Loftus (1855) was discussed by Barnett (1957), Reade (1968), Turner (1970), and Postgate and Reade (1976–80). Only Barnett and Postgate/Reade, however, refer to the inscribed slabs, and both wrongly identify them with two related but distinct slabs published by Rawlinson, which probably derive from Loftus's excavations nearby.

Users of the Assyriological literature, therefore, are not made aware that this text was found on thresholds in a palace reception room, while readers of the archaeological literature have no way of knowing the identity and content of the inscriptions. Readers of Layard will readily see the connection between the architecture and inscriptions but may be unaware of the identity of the king, whose name Layard could not read. This lack of attention to context in the Assyriological literature and to content in the archaeological literature is unfortunate, since the inscription is much more interesting in the doorway of a royal reception room than it is in isolation. By itself, it is an unusually extended genealogy that lists a few of Adad-nirari III's predecessors, but in its palatial context, its focus on the previous Adad-nirari, on the Middle Assyrian founder of Kalhu, and on the first Old Assyrian king known from inscribed bricks all serve not only to establish Adad-nirari's authority but also to identify his palace at Kalhu as a legitimate seat of that authority. Furthermore, if the two slabs published by Rawlinson were in fact from Loftus's excavations, and not from Layard's "upper chambers," then this would indicate that the plans of the two excavations represent parts of the same building, and this would give a much fuller idea of the layout of the palace than do the two plans taken separately.

In the study that follows, I have tried to establish the original physical context of every Neo-Assyrian palace inscription I could find and then to suggest types of studies that can exploit the knowledge of physical context. Its final form was influenced by a variety of opportunities and constraints and by a number of choices. The most fundamental choice was to deal only with inscriptions that were incorporated into the physical fabric of palaces—on gateway colossi, thresholds, wall slabs, and the like—since such inscriptions are almost certainly in their intended context. Inscriptions on steles and other movable objects, however interesting they may be and regardless of whether they were found in a palatial context, are omitted, both because they may be in a secondary context and because it is not possible to determine whether they were ever intended for a specific location. For similar reasons, palace inscriptions found loose are omitted, unless their original context can be ascertained with a reasonable degree of certainty.

Another basic choice was to focus on inscriptions that were visible at the time the palace was in use and to omit those on such things as foundation cylinders, door sockets, and foundation deposits. The one exception here is inscriptions carved on the backs of wall slabs; though they would have been hidden after the palace was completed, I found that they are in some cases so closely related to visible texts that to omit them would be to omit evidence basic to an understanding of compositional and decorative sequence. Another choice involves terminology. Throughout this study, I have tried to be consistent in the usage of the terms "text" and "inscription." A "text" is a verbal composition, while an "inscription" is the physical result of replicating all or part of such a text in a durable medium. The only exception to this terminological convention is the "Standard Inscription" of Assurnasirpal II, which I will refer to by its common designation, though it is in fact a "text." In referring to types of texts, "annalistic" denotes a historical text that is arranged chronologically, while "summary" refers to a text that is arranged nonchronologically. The book is organized chronologically, with each chapter devoted to one king. To help establish general contexts, each begins with a brief summary of that king's palace building activity. Within chapters, inscriptions are presented in roughly chronological order according to when they were composed or inscribed. Most of the chapters draw on both published and unpublished data.

Chapter 2, "Assurnasirpal II," deals with inscriptions in six general locations: (1) the backs of wall slabs, (2) the faces of wall slabs, (3) the throne base, (4) doorway colossi, (5) thresholds/doorway pavements, and (6) bronze doors. Much of the material here is new. I have for some time been interested in determining which texts appeared on pavements in doorways in Assurnasirpal's Northwest Palace, and very little has previously been published on the subject. While in Iraq in 1990, I studied most of these pavements *in situ* and my results are given here. The significance of the text on the backs of the wall slabs, which had previously not been recognized as a distinct text, is considered, and the inscriptions on the colossi *in situ* in Assurnasirpal's palace are published for the first time. The "Standard Inscription" on the front of the wall slabs, the throne base inscription, and the inscriptions on the bronze gates from Balawat, all previously published, are analyzed at length and the relationships among the various Northwest Palace inscriptions are explored.

In Chapter 3, "Shalmaneser III," inscriptions on throne bases, a glazed brick wall panel, and thresholds from Fort Shalmaneser, a pair of bull colossi from Kalhu citadel, and a pair of bronze gates from Balawat are considered. While all of this material has previously been published, it is scattered among a variety of sources and has not been collected before. A variety of misconceptions in the literature about the long annalistic inscription on the "Centre Bulls" are also cleared up. Chapter 4, "Adad-nirari III," focuses on a single threshold text of that king, as discussed already briefly above. In Chapter 5, "Tiglath-pileser III," two types of texts on the wall reliefs—annals and epigraphs—are considered. Since these reliefs were found out of context in various places on Kalhu citadel, the annalistic inscription becomes an important tool in reconstructing the number of relief series represented and the sequence of the slabs in each series. Possible reasons are suggested for the use of an annalistic text on these reliefs, in contrast with the summary inscription used in the same context by Assurnasirpal, and the role of epigraphs, which are used on wall reliefs for the first time in this palace, is discussed.

Chapter 6, "Sargon II," presents the numerous and varied inscriptions from Sargon's palace at Dur Sharrukin: from the backs of slabs, doorway colossi, thresholds, the face of the wall slabs, and epigraphs on the wall reliefs. The various types of texts used are identified and characterized, and possible criteria for the selection of different types of texts for different locations are suggested. Chapter 7, "Sennacherib," an area in which I have already published a book (Russell 1991), is an opportunity to offer solutions to several mysteries that had previously eluded me. There is a considerable amount of new material here, particularly in the sections on colossus inscriptions, where my fieldwork at Nineveh and archival work in the British Museum turned up several new texts, and on epigraphs, where the newly discovered original texts of several important epigraphs dealing with palace construction are published, along with my latest thoughts on the reading of a long epigraph in the throne room.

Chapter 8, "Esarhaddon," presents inscriptions from four different palaces worked on by Esarhaddon. Several of these texts have not previously been published. Though none of them are very long, taken together they suggest a chronology for the building of the palaces in which they were found. Chapter 9, "Assurbanipal," is a project that I have long wanted to carry out: a close analysis of the epigraphs and reliefs in Room XXXIII of the Southwest Palace at Nineveh and their relationship to the extensive collections of related epigraphs on clay tablets from Nineveh. The result was, for me, a surprisingly suggestive picture of the planning and execution of a narrative relief cycle and of the role of epigraphs in that process.

Despite the focus here on the work of individual kings, clear chronological patterns can be seen to emerge. The most striking of these is the decrease in the number of palace inscriptions from the palace of Assurnasirpal II, where almost every stone surface carried some sort of text, to that of Assurbanipal, where the only visible inscriptions were brief captions on the wall reliefs. Concurrent with this is a change in the locations favored for inscriptions, from Assurnasirpal's palace, where inscriptions appeared almost everywhere *except* on the carved wall relief surface, to Assurbanipal, where this was the *only* place that inscriptions were carved. Other features that vary through time are the length of inscriptions in particular locations, for example on doorway colossi, and the abrupt truncation of texts to fit a surface, a common feature in Assurnasirpal's palace that occurs only rarely later. Such patterns of change are more fully explored in the conclusions, followed by some preliminary observations on the further utility of this sort of research.

Chapter 2

Assurnasirpal II (883–859 B.C.)

The first of the great decorated Neo-Assyrian palaces was that of Assurnasirpal II in the Assyrian city of Kalhu (modern Nimrud, Xenophon's "Larissa"), located on the east bank of an ancient bed of the Tigris River some 35 kilometers south of Nineveh (modern Mosul) in northern Iraq. This palace was discovered in 1845 by Austin Henry Layard, who excavated at Kalhu in two campaigns, 1845–1847 and 1849–1851. Subsequent excavations in the palace were carried out by Hormuzd Rassam (1853–1854), M. E. L. Mallowan (1949–1957), the Iraq Department of Antiquities and Heritage (1969–present), and Janusz Meuszynski (1974–1976).[1] The monumental task of cataloging the reliefs in each room of the palace was begun by Meuszynski (1981) and continued by Paley and Sobolewski (1987, 1992).

Sometime around his fifth year, Assurnasirpal II moved the chief royal residence and administrative center of his realm from Assur to the Middle Assyrian provincial capital of Kalhu and began rebuilding the city on a massive scale. The largest structure he built there was his palace—called the Northwest Palace by Layard—which filled most of the northwest quarter of the citadel mound (fig. 5). Its excavated area measures 200 meters north-to-south and 120 meters east-to-west. Its southern limit has not yet been determined, and it may have extended farther to the east as well.[2]

Its northern third was a large outer court, entered from the east and surrounded on the north and, probably, east and west sides by offices and storerooms (fig. 6). The south side of the outer court was the throne-room façade (ED), decorated with five pairs of human-headed bull and lion colossi, one pair in each of its three doors, and one pair on each of the two gate towers. Beyond this was the throne room (B) and a smaller inner court (Y), surrounded by large state

1. The bibliography of the excavations is summarized in the excellent survey of the site by Postgate and Reade 1980: 304–7.
2. Postgate and Reade 1980: 311.

Fig. 5. Kalhu, Northwest Palace of Assurnasirpal II, view from the ziggurrat (photo: author).

apartments (G, S, and WG; fig. 7). The walls of all of the rooms in this part of the palace were lined with stone slabs, and most of these were carved in relief with protective deities and images of the king performing rituals. In the throne room and the rooms to the west of the inner court (WG, WH, BB), these subjects were augmented by reliefs showing Assurnasirpal on campaign and hunting. The areas above the wall reliefs were decorated with wall paintings and glazed bricks, but these have survived only in fragments.

The wall reliefs and the inscriptions on them were for the most part well preserved, because the destruction of the palace seems not to have been accompanied by extensive burning. The Iraq Department of Antiquities and Heritage has restored the area of the decorated state apartments as a site museum where visitors may view a large number of reliefs and inscribed slabs in their original context. The largest group of Northwest Palace reliefs outside Iraq is in the British Museum, but the site was extensively mined for reliefs in the 19th century and representative examples, often sawn into pieces to eliminate unsculptured inscribed areas, found their way into a large number of collections.

The throne-room façade and several other major entrances in the palace were decorated with human-headed bull and lion colossi (fig. 8). Apart from their size—the largest were nearly 6 meters in length and height—their most striking feature is their combination in a single figure of two distinct relief im-

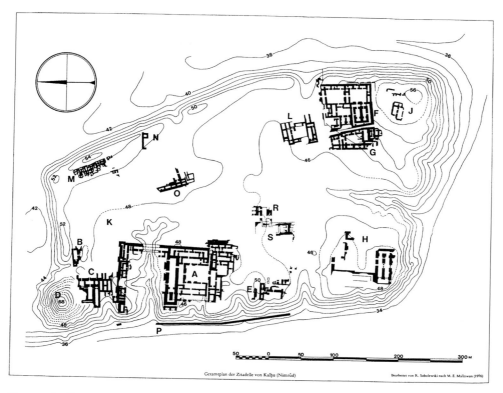

FIG. 6. Kalhu, citadel, general plan. A = Northwest Palace of Assurnasirpal II,
C = Ninurta Temple, E = Upper Chambers of Adad-nirari III, H = Southwest Palace of
Esarhaddon, R = location of Shalmaneser III bulls, S = site of Central Palace of Tiglath-
pileser III. Drawn by Richard Sobolewski (after Meuszynski 1981, plan 1; courtesy R. P.
Sobolewski).

ages: a static frontal view showing two legs, and a striding side view showing four
legs, the result being a five-legged creature. The spaces between the legs and behind the tails of these colossi were carved with a text that identifies the king and
summarizes some of his accomplishments.

The walls at both ends of the throne-room façade were paneled with slabs
carved with images of western foreigners presenting tribute to the king (fig. 9). At
the west end of the façade, these tributaries were shown before an image of the
king, while at the east end, two tribute processions converged on a doorway, beyond which was the enthroned king himself. Carved across the middle of each
slab and on every other wall slab in the palace was a text—usually the so-called
"Standard Inscription"—that gave the name, titles, and epithets of the king, summarized his military achievements, and described the appearance of the palace.

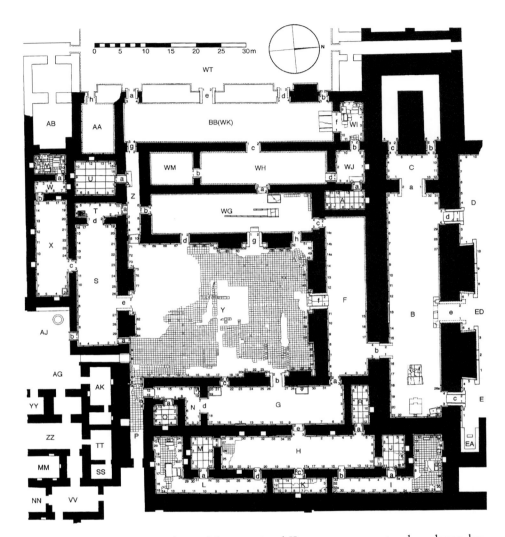

FIG. 7. Kalhu, Northwest Palace of Assurnasirpal II, state apartments, plan, drawn by Richard Sobolewski (adapted from Paley and Sobolewski 1987, plan 2; courtesy R. P. Sobolewski).

The walls of the throne room (B) were also covered with reliefs. Directly opposite the central door of the façade (ED) and at the east end of the room behind the inscribed throne base were niches raised somewhat above floor level, each carved with a similar scene (figs. 10, 11). On both, the images of the king and a winged deity are shown twice, symmetrically flanking a stylized palm tree (called the "sacred tree" in the modern literature). Variations of this motif, which must represent the role of the king in assuring the prosperity of Assyria, are repeated in the palace decoration of later kings. In the corners of the throne room and beside doorways are more images of sacred trees and winged deities. The slabs on the long walls were divided into three unequal registers (fig. 12). The wider upper and lower registers displayed a continuous series of images that are usually termed "narrative," while on the narrower central register, not shown in fig. 12, the Standard Inscription was carved, usually in its entirety, on each slab. All but one of the narrative reliefs from the south wall and a few from the mostly destroyed north wall were brought to the British Museum, though to save weight Layard sawed away the inscribed central register, thereby substantially altering their proportions and effect as an ensemble. Their subject is royal hunts and royal military conquests. Several attempts have been made to identify the cities and regions shown in the military scenes, but because the images carry no written captions and bear no direct relationship to the accompanying Standard Inscription, these efforts remain speculative.[3]

Military conquest and hunts were also the subjects of at least some of the reliefs in the suite of rooms west of the inner courtyard, the walls of which Layard was unable to trace because the reliefs had for the most part been removed for reuse in Esarhaddon's Southwest Palace. A different subject was depicted in Rooms G and H, on the east side of the inner court, where the king, accompanied by attendants, was shown sitting or standing, holding a bowl, engaged in an activity that may most plausibly be identified as pouring libations (fig. 13). The remaining sculptured rooms were all decorated with variations of a single subject: the "sacred tree" flanked by winged deities, some with human heads and others with heads of birds. In most cases these figures are the entire height of the slab, but in Room I the slabs were again divided into registers with the Standard Inscription in the middle (fig. 14). The walls of a number of smaller rooms, and also of Court Y, were paneled with unsculptured slabs. These too carried inscriptions, as did the plain stone pavement slabs that were placed in each of the palace doorways and that covered the floors of bathrooms.

A tremendous number of inscriptions are preserved on the wall slabs, pavement slabs, and doorway colossi in Assurnasirpal's palace—certainly the largest single collection of palace inscriptions now on view. Unfortunately, while most of the texts that form the basis for these inscriptions were published long ago, only a fraction of the individual inscriptions themselves have been published. This is in part because most of the inscriptions are what are usually called "duplicates"—a term that often conceals the fact that even short "duplicates" of the same text may vary from one another in dozens of small but significant ways—and in part because of the expense and time that would have to be invested in order

3. Winter 1981: 15; Winter 1983: 22–23; Reade 1985: 212–13.

Fɪɢ. 8. Kalhu, Northwest Palace of Assurnasirpal II, throne-room façade, Court E, Door c, view (photo: author).

to publish each of these hundreds of inscriptions adequately. Therefore, while the message expressed by the content of these inscriptions is easily accessible in several editions of these texts, the messages implicit in their physical context are only gradually coming to light. Especially in Assurnasirpal's palace, with its hundreds of "duplicate" inscriptions, each having its own set of variants, such contextual analysis has tremendous potential, for in the gap between a body of master texts and a palace full of inscribed stone slabs exist the king, his advisers, and his builders, sculptors, and scribes.

Chronology

In the discussion that follows, major events in Assurnasirpal's reign are used to determine the sequence and date of composition of his palace inscriptions. Unfortunately, the two pivotal events for these purposes—the campaign to Carchemish and the Mediterranean on the one hand and an apparent reference to a campaign to Urartu on the other—cannot be precisely dated. The political history of Assurnasirpal's reign is known almost exclusively from his building inscriptions, the primary function of which was to display prominently the geo-

FIG. 9. Kalhu, Northwest Palace of Assurnasirpal II, Court D, Slab 7, western tributaries, width 214 cm. British Museum, WA 124562 (photo: Trustees of the British Museum).

graphical extent of the king's rule and the variety of his deeds at home and abroad. They are not intended as an annual chronicle, and they pose serious difficulties when used as such. The most extensive "history" of Assurnasirpal's reign is an annalistic text carved on a series of pavement slabs in the Ninurta Temple at Kalhu.[4] This text gives a year-by-year account of campaigns from Assurnasirpal's accession

4. Grayson 1991a: 191–223.

FIG. 10. Kalhu, Northwest Palace of Assurnasirpal II, Room B (throne room), view toward east (photo: author).

FIG. 11. Kalhu, Northwest Palace of Assurnasirpal II, Room B, Slab 23, relief behind throne base, width 423 cm. British Museum, WA 124531 (photo: Trustees of the British Museum).

FIG. 12. Kalhu, Northwest Palace of Assurnasirpal II, Room B, Slabs 17–18 as installed in the British Museum, WA 124536–124539 (photo: author).

FIG. 13. Kalhu, Northwest Palace of Assurnasirpal II, Room G, Slabs 7–8, the king making a wine offering, width 465 cm. Metropolitan Museum 32.143.4, 32.143.6 (photo: Metropolitan Museum of Art, Gift of John D. Rockefeller, Jr., 1932).

FIG. 14. Kalhu, Northwest Palace of Assurnasirpal II, Room I, Slab 30, inscribed wall relief, width 211 cm. Metropolitan Museum 32.143.3 (photo: Metropolitan Museum of Art, Gift of John D. Rockefeller, Jr., 1932).

year (882 B.C.) through his sixth year (878). It then describes three more campaigns, giving the month and day on which each started but omitting the year. The historical portion of the Ninurta Temple annals then concludes with an account of the campaign in the eighteenth year (866); since no further campaigns are mentioned, it seems a reasonable supposition that this text was composed shortly after 866.

The third of the three undated campaigns is the campaign to Carchemish and the Mediterranean, which is also mentioned in all of Assurnasirpal's palace inscriptions. Since all three of these campaigns started out at about the same time of year, it is clear that they took place in three different years. The earliest possible date for the Mediterranean campaign, therefore, would be Assurnasirpal's ninth year (875), assuming that he had continued the pattern of one campaign per year. The year may have been omitted from the Ninurta Temple annals after 878, however, precisely to camouflage the fact that campaigns were no longer annual affairs. If so, then the Mediterranean campaign could have taken place anytime between 875 and 867. The fact that this campaign is mentioned on every inscription in the palace, including those placed in its walls during construction, would seem to favor a date toward the earlier end of the range, but on the basis of present evidence greater certainty eludes us.

The Ninurta Temple annals make no mention of Urartu, but a number of the palace inscriptions do, and it has been suggested that this can be accounted for either by positing a campaign to Urartu after the eighteenth year, or by a change in Assyrian terminology, perhaps reflecting the rise of the kingdom of Urartu late in Assurnasirpal's reign. Assurnasirpal had campaigned in the vicinity of Urartu already in his second and fifth years, though in his annals he refers to the region by its traditional Assyrian name, "the lands Nairi." His later claim that his conquests stretched to Urartu, therefore, could be a different form of reference to these early campaigns. As de Filippi observed, however we interpret the Urartu reference, the texts that contain it probably postdate the Ninurta Temple annals, that is, year 18.[5] With this background, let us now turn to a more detailed look at the palace texts themselves.

Slab Backs

A single text was carved on the backs of many—probably all—of the wall slabs and colossi in Assurnasirpal's Northwest Palace at Kalhu. This is one of the most striking examples of a text that lost its context because of the way in which it was published. There must originally have been hundreds—perhaps more than a thousand—exemplars of this text in the palace, and because of their protected position, turned against the walls, many survived until Layard's day. These were among the first inscriptions he discovered, at first in the unfinished Southwest Palace of Esarhaddon (where the slabs on which they were carved had been reused), and then in the Northwest Palace. His notebook for 1845–47 includes full copies of 31 exemplars and notes on the variants for 6 more, more than for

5. Grayson 1991a: 202–3, 209; Paley 1976: 145–46; de Filippi 1977: 30.

FIG. 15. Kalhu, Northwest Palace of Assurnasirpal II, West Wing (Room WG?), back of corner slab, width 86 cm. British Museum, WA 124557 (photo: Trustees of the British Museum).

any other text.[6] Instead of publishing the full text, however, he submerged it in his comprehensive "Table of Variants" that compares different versions of the "Standard Inscription." Though Layard did not specify the source of any other variants in this table, he made an exception with this text, identifying its most important variants as from "Inscriptions on the backs of Slabs."[7]

Unfortunately, this form of publication was not sufficient to ensure that the text retained its distinctive identity, and in subsequent text editions by other scholars, Layard's references to its location were neglected and the text was presented as just another disembodied variant of the Standard Inscription. Thus LeGac, who published five exemplars of this text on paper casts in the British Museum, gave no information about the origin of the casts, identifying the text simply as "Abridged Version B" of the "Standard Inscription." Likewise, Schramm's study of "Abridged Version B" gave it no provenience, while Grayson's full edition of the text is prefaced only by the statement that it was found on stone slabs originally from the Northwest Palace at Kalhu.[8] Furthermore, the number of ex-

6. Layard, Ms A, 13–29, 37–44, 47–54, 61–62, 70–71, 75–76, 80–81, 84.

7. Layard 1851: pls. 2:1–3:8 (note 4), 5:21–7:29 (note 1), 10:1a–11:6a.

8. LeGac 1907: 166–68; Schramm 1973: 43, "l"; Grayson 1991a: 301–2. The broken beginning of the text as published by LeGac and Grayson is preserved in Layard 1851: 10:1a–2a.

Fig. 16. Kalhu, Northwest Palace of Assurnasirpal II, palace wall foundation tablet, width 23 cm. British Museum, WA 90979 (photo: Trustees of the British Museum).

emplars of the text available for study was dramatically reduced by the nineteenth century practice of sawing off the backs of wall slabs to reduce weight before shipping them to museums and collectors. In consequence, to my knowledge, only two of Assurnasirpal's sculptured slabs now outside Iraq retain the inscription on their backs; if any others survive, the practice of building the slabs into the walls where they are displayed makes their back surfaces inaccessible.

As far as I am able to determine, the first scholar after Layard to mention a text on the backs of the palace wall slabs was de Filippi, who referred to an unpublished fragmentary example on the back of a corner slab (British Museum, WA 124557–124558; fig. 15).[9] Though she did not publish this inscription, and though she evidently did not recognize that it was the same as the text published by LeGac and Layard, she nevertheless made useful observations on its chronological and formal relationship to other Assurnasirpal II palace texts. More recently, Reade identified

9. De Filippi 1977: 32 n. 137, 39 n. 191, 40–41, 43. WA 124557–124558 is a corner slab from the West Wing, perhaps WG-1, that shows the king in his chariot in a mountainous landscape (Paley and Sobolewski 1987: 77; Budge 1914: pl. 25.1, 25.2). Megan Cifarelli and John MacGinnis checked the inscription on the back for me, for which I am very grateful, and confirmed that the text is carved once on each half of the slab. The top of the text is lost on both fragments. On 124557 it begins *la-qe-e* and on 124558 KUR *la-qe-e* (Grayson 1991a: 302:4) and continues on both to the end of the text.

LeGac's "Abridged Version B" as the text on the backs of Assurnasirpal II wall slabs and gave a full list of the Layard copies.[10] Reade's valuable contribution seems not to have received the attention it deserves, however, as neither his observations concerning its usual location nor Layard's numerous hand copies were mentioned in the most recent publication of this text.[11] Therefore a summary of de Filippi's and Reade's observations, together with my own based on my study of Layard's copies, seems to be in order.

The text, which I will call the "Slab Back Text," is closely related to another one, also published by LeGac as an abridged variant of the Standard Inscription, again without commenting on its origin.[12] This latter text was also published by King, who based his edition on three small (ca. 23 × 23 cm) limestone tablets in the British Museum (fig. 16).[13] The text on these is the same as an "inscription on small tablet," variants from which were copied by Layard and published in his "Table of Variants" to the Standard Inscription.[14] Presumably this is one of the British Museum examples. The text was republished by Grayson, who included three additional exemplars—from the dimensions given, it appears that one of these (21 × 21 cm) is also a small tablet, while the other two (61 × 41 cm and 76 × 46 cm) are larger slabs, perhaps paving stones.[15] This text appears also on the back of at least one wall relief slab, a narrow slab from the west wing of Assurnasirpal's palace carved with a lion hunt.[16]

Though the provenience of these tablets is not given in their various publications, Ellis convincingly suggested that they are the small alabaster tablets that Layard discovered in the debris behind fallen colossus B-*d*-2 and sent to the British Museum. Concerning their original location, Layard reported that they appeared "to have been built up inside the walls above the slabs, or to have been placed behind the slabs themselves, and this conjecture was confirmed by subsequent discoveries."[17] These subsequent discoveries were in the wall of Room G, south of Door *b*: "Whilst clearing away the wall of unbaked bricks, I discovered

10. Reade 1985: 205.

11. Grayson 1991a: 301–302.

12. LeGac 1907: 68 lower.

13. King and Budge 1902: 173–76. The tablets are British Museum, WA 90979, 90982 (not 90984; see Grayson 1991a: 300), and 92985.

14. Layard, Ms A, p. 117; Layard 1851: 11:1b–2b. Layard's published version accidentally(?) omitted part of the ending, from *ù* DAGAL.MEŠ to *eš-šú-te* (included in Layard 1851: 10:1a–2a).

15. Grayson 1991a: 299–300.

16. British Museum, WA 124579 (Paley and Sobolewski 1987: 76, "WFL-14." My thanks to Megan Cifarelli and John MacGinnis, who identified and collated this text for me. They reported that it varies from Grayson's edition of this text (1991a: 300) only in its omission of *mal-ki*.MEŠ *šá kib-rat* 4-*ta* at the end of line 5.

17. Layard 1849a: vol. 1, 115–16; Ellis 1968: 100, 193.

two small tablets, similar to those previously dug out in chamber B. On both sides they had the usual standard inscription, and they had evidently been placed where found, when the foundations of the palace were laid."[18] Because of the apparent find-spot of these tablets, I will refer to the text on them as the "Palace Wall Foundation Text." Both texts are given in full here in Table 2.1 (pp. 24–28).

The Slab Back Text and Palace Wall Foundation Text are very similar to one another. Both begin with a genealogy and basic titulary, continue with a brief summary of the geographic extent of the king's conquests, and conclude with a short account of the rebuilding of Kalhu. There are, however, two significant variants. The most substantial is the concluding passage that describes the building of the new palace. In both texts, this begins "The city Calah I took in hand for renovation." The Palace Wall Foundation Text continues: "I cleared away the old ruin hill (and) dug down to water level; I sank (the foundation pit) down to a depth of 120 layers of brick. I founded therein my royal palace."[19] By contrast, in the equivalent location in the Slab Back Text we find: "I founded therein my lordly palace. I built this palace for the eternal admiration of rulers and princes (and) decorated it in a splendid fashion. I made (replicas of) all beasts of mountains and seas in white limestone and *parūtu*-alabaster (and) stationed (them) in its doorways."[20]

The other significant variant is that some exemplars of the Slab Back Text include three royal epithets—"marvelous shepherd, fearless in battle, mighty flood-tide which has no opponent"—that are absent from the Palace Wall Foundation Text.[21] It is not possible to tell from the small number of unprovenienced exemplars published by LeGac and Grayson whether there is any pattern to the distribution of slabs with and without these three titles, but such patterns are discernible in the much larger number of provenienced exemplars copied by Layard. Relatively few of Layard's copies were made from slabs found *in situ* in the Northwest Palace, but their distribution is nonetheless suggestive: the two inscriptions from the backs of colossi from Room B and apparently all three on the backs of slabs from Room A had the three additional titles, while the single example from Room C or G omitted them.[22] Of less value because they were found in a secondary context, but still of interest, is the distribution of the two variants of this text on slabs found reused in Esarhaddon's Southwest Palace at Kalhu. The three titles in question were omitted from the following slabs [text continues on p. 28]:[23]

18. Layard 1849a: vol. 2, 91.
19. Grayson 1991a: 300:23–27.
20. Grayson 1991a: 302:8–10.
21. LeGac 1907: 166:2–3, and n. 5. Grayson 1991a: 301:2–302:3 and footnote.
22. Layard, Ms A, pp. 70–71, 75–76, 80–81, 84. The room of the example on p. 76 is uncertain; I read Layard's note to say Room "C", while Reade read "G" (Reade 1985: 205).
23. Layard, Ms A, pp. 13–15, 19–20, 22–23, 37–42, 54, 62.

Table 2.1. Comparison of Texts on Stone Tablets in the Palace Walls, on the Backs of Wall Slabs, and on the Fronts of Wall Slabs

Palace Wall Foundation Text	*Slab Back Text*	*Standard Inscription*
Palace of Assurnasirpal, great king,	Palace of Assurnasirpal, great king,	Palace of Assurnasirpal, vice-regent of Assur, chosen of the gods Enlil and Dagan, destructive weapon of the great gods,
strong king, king of the universe, king of Assyria, son of Tukulti-Ninurta, great king, strong king, king of the universe, king of Assyria, son of Adad-narari, great king, strong king, king of the universe, king of Assyria; valiant man who acts with the support of Assur, his lord, and has no rival among the princes of the four quarters,	strong king, king of the universe, king of Assyria, son of Tukulti-Ninurta, great king, strong king, king of the universe, king of Assyria, son of Adad-narari, great king, strong king, king of the universe, king of Assyria; valiant man who acts with the support of Assur, his lord, and has no rival among the princes of the four quarters,	strong king, king of the universe, king of Assyria, son of Tukulti-Ninurta, great king, strong king, king of the universe, king of Assyria, son of Adad-narari, great king, strong king, king of the universe, king of Assyria; valiant man who acts with the support of Assur, his lord, and has no rival among the princes of the four quarters,
	marvelous shepherd, fearless in battle, mighty flood-tide which has no opponent,	marvelous shepherd, fearless in battle, mighty flood-tide which has no opponent,
		the king who subdues those insubordinate to him, he who rules all peoples, strong male who treads upon the necks of his foes, trampler of all enemies, he who breaks up the forces of the rebellious, the king who acts with the support of the great gods, his lords, and has conquered all lands, gained dominion over all

Source: Grayson 1991a: 275–76, 300–302. Quoted courtesy of the University of Toronto Press.

Table 2.1. Comparison of Texts on Stone Tablets in the Palace Walls, on the Backs of Wall Slabs, and on the Fronts of Wall Slabs

Palace Wall Foundation Text	Slab Back Text	Standard Inscription
		the highlands and received their tribute, capturer of hostages, he who is victorious over all countries. When Assur, the lord who called me by name (and) made my sovereignty supreme, placed his merciless weapon in my lordly arms, I felled with the sword the extensive troops of the Lullumu in battle. With the help of the gods Shamash and Adad, the gods my supporters, I thundered like the god Adad, the devastator, against the troops of the lands Nairi, Habhu, the Shubaru, and the land Nirbu;
the king who subdued (the territory stretching) from the opposite bank of the Tigris to Mount Lebanon and the Great Sea, the entire land Laqu, (and) the land Suhu including the city Rapiqu. He conquered from the source of the River Subnat	the king who subdued (the territory stretching) from the opposite bank of the Tigris to Mount Lebanon and the Great Sea, the entire land Laqu, (and) the land Suhu including the city Rapiqu. He conquered from the source of the River Subnat	the king who subdued (the territory stretching) from the opposite bank of the Tigris to Mount Lebanon and the Great Sea, the entire land Laqu, (and) the land Suhu including the city Rapiqu. He conquered from the source of the River Subnat
to the interior of the land Nirbu.	to the interior of the land Nirbu.	to the land Urartu.
I brought within the boundaries of my land (the territory stretching) from the passes of Mount Kirruru to the land	I brought within the boundaries of my land (the territory stretching) from the passes of Mount Kirruru to the land	I brought within the boundaries of my land (the territory stretching) from the passes of Mount Kirruru to the land

Table 2.1. Comparison of Texts on Stone Tablets in the Palace Walls, on the Backs of Wall Slabs, and on the Fronts of Wall Slabs

Palace Wall Foundation Text	Slab Back Text	Standard Inscription
Gilzanu, from the opposite bank of the Lower Zab to the city Til-Bari which is upstream from the land	Gilzanu, from the opposite bank of the Lower Zab to the city Til-Bari which is upstream from the land	Gilzanu, from the opposite bank of the Lower Zab to the city Til-Bari which is upstream from the land
Zaban, from the city Til-sha-Abtani to the city Til-sha-Zabdani, (and) the cities Hirimu (and) Harutu (which are) fortresses of Karduniash.	Zaban, from the city Til-sha-Abtani to the city Til-sha-Zabdani, (and) the cities Hirimu (and) Harutu (which are) fortresses of Karduniash.	Zaban, from the city Til-sha-Abtani to the city Til-sha-Zabdani, (and) the cities Hirimu (and) Harutu (which are) fortresses of Karduniash.
Finally, I have gained dominion over the entire extensive lands Nairi.	Finally, I have gained dominion over the entire extensive lands Nairi.	I accounted (the people) from the passes of Mount Babitu to Mount Hashmar as people of my land. In the lands over which I gained dominion I always appointed my governors. They performed servitude.
		Assurnasirpal, attentive prince, worshiper of the great gods, ferocious dragon, conqueror of cities and the entire highlands, king of lords, encircler of the obstinate, crowned with splendour, fearless in battle, merciless hero, he who stirs up strife, praise-worthy king, shepherd, protection of the (four) quarters, the king whose command disintegrates mountains and seas, the one who by his lordly conflict has brought under one authority ferocious (and) merciless kings from east to west.

Table 2.1. Comparison of Texts on Stone Tablets in the Palace Walls, on the Backs of Wall Slabs, and on the Fronts of Wall Slabs

Palace Wall Foundation Text	Slab Back Text	Standard Inscription
The city Calah I took in hand for renovation.	The city Calah I took in hand for renovation.	The ancient city Calah which Shalmaneser, king of Assyria, a prince who preceded me, had built— this city had become dilapidated; it lay dormant. I rebuilt this city. I took people which I had conquered from the lands over which I had gained dominion, from the land Suhu, (from) the entire land of Laqu, (from) the city Sirqu which is at the crossing of the Euphrates, (from) the entire land of Zamua, from Bit-Adini and the land Hatti and from Lubarna, the Patinu. I settled (them) therein.
I cleared away the old ruin hill (and) dug down to water level. I sank (the foundation pit) down to a depth of 120 layers of brick.		I cleared away the old ruin hill (and) dug down to water level. I sank (the foundation pit) down to a depth of 120 layers of brick.
I founded therein my royal palace.	I founded therein my lordly palace. I built this palace for the eternal admiration of rulers and princes (and) decorated it in a splendid fashion.	I founded therein a palace of cedar, cypress, *daprānu*-juniper, boxwood, *meskannu*-wood, terebinth, and tamarisk as my royal residence (and) for my lordly leisure for eternity.
	I made (replicas of) all beasts of mountains and seas in white limestone and *parūtu*-alabaster (and) stationed (them) in its doorways.	I made (replicas of) beasts of mountains and seas in white limestone and *parūtu*-alabaster (and) stationed (them) in its doorways.

Table 2.1. Comparison of Texts on Stone Tablets in the Palace Walls, on the Backs of Wall Slabs, and on the Fronts of Wall Slabs

Palace Wall Foundation Text	*Slab Back Text*	*Standard Inscription*
		I decorated it in a splendid fashion; I surrounded it with knobbed nails of bronze. I hung doors of cedar, cypress, *daprānu-*juniper, (and) *meskannu-*wood in its doorways. I took in great quantities and put therein silver, gold, tin, bronze, iron, booty from the lands over which I gained dominion.

> Wall c, Slabs 1, 2
> Wall d, Slab 2
> Wall j, Slabs 3, 6, 7, 8, 9, 10
> Wall jj, Slabs 3, 4

They were present on the following:[24]

> Wall d, Slabs 1, 3
> Wall j, Slabs 1, 2, 4, 5, 11, 12
> Wall k, Slabs 13, 14, 15
> Wall m, Slabs 4, 5, 6, 7, 8, 9
> Wall jj, Slab 2
> Door d, Slabs 1, 2

In addition, the final sign of the inscription on both Slabs 1 and 3 of Wall d is *iz*. All the other examples copied by Layard end with *zi*.

It is readily apparent that these slabs tend to be grouped on the walls of the Southwest Palace according to the presence or absence of the three additional titles. This is precisely the arrangement we would expect, if we assume (a) that groups of adjacent slabs in the Northwest Palace, say in a single room or on a single stretch of wall, were carved with the same version of the Slab Back Text, and (b) that slabs were removed from the walls of Northwest Palace rooms and transported to the Southwest Palace in batches or stacks, with the result that

24. Layard, Ms A, pp. 15–18, 20–22, 24–29, 42–44, 47–53, 61–62.

neighboring slabs from the Northwest Palace tended to be reerected together in the Southwest Palace. According to this hypothesis, Slabs 6–10 of Wall j, for example, would have been from a Northwest Palace room in which the Slab Back Text lacked the three additional titles, while the other slabs on that wall would have been from one or more rooms where the text included these titles.

The differences between the Palace Wall Foundation Text and the Slab Back Text, and between the shorter and longer versions of the Slab Back Text, are of interest on several points. The less advanced stage of construction of the palace in the Palace Wall Foundation Text (palace foundations), as compared with that in the Slab Back Text (sculptural decoration of doorways), suggests that the latter was composed somewhat later than the former. This is the sequence that would be expected on the basis of their apparent original locations as well, since it seems clear that the inclusion of the tablets in the walls preceded the erection of the wall slabs. The significance of these variant endings also derives from their context—the text intended for the palace wall deals with the depth and solidity of its foundation, while that carved on the backs of the slabs and colossi describes the subjects and material of the colossi. Similarly, the absence or presence of the three additional royal epithets in the Slab Back Text suggests that it was carved on the slabs over a period of time, with the shorter version placed on slabs that were erected earlier than slabs that carried the longer version. If so, and if the distribution of inscriptions with and without the three additional titles was not random in the Northwest Palace, but rather grouped according to rooms or walls, then the presence or absence of this variant might provide evidence for the sequence in which rooms in the palace were furnished with wall slabs.

Almost everything in the Slab Back Text and Palace Wall Foundation Text is to be found also in the Standard Inscription as carved on the fronts of the wall relief slabs and in its further expanded form on the colossi. It is misleading, however, to consider these two texts "abridgments" of the Standard Inscription, as did LeGac, or to maintain that either text is "very similar" to the Standard Inscription, as did Grayson.[25] The Standard Inscription is a considerably longer text than the others, with a much expanded titulary and palace-building account and with numerous additional epithets. If we hypothesize that titularies and epithets are expanded over the course of time, though this is by no means certain in all cases, then these features may be taken to suggest that the Standard Inscription was composed after the Palace Wall Foundation Text and the Slab Back Text (Table 2.1). Certainly in this case, this proposed sequence of composition would be consistent with the sequence of construction of the architectural features with which they were associated. The Palace Wall Foundation Text would be the earliest, composed when the walls were built. Next would be the Slab Back Text, inscribed on the backs of the wall slabs before they were lifted into

---

25. LeGac 1907: 165; Grayson 1991a: 301.

place and sculpted. Finally would come the Standard Inscription, carved on the face of the wall slabs, in most cases after images had been carved on them.[26]

The Texts on the Wall Slabs

A horizontal band of text is carved across the middle of each of the decorated and plain wall slabs in Assurnasirpal's Northwest Palace. Where relief slabs are divided into two registers, the inscription is on a raised band between the registers; reliefs in one register have the inscription carved right across the relief decoration (see figs. 13, 14). In either case, the original visual effect was of a continuous band of inscription around the room. In most cases, this is a text known as the "Standard Inscription" and, space permitting, it appeared in its entirety on each wall slab.[27] This single text, repeated over and over, literally surrounds any visitor to the state apartments of the palace. In the throne room, for example, the Standard Inscription was on the reliefs of the outer wall flanking Doors *c* and *d*, on the unsculptured slabs of the inner jamb of these doors, and on each of the relief slabs within the throne room.[28] In addition, the text carved on the doorway

26. King and Budge published a text on three limestone slabs from Kalhu in the British Museum, one of which concludes with the statement that it was deposited "in its wall" (1902: 177–88). Since this is one of only three Kalhu texts that also includes a description of the city wall (the others are the Monolith and Ninurta Temple annals—Grayson 1991a: 223.iii.136, 252.v.10), and since the text does not begin with "Palace of" as is usually the case with Assurnasirpal's palace inscriptions, King concluded that these slabs were intended for the city wall. The text does, however, also include a description of Assurnasirpal's palace. Grayson noted that three other provenienced exemplars were found in the palace and argued that this text must originally have been intended for the palace walls (1991a: 278). All of these were clearly in secondary context, however, two covering a late eighth or seventh century grave and the other in the destruction layer on the floor of the throne room (Wiseman and Wilson 1951: 118, ND 816 and 817; Wiseman 1952: 66, ND 1121; Mallowan 1966: vol. 1, 114–15). Five more exemplars were found stacked against the wall of Room NE 26 in Fort Shalmaneser. It is difficult to account for their presence so far from the palace if they were in fact palace texts, and Mallowan's hypothesis that they had been disinterred in the course of Esarhaddon's work on the city wall in this area seems preferable (Mallowan 1966: vol. 2, 395). Since the city wall seems the most likely location for this text, I have not discussed it here.

27. Text: Layard 1851: pls. 1–11; LeGac 1907: 152–70. Text and transliteration: King and Budge 1902: 212–21. Transliteration and translation: Grayson 1991a: 268–76. Studies: Brinkman 1968: 390–94; Schramm 1973: 39–42; de Filippi 1977; Paley 1976; Winter 1981. The inscription is often legible in photographs of the reliefs (Budge 1914; Paley 1976).

28. Description of inner jambs of Doors *c* and *d* in Layard 1849a: vol. 1, 384.

colossi, throne base, and some thresholds also includes at least part of the text of the Standard Inscription.

The Standard Inscription begins with a section of royal titles and epithets, followed by a summary of the king's conquests, arranged geographically rather than chronologically, followed by another section of epithets. It concludes with an account of the construction of a palace at Kalhu (see Table 2.1). Its relative brevity and the frequency with which it occurred throughout the palace—Grayson listed 406 exemplars[29]—would make it an ideal subject for close analysis of variants for the purpose of clarifying the criteria that governed the selection of different variants of the text for particular locations, the sequence in which the inscriptions were carved in various rooms, and the number of scribes and stone-carvers involved in each stage of the process by which a body of source texts was transformed into a body of engraved inscriptions.

It is a great shame, then, that only a relatively small percentage of the total number of exemplars of the Standard Inscription have been adequately published, and nearly all of these are on sculptured slabs in museums.[30] The pattern was set by Layard, who copied 8 exemplars of the text in full and copied variant passages from 30 others, but published only a single exemplar in full (Room I, Slab 1), followed by a list of unidentified variants.[31] Essentially the same procedure was followed in King's edition of exemplars on sculptures in the British Museum, which gives the sources for neither the primary exemplar nor the selected variants that are listed, and LeGac's edition based on unidentified paper casts in the British Museum, which identifies variants only by cast number.[32]

The two most complete editions of the Standard Inscription to date are those of Paley and de Filippi, both of which give a primary exemplar of the text in full, along with full lists of variants, each identified by slab, from other exemplars.[33] From these editions it is possible to begin to see which variants tend to occur together on a given slab, as well as which ones may be characteristic of particular rooms or dates of composition. Unfortunately for these purposes, the size of their sample—12 reliefs for Paley, 21 for de Filippi—is too small and unrepresentative to serve as a basis for firm conclusions.

29. Grayson 1991a: 268–74.

30. In the case of a large, sharply-engraved monumental inscription such as the Standard Inscription, the best forms of publication are a clear photo, a good hand-copy, or a transliteration, in that order.

31. Layard, Ms A, pp. 89–91 (Room I, Slab 1) and passim; Layard 1851: pls. 1–11 (misidentified as Room A, Slab 1 in his table of contents). In Layard's primary exemplar (1851: pl. 1), either the scribe or Layard got lost at the beginning of line 5 and repeated a group of signs that do not seem to occur in any other exemplar.

32. King and Budge 1902: 212–21; LeGac 1907: 152–70.

33. Paley 1976: 125–44; de Filippi 1977: 4–17.

Now that the monumental task of cataloguing the wall reliefs from the Northwest Palace is nearly complete, such a study is finally possible.[34] Drawing on these catalogs, Grayson was able to utilize 406 exemplars, most of them collated either against the original or photos, for his recent edition of the Standard Inscription.[35] Despite his access to an unprecedented number of exemplars, however, limitations imposed by publication format prevented Grayson from including either transliterations of individual inscriptions or full lists of variants. Only a few major variants were included, without identification of their sources; even some variants that Paley and de Filippi considered to be of potential chronological significance were omitted. Therefore, nearly 150 years after the first exemplars of the Standard Inscription came to light, we still await an edition sufficiently definitive to permit it to be studied in context.

In the absence of that ideal edition, it is nevertheless possible to venture a few observations and hypotheses on the basis of the available material. In his study of exemplars in the Brooklyn Museum, Paley identified two sets of variants that he believed were characteristic of two chronologically successive "types" of Standard Inscription—"Type A" and "Type B"—and de Filippi likewise suggested that certain variants may have chronological significance. The single criterion that defines Types A and B is that Type A gives the northernmost extent of Assurnasirpal's conquests as "to the interior of the land Nirib" (*adi māt Nirib ša bītāni*), while Type B has "to the land Urartu" (*adi māt Urarṭi*).[36] Other variants that may occur consistently are the spellings of the name of the king of Patinu (*Li-bur-na* in Type A, *Lu-bar-na* in Type B) and of the Euphrates (*pu-rat-te* in Type A, A.RAD in Type B).[37]

The difficulty with these definitions of variant "types" of the Standard Inscription is the very small size of the sample for Type A—only four exemplars have been published, some only in small photos, all of them from Room I.[38] Even from this small sample it is clear that some of the variants Paley used to distinguish Types A and B do not occur consistently, notably the supposed omission in Type A of the reference to "palaces of cedar, cypress, and juniper" and of "iron" from the list of goods kept in the palace.[39] Another of Paley's Type A variants,

34. Meuszynski 1981; Paley and Sobolewski 1987; Paley and Sobolewski 1992.
35. Grayson 1991a: 268–76.
36. Grayson 1991a: 275:9 and n. 9; Paley 1976: 129; de Filippi 1977: 6.
37. Grayson 1991a: 276:16–17; Paley 1976: 131; de Filippi 1977: 6.
38. New York, Metropolitan Museum of Art, 32.143.3 (B. P. Mallowan, "Magic and Ritual in the Northwest Palace Reliefs," in *Essays on Near Eastern Art and Archaeology in Honor of Charles Kyrle Wilkinson*, ed. P. O. Harper and H. Pittman [New York, 1983] 34, fig. 2); Brooklyn Museum, 55.146 (Paley 1976: pl. 8 and plate following p. 114); Berlin, Vorderasiatisches Museum, VA 949 (L. Jakob-Rost, *Assyrien: Die Inschriften* [Berlin, 1982] 9–12, fig. 2) and VA 950 (Meuszynski 1975: 53, fig. 16).
39. Paley 1976: 132–33.

the listing of Til-sha-Zabdani before Til-sha-Abtani, seems to occur consistently in Type A inscriptions from Room I, but not in unpublished exemplars from other rooms.[40] Other significant variants that may be independent of the Type A/Type B classification are at the beginning of the inscription, where Assur is occasionally substituted for Ninurta and Adad-nirari's epithets "great king, strong king" are often omitted.[41] Even if such variants do not distinguish Types A and B of the Standard Inscription, they may ultimately be shown to have some chronological or organizational significance.

The small number of Type A inscriptions published may be attributed to the circumstance that the variant "to the interior of the land Nirib" apparently did not occur in any room with sculptured wall slabs other than Room I, and only sculptured slabs were transported to museums. Therefore, if further exemplars of Type A exist, they should still be *in situ* and are most likely unpublished. Reade observed, however, that Layard's notebook contains full copies or variant lists from 38 identified exemplars of the Standard Inscription, and his preliminary analysis of these copies indicated that at least 14 were of Type A inscriptions.[42] I recently looked over these copies myself, noting particularly the Nirib/Urartu variant and the order of Til-sha-Zabdani and Til-sha-Abtani. On the basis of the Nirib/Urartu variant, I classified each inscription as Type A or B, and then combined that data with the list of Type B inscriptions identified by Reade (1985) and the information on inscription type in Paley and Sobolewski (1987) to produce the highly provisional Table 2.2, which shows the distribution of inscription types on wall slabs in the palace. The first column gives the room number followed by the total number of slabs reported in that room, the second column gives the number of these slabs for which the inscription type has actually been identified and the source for this identification, and the third column lists the inscription type itself. The first entry, for example, shows that there were originally 17 single-register relief slabs in Room B, that Reade was able to identify the inscription type on only 4 of these 17 slabs, and that all four of these exemplars were Type B.

A few points are readily apparent from Table 2.2. First, as Reade observed, the Type B Standard Inscription seems to have been the version of choice for sculptured slabs in the palace.[43] The only exception is Room I, where Type B was used alongside Type A and the Palace Wall Foundation Text. Second, as Reade also suggested, Type A seems to have been preferred for unsculptured slabs, though the sample here is smaller and less representative.[44] In Room R, however,

---

40. Paley 1976: 129. The unpublished exemplars are discussed below.

41. Grayson 1991a: 275:1–2.

42. Layard, Ms A; Reade 1985: 205–6. Reade also generously shared with me his copious original notes made from Ms A, for which I am truly grateful.

43. Reade 1985: 206.

44. Reade 1985: 206.

Table 2.2. Inscription Types on Wall Slabs in the Northwest Palace

Room (Total Number of Slabs)	Number of Text Exemplars Identified (Source)	Inscription Type
Single-Register Relief		
B (17)	4 (Reade)	Type B
C (13)	1 (Reade)	Type B
D/E (13)	1 (Reade)	Type B
F (17)	3 (Reade)	Type B
G (31)	8 (Reade)	Type B
H (35)	7 (Reade)	Type B
L (36)	5 (Reade)	Type B
P (4)	3 (Ms A)	Type B
S (29)	4 (Reade, BaF 10)	Type B
T (10)	6 (BaF 10)	Type B
Z (10)	8 (Ms A, BaF 10)	Type B
WJ (11)	1 (Reade)	Type B
N (19)	0	unknown
Two-Register Relief		
B (15)	6 (Ms A)	Type B
I (35)	5 (Ms A, BaF 10)	PWFT
	13 (Ms A, BaF 10)	Type A
	7 (Ms A, BaF 10)	Type B
WM(?) (?)	1 (Reade)	Type B
WG (?)	0	unknown
WI(?) 11	0	unknown
Unsculptured Slabs		
A (13)	4 (Ms A)	Type A
M (12)	1 (Ms A)	Type A
R (12)	1 (Ms A)	PWFT
	2 (Ms A)	Type A
	1 (Ms A)[a]	(Type B?)

Inscription type: Type A = Standard Inscription, Type A; Type B = Standard Inscription, Type B; PWFT = Palace Wall Foundation Text.

Sources: Ms A = Layard, Ms A; Reade = Reade 1985: 206; BaF 10 = Paley and Sobolewski 1987.

a. Room R, Slab 4: I have little confidence in Layard's variant list for this inscription (MS A, p. 98), as it gives only a single small variant.

**Table 2.2. Inscription Types on Wall Slabs
in the Northwest Palace**

Room (Total Number of Slabs)	Number of Text Exemplars Identified (Source)	Inscription Type
V (11)	1 (MS A)	Type A
Y (85)	1 (MS A)	Type B
J (12)	0	unknown
K (14)	0	unknown
O (10)	0	unknown
U (16)	0	unknown
W (9)	0	unknown
X (24)	0	unknown
AA (9+)	0	unknown
BB (1+)	0	unknown

the Palace Wall Foundation Text and, less certainly, Type B were used together with Type A; in Court Y, the single slab for which Layard recorded the text seems to be Type B. Third, of the total number of slabs in each room, the percentage for which there is some record of the inscription varies considerably from room to room and is much higher in sculptured rooms than in unsculptured rooms, mainly because the former contained the slabs brought to museums. This bias could be corrected and the sample of both sculptured and unsculptured slabs greatly enlarged if the inscriptions on all the wall slabs *in situ* were recorded.

It is also clear from Table 2.2 that Room I stands apart from the others, both because it is the only known room decorated with sculptures of apotropaic figures in two registers and because it is the only sculptured room in which the wall slabs carry any text other than Standard Inscription Type B. Since the inscriptions on slabs from Room I are well represented in both Layard's Ms A and in Paley and Sobolewski (1987), I have been able to compile another table, this one showing the distribution of inscription types in Room I alone (see Table 2.3, p. 36).

Though the specific type of Standard Inscription on some slabs in Room I is open to question, the general pattern is clear enough (fig. 17). Type A was the version used on most of the western side of the room, appearing on Slabs 3–4, 7–13, and 16. The two gaps here were filled with narrow slabs—5, 5a, and 6 flanking a doorway, and 14–15 in the northwest corner—that did not have sufficient space for the full Standard Inscription, so a shorter text, the Palace Wall Foundation Text, was substituted and carved in its entirety on each of these narrow slabs. The

Table 2.3. Inscription Types on Wall Slabs in Room I

Slab Number	Inscription	Source
1	Type B	MS A
2	Type B	MS A
3	Type A	MS A
4	Type A	MS A
5	PWFT	MS A, BaF 10
5a	PWFT	BaF 10
6	PWFT	BaF 10
7	Type A	BaF 10
8	Type A	BaF 10
9	Type A	BaF 10
10	Type A	BaF 10
11	Type A	BaF 10
12	Type A	MS A, BaF 10
13	Type A	MS A, BaF 10
14	PWFT	MS A, BaF 10
15	PWFT	MS A, BaF 10
16	Type A	MS A
17	Type B	BaF 10
18	Type B(?)	BaF 10
19	Type B	MS A
20	Type B	BaF 10
21	Type B	MS A, BaF 10
22	Type B(?)	BaF 10
23	Type B(?)	BaF 10
24	Type A(?)	BaF 10
25	Type A	BaF 10

Inscriptions: Type A = Standard Inscription, Type A; Type B = Standard Inscription, Type B; PWFT = Palace Wall Foundation Text.[a]

Sources: Ms A = Layard, Ms A; BaF 10 = Paley and Sobolewski, 1987.

a. On Slabs 18, 22, 23, 24, 26, 27, 28, and 32 the Nirib/Urartu passage was not preserved, so Paley and Sobolewski's attribution was made on the basis of minor variants, usually in the epithet 'mighty' (*dan-nu* = Type A, *dan-ni* = Type B) of Tukulti-Ninurta in line 1. Since I am not certain whether this variant invariably characterizes Types A and B, I have marked such attributions with question marks.

Table 2.3. Inscription Types on Wall Slabs in Room I

Slab Number	Inscription	Source
26	Type A(?)	BaF 10
27	Type B(?)	BaF 10
28	Type B(?)	BaF 10
29	Type A	MS A
30	Type A	BaF 10
31	Type B (truncated)	BaF 10
32a	unknown	BaF 10
32	Type B(?)	BaF 10
33	unknown	BaF 10

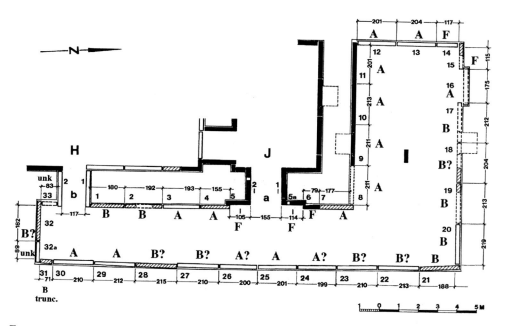

FIG. 17. Kalhu, Northwest Palace of Assurnasirpal II, Room I, distribution of Standard Inscription (source: author, after Paley and Sobolewski 1987, plan 4; courtesy R. P. Sobolewski).

same text was also carved instead of the Standard Inscription in a similar location in Room R, on Slab 1, a narrow unsculptured slab adjacent to the door. This text is not known to have been used on sculptured slabs elsewhere in the palace, however, where the preference instead was to engrave narrow slabs with as much of the Standard Inscription as would fit in the allotted space and then truncate it, often in the middle of a sentence. Indeed, this latter procedure was used in Room I on Slab 31, a narrow slab in the southeast corner, where the Type B Standard Inscription abruptly terminates at Til-sha-Zabdani.[45] The Type B Standard Inscription seems to have been the preferred version for the eastern side of Room I, appearing on all or most of Slabs 1–2, 17–23, 27–28, 31, and 32. Here, however, it alternates with Type A, which was certainly on Slabs 25, 29, and 30, and possibly also on 24 and 26.

The pattern of inscription types in Room I is interesting. As Reade pointed out, while it is certain that the inscription was carved after the sculptures in all of the rooms decorated with a single register of relief, in Room I the carving of the inscriptions and sculptures could well have been independent of one another.[46] If Standard Inscription Type A predates Type B, which seems a reasonable hypothesis, then the pattern of inscriptions in Room I suggests a sequence of events something like the following:[47]

After Assurnasirpal's ninth year (875), but before the introduction of the Urartu reference after his eighteenth year, Standard Inscription Type A was carved on the wall slabs in most or all of the rooms paneled with unsculptured slabs. Presumably while scribes were busy in the unsculptured rooms, sculptors were at work in the rooms that are decorated with reliefs. At this early stage of the proceedings, the scribes were apparently reasonably conscientious about getting the entire text on each slab; I know of no truncated examples of Standard Inscription Type A. On slabs that were too narrow to permit squeezing in the whole Standard Inscription, a shorter alternative text, the Palace Wall Foundation Text, was used, also in its entirety. The inscriptions in the space between the two relief registers on wall slabs in the western part of Room I must also have been carved at that time. The Urartu reference must have been incorporated into the Standard Inscription while slabs in the eastern part of Room I were being inscribed, which would account for the mixture there of Type A and B inscriptions. At this point the decision was apparently made to use the Type B inscription exclusively, truncated where necessary, as on Slab 31. The single-register reliefs in other rooms must have begun to be finished about this time or soon thereafter, and the Type B inscription was then carved, whole or truncated, across the sculpted face of every one of them.

45. Paley and Sobolewski 1987: 28; Grayson 1991a: 275:10.
46. Reade 1985: 206.
47. This is an elaboration of a scenario proposed by Reade 1985: 206–7.

As already mentioned, one of the more remarkable features of the Standard Inscription in the Northwest Palace is the fact that it is often left incomplete, breaking off in mid-sentence, when its allotted space has been filled.[48] In the throne room (B), for example, this truncation occurs on five of the twenty slabs on which the inscription is preserved and probably occurred on at least two others, while in the throne room entrance court (E), two out of three preserved inscriptions are truncated and one other probably was as well.[49]

The width of a slab seems to have been the primary, if not the sole, determinant of how much of the Standard Inscription would be carved on it. Most of the wall slabs in the Northwest Palace are roughly 2.2 meters wide; this seems to have been the standard selected by the masons who dressed the stone.[50] The Standard Inscription is almost never truncated on slabs of this width. In the throne room and most other rooms in the palace, these standard-width slabs are placed along long stretches of wall, usually beginning at a corner. If a break in the wall, such as a doorway or corner, occurs at a distance other than a multiple of the standard slab width, the remaining space is filled with a narrower slab cut especially for it. Since the number of lines available for inscribing is standardized for all the slabs in a given room, and since the inscription almost never runs over onto an adjoining slab, the total amount of space available for inscribing may be significantly less on these narrower slabs, with the result that on them the Standard Inscription is often truncated.[51] This is why the truncated inscriptions seem most often

48. Of 18 reliefs in the British Museum published by Budge, four (nos. 1, 18, 32, 34) have truncated inscriptions (Budge 1914: pls. 10, 27, 39a, 39b). Likewise, of the 12 reliefs in the Brooklyn Museum published by Paley (1976), the inscriptions of nos. 55.145, 55.149, and 55.150 are truncated.

49. *Room B:* The inscription is certainly truncated on Slabs 1, 16, 24, 26, and 32, and probably on 22 and 26a (Meuszynski 1981: 20–25). Meuszynski did not report the amount of the inscription on the narrative slabs (3–11, 17–20, 27–28) because Layard sawed away the text register. Note, however, that the last line—which indicates whether the inscription has been truncated—is often preserved at the top of the lower register. Budge's photographs (1914: pls. 18–24) show that the full inscription was on Slabs 3, 4, 8–11, and 17–20. Meuszynski's photos of Slabs 6 and 28 indicate that the inscription was complete on these slabs also (1975: figs. 2, 17a). The last line is lost on Slabs 5, 7, and 27.

Court E: Slabs 3 (Meuszynski 1975: fig. 22) and 4 (Meuszynski 1981: 34) carried truncated inscriptions, and Slab 2 probably did also. In Court D, however, the inscription was apparently entire on all eight slabs (Meuszynski 1981: 32–33).

50. For slab widths, see Meuszynski 1981; Paley and Sobolewski 1987. This would be four cubits, assuming that Assurnasirpal's cubit was the same length as Sennacherib's, i.e., 55 cm (Powell 1978–90: 474–75; Russell 1991: 79).

51. According to Meuszynski 1981: 12, a single inscription is spread over two slabs only in Room H, Slabs 11–12, and Room L, Slabs 21–22.

to be associated with doorways, corners, and short walls.[52] It also explains why the truncated inscription is most often found on slabs decorated with genies, since these are the figures that flank doorways, while it is apparently never found on narrative slabs or on formal slabs with representations of the king, since these most often occur on the longer stretches of wall. In the rare cases where the representation of the king is carved on a narrow slab, as in Room G, Slab 11, the Standard Inscription is included in its entirety, even though this results in overcrowding of the signs. On Slab 9 of the same room, decorated with a courtier, the inscription is truncated, even though this slab is only 7 cm narrower than Slab 11.[53] Thus, while the truncated version of the Standard Inscription does occur relatively frequently throughout the Northwest Palace, it rarely or never occurs on slabs that might be expected to be of most interest to a viewer, namely, the narrative and formal images of the king, and this is surely by design rather than by accident.

The significance and meaning of the Standard Inscription and its relation to the images carved with it have been discussed by Winter, and I will add only a few observations here.[54] The physical proximity of these images and texts would insure that they would be viewed together, and we must assume that their makers considered this juxtaposition to be significant. For a nonliterate viewer, the content of the text would be immaterial, but its connotations and context would insure that certain messages would be transmitted nonetheless. Among the things connoted by the palace inscriptions are authority, as evidenced by the resources and influence required to have the means to compose such texts and have them engraved in stone, and power, derived from the enormous quantities of information at the disposal of the one who controls the scribes. In terms of physical context, the Standard Inscription was sandwiched between narrative images of the king's conquests or was carved across images of the king performing various ceremonial functions—images whose basic message of power and authority would be clear to any viewer. For the nonliterate viewer, then, the connotations of the texts, power and authority evidenced by the control of writing, complement their context, accompanying images that evidence power and authority through control of the military and exercise of state ritual.[55]

This is very much the way the Standard Inscription would have functioned for a literate audience as well. One of the more interesting aspects of the juxtaposition of this text with these images is that the text "explains" little about the images, nor do the images really "illustrate" the text. The images appear for the

52. Note that in Room C, which had short walls, every preserved example of the Standard Inscription is truncated (Meuszynski 1981: 28–30).

53. Meuszynski 1981: 45–46; illustrated in Stearns 1961: pl. 5.

54. Winter 1981: 18, 21–22, n. 18.

55. On the function of these inscriptions for illiterates, see Russell 1991: 8–10.

most part to deal with specific events and procedures, while the text, except for the portion devoted to the palace-building account, deals with abstracts and generalities. It is true that some of these abstracts seem to find a sort of concrete expression in some of the images, but making this equation requires the reading of the images at the same abstract, nonliteral level as the text.[56] To be sure, this abstract level is a legitimate reading of the images, but so too is the literal reading, and it is at this level that the text provides no help.

Thus, for the literate viewer as for the nonliterate, the Standard Inscription complements, rather than duplicates, the images. For the literate viewer the abstracts denoted by the text help to focus the abstracts connoted by the images, but these abstracts are implicit in the images and are readily perceptible to a nonliterate as well. To be sure, the literate viewer would derive more information from the text than would the nonliterate, but the basic message of royal power and authority remains the same for both, and consequently the message conveyed through the interaction of text and image is essentially the same for both audiences.

There is, however, one passage in the Standard Inscription that *does* have an exact visual counterpart. This passage, at the end of the text, describes the appearance of Assurnasirpal's palace.[57] Its visual equivalent, interestingly, is not to be found in the accompanying reliefs, but rather in their context, the palace itself, the physical presence of which would have been a tangible affirmation of the truth and accuracy of the building account, suggesting by association the veracity of the remainder of the text as well.

The Throne-Base Text

A single text was used on Assurnasirpal's throne base, on all but one of the inscribed colossi, and on some of the thresholds in his Northwest Palace at Kalhu. The only preserved monument that contains the full text is the inscribed throne base from the east end of Room B, the principal throne room (fig. 18). This object was first uncovered by Layard, who published the part of the inscription that diverges from the Standard Inscription. His manuscript copy is more complete, but also lists only variants for the part that duplicates the Standard Inscription. It was reexcavated in 1951 and transferred to the Mosul Museum as ND 1122. A comparison of Layard's published version of the text with Postgate's transliteration made from the original reveals that Layard's published copy is a hybrid text: the line divisions in his lines 1–8 do not follow those of the original,

56. Winter 1981: 21.
57. Grayson 1991a: 276:14–22.

and he sometimes substituted variants for the signs actually on the slab. Layard's published copy was edited by LeGac, together with eleven paper casts in the British Museum of portions of the text. Though LeGac did not identify the source of any of the squeezes, his notes of variants for his E. 107 (lines 1–49), E. 87 (lines 18–49), and E. 86 (lines 44–62) and the large amount of text on each suggest that these were squeezes respectively of the first, middle, and final parts of the inscription, made from the throne base itself. The need for three partial squeezes of the slab can be attributed to its large size (247 × 336 cm) and to the presence of a step on its surface that disrupts lines 44–49.[58]

The beginning of this text, which I will call the "Throne-Base Text," is identical to the first two-thirds of the Standard Inscription, that is, titles and epithets of the king followed by a summary of the king's conquests, arranged geographically rather than chronologically, followed by another section of epithets.[59] At this point the Throne-Base Text diverges from the Standard Inscription, a section being inserted that begins with yet more royal epithets and continues with accounts of a campaign to the Mediterranean, the breeding and hunting of animals, and a campaign against Carchemish.[60] The Throne-Base Text concludes with the remaining third of the Standard Inscription, recounting the building of a palace at Kalhu.[61]

The Throne-Base Text seems to have been developed as a standard text, much like the Standard Inscription, to be reproduced in locations having an area too large for the Standard Inscription alone to fill, such as the throne base, colossi, and some of the larger thresholds. The text includes all of what is probably the final version of the Standard Inscription and, like it, places the northern limit of Assurnasirpal's conquests as "the land of Urartu" instead of "the interior of the land Nirib," as found in Room I.[62]

The Throne-Base Text augments the Standard Inscription by inserting further passages of two types. The first is a type characteristic of the annals of early ninth-century Neo-Assyrian kings. This example records a campaign to the Mediterranean and Carchemish. Grayson has characterized this type of military display as "a show of strength," the purpose of which was to collect tribute without military engagement. The two passages used here are excerpted from a more

---

58. Original discovery: Layard 1849a: vol. 2, 133–34 Layard's published version: Layard 1851: pls. 43–45. Layard's manuscript copy: Ms A, pp. 73–75. Reexcavation: Wiseman 1952: 66. Transliteration: Postgate 1973: no. 267. Transliteration and translation: Grayson 1991a: 223–28 and microfiche 372–93, "Ex. 1". Paper casts: LeGac 1907: xviii, 172–79. Location of step: Postgate 1973: 240.

59. Grayson 1991a: 224:1–225:21.

60. Grayson 1991a: 225:21–227:51.

61. Grayson 1991a: 227:52–228:62.

62. Grayson 1991a: 225:13, 275:9 and note to line 9; Paley 1976: 153:no. 24.

FIG. 18. Kalhu, Northwest Palace of Assurnasirpal II, Room B, throne base, 247 × 336 × 36.5 cm. Mosul Museum, acc. no. 1 (photo: author).

complete account of this campaign preserved in the Ninurta Temple Annals: in the Throne-Base Text, the Carchemish campaign account was abridged somewhat, while the Mediterranean part was used almost verbatim. In the Throne-Base Text, however, the order of the two episodes is reversed from their actual chronological order and they are separated by the account of hunting and breeding of exotic animals, with the result that any sense of continuity between the two, either chronological or narrative, is lost. The two episodes are thereby transformed from parts of a continuous story into independent displays of royal power.[63]

The other type of passage incorporated into the Throne-Base Text describes the formation of herds of wild beasts and the hunting of these animals. This type

63. "Show of strength": Grayson 1991a: 145, 153:105–154:119 (Adad-nirari II), 173:41–178:127 (Tukulti-Ninurta II). Throne-Base Text: Grayson 1991a: 226:25–31 (Mediterranean), 227:43–51 (Carchemish). Ninurta Temple Annals: Grayson 1991a: 216:56–218:77 (Carchemish), 218:84–219:88 (Mediterranean). This campaign dates between 875 and 867 B.C. (Schramm 1973: 31).

of passage first appears in the annals of Tiglath-pileser I (1114–1076 B.C.) and occurs occasionally thereafter. Its only parallel in Assurnasirpal II's other inscriptions, save for a very brief hunting account in the annals, is in the so-called "Banquet Stele," which was carved to commemorate the construction and dedication of the Northwest Palace.[64]

Thus the Throne-Base Text is somewhat broader in scope than the Standard Inscription alone. To the Standard Inscription's affirmation of the divine source and great geographical extent of the king's authority, it adds relatively extensive references to the king's ability to exact tribute, and to his role as shepherd. Both of these themes are particularly appropriate to the throne room. The references to peaceful collection of tribute in the inscriptions of the throne base and throne-room colossi complement the carved images of tribute bearers that are shown approaching throne-room Doors c and d on courtyard façade ED.[65] These verbal and visual messages emphasize the voluntary giving of tribute as symbol of the universal recognition of the authority of the Assyrian king.

Likewise, the references to herds of diverse wild beasts probably indicate more than mere zoological curiosity. The royal epithet *rē'û* ('shepherd') appears twice in the relatively brief span of the Standard Inscription.[66] The animals listed in the Throne-Base Text came from all parts of the empire and beyond, some as tribute, others captured on hunting expeditions. Indeed, the arrival of some of these animals (apes) is shown on slab D-7 of the throne-room façade.[67] Assurnasirpal II explicitly states that he displayed herds of these animals "to all the people of my land."[68] Viewing these animals, his subjects would be reminded in a very direct way of the king's role as shepherd, and may well have seen in these heterogeneous animals from diverse regions, brought together in the capital and cared for by the king of the realm, a metaphor for the various peoples of the empire, united and protected by that same authority. The text carved on Assurnasirpal's throne base, then, complements the images and other texts in and about the throne room, emphasizing both general and specific attributes of the king.

---

64. List of hunting and animal breeding accounts: Grayson 1991a: 7–8. Throne-Base Text: Grayson 1991a: 226:31–227:42. Ninurta Temple Annals: Grayson 1991a: 215:48–216:49. Banquet Stele: Grayson 1991a: 291:84–292:101. Because of their inclusion of Urartu in the list of conquered territories, de Filippi (1977: 37, 45) argued that the Standard Inscription, Throne-Base Text, and "Banquet Stele" were composed at about the same time and in that order, sometime after Assurnasirpal's 18th regnal year.

65. Meuszynski 1981: Taf. 5, 6, plan 2.

66. Grayson 1991a: 275:2, 276:13.

67. Meuszynski 1981: Taf. 5; Budge 1914: pl. 28.

68. Grayson 1991a: 226:37–38.

Colossus Inscriptions

The same text that was on Assurnasirpal's throne base was also used on all but one of the inscribed colossi in his Northwest Palace at Kalhu. According to Layard, this text appeared "on Bulls and Lions at Entrances *a*, *c*, and *d*, Chamber B; Entrances *b*, *c* [actually *e*] and *f*, Chamber Y [i.e., G-*b*, S-*e*, and F-*f*]; and Entrance *a*, Chamber BB." It was also found on the colossi on the throne-room façade and in Door *b*, Room B. It is not clear how many of these colossi Layard actually used in compiling the variants listed in his published edition of the Throne-Base Text: he apparently did not copy any of the inscriptions on colossi B-*b*-1, D-*o*, E-6, F-*f*-1, F-*f*-2, and S-*e*-1. Among the paper casts in the British Museum were single columns of F-*f*-2 and S-*e*-1, however, and these may already have been available to Layard when he was preparing his edition of the text. Eight of these paper casts made from colossi were published by LeGac, though only one (E. 85) was actually labeled as a bull inscription, without giving its original location. I have been able to determine the source of all but one of these casts (E. 12) and have included this information in the notes to each colossus.[69]

The inscriptions on the colossi are not carved across the modeled portions of the figures, as they are in the case of single-register relief slabs in the same palace, but rather are arranged in four columns, placed in the three empty spaces between the legs and in the area beneath the wing behind the tail (see fig. 83). These inscriptions run from left to right; on a colossus facing left, the inscription begins between the forelegs, while on one facing right, it begins beneath the wing at the back.[70] A curious feature is that no effort has been made to fit the entire Throne-Base Text onto any of the known colossi, nor is the text usually tailored to the space at hand. Rather, all the inscriptions are carved with roughly the same line spacing and character size; when the space is filled, the inscription terminates abruptly, often in the middle of a sentence.

Details of each colossus are given in Catalog 1. To summarize, of the nine pairs of colossi for which we have some record of the inscription, none of them carried the complete Throne-Base Text. Only on B-*d*-1, F-*f*-2, S-*e*-1, and BB-*a*-2 does the inscription conclude at a natural break in the text. On B-*c*-2, B-*d*-2, D-*o*, E-6, F-*f*-1, G-*b*-1, S-*e*-2, and BB-*a*-1, it terminates at the end of a sentence, but in the middle of a section. On B-*a*-1, B-*a*-2, B-*b*-1, B-*c*-1, and G-*b*-2, it ends in the middle of a sentence. On B-*b*-2, the inscription is cut off in the middle of a place name. In addition, at the end of Column iii, the G-*b*-2 inscription is interrupted in the middle of a sentence, skips a section of text, and then resumes at

---

69. Layard 1851: pl. 45; LeGac 1907: iv, xviii, 172–79. LeGac's "E. 12" may belong to a pavement slab, because it does not seem to fit any of the colossi.

70. An exception is G-*b*-2 (see Catalog 1).

the beginning of a new section with Column iv. Similarly, in BB-*a*-2, most of one sentence was omitted in the transition between Columns ii and iii.

King suggested that, in cases where the text breaks off in the middle, it "was probably continued on a neighbouring slab," but it is hard to imagine where these slabs might have been located and how Layard could have overlooked them in compiling his copy of the text.[71] With only one exception (G-*b*-2), these inscriptions are always arranged from left to right. If the inscription were concluded on an adjacent slab, then we should look for this part of the inscription in front of a colossus facing right, and to the rear of a colossus facing left. In the case of B-*a*-1, a lion facing right, the inscription would be expected to be carried over to Slab 32 in the throne room. But there we find, not the conclusion of the Throne-Base Text, but rather the first half of the Standard Inscription, another example of a standard text repeated only in part and breaking off in mid-sentence.[72] The cases of the inscribed colossi of throne-room Doors *c* and *d* are similar. The inscriptions on B-*c*-2 and B-*d*-2, which face right, should be continued on Court D, Slab 4, and Court E, Slab 3, but in fact Court D, Slab 4 contains only the Standard Inscription, this time in full, while Court E, Slab 3 displayed the Standard Inscription, again truncated.[73] The slabs contiguous to the rears of B-*c*-1 and B-*d*-1, the left-facing colossi from the same doors, were also inscribed with the Standard Inscription.[74] The same holds true for the other palace colossi as well.

Paley and Sobolewski suggested that the Throne-Base Text was concluded on the backs of the colossi, that is, on the side against the wall, and there would be a parallel for this in Shalmaneser III's "Centre Bulls" (discussed later).[75] Layard copied the inscriptions on the backs of B-*b*-2 and B-*d*-2, however, and B-*b*-1 and B-*b*-2 are now on display with their inscribed backs visible. In all three cases, the

---

71. King and Budge 1902: 198 n. 12; 199 n. 2. Grayson (1991a: 223) repeated this suggestion.

72. According to Meuszynski (1981: 25:B-32), the inscription on Slab 32 runs through *ina* KUR.KUR.MEŠ ('in the lands'; Grayson 1991a: 276:11), part way through the Standard Inscription. For B-*a*-2, the lion facing left in the same door, the text should be continued on Slab 1 of Room C, but this cannot be determined because the inscribed part of this slab is lost (Meuszynski 1975: 67, fig. 25.

73. Court D, Slab 4: Meuszynski 1981: 33:D-4. Court E, Slab 3: Meuszynski 1981: 34:E-3; and Meuszynski 1975: 57, fig. 22. It is not possible to tell precisely how much of the Standard Inscription was originally incised on Slab E-3, since the lower part is broken away. On the neighboring slab E-4, the inscription was carved in 18 lines, and this must likewise have been the case with Slab E-3 (Meuszynski 1981: 34:E-4). Meuszynski's photo of E-3 (1975: fig. 22) shows that the 15 preserved lines contain the Standard Inscription through *li-i-ṭí šá-kín*, roughly the first quarter of the text (Grayson 1991a: 275:5).

74. Meuszynski 1981: 33:B-*d*-3 and 4, and 34:B-*c*-3 and 4.

75. Paley and Sobolewski 1987: 49.

text is not a continuation of the one on the front but rather the fullest version of the text found also on the backs of the wall slabs.[76]

It is possible that one pair of colossi was inscribed with considerably more of the Throne-Base Text than was found on any of the surviving examples. This is the pair in the central door, now lost, of the throne-room façade.[77] The colossi in this location at Dur Sharrukin and in the Southwest Palace at Nineveh were the largest examples in their palaces, and this would probably have been the case in Assurnasirpal's palace also. If the Throne-Base Text were carved complete on any colossi in the Northwest Palace, one would expect it to have been here, both because of the large size of these bulls and because of the importance of their location, in the main entrance to the throne room.

It remains to consider briefly the nature and function of the colossus inscriptions. As mentioned in the discussion of the Throne-Base Text, the content of these inscriptions should complement that of the images and other texts in the palace, drawing attention to both general and particular attributes of the king. In fact, however, they cannot have fulfilled this function as effectively as they might, since the text seems never to appear in its entirety on the colossi. As with the Standard Inscription, which is often similarly truncated, the power of these inscriptions must reside not primarily in their content but rather in the very fact of their existence.

Thresholds

Inscribed stone thresholds—a term I will use for convenience to refer to any pavement slabs in doorways—seem to have been a common, though perhaps not invariable, feature of monumental doorways in the palace of Assurnasirpal II at Kalhu (see fig, 93). Layard observed that "between the lions and bulls forming the entrances, was generally placed one large slab, bearing an inscription."[78] He specifically mentioned the inscribed thresholds in Doors *c* and *d*, the two flanking entrances leading from the great outer court (D/E) into the throne room (B), and published the inscription in Door *c*.[79] These and a number of other inscribed thresholds are now visible *in situ* in the palace. The inscriptions I have been able to identify are discussed in detail in Catalog 2. To summarize, the thresholds in Assurnasirpal's palace were carved with a variety of texts, the locations of which are shown in Table 2.4.

76. Layard, Ms A, pp. 80–81, 84, and personal observation.
77. The probable original size and appearance of these colossi are discussed in Paley and Sobolewski 1992: 17–21, pl. 4.
78. Layard 1849a: vol. 2, 261.
79. Door *d*: Layard 1849a: vol. 1, 115. Door *c*: Layard 1851: pls. 48 and 84 lower.

Table 2.4. Texts Used on Assurnasirpal II Palace Thresholds

Palace Wall Foundation Text

Room A, Door *a*

Room J, Door *a* and wall niche

Room O, Door *a*

Room R, Door *a*

Room U, Door *a*

Standard Inscription, Type A, in full, with variant "to the interior of the land Nirib"

Room M, Door *a* and wall niche

Standard Inscription, Type B or Throne-Base/Colossus Text, truncated, abridged third generation, variant "to the land Urartu"

Room B, Door *b*

Room H, Doors *b, c*

Room N, door to Room P

Room T, Door *a*

Unknown 3

Standard Inscription or Throne-Base/Colossus Text, truncated, abridged third generation, Urartu/Nirib variant illegible

Room S, Doors *a, b*

Standard Inscription or Throne-Base/Colossus Text, truncated, abridged third generation, stops before Urartu/Nirib

Room B, Door *e* (on west doorpost seat only)

Room G, Door *a*

Room V, Door *a*

Unknown 1 (on doorpost seats and doorsill only)

Unknown 2 (probably Room W, Door *b*)

Throne-Base/Colossus Text, truncated

Room B, Door *d*

Room F, Door *f*

Annals

Room B, Door *c* (fifth year)

Room B, Door *e* (doorsill only, fourth year)

Room BB(WK), Door *f* (first year)

The inscription is on the main threshold slab unless noted otherwise.

Table 2.4. Texts Used on Assurnasirpal II Palace Thresholds

Uninscribed or Obliterated

Room G, Door *c* (obliterated)

Room H, Doors *d, e* (uninscribed)

Room Z, door to Court Y (floral pattern)

No Threshold Slab in Situ

Room B, Door *a*

Room C, Doors *b, c*

Room G, Doors *b, d*

Room S, Doors *c, d, e*

On the basis of this table, a few general observations occur to me. The Palace Wall Foundation Text, which I consider to be of relatively early date because examples of it were found on tablets buried in the palace walls, occurs only on the thresholds (and in a wall niche) of rooms that are paved with stone slabs (A, J, O, R, U). In Room M, which was also paved with stone slabs, the threshold and wall niche slab are carved with the full Standard Inscription Type A. The variant "to the interior of the land Nirib" that occurs in the text on these slabs, and which also occurs in the Palace Wall Foundation Text, may indicate a relatively early date for this version of the Standard Inscription. As I recall, each pavement slab in these rooms also carries a short inscription, possibly the same text that is in the doorway. Unfortunately, the only interior pavement slabs I photographed were the floor slabs in the wall niches in Rooms J and M. In these two cases, at least, the inscription was the same as the one on the threshold in that room.

The majority of preserved thresholds carry the text that I refer to in Table 2.4 as the "Standard Inscription or throne-base/colossus text, truncated." The first part of the Standard Inscription—the only part that is carved on these thresholds—is essentially identical to the beginning of the "throne-base/colossus text," which was the text used on two of the largest thresholds. Note in particular that these truncated inscriptions on the thresholds have an abridged genealogy in the third generation. This is not characteristic of the Standard Inscription as it appears on most of the wall slabs, but is the variant that is usually found on the colossi. It seems probable, therefore, that the base text for all these thresholds was the "throne-base/colossus text," truncated to fit the space available.

An annalistic text was apparently chosen for three of the largest thresholds in the palace: two of the three doorways of the throne-room façade and possibly in the central doorway of the western façade. The most obvious way to explain the use of annalistic texts in these locations is to suppose that the slabs were too large for the other available texts. In Room B, however, the thresholds in Doors *c* and *d* were the same size, yet one carried an annalistic text and the other the truncated "throne base/colossus text." Another explanation for the use of the annals texts in the throne room was proposed by Paley at a time when only the inscription from the Door *c* threshold was known. He suggested that each of the throne room's five doorway thresholds was inscribed with an account of a different year, which taken together would constitute a narrative of the first five years similar to that on the Nimrud Monolith.[80] The subsequent publication of the Door *e* threshold provided some support for this appealing hypothesis, but the threshold text in Doors *b* and *d* is not annalistic, and there is now no way to determine if there was ever an inscribed threshold in Door *a*.

It is also not clear to me why the annalistic texts chosen for the doors in the throne-room façade were the accounts of the fourth and fifth years. It may be that these were the most recent campaigns for which prepared accounts were available at the time the inscription was carved. Assurnasirpal's annals are preserved in two editions. The first, for which the principal exemplar is the Nimrud Monolith, records the king's first five years and was apparently composed immediately after the fifth year.[81] Presumably the stimulus for the composition of this edition of the annals was Kalhu's transformation into a royal residence, the date of which can be deduced from the Ninurta Temple annals.[82] The other edition of the annals, preserved in wall and pavement slabs from the Ninurta Temple at Kalhu, repeats the Nimrud Monolith account of years one to five, and adds to it an account of years six to eighteen. Presumably this edition was composed soon after the eighteenth year.[83] There is no evidence that updated editions of the annals were compiled between years five and eighteen. If the Door *c* threshold was carved with an annalistic text sometime between the sixth and eighteenth years, then the accounts of the first five years may have been the only ones that were available for use. Evidence that the thresholds were carved before year eighteen may be seen in the scribal variants in the threshold inscription, which frequently

80. Paley 1976: 152, no. 23; and 155, no. 33.

81. Grayson 1991a: 237–54, no. 17. The date of composition can be deduced from the fact that while Assurnasirpal also campaigned in his sixth year (ibid., 212:iii:1), that campaign is not included in the Nimrud Monolith inscription. See also Olmstead 1916: 16–18.

82. The royal campaigns of Assurnasirpal's first, second, and fourth years originated from Nineveh (Grayson 1991a: 198, 200, 205). No point of origin is recorded for the campaigns of the third and fifth years (ibid., 203, 208). People subjected during the fourth-year campaign were put to work at Kalhu (ibid., 208). The campaigns of the sixth and all subsequent years originated from Kalhu (ibid., 212). Therefore the king apparently moved to Kalhu in his fifth or sixth year.

83. Grayson 1991a: 191–223, no. 1.

agree with those of the Nimrud Monolith inscription while disagreeing with those of the Ninurta Temple inscription.[84]

Whatever the text, these inscriptions would have functioned at at least two levels. For those able to read them, they summarize the territorial and architectural accomplishments of the king. For all viewers, literate or not, the threshold inscriptions symbolize the power that ordered their creation. This sense of power would be greatest at the monumental portals, where the effect of the threshold inscriptions in the horizontal dimension would be complemented by that of the colossus inscriptions in the vertical dimension, creating a space charged with the power connoted by the surrounding inscriptions.

A number of doorways do not have inscribed thresholds. Two doors in Room H have thresholds that were apparently never inscribed. I cannot account for this. Four rooms, excluding the poorly recorded west wing, have doorways that lack stone threshold slabs. One of these (C) is a stairwell that, like passageways, may never have had threshold slabs in its entrances. The other three are outer reception rooms, each of which has a wide, thresholdless doorway at one of its short ends (B:*a*, G:*d*, S:*d*). Perhaps doorways in this position were not usually equipped with threshold slabs. In addition, however, each of these three rooms has one doorway that should have a threshold slab but does not (B:*b*, G:*b*, S:*e*). In the case of the threshold in Room B, Door *b*, Layard copied its inscription, but the slab has now disappeared. In the cases of the other two doorways (G:*b*, S:*e*) there is no record of a threshold slab ever being there. What these three doorways have in common is that they all originally contained colossi that were removed from the palace in modern times. I suspect that in each case the threshold slab, or what was left of it, was removed by the excavators to facilitate the lowering of the colossi.

In the cases of colossi S-*e*-1 and G-*b*-2, which were removed intact in spring 1847 and sent to the British Museum, Layard reported that he removed a section of wall behind each colossus, dug out the earth underneath it, and then lowered it onto its back.[85] He may have removed the thresholds at this time to prevent the bases of the colossi from being damaged as a result of binding against the edge of the threshold slabs as the colossi pivoted over. An alternative possibility is that these two thresholds remained in place until the other two colossi in

84. Olmstead 1916: 16. The reference to Urartu would imply a gap between the carving of the Door *c* threshold inscription, between years 5 and 18, and the Door *d* threshold, colossi, and Standard inscriptions in the throne room, after year 18 (de Filippi 1977: 37–39). If these dates are accepted, then this is evidence for the sequence in which the inscriptions were carved in the throne room. Intuitively, however, the threshold inscriptions might be expected to have been carved last, since they would be the most vulnerable to the passage of workers and construction materials through the doorways.

85. Layard 1849a: vol. 1, frontispiece; vol. 2, 79–80, 90–91.

these doorways, S-*e*-2 and G-*b*-1, were removed by Layard in 1850–51 for the "Nineveh Porch" of Canford Manor, the residence of Sir John Guest.[86] Layard's published works do not mention the removal of these colossi, but it appears that unlike the ones sent to the British Museum, these two were lowered into the doorway with their carved side down.[87] The threshold slabs could have been removed in the course of this operation, either to provide a softer surface for the sculptured face of the colossi to be lowered onto, or to permit the excavation of a shallow pit for a cart to receive the colossi, which was the procedure Layard had followed in 1847 with colossus G-*b*-2.[88] If any of these thresholds were removed in modern times, there seems to be no record of where they are now.

Another possibility is that the slabs missing from Rooms G and S were removed in antiquity. Layard found at least one inscribed Assurnasirpal II threshold reused as a wall slab in the Southwest Palace at Kalhu (see "Unknown 3"). These thresholds seem to be less likely candidates for this type of spoliation, however, than those in the more convenient West Wing (numerous slabs from which were found in the Southwest Palace), since they would have to be extracted from deep in the interior of the palace.

The Northwest Palace Inscriptions—Conclusions

Table 2.5 is compiled from Tables 2.2 and 2.4 as an attempt to relate the versions of texts found on the wall slabs to those on the threshold slabs in each room. Though it would be nice to have more data, particularly on the unsculptured rooms, this table does suggest patterns that are consistent with those seen in the individual text types. Of the unsculptured rooms, three of the four known to have had the earlier version of the Standard Inscription (Type A) on their walls (Rooms A, M, and R) also had an early text—either Type A or the Palace Wall Foundation Text—on their threshold slabs, and this was probably the arrangement also in Rooms J, O, and U. In the cases of the thresholds inscribed with the Palace Wall Foundation Text, the selection of that text might indicate either that the thresholds were inscribed first, before the Standard Inscription Type A was in use, or that the Type A text was deemed too lengthy for small threshold slabs. In Room V, by contrast, the truncated Standard Inscription Type B/Throne-Base

86. See John M. Russell, *From Nineveh to New York* (London, 1997).

87. That they were not lowered onto their uncarved backs, as were the British Museum examples, is evident from fig. 7, where the section of wall behind these two colossi is shown as still intact and was therefore not removed by Layard.

88. Layard 1849a: vol. 2, 90–91. In early 1850, however, Layard used a method that did not involve digging pits when he loaded the larger colossi B-*a*-1 and 2 onto carts (Layard 1853a: 202–3).

Table 2.5. Texts on Wall Slabs and Thresholds in the Northwest Palace

Room	Wall Slab Text	Door: Threshold Text
Unsculptured Rooms		
A	Type A	A-*a*: PWFT
J	unknown	J-*a*: PWFT
K	unknown	H-*c*: Type B/Throne-Base Text, truncated
M	Type A	M-*a*: Type A, complete
O	unknown	O-*a*: PWFT
R	PWFT, Type A, Type B(?)	R-*a*: PWFT
U	unknown	U-*a*: PWFT
V	Type A	V-*a*: Type B(?)/Throne-Base Text, truncated
W	unknown	W(?)-*b*(?): Type B(?)/Throne-Base Text, truncated
X	unknown	S-*c*: lost(?)
Y	Type B	courtyard
AA	unknown	unknown
BB(WK)	unknown	BB(WK)(?)-*f*(?): annals, first year
Sculptured Rooms		
B	Type B	B-*c*: annals, fifth year B-*d*: Throne-Base Text, truncated B-*e*: annals, fourth year
C	Type B	B-*a*, C-*b*, *c*: no slab
D/E	Type B	courtyard
F	Type B	B-*b*: Type B/Throne-Base Text, truncated F-*f*: Throne-Base Text, truncated
G	Type B	G-*a*: Type B(?)/Throne-Base Text, truncated G-*b*: lost(?) G-*c*: obliterated
H	Type B	H-*e*: uninscribed
I	PWFT, Type A, Type B	H-*b*: Type B/Throne-Base Text, truncated
L	Type B	H-*d*: uninscribed

Type A = Standard Inscription Type A
Type B = Standard Inscription Type B
PWFT = Palace Wall Foundation Text.

Table 2.5. Texts on Wall Slabs and Thresholds in the Northwest Palace

Room	Wall Slab Text	Door: Threshold Text
N	unknown	G-*d*: no slab N/P: Type B/Throne-Base Text, truncated
P	Type B	P/Y: no slab
S	Type B	S-*a*: Type B(?)/Throne-Base Text, truncated S-*b*: Type B(?)/Throne-Base Text, truncated S-*e*: lost(?)
T	Type B	T-*a*: Type B/Throne-Base Text, truncated S-*d*: no slab
Z	Type B	Z/Y: floral (Sargon II?)
WG	unknown	unknown
WI(?)	unknown	unknown
WJ	Type B	unknown
WM(?)	Type B	unknown

Text on the threshold suggests that it was inscribed after the wall slabs, which carry Type A, and this may also have been the case in the neighboring Room W and in Room K.

All but three of the surviving inscribed thresholds in the sculptured rooms have the truncated Standard Inscription Type B/Throne-Base Text and were presumably carved at about the same time that the Type B text was placed on their walls, after the sculptures were completed. Even in the case of Room I, where earlier and later texts appear on different stretches of wall slabs, the Type B text on the threshold is flanked by Type B inscriptions on the wall slabs to either side of the door. The three exceptions are very large thresholds—two in Throne Room B and the other in Room BB(WK), probably in secondary context—that are inscribed with annals of the first, fourth, and fifth years. The primary requirement here was for a text long enough to fill the space. The selection of annals texts from early in the king's reign suggests that these thresholds may have been carved before the king's eighteenth year, when the annals were updated for the Ninurta Temple; before the introduction of the reference to Urartu, which apparently postdates the eighteenth year; and, consequently, before the Standard Inscription Type B and Throne-Base Text were compiled. If this admittedly tortured logic is sound, then these three thresholds may have been inscribed some time before those with the Standard Inscription Type B/Throne-Base Text, and therefore also before the colossi that adjoin them were inscribed.

These are only the crudest examples of the sorts of information that might be deduced from a close study of physical context and textual variants in Assurnasirpal's Northwest Palace inscriptions. When all of these inscriptions are adequately published, then the data will be available for a much more nuanced and detailed study of the production of an inscribed palace.

Epigraphs

In 1878 Hormuzd Rassam found bronze strips that had decorated two pairs of wooden gates in what was probably a palace of Assurnasirpal II at Balawat (ancient Imgur Enlil), a way station on the road to Babylon some 28 kilometers southeast of Nineveh. One pair of gates had reliefs and inscriptions of Shalmaneser III and the other of Assurnasirpal II. Such doors are mentioned frequently in building accounts and seem to have been a common feature of Assyrian palaces and temples, but the two in the Imgur-Enlil palace, together with another one of Assurnasirpal II found in the neighboring temple of Mamu, are the only well-preserved examples discovered to date.[89] The Assurnasirpal gate was composed of sixteen bronze bands, eight on each gate, each decorated in repoussé with a single register of relief with a floral border (fig. 19). Four of the bands showed the king hunting lions and wild oxen and the remainder depicted military conquest and tribute.[90] The gate carried two types of inscription. On the vertical edge of each door leaf was a strip of bronze inscribed with a variant of the Standard Inscription that concludes with a report on the building of the town wall and palace in Imgur-Enlil.[91]

The other type of inscription was epigraphs—brief captions—one on each of the relief bands. The content of each of these epigraphs is summarized in the following chart, where each epigraph is juxtaposed with a schematic description of its subject, in order to place it in its compositional context. The bands are listed in the order in which they are now on display in the British Museum. Table 2.6 was compiled from observation of the originals, and because of their poor preservation, it must be considered tentative pending the publication of detailed photographs and drawings of the reliefs.

A few preliminary observations on the epigraphs suggest themselves. All of the epigraphs include a brief descriptive passage, but only seven begin with the

89. Palace doors: Rassam 1897: 200–220; Rassam 1882: 50. Temple door: D. Oates 1974. For textual references to such doors, see Grayson 1991a: 321.

90. British Museum, WA 124685–124700. Only five of the bronze strips have been published to date: King 1915: 35–36, pls. 78–80 (WA 124687, 124688); Barnett 1973 (WA 124685, 124697, 124698).

91. Grayson 1991a: 321–23, no. 51.

FIG. 19. Balawat, bronze gates of Assurnasirpal II, sculptured strip, drawing by

Table 2.6. Summary of Epigraphs on British Museum WA 124685–124700

Left Leaf	
tribute→	"tribute from the city Sarugu" tribute→ ←**king** ←chariot ←horse (124689)
enemy→ enemy→	"the city Ulluba of Sagara, king of Hatti, I captured" city ←**king**'s(?) chariot ←chariot (124695)
booty→ booty→	"booty from Sangara of Hatti" booty→ booty→ ←**king** (124685)
titulary city ←booty	"booty from the land Hatti" ←booty ←booty ←**king**'s(?) chariot ←chariot (124690)
chariot→	"battle against the city Marinâ in Bit-Adini" city enemy→ ←**king**'s(?) chariot ←chariot (124686)
chariot→ enemy	"the city Ialligu(?) in Bit-Adini, I captured" ←chariot enemy ←**king**'s(?) chariot ←chariot (124692)
swamp swamp	"wild oxen by the Euphrates, I killed" ←oxen ←**king**'s chariot ←chariot (124697)
swamp swamp	"lions by the Balih River, I killed" lions ←**king**'s chariot ←chariot (124698)

The vertical bar marks the division between the curved and flat parts of the band. Concerning my designation "king's(?) chariot," if the king was not present elsewhere in a band, I tentatively designated the lead chariot as his, even if poor preservation made it impossible actually to identify his figure in it. Translations from Grayson 1991a: 345–50, nos. 80–95.

Marjorie Howard. British Museum, WA 124685 (photo: Trustees of the British Museum).

Table 2.6. Summary of Epigraphs on British Museum WA 124685–124700

Right Leaf	
"tribute from the city [. . .]ga city tribute→ tribute→	[. . .]" ←king (124694)
titulary "booty from the horse→ chariot→ **king**→ ←booty	city Ellipu in Hatti(?)" ←booty (124687)
"the city Magarisu(?) chariot→ **king**'s(?) chariot→ enemy city	in Bit-Iahiri, I captured" enemy ←chariot (124688)
titulary "booty from the city chariot→ **king**'s chariot→ booty→	Mariru(?) in Hatti(?)" booty→ city (124696)
titulary "the city Rugulutu(?) chariot→ **king**'s(?) chariot→ enemy city	in Bit-Adini, I captured" enemy ←chariot (124691)
titulary "tribute from horse→ chariot→ **king**→ ←tribute	the land Suhu" ←tribute (124693)
titulary "lions by the Balih chariot→ **king**'s chariot→ lions	River, I killed" lions (124699)
titulary "wild oxen by the chariot→ **king**'s chariot→ oxen	Euphrates, I killed" oxen (124700)

titulary: "Palace of Assurnasirpal, king of the universe, king of Assyria, son of Tukulti-Ninurta, king of Assyria, son of Adad-nirari, king of Assyria," while the other nine omit this. The content of the descriptive passage that follows the titulary seems to play no part in determining whether or not a titulary is included, since with the Euphrates and Balih hunting epigraphs, for example, the same text appears twice, once with and once without the titulary.

The distribution of titularies is neither random nor even, however, as all but one occur on the right leaf of the gate. A look at the table suggests why this is so. In every case on the right leaf, the titulary either brackets the head of the king or precedes it at the left (this relationship is shown on the chart). Moreover, though the titulary, when it occurs, always precedes the descriptive part of the epigraph, it is occasionally separated from the descriptive passage by a considerable space. This gives the titulary and descriptive part the appearance of being two distinct epigraphs (an effect that is nullified in text publications by the common practice of running together all texts that are on a single band, regardless of the spaces that separate them).[92] The placement of the titulary in each of its occurrences on the right leaf, therefore, suggests that its function is not primarily to introduce the descriptive passage, but rather itself to serve as an epigraph that labels the figure of the king.

These observations are borne out as well by at least one of the two bands without a titulary on the right leaf. On band 124694, the figure of the king is at the far right of the composition. The titulary was apparently omitted here because the composition would not permit it to precede the descriptive passage that identifies the source of the tribute. It appears that if the king's name could not be given precedence, then it was left out. The situation with the other band without a titulary on the right leaf, 124688, is not so clear. It may be that the king's figure was not on this band at all (it is not recognizable there now). If the king was not shown, then no titulary would have been required to identify him.

The situation on the left leaf is similar to that on band 124694. In every case, the figure of the king is to the right, so that if the titulary were to label the king himself, it would have to follow the descriptive passage. On the single band where there is a titulary, it is at the far left, over the image of a city that is the focus of a booty procession approaching from the right. Since the titulary commences "Palace of Assurnasirpal," it seems likely that this city is Imgur Enlil and that the titulary labels the palace itself.

The brief descriptive portion of these epigraphs, whether standing alone or preceded by a titulary, focuses on the names of places and people, while giving only the briefest reference to the action ("I conquered, I killed") or subject (battle, booty, tribute). It seems clear that the emphasis in these epigraphs is pri-

---

92. There is a gap between the titulary and descriptive text on 124687, 124690, and 124693.

marily on establishing the setting. Of fourteen place names specified in the epigraphs as restored by Grayson, six are not mentioned in any other known text of Assurnasirpal II.[93] The implications of these unique occurrences will be considered in the discussions of epigraphs of later kings.

Though epigraphs are a standard feature of the small-scale reliefs on Assurnasirpal II's bronze doors and obelisks, they are not found on the palace wall reliefs.[94] The reason for their omission from the wall reliefs is unclear. It appears from the inclusion of an epigraph on the White Obelisk that at least one of Assurnasirpal's monument makers was familiar with the idea of epigraphs already at the beginning of the king's reign, so one could hardly suggest that epigraphs weren't "invented" until after the palace reliefs were carved.[95] Two possible explanations for Assurnasirpal's omission of epigraphs from his narrative palace reliefs suggest themselves to me.

93. Mentioned in other texts of Assurnasirpal II: Bit-Adini, Bit-Iahiri, Euphrates, Hatti, Magarisu(?), Mariru(?), Suhu, Ulluba. Mentioned only in bronze door epigraphs: Ellipu, Marinâ, Sarugu, Rugulutu(?), Ialligu(?), Balih River (source: Grayson 1991a: 345–50). Grayson did not attempt to restore the name of the city [. . .]*gal*[. . .] (1991a: 348, no. 89).

94. In addition to the Imgur-Enlil palace doors, the following Assurnasirpal II monuments have epigraphs:

Bronze doors, from the Mamu Temple at Imgur-Enlil (Baghdad, Iraq Museum): Barnett 1973; J. Oates 1983. Only two of the epigraphs are published, both from the same band: "the city Imgur-Enlil" and "tribute of Kudurru of the land Suhu" (Grayson 1991a: 351). Two more (Bit-Adini, Carchemish) are mentioned by Barnett (1973: 21).

The *"White Obelisk,"* from Nineveh (British Museum WA 118807): Sollberger 1974; Reade 1975; Grayson 1991a: 254–56. The single epigraph refers to rituals performed at the *bīt nathi* in Nineveh.

The *"Rassam Obelisk,"* from Kalhu (British Museum WA 118800 + 90925 + 132013): Reade 1980c; Grayson 1991a: 277–78, 342–44. Fragments of eight epigraphs are preserved. All seem to be tribute lists. No personal or place names survive.

95. The argument that the use of epigraphs on Assyrian monuments predates Assurnasirpal II's palace reliefs holds true even if the White Obelisk dates to the reign of Assurnasirpal I (1049–1031 B.C.), or to some other king considerably earlier than Assurnasirpal II, as some scholars believe (for a summary of the literature, see Börker-Klähn 1982: vol. 1, 179–80). I am convinced by Sollberger's (1974) arguments that the inscription at least belongs to Assurnasirpal II. I am not persuaded by attributions based on differences between the White Obelisk reliefs and the wall reliefs of Assurnasirpal II's Northwest Palace at Kalhu, in part because of the different scale of these two sets of reliefs, and in part because of their different dates of execution: the White Obelisk inscription records Assurnasirpal II's first two years only, and so must date ca. 881 B.C.; the Northwest Palace reliefs were carved sometime after the ninth year, which is the earliest possible date of the Mediterranean campaign mentioned in the inscription on the back of the wall slabs, and probably not until after the king's eighteenth year (Reade 1985: 206–7).

The first is tied to the innovative nature of Assurnasirpal II's throne room re-liefs, which are the first in Near Eastern art to combine "sequence, action, and particularity" to achieve what Winter has identified as continuous historical nar-rative.[96] Since this was a new and somewhat unfamiliar form of expression, its designers could not yet have been fully aware of its possibilities and limitations. It has been suggested that each of the several distinct narrative episodes that comprise the throne room relief series was intended to represent a highly specific subject, that is, a particular city in a particular region, similar in its specificity to the city by city record of the campaigns in the written annals.[97] The designers of the reliefs may have felt that in these relatively large-scale images, the incorpo-ration of particularizing details such as costume, scenery, and architecture would have made the images sufficiently specific to be readily recognizable, without the necessity of incorporating explanatory labels. Indeed, it may have been felt that captions placed on the picture surface, outside the central space reserved exclu-sively for text, would be overly intrusive, disrupting the flow of the narrative and detracting from the verisimilitude the images are striving to achieve. That the images were unsuccessful in attaining this high level of specificity is suggested by the palace reliefs of later kings, which, tentatively at first, then more openly, place ever greater reliance on the epigraph to ensure identification of the subject.

Another possible explanation for the omission of epigraphs in Assurnasirpal's narrative palace reliefs derives from the character of the reliefs themselves. In looking at the entire narrative relief series from the throne room, one is struck by its episodic character. This is to say that, while two, three, or four slabs may be devoted to a single subject and exhibit considerable continuity from slab to slab in their depiction of that subject, the series as a whole consists of a number of compositionally unconnected episodes, and the differing costumes and scenery from episode to episode likewise suggest that the events depicted may be widely separated in space and time. So that while there is narrative continuity within episodes, this continuity does not extend to the series as a whole. This episodic and nonchronological series of representations is much closer in spirit to the summary account of the king's achievements recorded in the Standard Inscrip-tion—carved across the middle of all the wall relief slabs—than it is to the an-nals. One goal of a summary account is to be all-encompassing, and one way it achieves this, in contrast to annals, is by speaking in generalities ("I conquered the land Nirbu"), instead of specifics (the annals of the second year detail the capture of the cities Kinabu, Mariru, Tela, and Ishpilipria, all in the land Nirbu).[98] A visual record that was striving for the narrative continuity of the an-nals might be expected to show Assurnasirpal's conquest of some or all of these

96. Winter 1981: 12.
97. Winter 1981: 15; Reade 1985: 212–13.
98. Standard Inscription: Grayson 1991a: 275:7; the annals: ibid., 200:101–203:19.

cities, arranged in a narrative series with each city labeled by an epigraph to prevent confusion. A visual account with the all-encompassing intent of the summary inscriptions, by contrast, might choose a single city to represent the entire campaign, showing it in a manner that combines geographical specificity, through scenery and costumes, with ambiguity concerning the precise site depicted, through omission of captions, thereby assuring that the images are taken as regional, rather than local, indicators. According to this explanation, then, the captions would have been omitted in order to ensure that the images would not be read *too* specifically.

It is not difficult to imagine a possible reason for this. If one assumes that the throne room reliefs were intended to appeal to a range of foreigners, as is suggested by the reliefs of different foreigners bearing tribute placed at both of the side entrances to the throne room from the outer court, then one way of achieving this appeal is to ensure that the images operate at the minimum possible level of specificity that will still serve to convey the message. For example, to return to the second year campaign against Nirbu, if in the reliefs the episode devoted to this campaign depicted what was clearly a specific city, for example, Tela, then an envoy from Tela might be impressed, while one from Kinabu, also in Nirbu, might not, since the city shown is not his. If, by contrast, the relief devoted to Nirbu clearly evoked, through costume and scenery, a city in Nirbu, without unambiguously specifying *which* city was represented, then any envoy from Nirbu might be expected to get the message. Through use of this minimum level of specificity, then, a wide audience can be reached through a relatively small number of relatively specific images.

These two explanations can be harmonized somewhat by suggesting that the designers of the images were in fact working from detailed descriptions of particular cities recorded in the annals, but that the planners of the inscriptions, which were added after the reliefs had already been finished, failed to include epigraphs either through neglect or deliberately, to ensure that the images would have the same general character as the Standard Inscription.

Summary: Assurnasirpal II

For Assurnasirpal II, there is a large corpus of palace inscriptions preserved in or recorded from his Northwest Palace at Kalhu, but relatively few individual examples have been published. I looked here at inscriptions from five general locations in that palace: the backs of wall slabs, the faces of wall slabs, the throne base, doorway colossi, and thresholds. The visitor to the state apartments of this palace would literally have been surrounded by texts, below and on every side. For the nonliterate visitor, this surfeit of inscribed surfaces forms an impressive

display, connoting the vast power and authority of the king who ordered its execution. The literate visitor would be likewise impressed, but would soon detect
the seemingly endless repetition of the same texts.

The architectural context of the text on the back of the wall slabs, for which
there may have been more exemplars than for any other Assurnasirpal palace inscription, has previously been almost universally ignored, and the text itself identified as just another variant of the Standard Inscription. A close look at the text
itself, however, demonstrates that it is different from and probably earlier than
the Standard Inscription, as would be expected from its context on the backs of
slabs against the mudbrick walls. Attention was also drawn here to Layard's numerous copies of exemplars of this text, which have unaccountably been ignored
by most scholars, and to a related text inscribed on stone tablets that were buried
in the walls.

The text on the front of Assurnasirpal's wall slabs is usually the so-called
Standard Inscription. A number of combined editions of this text have been published, but very few of these identify the specific slabs in which individual variant
readings occur. I have argued here that the time has come to look at all of the
variants in each exemplar of the Standard Inscription for evidence that might assist us in determining the sequence in which different rooms in the palace were
decorated. Some preliminary observations on apparent sequence were offered,
based on available published inscriptions and unpublished Layard copies.

A single basic text was inscribed on the throne base and on the gateway colossi. The result, however, differs in the two locations, because only on the
throne base does the text appear in its entirety. On the colossi, the text is always
truncated, often in mid-sentence. It has repeatedly been suggested that the "conclusion" of the colossus inscriptions must have been carved somewhere nearby,
even though no such conclusion has been located in the archaeological record
for any of the colossi. Instead, this is an example of a text that has been cut to fit
the space available, without regard for completeness, a treatment also often accorded the Standard Inscription when it was carved on narrow wall slabs. The
previously unpublished inscriptions *in situ* on a number of the Northwest Palace
colossi have been presented here in detailed photographs in Catalog 1, and an
unlabeled Layard drawing of an otherwise unknown colossus is identified on the
evidence of his labeled hand copy of its inscription. A number of unlabeled paper
casts formerly in the British Museum that were published by LeGac were also
matched here with specific colossi.

Very little work had previously been done on the inscribed thresholds of Assurnasirpal's palace—only one was published by Layard and part of another by
Paley. I have here been able to identify the inscriptions on a considerable number
of thresholds that survive *in situ*. It turns out that a greater range of texts appeared on the thresholds than in any other palace location, including annalistic
texts, which were not reported anywhere else in the palace. It appears that the

criteria for selecting a text for a given threshold may have depended in part on the date when the inscription was carved and in part on the size and, perhaps, location of the threshold. In conclusion, the texts on the thresholds were correlated with those on the wall slabs in each room and the patterns of selection that emerged were noted.

Though door leaves bound with sculptured bronze bands have not been published from Assurnasirpal's palace at Kalhu, a pair were discovered in his palace at Imgur Enlil (Balawat). Though only a few of the bronze reliefs from these doors have been published, the summary text and epigraphs on them are fully published and the reliefs themselves are on view in the British Museum. I presented a schematic diagram that relates the epigraph on each band to the representation that accompanies it, and this highlighted the nature of the interdependency between text and image in these narrative compositions.

Chapter 3

Shalmaneser III (858–824 B.C.)

Shalmaneser III, Assurnasirpal's son and successor, also built extensively at Kalhu (Nimrud). His largest project for the capital was the arsenal—called the "review palace" by the Assyrians and "Fort Shalmaneser" by its excavators—a huge new palace that seems to have served as a storehouse for military equipment and booty, and as the assembly point for the army (fig. 20). It was located at the southeast corner of the city, just inside the city wall, and measured some 200 by 300 meters. It was planned around four large courtyard areas: two outer courtyards on the north side surrounded by storerooms and offices, a southwest inner courtyard subdivided into a block of smaller courts and long rooms, and a southeast inner court that had the throne-room suite on its south side. The building had no wall reliefs at all, but at the east end of the throne room was a large stone throne base that was decorated on its sides and front with scenes of tribute being brought before the king, each labeled with a brief text describing the origin and type of tribute shown. Inscribed on top of the throne base is a lengthy text summarizing the king's first 13 years of rule. Above the south outside entrance to the throne-room suite was a 4-meter-tall brick mosaic panel comprising over 300 glazed bricks, decorated with symmetrical images of Shalmaneser flanking a god in a winged disk and bulls flanking a stylized tree. This is the most complete Assyrian glazed-brick mosaic panel yet recovered.

Another of Shalmaneser's projects was at the center of the Kalhu citadel, where there is a pair of bull colossi inscribed on front and back with a text recounting the king's first 18 years. These should have marked the entrance to a palace or temple, but the building itself has disappeared. The most extensive group of Shalmaneser III reliefs was 16 bronze bands that embellished a pair of wooden doors that he erected in his father's palace at Balawat. Each band was divided into two registers, decorated in repoussé with lively images of royal military campaigns and delivery of tribute. The subjects are drawn from the king's first 11 years, each labeled with a brief epigraph giving the location of the event. A long text summarizing Shalmaneser's first 13 years was engraved on two bronze strips, one on the edge of each door.

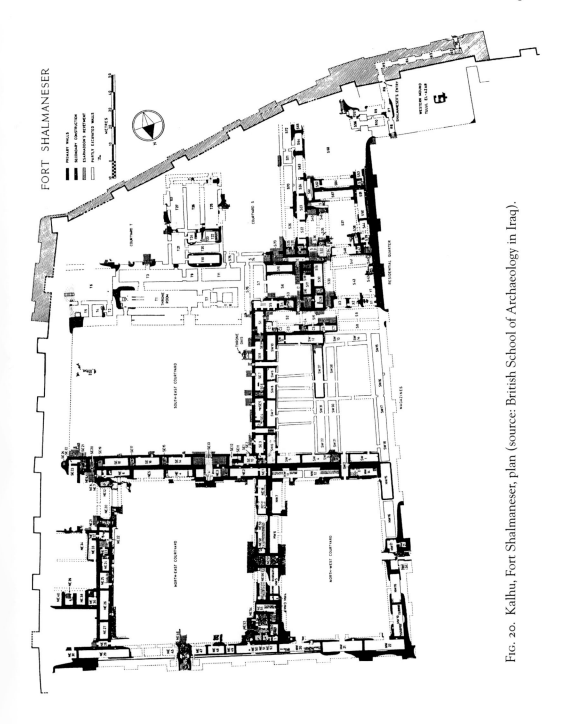

FIG. 20. Kalhu, Fort Shalmaneser, plan (source: British School of Archaeology in Iraq).

Fig. 21. Kalhu, Fort Shalmaneser, Room T1, decorated throne base, 228 × 382 cm (after A. Moortgat, *The Art of Ancient Mesopotamia*, 1969, fig. 269).

Throne Bases

Two inscribed throne bases were found during excavations in Fort Shalmaneser. The better-preserved base was against the wall at the east end of Room T1, the main throne room (fig. 21).[1] It was composed of two stone blocks, both of them inscribed. The texts were a nonchronological account of selected events from the first 13 years, two epigraphs that labeled pictures carved on the sides, a longer text that refers to an image on the front of the base, and a label or tag.[2] The main historical account began in a framed panel at the north side of the east block, continued in a similar panel at the south side of the east block, continued with two lines of text that framed the upper step on the west block, and concluded with two lines framing the lower step on the same block.

The main text begins with an interesting titulary (discussed below) and continues with a historical summary of Shalmaneser's accession year and first six years, arranged in a modified chronological order. The historical portion begins with the campaign of the accession year, which proceeded northward to the land Nairi and Lake Van. The next section continues with brief descriptions of three decisive (he claims) campaigns to the west: to Hatti, the Amanus, and the Medi-

1. Baghdad, Iraq Museum 65574. Mallowan 1966: vol. 2, 444–50.
2. Hulin 1963; Grayson 1996: 101–4, 137–40.

terranean in the first year, to Bit-Adini in the first campaign of his fourth year, and against the Hamath coalition at Qarqar in his sixth year. The section on western conquests concludes with a summary statement that in his thirteen years Shalmaneser crossed the Euphrates ten times and conquered the west from the Euphrates to Phoenicia. This reference to the thirteenth year is the latest date in the text and suggests the date of its composition. The text then returns to a summary of campaigns to the north and east, again arranged chronologically: to the northeast to Urartu during the third year, to the east to Zamua and Lake Zeribor in the second campaign of his fourth year, and to the north to Shubria in his fifth year.[3]

A separate text of three lines, written in smaller signs along the east edge of the east block at the very back of the throne base, records Shalmaneser's campaign to Babylonia to help the Babylonian king, Marduk-zakir-shumi, defeat his rebellious brother (years 8, 9). This clearly refers to the otherwise unlabeled picture carved on the front of the base, which shows Marduk-zakir-shumi taking the hand of Shalmaneser III. Though this text is too long and too far away from the corresponding image to be considered an epigraph, the two are nevertheless closely related in subject, and the text may perhaps be seen as a commentary on the image.

The two epigraphs are carved directly above the images they label. The epigraph on the north side, which records an event from year 11, reads: "Tribute of Qalparunda of the land Unqu: silver, gold, tin, bronze, bowls of bronze, elephant tusks, ebony, logs of cedar, bright-colored garments and linen, horses trained to harness, I received from him." The one on the south side refers to year 9: "Tribute of Mushallim-Marduk son of Ukani (and) of Adini son of Dakuri: silver, gold, tin, bronze, elephant tusks and hides, ebony, sissoo-wood, I received." This type of lengthy list occurred only once in Shalmaneser's earlier bronze door epigraphs, but it is also the type found in the later Black Obelisk. Marcus has observed that there is a striking contrast between the content of the historical text, with its emphatically militant focus on the establishment of military supremacy in the first few years, and the visual images of stability and prosperity in the reliefs, which depict the current economically beneficial results of that military dominance.[4]

The label or tag, above the relief at the rear part of the south side, labels the throne base itself: "This Mt. Tunu *parūtu*-stone, for the throne of Shalmaneser, king of Assyria, his lord, Shamash-bel-usur the governor of Kalhu set up for ever."[5] On the underside of the east block was a short text that gave the name and titles of Shalmaneser, followed by the statement "Shamash-bel-usur, governor of

---

3. According to Hulin (1963: 64), the scribe ran out of space at the end of the last line on the lower step and had to omit the final verb. Between the third and fourth campaigns, line 42 inserts a reference to the king washing his weapons in the Mediterranean, an event of the first campaign that seems out of context in this location.

4. Hulin 1963: 56:48–49; Grayson 1996: 139; Marcus 1987: 87.

5. Hulin 1963: 56:50; Grayson 1996: 139–40.

Kalhu, made (it)."[6] Shamash-bel-usur's name also appears on four inscribed pavements in doorways in Rooms T3 and T25, all in the vicinity of the throne room.[7]

The titulary section of this inscription presents some interesting features that
indicate it was composed with this specific location in mind. It begins "Palace of
Shalmaneser," meaning that it was intended for the palace, and continues with
three general epithets ("king of all peoples, prince, priest of Assur"), a brief genealogy, and references to his favor with the gods. These are all standard elements
of Shalmaneser's titularies, though several standard epithets are omitted and one
is added—"the one who cares for the shrines of the gods in the temple Esharra"—
which seems to be unique and may refer to work on the Assur Temple in Assur.
Five more standard epithets follow, two of which, however, seem particularly appropriate in this context. One of these, "the one who treads on the summits of
the mountain regions," evokes the location of the inscription itself, which is also
under the king's feet. The other, "the one who receives the tribute and gifts of all
regions," relates directly to the imagery and epigraphs on the side of the throne
base.[8]

The titulary concludes with four titles that, among Shalmaneser's texts, occur
only here and on one of his threshold slabs: "the one who treads on the neck of
his enemy, who shatters the armies of the insolent, who tramples all his enemies,
who, with the help of Assur his lord, tramples all countries under his feet like a
footstool." The first three of these titles are lifted directly from the Standard Inscription of his father, Assurnasirpal II, where they also occur together, but in a
slightly different order. The wonderfully specific final epithet occurs previously
only in variant form in an inscription of Tukulti-Ninurta I.[9] On both the throne
base and the threshold, the names of Assurnasirpal's enemies are literally "underfoot," and one wonders if the scribe, or someone, struck by the aptness of the
"treads on the summits" epithet, went in search of further examples. The "shatters the armies of the insolent" epithet is not so clearly appropriate here but may
refer to the subject of the relief carving on the front of the throne base.

The other throne base was at the southwest corner of the South-East Courtyard, along the west wall. It was also composed of two stone blocks, each with its
own inscription. The inscription on the west block, against the wall, was the
better-preserved of the two. Grayson's edition, based on Hulin's draft transliteration, supersedes the partial edition published by Laessøe.[10] The text is a historical

6. Hulin 1963: 68–69; Grayson 1996: 137.

7. Hulin 1963: 67. Published by Grayson 1996: 106–9.

8. Shalmaneser III's standard titles are analyzed by Schneider (1991: 256).

9. Assurnasirpal II: Grayson 1991a: 275:3–4. Tukulti-Ninurta I: Grayson 1987: 245:
62. Threshold: Grayson 1996: 107.

10. Context: Mallowan 1966: vol. 2, 380, 424, fig. 353. Inscription: Laessøe 1959:
40–1; Grayson 1996: 104–6. Study: Schramm 1973: 86–7.

summary, in two framed panels, each containing 24 lines. The right panel was much better-preserved than the left, but the full text could be reconstructed on the basis of parallels with the threshold texts. It begins on the left panel with a simple three-generation genealogy. A historical summary follows, arranged roughly geographically rather than chronologically. This begins in the west with the conquest of Hatti (year 1) and Bit-Adini (year 4), the third defeat of the Hamath coalition (year 11), and excursions to the Mediterranean Sea (years 1, 6), to Mt. Amanus for timber (years 1, 11, 17), and to Mt. Lallar (year 1). The focus then shifts clockwise, north to the conquest of Nairi from the source of the Tigris to the source of the Euphrates (year 15), northeast to Urartu (year 3), east to Zamua (year 4), and southeast to Babylonia (year 8) and Chaldea (year 9). The latest certain date is the campaign of year 15, which suggests a date of composition shortly thereafter. The inscription on the east block of this throne base was evidently illegible except for the fragment "[. . .], king of all peoples, prince, [. . . (?)], son of Assurnasirpal" in line 1, which identifies the owner as Shalmaneser III and suggests that this was not a continuation of the inscription on the section next to the wall but rather a separate text with its own titulary.[11]

Thresholds

Thirteen inscribed threshold slabs were reported from Fort Shalmaneser. The inscription on one of them, from NE3, a gate chamber opening into the northeast court, was illegible, but the excavator suggested it was Shalmaneser's.[12] Another was in S4, a small chamber in the southern residential wing, to the west of the throne-room suite.[13] The remainder were all in the projecting wing of the throne-room suite, in T21, 25, 26, and 27.[14] The texts on four of these latter slabs, Grayson's nos. 30, 31.1, 31.2, and 31.3, say that they were commissioned by Shamash-bel-usur, the governor of Kalhu, who also commissioned the throne base. The latest dated events in these texts are from year 15, mentioned in all but one of them and therefore presumably the date when they were composed. The texts all consist of a titulary and some combination of historical or geographical passages similar to those on the two throne bases.

The longest of these texts (Grayson's no. 30) is in the doorway between Courtyard S and Room T25, on a large slab commissioned by Shamash-bel-usur.[15]

11. Titulary in Laessøe 1959: 41, augmented by Hulin 1963: 58. Laessøe and Hulin disagree about how much of the titulary was legible.

12. Mallowan 1966: vol. 2, 393, fig. 319.

13. Laessøe 1959: 38–40; Grayson 1996: 111–12. See also Schramm 1976: 86, no. 5a.

14. Grayson 1996: 106–14. Grayson is to be warmly thanked for publishing all of these texts from Hulin's draft transcriptions.

15. Grayson 1996: 106–8.

Its titulary is almost identical to that on the main throne base, including the un-usual references to treading, trampling, and conquered lands as a footstool, again highly appropriate for a text that would literally have been underfoot. Unlike the throne-base texts, the historical summary here is arranged chronologically, presenting a selection of campaigns: Urartu (year 3), Bit-Adini (year 4), the Hamath coalition (year 6), and Babylonia and Chaldea (years 8 and 9). The Bit-Adini passage is introduced with the general statement that the king crossed the Euphrates twelve times in fifteen years and conquered Hatti. The other texts are shorter, consisting of a genealogy, a few brief references to the extent of the realm ("from. . .to. . ."), and brief summaries of one, two, or three specific campaigns, selected from years 1, 3, 4, and 15.[16]

With the exception of year 15, all of the campaigns mentioned in the thresh-old texts are included in the text on Shalmaneser's throne base, from the prin-cipal throne room of Fort Shalmaneser.[17] The latest date mentioned in the throne-base text is year thirteen, and this must have been when it was composed. The latest date on the threshold texts indicate that they were compiled two years later. Their authors appear to have abstracted selected passages from the throne base text or from other similar texts, updating them when necessary to reflect events through year fifteen, as for example when the number of regnal years is changed from "13" to "15" and the number of Euphrates crossings from "10" to "12." To this is added a brief summary of the conquests of year 15.

Thus Shalmaneser's threshold inscriptions, like those of Assurnasirpal II, seem to have been based on an extant text. Unlike Assurnasirpal's texts, how-ever, which seem to have been applied with no consideration for completeness, the Shalmaneser examples were apparently compiled specifically for their in-tended location, with special care taken that they constitute a complete and in-telligible whole. This is precisely the same sort of transformation that will be seen in comparing the Shalmaneser III and Assurnasirpal II bull inscriptions and per-haps reflects the growth of a larger literate audience, for whom an inscription ex-ists to be read.

16. Grayson 1996: 108–14. Content: Nos. 31.1, 31.2, 31.3, 32, 33—years 15 and 3; No. 34—years 15, 4, and 1; Nos. 35, 36—year 15; No. 37—no specific year. Locations: No. 31.1—in the door between T25 and 26; Nos. 31.2 and 31.3—in the door between T3 and 21; No. 32—Hulin's notes say it is from the door between T27 and 28, but this area was not excavated; it is most probably from the central door between T27 and Courtyard T (which Hulin may have thought was T28, following the pattern of number-ing these rooms from west to east); No. 33—in the northern door between T27 and Courtyard T; No. 34—in the door between S3 and 4; No. 35—in the door between T21 and 27; Nos. 36.1 and 37—in the door between T23 and 26; No. 36.2—in the door be-tween T21 and 24.

17. Grayson 1996: 101–4.

Fig. 22. Kalhu, Fort Shalmaneser, glazed brick panel, drawing (courtesy Julian Reade).

Glazed Brick Wall Panel

A large-scale arched panel of Shalmaneser III, originally more than 4 meters high and made up of more than 300 glazed bricks, was found in Courtyard T of Fort Shalmaneser, evidently fallen from the outer wall above the door to Room T3. Reade's painstaking analysis of the fragments and reconstruction of the composition is one of the triumphs of the Fort Shalmaneser excavations (fig. 22). The panel showed symmetrical images of the king flanking a god in a winged disk, above which were bulls flanking a stylized tree, all framed by a border of floral and animal motifs. In the space between the winged god and the stylized tree was a 4-line inscription: "Palace of Shalmaneser, great king, mighty king, king of the world, king of Assyria; son of Assurnasirpal, great king, mighty king, king of the world, king of Assyria; son of Tukulti-Ninurta, great king, mighty king, king of the world, king of Assyria."[18] This is the only glazed brick composition that has been fully reconstructed to date, but bricks from another glazed panel were excavated in Room T20 of Fort Shalmaneser in 1989, and some of these carried parts of a similar inscription.[19] In addition, individual glazed brick fragments, often decorated with a few isolated signs from inscriptions that originally covered many bricks, have been found in every Assyrian palace. This suggests that glazed brick wall facings, and presumably also wall paintings, would have been common locations for palace inscriptions.

Colossi

A pair of five-legged, human-headed bull colossi of Assurnasirpal II's son, Shalmaneser III, are known to us, though their architectural context is uncertain (fig. 23). They were discovered in the center of the mound at Kalhu by Layard, who gave their dimensions as 14 feet at the base.[20] Sobolewski, who helped re-excavate these bulls in 1975, suggested that they had been moved from a nearby doorway to their present location, which is dissociated from any distinguishable architectural features.[21]

The bulls are each inscribed with the same text, which originally consisted of an introduction, giving the king's name, titles, and conquests, and an annalistic

18. Reade 1963: 44 and pl. 9; Grayson 1996: 169.

19. J. Curtis et al., "British Museum Excavations at Nimrud and Balawat in 1989," *Iraq* 55 (1993) 26.

20. Layard 1849a: vol. 1, 47.

21. Sobolewski 1982a: 258–60, fig. 6; Sobolewski 1974–77: 232, figs. 4, 5; Sobolewski 1980: English section, 155, fig. 4; Sobolewski 1982b: 329–40, figs. 4, 10.

FIG. 23. Kalhu, Centre Bulls, general view (courtesy R. P. Sobolewski).

account of years 1 through 15 (years 1–3 are now lost) and 18.[22] The three spaces between the legs contain the introduction and account of year 18, while the account of years 1–15 is inscribed on the back of the slab, on the unsculptured part that was originally against the wall (fig. 24).[23] Though the same text was the basis for each bull inscription, each bull omits part of the text.[24] Bull 1 contains more of the text than Bull 2, omitting only lines 48–52, listing the booty of

22. Manuscript copy: Layard, n.d., Ms A, 55–61, 119–21. Published text: Layard 1851: pl. 12–16, 46–7. Transliteration and translation: Delitzsch 1908, Grayson 1996: 42–48. Study: Schramm 1973: 76–77.

23. The text distribution may be seen in the photos in Sobolewski 1974–77: figs. 4, 5; and Sobolewski 1980: fig. 4.

24. The excavator's statement (Sobolewski 1982a: 260; and 1982b: 331, 335–36) that the inscription begins on the back of one colossus and ends on the other must be in error, assuming these are indeed the same colossi excavated by Layard. The publication of the inscription excavated by the Poles would clarify this matter.

FIG. 24. Kalhu, Centre
Bulls, view of inscribed
back (courtesy R. P.
Sobolewski).

Hazael of Damascus (year 18), and lines 106–7, which record the tribute of Asia
of Daianu (year 15).[25] Bull 2 contains a much more substantial omission, from
the middle of line 94 to the middle of line 100, including the second half of the
description of year 11, all of years 12 and 13, and the first half of year 14.[26]

Though this bull text, as transliterated and translated by Delitzsch and Grayson, appears to be substantially different from that of Assurnasirpal II, in reality

25. Line nos. from Delitzsch 1908: 148, 151; equivalent to Grayson 1996: 48:10″–
13″ ("I put to the sword . . . military camp"), and 48:50b′–51′ ("washed the weapons . . .
his city").

26. Line nos. from Delitzsch 1908: 147–48; equivalent to Grayson 1996: 47:39b′ ("I
took from them . . . ") through 45b′ (". . . 120,000 troops").

this is not the case. The publications of Delitzsch and Grayson reorder the text to conform to a chronological scheme that is not present in the original. Their translations present the introduction, account of years 1–15, and account of year 18 in that order, tending to obscure the fact that unless these bulls were originally free-standing, the account of years 1–15, carved on the back of the blocks, would have been invisible, turned against the wall.[27]

In effect, therefore, these bulls are inscribed not with a single continuous text, distributed discontinuously, but with two texts. The text on the back, an annalistic account of the first 15 years (with the introduction and accounts of the first two years broken away), is a duplicate, with minor variants, of a major part of Schramm's Recension C, an account of the first 16 years, preserved in numerous exemplars, most of them from Assur.[28] Of particular interest, however, is a fragmentary tablet containing part of this text found in the Nabu Temple at Kalhu, written in the script characteristic of Neo-Assyrian monumental inscriptions, and which Wiseman suggested "may have been a draft for the mason."[29] Perhaps this very tablet served as the guide for the cutting of the inscription on the backs of the Shalmaneser III bulls. This must remain conjectural, however, because the preserved portion of the tablet records only the accession and first years, parts that are destroyed in the bull inscriptions.

In the other text, carved on the front of the slab in the spaces between the legs, the passages giving titles and the resume of conquests are also taken from Recension C. Only the account of year 18 derives from a different text, a more complete example of which was published by Rawlinson.[30] Viewed as a whole, the text on the front of the Shalmaneser bulls is quite similar in form to the text on Assurnasirpal II's throne base and colossi. Like the Assurnasirpal text, it begins with the king's name and titles, continues with a resume of the king's conquests, arranged geographically rather than chronologically, and then proceeds to a more detailed account of a specific campaign, in this case against Syria. The

27. Delitzsch (1908: 144) indicates the correct order in his introduction to the text. I know of no evidence for free-standing colossi of this type. The free-standing gateway figures that occur later, in Esarhaddon's Southwest Palace at Kalhu, are sculptured on all sides (Barnett and Falkner 1962: pl. 108).

28. Schramm 1973: 73–76. The only complete example of this text is published by Cameron (1950). Six fragmentary examples are published by Schroeder (1922: nos. 109, 110, 112–115). Transliteration and translation in Grayson 1996: 32–41.

29. Wiseman 1964: 118, pl. 26; Grayson 1996: 32, "Ex. 11." Wiseman's reading is corrected and improved by Schramm (1973: 75–76).

30. "Rezension C": Cameron 1950: 10:I:11–27 and 17:IV:26 to 18.IV.36 (also Grayson 1996: 33:i:11–34:i:27, 41:iv:26–36). Rawlinson 1870: 5, no. 6; translated by Oppenheim in Pritchard 1969b: 280 (also Grayson 1996: 48, "Ex. 3"); further bibliography in Schramm 1973: 77; a paper squeeze is (or was) in the British Museum (*Guide to the Babylonian and Assyrian Antiquities* [3d ed., London, 1922] 47).

only sections of the Assurnasirpal text that do not have counterparts in the Shalmaneser III bull text are the passage describing the breeding and hunting of animals and the concluding account of the building of the palace.

Concerning the latter, it should be remembered that even though Assurnasirpal's Throne-Base Text concluded with a palace-building account, the truncated version that was inscribed on his colossi omitted that section in every case but one (B-c-2; see Catalog 1). If Assurnasirpal's colossus text served as Shalmaneser's model, then the omission of a building account would be expected. Furthermore, the function of "Shalmaneser's Building," of which these bulls were evidently a part, is unclear due to extensive disturbance of its remains by later building activity. That it may not be a palace may be inferred from the beginning of the bull inscription itself, which commences immediately with the king's name, omitting the word *ekallu* ('palace') found at the beginning of the palace inscriptions of all Assyrian kings, including other Shalmaneser III examples from Fort Shalmaneser. If this is not in fact a palace, then the absence of the palace-building account would not be surprising.[31]

The absence of the breeding and hunting accounts may best be attributed to lack of space, though it should be noted that hunting accounts do not figure as prominently in the records of Shalmaneser III's reign as they do in the records of Assurnasirpal II. While Assurnasirpal II's bronze gates from Balawat include hunting scenes, those of Shalmaneser III from the same site show only conquest and tribute. Nonetheless, hunting accounts of Shalmaneser III are preserved in the texts of Schramm's Recension C and Recension E. No account of breeding animals from Shalmaneser III's reign is known to me, but indirect evidence for the practice is seen in the reliefs of the "Black Obelisk" that show exotic animals, tribute from the land of Musri.[32]

A detailed analysis of the function of Shalmaneser III's bull inscriptions is not possible without a knowledge of their original context. A few general observations, however, may be offered. The fact that the text on the back of the slab ends with year 15 suggests that it was carved before the one on the front. As with the apparent sequence of the texts carved on the backs and fronts of Assurnasirpal II's colossi, this assumption is consistent with the presumed sequence of erection for these figures: the text on the back would have been carved before the blocks were erected against the jambs, sometime after year 15, while that on the front would not have been inscribed until after the figures were completed, after year 18.

31. Condition of remains: Sobolewski 1982a: 259–60. Fort Shalmaneser inscriptions that begin with "*ekallu*": Laessøe 1959: 38; Hulin 1963: 52.

32. "Rezension C": Cameron 1950: 18, 25; "Rezension E": Safar 1951: 11:41–45 and 12:19–22; Schramm 1973: 73, 77–78. Exotic animals from Musri: Pritchard 1969a: figs. 351–54.

As already noted, the visible portion of these inscriptions is similar in form to the bull inscriptions of Assurnasirpal II, and they probably functioned similarly, stating the nature, source, and extent of the king's authority, followed by a specific example of the force of the king's arms. In the case of the Shalmaneser bulls, the example chosen was the campaign of the eighteenth year, which suggests that the bull inscriptions were probably carved soon after that campaign. Indeed, the account of the eighteenth year found on the bulls was apparently the official version until the twentieth year. It is the version found on Shalmaneser's "Kurba-il Statue," which recounts events of years 18 to 20, but a new edition of the annals compiled in year 20 gives a somewhat more detailed account of year 18, including the name of the Tyrian king and a report of the setting up of a stele on Mt. Lebanon. Thus the bull inscriptions were probably carved between the eighteenth and twentieth years.[33]

While the visible text on the Shalmaneser III bulls is similar to the Assurnasirpal II throne-base/colossus text, there seems to be a significant difference in the way the text was applied. The Assurnasirpal II text breaks off, often abruptly, when the allotted space is filled. By contrast, the Shalmaneser text seems to be edited for the space at hand, giving a sense of completeness that the Assurnasirpal II colossus inscriptions often lack. Perhaps this text was arranged specifically for these particular bulls, rather than being an all-purpose text, as was the Assurnasirpal II throne-base/colossus text. As Pamela Gerardi has observed, this would imply a greater professionalism on the part of the scribes—with Assurnasirpal's palace now behind them, they would have been better-prepared to deal with the problems of length and location posed by the integration of texts into a palace's decorative program.[34] It is also possible that the expanding bureaucracy accompanying the expansion of the empire resulted in a larger literate audience for these inscriptions, with the consequence that the mere presence of an inscription was no longer enough; it now had to read well also.

Another difference between the inscriptions on the Assurnasirpal II and Shalmaneser III bulls is the extended annalistic inscription on the back of the latter. If these bulls were installed in the usual way, flush with the door jambs, this inscription would not have been visible. We are presented, therefore, with the question of the intended audience for this invisible inscription. Two possible audiences suggest themselves, though there is no specific evidence for either. First, these inscriptions could be intended for the eyes of a 'future prince' (*rubû arkû*) who would find it after the collapse of the building of which it was a part. Messages of this sort, which were intended to identify the builder of a structure even after it had fallen into ruins, are a common feature of Neo-Assyrian royal building

---

33. Wilson 1962: 94:21–30; Safar 1951: 11:45–12:15.
34. Personal communication, letter of 15 November 1995.

FIG. 25. Balawat, bronze gates
of Shalmaneser III, view of
restored replica in the British
Museum (photo: author).

inscriptions.[35] Inscriptions intended for future princes, however, usually conclude with a request that the associated building be restored, thereby perpetuat-
ing the memory of the writer of the inscription, and no such request is preserved
in the Shalmaneser III bull text.

A second possible audience is a god or gods. In this case the invisible inscription would presumably be intended to inform the god of the king's accomplishments. This was the audience for the inscription on Shalmaneser III's "Kurba-il

35. For examples of Shalmaneser III, see Grayson 1996: 99:34–36, 101:13–15, 116:
11–14, 121:10–13, 123:9–12, and passim.

Statue," addressed to the god Adad.[36] I assume that the inscription on the back of the bulls could be known to a god, even if it was not visible to mortals, especially if the building these colossi adorned should prove to have been a temple. Unfortunately, if this message was originally addressed to a god, that information was lost with the first lines of the inscription.

Bronze Doors: Epigraphs

Though no wall reliefs are known from the reign of Shalmaneser III, he did continue his predecessor's practice of labeling his small-scale reliefs with epigraphs. The largest collection known is on a pair of door leaves from the palace at Imgur-Enlil, where similar doors of Assurnasirpal II were also found. The pair of doors comprised 16 bronze bands (figs. 25, 26). Each was divided into two registers of relief, the subjects of which were mainly military conquest and the delivery of tribute. As with the Assurnasirpal II doors, there were two types of inscription. On the vertical edge of each door leaf was a strip of bronze inscribed with an annalistic account of years 1, 3, 4, 8, and 9. This is Schramm's Recension B, the second edition of the annals, composed sometime after year 9.[37] In addition, each of the bronze relief bands carried at least one epigraph; some had two and one had three. A total of 24 epigraphs are preserved, listed in the table on pp. 80–81 according to their form.[38]

Most of these epigraphs are similar to the epigraphs on the doors of Assurnasirpal II in the same palace. Those beginning "tribute from . . ." or "battle against. . . ," and those ending with ". . . I captured" or ". . . I received," have the same form as the descriptive portions of Assurnasirpal's epigraphs. An important difference, however, is that Shalmaneser's bronze door epigraphs are purely descriptive. None of them begin with a titulary, as do nearly half of Assurnasirpal's. The omission of the titulary has the effect of placing the focus of the epigraph solely on the subject depicted. This act of focusing is facilitated by the brevity of most of these epigraphs, which are much shorter than the epigraphs of Assurnasirpal that begin with a titulary and therefore can be taken in at a glance. Their brevity also has the effect of making them *appear* more accessible, so that they are more likely to be read than a longer text.

36. Wilson 1962: 93:1, 96.

37. Transliteration and translation: Michel 1959: 408–17; Michel 1967: 29–35; Grayson 1996: 27–32. Studies: Schramm 1973: 72–73; Marcus 1987; Schneider 1991: 176–79.

38. Transliteration and translation: Michel 1967: 34–37; Grayson 1996: 140 48. Photos and discussion: King 1915; Unger 1920. Registers I/IX:a and J/X:b each have two epigraphs; these are run together in Michel's edition.

FIG. 26. Balawat, bronze gates of Shalmaneser III, Band II, width of flat (left) part: 145 cm.

English Translation, from Michel's Transliterations	Michel's Letter	King's Roman Numeral	British Museum Number	a=above/b=below
"Battle against the city Baqanu(?) in Chaldea."	O			
"Battle against the city Dabigu, belonging to Ahuni of Bit-Adini."	D	IV	124658	a
"Battle against the land Hamath."	P			
"Battle against the city Hazazu."	C	III	124661	b
"Battle against the land Urartu."	B	II	124659	a
"Tribute from Adini of Bit-Dakuri, the Chaldean."	K	XI	124660	a
"Tribute from Sangara of Carchemish."	F	VI	124653	a
"Tribute from the land Gilzanu."	G	VII	124652	b
"Tribute from the land Unqu(?)."	E	V	124651	a
"The city belonging to Arame of Urartu, I captured."	G	VII	124652	a
"The city Arne, belonging to Arame, I captured."	L	XII	124654	a
"The city Sugunia, belonging to Arame of Urartu, I captured."	A	I	124662	b
"The city [. . .]agda, belonging to Arame of Bit-Agusi, I captured."	L	XII	124654	b
"Ashtamaku, the royal city of Irhuleni of Hamath, together with 86 cities, I captured."	M	XIII	124657	a
"The city Ada, belonging to Urhileni of Hamath, I captured."	I	IX	124655	a
"The city Qarqar, belonging to Urhileni of Hamath, I captured."	I	IX	124655	b

British Museum, WA 124659 (photo: Trustees of the British Museum).

English Translation, from Michel's Transliterations	Michel's Letter	King's Roman Numeral	British Museum Number	a=above/b=below
"The city Parga, I captured."	I	IX	124655	a
"The city Ubumu, belonging to Anhiti of Shubria, I captured."	H	VIII	124663	a
"Kulisi, the royal city of Mutzuata, I captured, I burned with fire."	J	X	124656	b
"Tribute from the ships of Tyre and Sidon, I received."	C	III	124661	a
"Tribute from Tyre and Sidon: silver, gold, tin, copper, and scarlet wool, I received."	N			b
"I entered the sources of the river, I offered sacrifices to the gods, I set up my royal image."	J	X	124656	b
"I set up an image on (the shore of) the sea of Nairi; I offered sacrifices to the gods."	A	I	124662	a
"My royal image . . . "	N			a

Another difference is that a few of Shalmaneser's epigraphs give different sorts of information than do Assurnasirpal's. Three deal with the erection of royal images. Another specifically identifies the types of goods received as tribute from Tyre and Sidon. Interestingly, all seven of the king's later epigraphs—two on the throne base from Room T1 in Fort Shalmaneser (after year 13) and five on the Black Obelisk from Kalhu (after year 31)—are tribute lists of this latter type.[39]

39. Black Obelisk (British Museum, WA 118885), photographs: Pritchard 1969a: figs. 351–54; transliteration and translation: Michel 1955: 140–43; Grayson 1996: 148–51.

Also in contrast to the epigraphs of Assurnasirpal, the place names in Shalmaneser's epigraphs nearly all also occur in his annalistic texts.[40]

Summary: Shalmaneser III

The total number of Shalmaneser III palace inscriptions was much smaller than for Assurnasirpal II, but they were found in most of the same sorts of locations. The content and complicated arrangement of the long inscription and the various tags and epigraphs on Shalmaneser's main throne base from Fort Shalmaneser were analyzed and compared with his inscribed thresholds. Attention was also drawn to a brief inscription on a wall panel of glazed brick that, while not particularly informative by itself, reminds us that many texts must originally have been displayed on wall paintings and glazed bricks, now lost or dispersed.

A pair of inscribed Shalmaneser bull colossi in the center of Kalhu citadel in the area later occupied by Tiglath-pileser III's palace may have belonged to either a palace or temple of Shalmaneser. These texts, while fully published by Layard, have suffered subsequently at the hands of philologists and archaeologists, both (1) by being reordered in later publications to conform to a chronological arrangement and (2) by being misidentified in preliminary publications that report on their recent reexcavation. These misrepresentations were rectified here and the texts were analyzed in their correct contexts, on the fronts and backs of the colossi. The text on the front of the colossi was similar in form to that on Assurnasirpal's bulls, but unlike Assurnasirpal's, the back was carved with an annalistic account of Shalmaneser's first fifteen years. Finally, the epigraphs on Shalmaneser's bronze doors from Imgur Enlil were presented in full and discussed in terms of their form and their relationship to the epigraphs of Assurnasirpal. In cases where more than one epigraph appears on a single relief, the common practice of publishing the separate epigraphs all together as a single text was noted and such examples were here presented as individual texts.

40. The only exceptions are the cities Parga, Ada, and Kulisi, which according to Parpola (1970) occur only here.

Chapter 4

Adad-Nirari III (810–783 B.C.)

Following the death of Shalmaneser III, Assyria went into a period of decline for some 80 years. The only relatively powerful monarch during this time was Adad-nirari III, who ruled from Kalhu and left his mark on that city in the form of the Nabu Temple and neighboring "Burnt Palace," a palatial building at the northwest corner of the city wall, and an addition to the south side of Assurnasirpal II's palace. At Nineveh, Adad-nirari III built or rebuilt the Nabu Temple and finished a palace, and at Assur he reinforced a stretch of the quay wall.

At the western edge of the Kalhu citadel, just to the south of Assurnasirpal's palace, Layard found a suite of rooms, which he called the "upper chambers" (fig. 27).[1] This consisted of four rooms arranged in a T-shaped plan. The top of the T was formed by three small rooms laid out from east to west and connected to one another by two doorways (*b* and *c*). The middle room communicated via another doorway (*a*) with a large reception room to its south (the stem of the T). Only the north end of this room was preserved. It was furnished with a dais and two sets of "tramlines," evidently tracks for a wheeled brazier. The rooms were decorated with two layers of wall paintings. In 1854–55, William Loftus excavated some additional rooms that may be part of the same structure.[2] The plans of both excavations appear flawed, but Turner observed that they can be combined and restored to show a typical Assyrian reception suite.[3]

---

1. Layard 1849a: vol. 2, 14–17 and plan 4.

2. Loftus's rooms may, however, belong to a different level. The excavations of 1854–55 have never been fully published; the work in the vicinity of the "upper chambers" is recorded on a plan (Barnett and Falkner 1962: pl. 130) and referred to briefly in the second "Report of the Assyrian Excavation Fund" (reproduced in Gadd 1936: appendix, p. 4).

3. Reade (1968: 69–70) and Turner (1970: 198–99 and pl. 43) discuss the problems posed by the plans and Turner included a restoration.

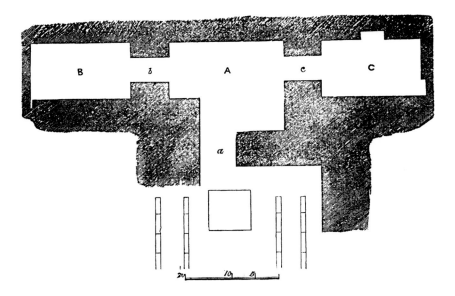

Fig. 27. Kalhu, Upper Chambers of Adad-nirari III, plan (after Layard 1849a: vol. 2, plan 4).

In two of the doorways (*a* and *b*) Layard found stone threshold slabs inscribed with two variants of a text of Adad-nirari III (fig. 28).[4] Layard published the full text of the inscription in Door *a* and listed variants from Door *b*.[5] These are the only Adad-nirari palace inscriptions known to have been found in a clear architectural context. They probably indicate that he was the builder of this structure, which may be an addition to Assurnasirpal's palace. Another, slightly longer, variant was published by Norris from a cast or copy in the British Museum, identified only as "from a pavement slab . . . found at Nimrud, at the edge of the mound, between the N.W. and S.W. Palaces," which is also the area of the "upper chambers."[6] If, as seems likely, this slab derives from Loftus's excavations,

4. Layard 1849a: vol. 2, 16.

5. Layard 1851: 70. His original copy of the full Door *a* text is Ms A, 122–23. He copied only variants for the Door *b* text (Ms A, 123). The slab from Door *a* is British Museum, WA 118925 (acc. no. 51-9-2, 35; former no. 611; contra Bezold 1889–99: vol. 5, "1R 35, no. 3").

6. Text: Rawlinson 1861: vol. 1, pl. 35:3; republished in F. Delitzsch, *Assyrische Lesestücke* (5th ed., Leipzig, 1912) 61. Transliteration and translation: Grayson 1996: 201–3. The slab itself is not in the British Museum (contra Bezold 1889–99: vol. 5, "1R 35, no. 3").

FIG. 28. Kalhu,
Upper Chambers,
threshold of Adad-
nirari III. British
Museum, WA 118925
(photo: Trustees of
the British Museum).

then the appearance of the same text in both the "upper chambers" and Loftus's rooms would strongly suggest that both groups of rooms belonged to the same structure.

The text, basically a genealogy, is a traditional enough type of Assyrian palace inscription but is unusual in its length and scope. The longest version of the text, on the exemplar published by Norris, begins with "Palace of Adad-nirari" and a few standard titles and epithets. Then follows the list of his predecessors, each with one or two brief titles or epithets: his father Shamshi-Adad V, his grandfather Shalmaneser III, his great-grandfather Assurnasirpal II, and their predecessors Adad-nirari II (911–891 B.C.), Tukulti-Ninurta I (1243–1207 B.C.), Shalmaneser I (1273–1244 B.C.), Enlil-kapkapi, and Sulili. The two variants from doors *a* and *b* of the "upper chambers" are the same text, but slightly truncated: both omit Sulili and Door *a* also omits Enlil-kapkapi.

According to the Assyrian King List, these last two kings predate the Old Assyrian period. Sulili (ca. 2000 B.C.), number 27 on the list, is given as the first of a group of six kings, the latter three of whom are the first kings of the Old Assyrian dynasty. The label for this group of kings associates them with bricks—probably something like "6 kings [who are known from] bricks, but whose eponymies are *unknown*(?)," that is, their bricks had been recovered, but not an eponym list that would give the lengths of their reigns.[7] The name "Enlil-kapkapi" is not attested elsewhere, but must be the same king as Ilu-kabkabi, number 25 on the king list, who is rather improbably listed both as the grandfather of Sulili and, more accurately, as the father of Shamshi-Adad I (1813–1781 B.C.; number 39 on the list), the first Amorite king after the Old Assyrian dynasty.[8] Adad-nirari III, who must have based this part of his "genealogy" on the king list, seems here to be claiming descent both from the indigenous Assyrian line (Sulili) and from the Amorite Shamshi-Adad line (Ilu-kabkabi).[9] In addition, the context makes it appear that these kings are being contrasted with the first 17 on the list, who "lived in tents," and Adad-nirari may have understood Sulili to be the first Assyrian king to live in a palace of brick.

This is a remarkable text. In the threshold inscriptions of Adad-nirari's predecessors, the emphasis had been on royal epithets and the king's supremacy over foreign lands, and this was in fact the subject of an Adad-nirari III palace inscription on a broken (pavement?) slab, also found out of context "at Nimrud, at the edge of the mound, between the N.W. and S.W. Palaces."[10] The emphasis in the slabs from the "upper chambers," by contrast, is on Adad-nirari's inherited right to rule. This is established by tracing his lineage back to Assurnasirpal II, the

7. Translation and bibliography: Pritchard 1969b: 564. Commentary in Larsen 1976: 34–39. The uncertain passage reads: PAP 6 LUGAL.MEŠ-*a-ni* [x x x] ʳxʾ SIG₄ *šá li-ma-a-ni-šú-nu la-u-ṭu-ni* (I. J. Gelb, "Two Assyrian King Lists," *Journal of Near Eastern Studies* 13 [1954] 213:24–25). Sulili may be the same as Ṣilulu, whose name appears on an Old Assyrian seal impression (Grayson 1987: 12–13).

8. The only significant difference between Ilu-kabkabi (ᵐDINGIR-*kab-ka-bi*) and Enlil-kapkapi (ᵐᵈBAD-*kap-ka-pi*) is the BAD sign, which may have been added erroneously on Adad-nirari's version of the king list or during the compilation of the master copy of the threshold text (for references, see Borger 1961: 12; W. Röllig, "Ila-kabkabu," *Reallexikon der Assyriologie*, vol. 5 [Berlin, 1976–80] 48). In addition, Kirk Grayson points out that "since Enlil was pronounced Ellil in Neo-Assyrian, a confusion with Ilu is quite understandable" (personal communication, letter of 31 January 1996). He does seem to have been Shamshi-Adad I's father (Grayson 1987: 60–61).

9. An observation I owe to Jerrold Cooper (personal communication, letter of 6 May 1994).

10. Text: Rawlinson 1861: vol. 1, pl. 35:1. Transliteration and translation: Grayson 1996: 212–13. Translation: Pritchard 1969b: 281–82. According to Bezold (1889–99: vol. 5, "1R 35, no. 1"), the slab is "not in Europe."

modern rebuilder of Kalhu; then back to Adad-nirari II, his namesake; on back through famous Middle Assyrian kings, including Shalmaneser I, who according to Assurnasirpal II was the original founder of Kalhu; and finally, back to the two original Assyrian royal lines and what he may have believed to be the first Assyrian king to rule from a palace. It is a powerful statement of royal authority. It is also, to my knowledge, unique among Assyrian display inscriptions in its extensive and single-minded focus on royal succession.

Of course, this full message was only conveyed on one of the three published slabs. The other two were truncated: Door *a* in the middle of Shalmaneser I's epithets, Door *b* in the passage that introduces Sulili. In both cases this truncation does violence to the text, especially in the case of Door *b*, where the break occurs in mid-sentence. The Door *a* slab is very well preserved; there is no possibility that lines were lost. The text does, however, cover all the available surface. It may be that here, as in the truncated inscriptions of Assurnasirpal II in the older part of the palace right next-door, the available space determined the amount of text to be included, without regard for completeness.

Summary: *Adad-Nirari III*

The only palace text of Adad-nirari III to be found in a good architectural context was carved on three thresholds in his palace at Kalhu. This is another example of the philological and archaeological traditions going their separate ways, but when the two are reunited, the result is a complex and, I believe, deliberate interplay between the genealogical text and its palatial context.

Chapter 5

Tiglath-Pileser III (744–727 B.C.)

In the time of Tiglath-pileser III, Assyria's expansionist policy was renewed, with a change in emphasis from control of trade and resources to actual political domination of foreign lands and peoples. The Assyrians were so successful in this regard that by the time of Esarhaddon (680–669 B.C.) the empire included all of what is now Iraq, Syria, the Levant, Egypt, and large parts of Turkey and Iran. Tiglath-pileser III ruled from Kalhu, where he built a new royal palace decorated with wall reliefs in the manner of Assurnasirpal II's palace. Little has been recovered of the plan of this palace, which Layard called the Central Palace. Tiglath-pileser says it was on the west side of the citadel mound, facing the Tigris, and it may have extended into the center of the citadel as far as Shalmaneser III's bull colossi, near which Layard found a number of Tiglath-pileser wall reliefs stacked in piles awaiting reuse in Esarhaddon's palace.[1] Layard was unable to locate any palace walls in this vicinity, however. Meuszynski located fragmentary remains of a monumental late building in this area, but Sobolewski, who published these finds, doubted that they belonged to Tiglath-pileser's palace.[2]

The Wall Slab Text

The walls of some rooms in Tiglath-pileser's palace were lined with relief slabs, but these had been removed from their original position by Esarhaddon for reuse in his Southwest Palace. They were found by Layard stacked in the Central Palace, in preparation for being moved, and in the Southwest Palace, some already on the walls and others lined up on the floor in front of the walls. Since the slabs were not in position, Layard was unable to trace the walls of the Central Pal-

1. Postgate and Reade 1976–80: 314–15.
2. Sobolewski 1982a: 261.

88

FIG. 29. Kalhu, Central Palace of Tiglath-pileser III, the booty of Astartu, width 195 cm. British Museum, WA 118908 (photo: Trustees of the British Museum).

ace to determine how many rooms might have been decorated. Layard shipped a selection of the reliefs to the British Museum and made drawings of a number of others he left behind, but Meuszynski's reexcavation of the Central Palace showed that some slabs were not recorded at all.[3]

3. Meuszynski 1976. The surviving slabs and drawings are assembled in Barnett and Falkner 1962.

Some of the reliefs were found stacked in the order in which they had been removed by the Assyrian workers who dismantled the palace, and this together with an analysis of overlaps in the inscription and stylistic criteria were used by Tadmor to propose a reconstruction of parts of five or six inscribed relief series, each of which may have decorated a different room.[4] Most of the published reliefs, including two of Tadmor's series and an uninscribed series assembled by Reade, depict military activity. The format of these slabs was the same as that of the military reliefs of Assurnasirpal II: two registers of relief separated by a central register of text (fig. 29). Tadmor distinguished between the two inscribed series of military reliefs on the basis of the number of lines in the inscription: his "Series A" has seven lines, while "Series B" has twelve. The reliefs in each of these series may be summarized as follows (numerals are plate numbers in Barnett and Falkner 1962):[5]

Table 5.1. Tadmor's Series A ("the seven-line series")

	72		80		37+39		69		62	
gap	inscr.	gap	inscr.	gap	inscr.	gap	inscr.	gap	inscr.	gap
	73		48		50+52		69		63	

Table 5.2. Tadmor's Series B ("the twelve-line series")

	88		89		81			
	88		89		81		65	
gap	inscr.	gap	inscr.	gap	inscr.	inscr.	inscr.	gap
	88		89		82	85		

At least one more military series is represented by a group of reliefs that have the central strip prepared for an inscription that was never added (figs. 30, 31).[6] This may indicate that the palace was uncompleted at Tiglath-pileser's death.

Initially, Tadmor (1968) distinguished four more relief series: C_1-C_2, D, and E. Only the reliefs from Series D have been published, but the subjects on the remainder are mentioned by Layard (1851, abbrev. ICC; see Table 5.3).

More recently, Tadmor (1994) has expressed reservations about the subdivision of C_1, C_2, and D, since "their fragmentary condition, the many lacunae and the absence of most of the originals makes such a distribution rather con-

---

4. Tadmor 1968: 177–86; Tadmor 1994: 24–25, 238–59.
5. Tadmor 1994: 238–59.
6. Reade 1979b: 72–76.

FIG. 30. Kalhu, Central Palace of Tiglath-pileser III, booty of an unnamed city, width 290 cm. British Museum, WA 118882 (photo: Trustees of the British Museum).

Table 5.3. Tadmor's Series C₁–C₂, D, and E

Series C$_1$	ICC, 71–72a, "across Winged Figures" ICC, 45b, "Across Colossal Figure holding a Mace" Rawlinson 1870: 9, no. 1 (no description) ICC, 29, "on Winged Figure"
Series C$_2$	ICC, 65, "Across a Winged Figure" ICC, 72b-73a, "Across three Colossal Figures of Eunuchs"
Series D	Barnett and Falkner 1962, pls. 97 + 98
Series E	ICC, 66, "Across a Figure carrying a Mace"

jectural."[7] I have nevertheless retained his designations here because the distinctions they highlight may prove to be valid. According to Tiglath-pileser's building account, his palace decoration included bull and lion colossi and apotropaic figures.[8] Layard reported winged deities and figures holding maces but didn't draw any examples, and only a fragment of one survives.[9] Three of Tadmor's proposed relief series (C$_1$, C$_2$, E) featured figures of these types. Two inscribed fragments in the British Museum from another series (D) show the king and an

7. Tadmor 1994: 24.
8. Text: Rawlinson 1866: pl. 67; Rost 1893: pl. 38, pp. 72–77. Translation: Luckenbill 1926: §804.
9. Barnett and Falkner 1962: 26, pl. 104.

attendant, and Meuszynski found another inscribed slab with courtiers from the same series.[10] All of these formal subjects were composed in one register with the text carved across the image. Colossal winged human-headed bulls carved in low relief and colossal wingless humans holding plants were also found but seem to have been uninscribed.[11]

The inscription on all of these reliefs was not a short text repeated on each slab, as with Assurnasirpal's "Standard Inscription," but instead was a long annalistic text (or summary text in the case of Series E) that continued from slab to slab, apparently around the entire room. Also unlike Assurnasirpal's inscribed wall slabs, the column divisions of Tiglath-pileser's annals only rarely correspond to the slab edges, so that a single column of text is often spread across two slabs. The surviving exemplars of this text, though fragmentary and incomplete, constitute our most detailed source for the events of Tiglath-pileser's reign.[12] In addition to the register of annalistic text, at least one relief series included brief captions on the images themselves, giving the names of the cities represented.

There are serious obstacles to determining the precise relationship between image and text in the reliefs of Tiglath-pileser III. Layard apparently discovered, or recorded, only a small portion of the reliefs originally in the Central Palace, every relief series known to us has major lacunae, and most are known only from a very few slabs. Furthermore, there seems to be no way to determine the original location of any relief series, because the plan of the Central Palace itself is unknown. Finally, the events of the reign of Tiglath-pileser III are but imperfectly known to us, due in large part to the fragmentary nature of the annals carved on the palace wall slabs.[13] Nonetheless, a few observations may be ventured on the basis of the available material.

First, it appears that there is not necessarily any direct relationship between the text on a given slab and the images immediately above and below.[14] With the exception of Series E, all of the inscriptions preserved on wall reliefs seem to be annalistic in form. In rooms decorated with formal subjects—as on Tadmor's Series C_1-C_2, D, and E—there was apparently no direct connection between the narrative text and the large-scale figures of winged genies, eunuchs, and the like. Even in rooms decorated with narrative images, there seems to have been little concern with placing texts and images devoted to the same subject in close prox-

10. Sobolewski 1982a: 263–64.

11. Barnett and Falkner 1962: 25–26, pls. 105–7; Meuszynski 1976: 41, pls. 12:a, 13; Sobolewski 1982a: 264–66.

12. Tadmor (1994) has published all the source material.

13. These problems may be at least partially cleared up when the many recently re-excavated reliefs from the area of the "Central Palace" are fully published (Meuszynski 1976; Sobolewski 1974–1977; Sobolewski 1980; Sobolewski 1982a). See also the reconstruction essay in Tadmor 1994: 238–59.

14. *Contra* Barnett and Falkner 1962: 29, no. 3b.

imity to one another. In Tadmor's Series A, for example, one slab shows the siege of what is apparently an Eastern city (labeled U-pa?) in the upper register and an unknown city in the lower register. The accompanying text band records the campaigns of the eighth year, to the west, and the ninth year, to Media. This latter portion of the inscription may in fact refer to the campaign illustrated above it. Proceeding further in the series, however, we encounter two slabs also showing labeled cities, Astartu and Gezer, both undoubtedly in the west, yet the accompanying texts refer to the campaigns of the eleventh year (to Urartu) and the fifteenth year (to Babylonia) (see fig. 29).

Similarly, in Tadmor's Series B, the first two preserved slabs depict a western campaign in the upper and, probably, lower registers, but the text records the campaigns of the first year, to Babylonia, and the second year, to Media. Further along, three connected slabs show campaigns that Barnett identified as Urartu (above) and Media (below), though neither identification is certain.[15] The text band records the campaigns of the eighth year (to the west) and ninth year (to Media), so that here too there is a possible partial parallel between image and text. Thus the admittedly fragmentary evidence leaves one with the impression that, while the text band and associated images *may* refer to the same event, they often do not; thus, an occasional correspondence is more likely to be attributed to accident than design. In other words, it appears that the relief decoration and wall text of a room were planned independently of one another; when parallels between the two occur on a given slab, this is coincidental.

Second, it seems clear that the narrative decoration of a single room of Tiglath-pileser III's palace could include scenes from several of the king's campaigns. This can be seen both in Series A, which apparently contains scenes of both east and west, and Series B, which depicted campaigns that have been identified as western, northern, and eastern, the latter two on the upper and lower registers, respectively, of the same slab. This same combination of a number of campaigns in the decoration of a single room can be seen in the extended series of uninscribed narrative slabs in two registers discussed by Reade (figs. 30, 31).[16] Here, the upper register was devoted to a Babylonian campaign, while the lower showed Syrian and Arab tributaries and possibly an Arab campaign as well. On the basis of these examples, it appears that a consistent correspondence between text and image on a given slab cannot have been a significant priority for a relief designer who regularly shows one campaign at the top of the slab and a different campaign at the bottom.

Finally, the narrative series showing the Babylonian, Syrian, and Arab subjects, because it is the most completely preserved relief series from the Central Palace, illustrates the reason why a precise correspondence between text band

15. Barnett and Falkner 1962: xx, xxiv, 41–42.
16. Reade 1979b: 74–75.

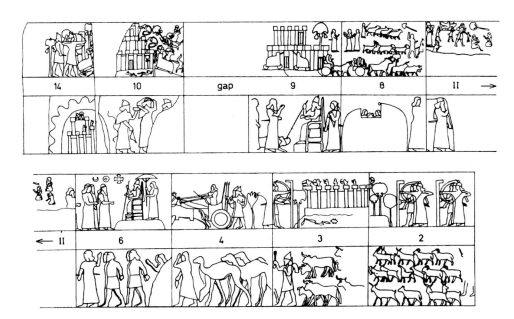

Fig. 31. Kalhu, Central Palace of Tiglath-pileser III, drawing of uninscribed relief series (source: J. Reade).

and image might not have been desirable. The narrative of a Babylonian campaign here occupied the upper register of at least eleven contiguous slabs, nine of which survive, and may have continued further, beyond either end of this preserved portion of the series. A written account of the same events, by contrast, would have covered the central text band of no more than two or three slabs.[17] The issue here is the different amount of space required for verbal and visual narratives. A written account of a series of events can compress a considerable amount of information into a relatively small space. Thus it was possible to inscribe the entire annals of Tiglath-pileser's first fifteen years of rule on the text band of each decorated room, as was apparently done in the Central Palace. A pictorial narrative, by contrast, requires a considerably greater space to illustrate even a limited number of events.

To be sure, the Assyrian artist could have selected from each campaign a single event, which would then "stand for" the entire campaign, and thereby include every campaign in the pictorial decoration of a room. There are possible problems with this approach, though. First, if these scenes were arranged in chro-

17. This length is of necessity an estimate, since no complete account of any of Tiglath-pileser III's campaigns is preserved. See Tadmor 1968: 186.

nological order, the lack of continuity from one scene to the next would be confusing for the viewer. Second, the limited amount of space available for each episode would limit the number of particularizing details that would be added to facilitate the viewer's recognition of the subject. Finally, if we recall the stipulation of Güterbock and Winter that historical narrative must "incorporate some coherent progression of events," that is, "the story must be 'told,' not 'implied,'" it becomes clear that the representation of a single event from a campaign is in no sense the equivalent of the verbal narration of that campaign.[18] Indeed, it is quite the opposite, for "sequence" is the most basic requirement of an annalistic narrative. These three drawbacks of episodic narrative—lack of continuity, limited number of particularizing details, and absence of sequence—are the main reasons why the narrative representations in Assurnasirpal II's Northwest Palace throne room are so difficult to read accurately. Thus we see that, assuming that the Assyrian artist wished to convey the same type of information in his visual narratives that the Assyrian scribe included in his verbal narratives, the former would require much more space than the latter, necessitating the inclusion of fewer campaigns in the pictorial portion of the decoration than in the written.

To summarize the relationship of text to narrative image in the wall relief decoration of Tiglath-pileser III's palace then, it appears from the fragmentary surviving evidence that the message presented in both media was roughly the same. Most rooms contained a complete written narrative account of the king's reign, and this was paralleled in several rooms by a pictorial narrative account of selected campaigns. The only benefit of literacy in such a room was that it would permit an appreciation of the full extent of the king's accomplishments, rather than the less complete version presented by the selection of campaigns represented pictorially. This would hardly seem to be a significant difference, however, since the same full picture could be achieved by a nonliterate viewer walking through two or three rooms, each decorated with a different selection of campaigns. The only notable difference between the two accounts would be that the overall sequence of campaigns might be clearer from the text than from the images. Other rooms were decorated with formal scenes of winged genies, the king and courtiers, and the like, across which was carved the same annalistic account of the king's reign. Clearly, the content of image and text were different from one another in these rooms.

In conclusion, it should be noted that Tiglath-pileser III's annalistic text, carved once around the walls of a room, has one disadvantage when compared to the short summary text carved on every slab of Assurnasirpal II's palace: the important passage that gives the name and titles of the king—and thereby identifies the protagonist of the texts and reliefs both for contemporaries and, especially, posterity—apparently occurs only once, at the beginning of the wall inscription,

18. Winter 1981: 2; Güterbock 1957: 62.

in each room of the Central Palace. Since one of the primary reasons for including a text with an image is the ability of the text to particularize the image (for
example, "this is Tiglath-pileser III," instead of "this is a king"), this infrequent
occurrence of the king's name is potentially serious, for if the slab bearing the
royal name is overlooked or damaged, then the events described and depicted on
all of the reliefs in that room lose their specific historical context.[19]

Epigraphs

The reliefs of Tiglath-pileser III mark the first known appearance of epigraphs on the wall reliefs of an Assyrian palace. Only three of these epigraphs
have been reported, all from Tadmor's Series A. Each consists only of a single city
name—U-pa(?), Gezer, and Astartu—written directly above the walls of the city
it labels (see fig. 29).[20]

There are two features that distinguish these epigraphs from the earlier examples on the small-scale reliefs on the bronze doors of Assurnasirpal II and
Shalmaneser III. First, the Tiglath-pileser III epigraphs are briefer. The epigraphs
of Shalmaneser and Assurnasirpal are typically in the form of a declarative sentence: "The city GN$_1$ in the land GN$_2$ I captured," or "The tribute of PN of the
land GN." Tiglath-pileser's preserved epigraphs, by contrast, consist of only a
single word, the name of the identified city. Second, Tiglath-pileser's epigraphs
seem to occur less frequently than do those of his predecessors. In the bronze
doors and obelisks of Assurnasirpal and Shalmaneser, virtually every city and
tribute procession is labeled. In the palace reliefs of Tiglath-pileser III, representations of some twelve cities are known from preserved reliefs or drawings, yet
only three of these are certainly identified by epigraphs. To be sure, in some of
these cases an epigraph might have been broken away or omitted in the drawing,
but in others the epigraph was apparently never there at all.[21] Furthermore, the
three preserved epigraphs all seem to have been from a single room, and even this
relief series included at least one unlabeled city scene.[22]

19. See Barthes 1977: 38–40.
20. URU *ú-p[a]*(?) (Barnett and Falkner 1962: xix, 41, pl. 38); URU *ga-az-ru* (ibid.,
pl. 62); URU *aṣ-tar-tu* (ibid., pl. 69).
21. Original relief fully preserved, no trace of epigraph: Barnett and Falkner 1962:
pls. 3, 45, 50, 90. Original relief only partially preserved, no trace of epigraph on preserved portion: ibid., pls. 34, 61, 79. Relief known only from drawing, no epigraph
shown: ibid., pls. 10, 56. Note that two of Layard's city drawings include the epigraph
(ibid., pls. 37, 62), while a third (pl. 68) omits the epigraph even though it is clearly visible on the original relief; thus Layard's omission of an epigraph in a drawing does not
necessarily mean that it did not exist on the original relief.
22. Barnett and Falkner 1962: pl. 51.

The palace reliefs of Tiglath-pileser III mark a shift from the use of a single narrative episode to evoke an entire campaign or region, as in the throne room reliefs of Assurnasirpal II, to more extended narrative series, each apparently devoted to the events of a single campaign, accompanied in the central text register by an inscribed annalistic text. In this context, it is possible to suggest two explanations for the appearance of brief epigraphs on Tiglath-pileser's reliefs. If the relatively generic appearance of the narratives of Assurnasirpal's reliefs was a deliberate attempt to provide an accurate visual parallel to the general message of the Standard Inscription, then the introduction of epigraphs into the reliefs of Tiglath-pileser III may be seen as a means of insuring that the reliefs convey the same high degree of specificity as does the accompanying annals text. If, on the contrary, Assurnasirpal II's narrative images were originally intended as highly specific representations of particular cities and events, which failed to function at the desired degree of particularity due to lack of epigraphs, then Tiglath-pileser's use of epigraphs could be seen as a remedy for this undesirable situation.

Assurnasirpal II's narrative palace reliefs may indeed have been sufficiently specific to be recognizable by members of and visitors to that king's court, viewers who either would already have a passing familiarity with the events of the day, or who could easily find someone who was. Whether Assurnasirpal's narratives were intended as regional generics or specific cities, a viewer could easily determine the subject, if he didn't readily recognize it, by asking around. Such may not have been the case, however, for Tiglath-pileser III and his court, living in Assurnasirpal's palace 150 years later. It is probable that by this time relatively few of Assurnasirpal's unlabeled images would have been recognizable, due to changing artistic conventions, the changing appearance of the cities in question, and the death long before of all those who could explain the images. For Tiglath-pileser, the "matching" of events recounted in Assurnasirpal's annalistic texts with the events depicted on the reliefs may have been nearly as uncertain a process as it is today. Thus Tiglath-pileser III may have been in the position to perceive what Assurnasirpal II could not: the difficulties of interpretation that unlabeled narrative images present for posterity. Tiglath-pileser's brief, unobtrusive epigraphs would have ensured that his narrative reliefs would have a high level of specificity both at the time they were carved and for years to come.

The question of why some of Tiglath-pileser III's narrative images bore epigraphs while others did not is complicated by the fragmentary nature of the evidence. In at least one room, the annalistic inscription was never carved on the central band, even though one must originally have been intended.[23] Thus it is perhaps not surprising that no epigraphs were carved on that series. In the room decorated with Series B, the text band was inscribed, but the accompanying reliefs are so defaced that it is not possible to be certain whether epigraphs were

23. Reade 1979b: 72–75.

originally included. In the room decorated with Series A, epigraphs do survive, but even here, one city in the lower register bears no epigraph even though the city, U-pa(?), in the upper register of the same slab does.[24]

The explanation for this selective use of epigraphs may perhaps be deduced from the wording of the annals text. Here, a frequent practice is to give the name of an important conquered city and add that other cities in the neighborhood were captured as well, leaving their number, names, and importance to the imagination of the reader: "Sibur, together with the cities of its environs, I captured."[25] This combination of a specific ("Sibur") with a generic ("the cities of its environs") may well be paralleled in the reliefs, in which case the important city would be labeled with an epigraph, while the smaller towns in its environs could be represented collectively by an unlabeled city picture associated compositionally with the labeled image.

Finally, it should be noted that none of the three city names recorded by the epigraphs are to be found in the preserved inscriptions of Tiglath-pileser III. In view of the very fragmentary nature of this king's historical records, it would not be prudent to make too much of this, but it should be noted that the epigraphs on the palace reliefs of Sargon II and Sennacherib also record a number of place names that are not mentioned in their much better-preserved annals.

Summary: Tiglath-Pileser III

Two types of texts were found on relief slabs from the walls of Tiglath-pileser's palace at Kalhu. One of these was a band of inscription, like that on the reliefs of Assurnasirpal. Unlike Assurnasirpal's inscriptions, however, Tiglath-pileser's inscriptions were annalistic, rather than summary, in form. This king's palace at Kalhu had been dismantled in antiquity and his wall reliefs were found out of context in various places on the Kalhu citadel. Tadmor's study of the annalistic inscription on these reliefs was used as the basis for grouping together slabs that belong to individual relief series and for determining the sequence of the slabs in each series. Layard's notations concerning relief subject on his copies of these inscriptions were used to identify the subjects of otherwise unpublished sculptures. The differences between Tiglath-pileser's brief epigraphs, which appeared on palace reliefs here for the first time, and their predecessors on the bronze door reliefs of Assurnasirpal II and Shalmaneser III were discussed, along with their limited but crucial role in the functioning of the pictorial narratives.

24. Barnett and Falkner 1962: pls. 38, 51.
25. Luckenbill 1926: §774. Text: Rost 1893: vol. 1, 28:164; vol. 2, pl. 16:12.

Chapter 6

Sargon II (721–705 B.C.)

Kalhu, the Northwest Palace

Early in his reign, Sargon II restored Assurnasirpal II's palace in the capital of Kalhu. One record of this work was a 22-line Sargon text that was inscribed above Assurnasirpal's "Standard Inscription" on each of the unsculptured jambs of Door *a*, Room U. The two inscriptions, which duplicate one another, were copied and published by Layard.[1] The text begins with a version of the royal titulary that omits the title "ruler of Babylon" and therefore presumably predates Sargon's conquest of Babylon in his twelfth year. This is followed by a brief resumé of conquests, drawn from the first eight years of his reign. The remainder of the text, about half its length, is devoted to an account of Sargon's restoration of Assurnasirpal's palace, which he calls the "Juniper Palace," and the festivities that attended its rededication. He states here that he filled the palace with plunder, in particular the booty from his conquest of Carchemish, and one gets the impression that the restoration of the palace at Kalhu was undertaken primarily to provide storage space for Sargon's booty. This is even stated explicitly toward the end, when Sargon says that he placed the gold and silver booty from Carchemish "into this storehouse" (*bīt nakkamtu*). This contrasts nicely with the conclusion of Assurnasirpal II's Nimrud Monolith inscription, where he curses the one who shall appropriate his palace "for a storehouse" (*bīt nakkamtu*).[2] It seems clear from the context of this inscription that Room U—a small, isolated room with a single entrance, stone pavement, and fittings for both inner and outer doors—is the room in which at least a part of the Carchemish treasure was meant to be stored.

---

1. Text: Layard 1851: 33–34. Layard's hand copy is Ms A, pp. 124–26. Transliteration: Winckler 1889: vol. 1, 168–73; vol. 2, no. 48. Translation: Luckenbill 1927: §§136–38. Study: Renger 1986.

2. Grayson 1991a: 253:35.

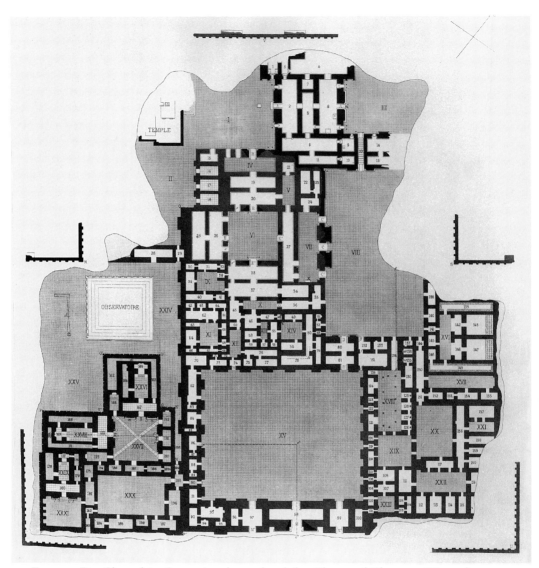

Fɪɢ. 32. Dur Sharrukin, Sargon's palace, plan (after Place and Thomas 1867: vol. 3, pl. 3).

Dur Sharrukin

In his fifth year, Sargon founded a new capital city called Dur Sharrukin ('Fortress of Sargon', modern Khorsabad) some 60 kilometers north of Kalhu and 18 kilometers north-northeast of Nineveh, where no city had been before. It is a site with no apparent strategic, political, or economic advantages and appears to have little to recommend it except its scenic beauty and rich farmland. Sargon's reasons for abandoning Kalhu in its favor are not clear; I will return to this question in the last chapter.

The largest structure in the city was the royal palace, which straddled the city wall on a terrace, measuring roughly 315 × 195 meters and averaging 7.5 meters high, at the northwest side of the citadel (fig. 32). This is the only late Assyrian palace to be completely excavated, its northwest end by Botta (1842–44), the remainder by Place (1852–54); some parts were reexcavated by Chiera and Loud (1929–32). The palace plan may be divided into three major sections, each of which was built around a large courtyard. Surrounding the outer court (XV) were numerous small rooms and courts that were apparently devoted to palace administration. These rooms were either undecorated or decorated only with paint. At the south corner of the palace, around Court XXX, were the palace temples (misidentified by Place as the "harem") and ziggurrat. To the northwest and southwest of the throne-room court (VIII) were the royal reception suites, including the principal and secondary throne rooms, and the royal apartments (fig. 33). This was apparently the only part of the palace in which the rooms and courts were decorated with wall reliefs, the subjects of which were military campaigns, banquets, hunts, processions, and apotropaic deities. The most recent edition of the Dur Sharrukin texts is by Fuchs (1994), and this will soon be joined by an edition of all the Sargon texts by Grant Frame.

The Text on the Backs of Slabs

Botta reported that the same text was carved on the back of every relief slab in Sargon's palace at Dur Sharrukin and that the characters of these concealed inscriptions were more carelessly executed than those visible on the slab fronts. He published copies of 16 exemplars of this short text, one of which was from the reverse of bull colossus no. 2 in Door *k*.[3] Other examples are on the backs of slabs in the Louvre and the bull in Chicago, and it is probable that every colossus in the palace originally had this text on its reverse side.[4]

3. Text: Botta and Flandin 1849–50: vol. 4, pls. 164–79; vol. 5, pp. 183–84. Transliteration: Fuchs 1994: 54–59. Translation: Luckenbill 1927: §§104–5.

4. According to Grant Frame, the Chicago example (Oriental Institute Museum, A 7369) has been published semi-officially via a translation made by J. A. Brinkman in an Oriental Institute Featured Object handout pamphlet (personal communication, letter of 18 July 1995). For the exemplars in the Louvre, see de Longpérier 1854: nos. 598–615, and B. André-Salvini, "Remarques sur les inscriptions des reliefs du palais du Khorsabad," in *Khorsabad, le palais de Sargon II, roi d'Assyrie*, ed A. Caubet (Paris, 1995) 15–45.

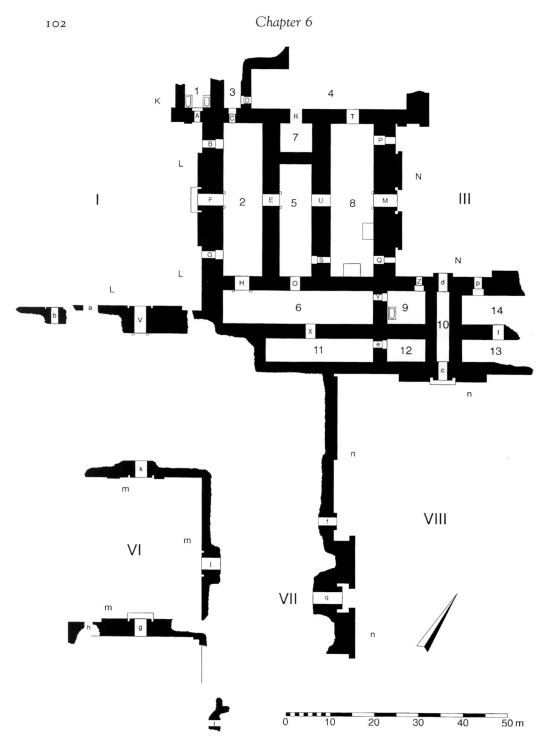

Fig. 33. Dur Sharrukin, Sargon's palace, state apartments, plan (source: author).

The text begins with Sargon's name and titles, followed by a list of cities to which the king had granted favors. There follows a brief reference to the king's prowess in battle, but without the usual extensive list of places conquered. The remainder of the text is devoted to a description of the building of Dur Sharrukin and the palace. This text, then, serves primarily to identify the building and its builder. Since it would only be visible in the future, after the slabs had fallen from the walls, its purpose was evidently to identify Sargon for posterity as a benevolent and wise ruler, a ruler whose works deserved restoration.

Hincks, one of the first scholars to make chronological inferences from variants in royal titularies, observed that in the text on the backs of the slabs, Sargon does not refer to himself as *šakkanakku* (ruler/governor) of Babylon, a title that appears in all of his visible palace inscriptions. Hincks knew that Sargon had become king of Babylon only in his twelfth year, after his victory over Merodach-baladan. He drew the interesting conclusion that the backs of the slabs had originally been the fronts of the slabs, and that the inscriptions found on them had first faced outward. Following his defeat of Merodach-baladan, Hincks supposed, Sargon turned these slabs over, with their outdated inscriptions against the wall, "with a view to bury in oblivion what he had written on these reversed slabs," and then had them reinscribed with a text that reflected his new status.[5] Hincks's observation that the titularies vary at this point was absolutely correct, though his explanation of how the earlier inscriptions came to face the wall is certainly wrong; the careless execution of these inscriptions and the absence of any sculpture on the reverse of the slabs make it clear that this side of the slabs had always been the back. A more probable explanation is that the reverse of the slabs was inscribed and they were placed against the palace walls before Sargon's twelfth year, while the carving of the texts on the obverse was done later, after the twelfth year.

The Colossus Inscription

The relief decoration of Sargon's palace was modeled closely on that of Assurnasirpal II's palace at Kalhu. The façade of the principal throne room ("Court" VII) was decorated with five pairs of human-headed bull colossi: one pair in each of the three doors and two antithetically posed pairs on the buttresses between the doors (fig. 34). Between each pair of buttress bulls was a colossal human figure holding a small lion. The same arrangement of figures was used also at the main exterior entrance to the palace, and a similar arrangement—without the figures holding lions—appeared on the façade of the subsidiary throne room. Pairs of

5. Hincks 1853: 365. For a more recent study of Sargon's titulary, see Renger 1986: 110–14.

Fig. 34. Dur Sharrukin, Sargon's palace, southwest wall of Court VIII, Façade *n*, Slabs 42–57, throne-room façade (after Botta and Flandin 1849: vol. 1, pl. 30).

human-headed bull colossi were also used in a number of important doorways in the palace and in several of the city gates. Like Assurnasirpal's colossi, these colossi also have five legs and in the spaces between the legs is an inscription.

Six inscribed colossi from Dur Sharrukin are preserved in museums: three from Sargon's palace, two from the inner citadel wall, and one from the outer city wall (fig. 35).[6] In addition, Botta published thirteen colossus inscriptions from the palace.[7] As with the palace colossi of Assurnasirpal II, all of Sargon's colossi

6. Collected in Albenda 1986: 49–50. Palace, Door *k*:2 (←): Louvre AO 19857 (Albenda 1986: fig. 2). Palace, Door *k*:1 (→): Louvre AO 19858 (E. Pottier, *Musée National du Louvre: Catalogue des antiquités assyriennes* [2d ed., Paris, 1924] pl. 1). Palace, Façade *n*:45 (→): Chicago, Oriental Institute A 7369 (Albenda 1986: fig. 5). Citadel wall, Gate B (probably): London, British Museum WA 118808 (←) and 118809 (→), both in Albenda 1986: figs. 4 and 3. City wall, Gate 3: Louvre AO 19859 (→), Albenda 1986: fig. 1. The two colossi from citadel wall, Gate A: Iraq Museum 72129 (←) and 72128 (→), both in F. Basmachi, *Treasures of the Iraq Museum* (Baghdad, 1975–76) figs. 141 right and left, were apparently uninscribed.

7. References are to Botta and Flandin 1849–50: vol. 3, pls. 22–62 (for location see Botta, vol. 1, pl. 6bis; note that later excavators at Dur Sharrukin did not use Botta's door and façade designations):

F:1	(Botta, 22–23):	panels 3–4 on bull 1 (→) only (labeled "bull 2" on Botta's plans)
M:1	(Botta, 24–25):	full text on single bull (→)
M:2	(Botta, 26–27):	full text on single bull (←)
N:10–9	(Botta, 54–57):	panels 1–2 on bull 10 (←), 3–4 on bull 9 (→)
N:18–17	(Botta, 58–61):	panels 1–2 on bull 18 (←), 3–4 on bull 17 (→)
c:2–1	(Botta, 28–31):	panels 1–2 on bull 2 (←), 3–4 on bull 1 (→) (numbering of bulls is reversed in Botta's plans)
d:2–1	(Botta, 32–35):	panels 1–2 on bull 2 (←), 3–4 on bull 1 (→)

FIG. 35. Dur Sharrukin, Sargon's palace, southwest wall of Court VIII, Façade *n*, Slab 45, throne-room façade colossus, width 480 cm. Chicago, Oriental Institute, A 7369 (photo: courtesy of The Oriental Institute of The University of Chicago).

f:1–2	(Botta, 36–39):	panels 1–2 on bull 1 (←), 3–4 on bull 2 (→)
g:1–2	(Botta, 40–43):	panels 1–2 on bull 1 (←), 3–4 on bull 2 (→)
j:2–1	(Botta, 44–47):	panels 1–2 on bull 2 (←), 3–4 on bull 1 (→)
k:2–1	(Botta, 48–51):	panels 1–2 on bull 2 (←), 3–4 on bull 1 (→)
n:47	(Botta, 62; mislabeled "N"):	panel 1 on bull 1 (←) only
δ:1–2	(Botta, 52–53):	panel 1 on bull 1 (←), panel 4 on bull 2 (→)
		(numbering of bulls is reversed on plan in Botta I: 46)

In addition, Lyon published text, transliteration, and translation for the two Louvre colossi from Door *k* (text also in Botta) and included in his notes variants from the third Louvre colossus and from a fragment in the Louvre (Lyon 1883: xii, 40–47). Full edition: Fuchs 1994: 60–74. English translation in Luckenbill 1927: §§92–94.

were apparently inscribed with the same text. Unlike the Assurnasirpal II colossus inscriptions, each Sargon inscription contains the entire text. With a single exception, the text in the recorded examples is distributed between the two bulls of each doorway or façade buttress, confined to rectangular frames located beneath the belly and between the hind legs of each bull. These inscriptions, therefore, occupy four spaces: beginning under the belly of the left-hand bull, continuing between the rear legs of the same bull, then to the space between the rear legs of the right-hand bull, and concluding under the belly of the right hand bull. The exception is the bulls in Door M of Room 8, the subsidiary throne room, where each colossus carries the entire text.[8] The space between the front legs of the bull is no longer used for inscriptions.

The Sargon II bull text is somewhat different in form from the examples of Assurnasirpal II and Shalmaneser III. It commences with a very brief titulary followed by a list of Babylonian and Assyrian cities to which Sargon granted special favors.[9] Next follows a summary of Sargon's conquests, arranged geographically rather than chronologically, beginning with the Medes and Manneans to the east; proceeding counterclockwise to the Urartians to the north; then Hattina, Cilicia, and the Levant to the west; and concluding with Chaldea, Elam, and Bit-Iakin to the south.[10] The text concludes with a lengthy account of the building of the new capital, Dur Sharrukin, followed by a brief blessing, asking the gods to protect the works of Sargon's hands.[11] The proportions of this text are noteworthy: fully two-thirds of its length is devoted to the building account, compared with less than a sixth of Assurnasirpal II's throne base/colossus text. Apparently, the primary function of Sargon's bull text, judging from the very sketchy historical section and the extended building section, was to commemorate the foundation of the new capital, emphasizing construction at the expense of conquest.

To get some idea of the types of variants that occur in these inscriptions, I compared the example from Court VI, Door *k*, edited by Lyon, with those from throne-room Door *f* and Façade *n*. The most notable variants thus identified were then checked in the other examples of the text published by Botta. Though this examination was not comprehensive, it did turn up variants of three general types, listed here in order of frequency. Most common are purely orthographic variants: variant sign forms, variant sign values, and the interchanging of logographic and phonetic writings of words. Less frequent, but still relatively common is the use of variant determinatives and synonyms. The examples I noted were the interchanging of URU ('city'), KUR ('land'), and LÚ ('people') before geographical

---

8. The text distribution may be seen in Botta and Flandin 1849–50: vol. 1, pl. 30, and vol. 3, pls. 22–62.

9. Fuchs 1994: 61:1 to 62:10.

10. Fuchs 1994: 62:11 to 66:36.

11. Fuchs 1994: 66:36 to 74:106.

names and the substitution in some exemplars of *epēšu* 'to practice' (treachery) for *dabābu* 'to speak' (treachery) in reference to the wicked Hittites.[12]

Least frequent seem to be omissions and additions. The reference to the "month of Tashritu" (September-October), given in the Door *k* text as the date when the gods were invited into the completed palace, does not occur in any other published Sargon bull inscription. The implication may be that the inscription on this pair of colossi was carved after the event itself occurred. Another variant of this type is that Kasku and Hilakku are omitted in the inscriptions from Doors *f* and *δ* but are included in every other published example.[13] This omission, too, may have historical implications, because it was in this region that Sargon was killed. It seems unlikely, but it is just possible that the Door *f* and *δ* inscriptions were carved after the king's death. A more probable explanation for this omission, however, would be to suppose that both inscriptions were copied from a single scribal draft in which these names were accidentally omitted.

These numerous minor variants, which are characteristic of all Neo-Assyrian palace inscriptions carved in stone, apparently are to be seen not as features of the original text but rather as relics of the process by which a "text" becomes an "inscription." Evidence for one stage of this process was noted by Place, who reported that the inscription on the bull colossi in Gate 6 of the city wall was painted on the stone with black paint. He suggested this was done as a guide for the stonecarver, but for some reason this inscription was never incised.[14] One may wonder who painted these preliminary guides. Nonliterate masons copying from a master text could hardly have been responsible for the types of variants noted above unless a different draft was prepared as a guide for each bull inscription. It seems more likely that the painted "underdrawing" of the inscription was the work of scribes. The variants could then be accounted for by supposing that the scribes either painted the text while it was being dictated to them or that

12. URU/KUR/LÚ variants in bulls from Door *f* and Façade *n* (Botta and Flandin 1849–50: vol. 3, pls. 36–39, 62), compared to Door *k* (Lyon 1883: 13–19), listed by door/façade and line number:

f,15:	URU ('city'), instead of KUR ('land' of Kummuhu; *k*,18)
f,20; *n*,22:	KUR ('land'), instead of URU ('city' of Gaza; *k*,23)
n,24:	KUR ('land'), instead of URU ('city' of Iamnai; *k*,25)
f,27; *n*,29:	KUR ('land'), instead of LÚ ('people' of Puqudu; *k*,29)
Dabābu	(references to Botta and Flandin 1849–50: vol. 3): Door M:1 (pl. 24:4), M:2 (pl. 26:13), *c* (pl. 28:18), *d* (pl. 32:17), *g* (pl. 40:22), *k* (Lyon, 1883: 13:19); Façade N:10–9 (pl. 54:19), N:18–17 (pl. 58:20).
Epēšu	Door *f* (pl. 36:16), *j* (pl. 44:18), *δ* (pl. 52:16); Façade *n*:47 (pl. 62:17).

13. Tashritu (ITI.DU$_6$): Lyon 1883: 18:98. Kasku and Hilakku (ibid., 14:21–22) omitted in Doors *f* and *δ* (Botta and Flandin 1849–50: vol. 3, 36:19, 52:19).

14. Place and Thomas 1867–70: vol. 2, 266–68.

they freely copied from a master, adapting and omitting to suit their own prefer-
ences and the space at hand.

Thresholds

Flandin's detailed plans of individual rooms show no fewer than 29 inscribed
thresholds, indicating their size, proportions, and format of the text.[15] Botta initially reported that the cuneiform signs of the Sargon thresholds were inlaid
"with copper or some coppery cement, still retaining great hardness, and which
has dyed green even the surface of the stone." He later retracted this view after
finding partially melted copper nails on some of the slabs, which convinced him
that the presence of copper on the slabs was the result of door fittings having
been melted by the intense fire that consumed the palace.[16] This may account for
the apparent presence of copper in at least one threshold in Assurnasirpal's palace at Kalhu as well.

Botta published copies of 21 of these inscriptions.[17] The inscriptions were
edited by Winckler, who noticed that each represented one of five different texts,

15. In addition, Loud (1936: 65, fig. 71) said that the threshold of Door *c* in Sargon's principal throne room, "Court VII," was inscribed, though it is unpublished. See
also "thresholds" in the "Index" of the same volume, where the Door *c*" threshold is
listed as "inscribed."

16. Mohl 1850: 9, 18; Botta and Flandin 1849–50: vol. 5, 68.

17. References to the room plans showing the placement of each threshold and to
the copies of the inscriptions are as follows (volume and plate nos. from Botta and Flandin 1849–50):

Door A	vol. 1, 48; vol. 3, 1; also Mohl 1850: pl. 9	*Door V*	vol. 1, 11; inscription unpublished
Door B	vol. 1, 51; vol. 3, 2; also Mohl, pls. 13–14	*Door X*	vol. 2, 137; inscription unpublished
Door C	vol. 1, 51; vol. 3, 3; also Mohl, pl. 15	*Door Y*	vol. 2, 121; vol. 3, 13
Door D	vol. 1, 79; inscription unpublished	*Door Z*	vol. 2, 121; inscription unpublished
Door E	vol. 2, 84; vol. 3, 4	*Door b*	vol. 1, 11; inscription unpublished
Door F	vol. 1, 51; inscription unpublished	*Door c*	vol. 2, 122; vol. 3, 14
Door G	vol. 1, 51; vol. 3, 5	*Door d*	vol. 2, 122; vol. 3, 15
Door H	vol. 1, 51; vol. 3, 6	*Door e*	vol. 2, 137; inscription unpublished
Door M	vol. 1, 26; vol. 3, 7	*Door g*	vol. 1, 42; vol. 3, 16
Door O	vol. 2, 84; vol. 3, 8	*Door j*	vol. 1, 42; vol. 3, 17
Door P	vol. 1, 26; vol. 4, 181:5? (Fuchs 1993: 271)	*Door k*	vol. 1, 42; vol. 3, 18
Door Q	vol. 1, 26; vol. 3, 9	*Door l*	no plan; vol. 3, 19
Door S	vol. 2, 84; vol. 3, 10	*Door p*	vol. 2, 144; vol. 3, 21
Door T	vol. 1, 79; vol. 3, 11	*Door r*	vol. 2, 139; inscription unpublished
Door U	vol. 2, 84; vol. 3, 12	*Door δ*	vol. 1, 46; vol. 3, 20

and they have recently been treated by Fuchs.[18] Winckler's threshold text no. 1 was the shortest, consisting of a brief titulary, followed by a summary of the boundaries of the empire, a slightly condensed version of the similar passage in the display text carved on the wall reliefs.[19] Threshold text no. 2, which is considerably longer, virtually repeats the text of no. 1, adding to it a detailed description of the building of the palace, very similar to the description incorporated into the texts carved on the wall reliefs.[20] Threshold text no. 3 also begins with the text of no. 1, but adds only a very brief account of the building and dedication of the palace.[21] Interestingly, while texts 1 and 2 are written in the third person, no. 3 is in the first person.

Threshold text no. 4, written predominantly in the third person, is the most common and also the longest of the threshold texts.[22] The first part of the text, which consists of a brief titulary, a list of tax concessions, a summary of the king's triumphs, and the summary of the borders of the empire found also in threshold texts 1–3, is a virtual duplicate of the beginning of the Room 14 display text.[23] The text concludes with a detailed palace building description and blessing, also apparently condensed from the Room 14 display text.[24] Threshold text no. 5 is

18. Summary of locations in Winckler 1889: vol. 1, x. Winckler omits mentioning the inscriptions from Doors *d* and *p*, both of which are variants of his "Pp 3," and gives an incorrect publication reference for Door G (should read "5," not "15").

19. Found in Doors A, C, and Y. Text and transliteration in Winckler 1889: vol. 1, 136–38; vol. 2, pl. 37; transliteration and translation in Fuchs 1994: 249–51; English translation in Luckenbill 1927: §96. The same text may occur in Palace F (the arsenal) in the door between Rooms 29 and 30 (Loud 1938: 77–78, 104 no. 4, pl. 40E). The similar passage in the display text is Luckenbill 1927: §§54 and 82.

20. Found in Doors B and G. Partial text and transliteration in Winckler 1889: vol. 1, 138–42; vol. 2, pl. 37; full transliteration and translation in Fuchs 1994: 251–54; partial English translation in Luckenbill 1927: §§97 and 74. The same text may occur in Palace F (the arsenal) on three (reused?) slabs on the wall outside Room 15 (Loud 1938: 77, 104 no. 5, pl. 41d). The editions of Winckler and Luckenbill, but not Fuchs, omit the final 2 1/2 lines of this text: (Images of) people from all countries, from east (44) "to west, who through the power of Assur he had conquered, (45) through the work of the sculptor, in the midst of that palace, (46) he caused to be placed as adornment."

21. Found in Doors O, Q, S, *d*, and *p*. Text and transliteration in Winckler 1889: vol. 1, 142–46; vol. 2, pls. 37–38; transliteration and translation in Fuchs 1994: 254–59; English translation in Luckenbill 1927: §98.

22. Found in Doors *E, H, M, T, U, g, j, k,* and *l*. Text and transliteration in Winckler 1889: vol. 1, 146–56; vol. 2, pls. 38–40; transliteration and translation in Fuchs 1994: 259–71; English translation in Luckenbill 1927: §§99–101. The first person is used in a few passages (Winckler, vol. 1, 151 n. 2, 153 n. 1, and 155 n. 2).

23. Luckenbill 1927: §§77–82. The only substantial change is the abridgment in threshold text no. 4 of the account of the defeat of Iamani of Ashdod (§§79–80).

24. Luckenbill 1927: §§84, 87–88.

only partially preserved.[25] It begins, as does text no. 4, with a titulary and summary of tax concessions for important Assyrian and Babylonian cities and then continues with the summary of borders found in the other four threshold texts. A detailed palace-building account, like that of threshold texts 2 and 4, followed; unfortunately, this text is broken in the middle of the description of the *bīt ḫilāni*, and the remainder of the text is lost. This text, like threshold text no. 3, is also written in the first person.

It may not be possible to recover all of the criteria that determined what text would be carved on a given threshold, but a glance at Botta's plan shows, not surprisingly, that the size of the threshold was a major factor.[26] The smallest thresholds, in Doors A, C, and Y, are inscribed with the shortest text, no. 1, while the largest thresholds, between the colossi of Doors M, g, j, and k, and in especially wide doorways like E, H, T, and U, are inscribed with the longest text, no. 4. Furthermore, it appears that texts of roughly the same length, namely nos. 2, 3, and 5, were not intermixed in the principal reception rooms. Thus, in Room 2 the medium-sized thresholds of Doors B and G were both carved with text no. 2, while in Room 8, the thresholds of Doors Q and S were carved with text no. 3.[27] It also seems probable that the threshold text reflects something of the function of the room it is inscribed in. It may be no coincidence that the thresholds of Room 8, Doors Q and S, are inscribed with text no. 3, which is the only version that mentions "princes of the four quarters (of the world), who had submitted to the yoke of my rule, whose lives I had spared," when the subject of the Room 8 reliefs is the punishment of errant rulers.[28] Likewise, the casting of this text in the first person may reflect the function of Room 8, which the presence of a throne dais indicates to be a subsidiary throne room. An exhaustive examination of the context of these slabs might reveal other such relationships.

To summarize, all of Sargon's published palace thresholds were inscribed with one of five texts. The longest of these, apparently derived from the display text of Room 14, was designed for monumental entrances. The remaining four texts represent various degrees of abridgment of this long text, with occasional additions which may reflect a text's intended function. The decision of which of these five texts to carve on a given threshold was influenced largely by the size of the threshold but probably by other factors as well, such as the function and decoration of the room.

25. Found in Doors c and δ. Text and transliteration in Winckler 1889: vol. 1, 158–62; vol. 2, pl. 40; transliteration and translation in Fuchs 1994: 271–75; English translation in Luckenbill 1927: §102.

26. Botta and Flandin 1849–50: vol. 1, pl. 6.

27. Note, however, that in Room 10 (a passageway) the apparently identical thresholds of Doors c and d were carved with texts 5 and 3, respectively.

28. Luckenbill 1927: §98.

It is noteworthy that, while Sargon's palace thresholds are inscribed in the traditional fashion, important thresholds in some of the neighboring buildings exemplify another fashion. Three stone thresholds from Residence L carry a short inscription identifying the building's owner as Sinahusur, Sargon's brother and vizier, but the inscription occupies only a small part of the surface, the remainder being covered by a pattern of small rosettes enclosed in a grid.[29] Three thresholds were also found in Residence K, and these carried no inscription at all but rather an elaborate ornamental pattern of rosettes and alternating cone and lotus.[30]

The antecedents, if any, of these floral patterned thresholds are unknown to us. Albenda has suggested that they may reflect an otherwise unknown tradition of placing floral patterned carpets in the principal doorways of important nonpalatial Neo-Assyrian buildings.[31] However that may be, it seems likely that the motifs on these slabs served an apotropaic as well as decorative function. This is particularly true for the rosette, which was found in large numbers, apparently as votive offerings to Ishtar, in the Middle Assyrian temple of Ishtar at Assur and which is worn as jewelry by both kings and deities in the Neo-Assyrian wall reliefs. Carved on the thresholds of important doorways, rosettes evidently became a permanent part of the building's security system. Though they were not found in the royal palace at Dur Sharrukin, these floral thresholds are nevertheless of interest, because in the palaces of Sennacherib and Assurbanipal, the floral threshold completely supplanted the traditional inscribed threshold seen in the palaces of Assurnasirpal II, Shalmaneser III, and Sargon II.

The Wall Slab Text

In Sargon's palace, extensive inscriptions were sometimes carved on a band across the middle of reliefs in two registers or across the lower portion of formal scenes in one register (fig. 36). These wall slab inscriptions were of two types: an annalistic account of the king's first fourteen years, and a historical resume in which campaigns were arranged geographically, beginning with the east, proceeding roughly counterclockwise around the empire, and concluding with the southeast. Both types of text conclude with an account of the building of the new palace at Dur Sharrukin.

Though we know that "Court" VII in this palace was Sargon's principal throne room, and though the walls of this room were excavated by Place, very little is known about their decoration and nothing about the accompanying

29. Loud 1938: pls. 36, 66; see also Albenda 1978: 12–13.
30. Loud 1938: pl. 30; Albenda 1978: 12–13.
31. Albenda 1978: 1–3.

FIG. 36. Dur Sharrukin, Sargon's palace, Room 7, Slab 10, royal banquet and hunt, width 251 cm. Chicago, Oriental Institute, A 11254 (photo: courtesy of The Oriental Institute of The University of Chicago).

inscriptions, if there were any. According to Place, the subject of the throne room reliefs was a procession of tall figures, presumably in a single register, march-ing toward the king.[32] These reliefs were poorly preserved, with only a few re-maining in place; the majority had fallen and broken or been thrown down and

32. Place and Thomas 1867–70: vol. 1, 52.

defaced, and some had apparently been removed by plunderers.[33] Place must have removed such reliefs as remained and included them in his ill-fated shipment down the Tigris, since none were found by the Chicago expedition that reexcavated the throne room later.[34]

In order to appreciate the role of wall slab texts in the decorative scheme of Sargon's palace, then, we must look to the better known portion of the palace, the northwest wing excavated and published by Botta. The wall inscriptions in this wing have been studied by Weissbach, and his observations are outlined here.[35] Four rooms (2, 5, 13, and the northeast portion of 14) each contained similar editions of the annals of the king carved on the central band between two registers of relief.[36] In each case, this inscription was associated with scenes of battle on the reliefs, though part of the upper register of Room 2 also showed a banquet. The relief slabs of five other rooms (1, 4, 7, 8, and 10) were carved with a nonchronological summary text, apparently the same in all five rooms, outlining the king's accomplishments.[37] The reliefs associated with these inscriptions were sometimes in two registers (Rooms 1, 7, and 10) and sometimes in one (Rooms 4 and 8) and contained a variety of subjects: war (Room 1), punishment

33. Place and Thomas 1867–70: vol. 1, 51. If Place had drawings made of the reliefs he uncovered, then none of them have been published. He may have felt that drawings were unnecessary, since he apparently removed most of the reliefs he discovered, intending to send them to Paris. The vast majority of these were lost in the Tigris accident of 23 May 1855 (Albenda 1986: 29–30).

34. It is puzzling that Loud makes no mention of Place's excavation of the walls of the throne room in the report of his own excavations. Nonetheless, it is clear from Loud's report that Place had been there before him, as for example in Loud 1936: fig. 82, which shows the location of fragments of painted plaster discovered by the Chicago excavators. None of these fragments were found closer than 1.5 meters from the wall (except for fragment no. 10, in a doorway), and this was also the width of Place's trench that ran along this wall (Pillet 1962: 51).

35. Weissbach 1918.

36. Weissbach 1918: 170–77. Text: Winckler 1889: vol. 2, nos. 1–54. Transliteration and translation: Winckler 1889: vol. 1, 2–79; Lie 1929: 2–83; Fuchs 1994: 82–188. English translation: Luckenbill 1927: §§ 4–51. In addition, Botta and Flandin (1849–50: vol. 4, pl. 163) published another portion of an annalistic text band for which the original location is unknown. The inscription on this fragment is in 14 lines and thus cannot originate in any of the rooms known to have had an annalistic text (Room 2 = 13 lines; Room 5 = 17 lines; Room 13 = 15 lines; Room 14 = 15 lines). The only room in this portion of the palace with an inscription possibly unaccounted for is Room 3, which also contained reliefs in two registers, and this fragment may have originated here, though the room would appear to have been too small to have accommodated the full annals.

37. Weissbach 1918: 165–70. Text and transliteration: Winckler 1889: vol. 1, 96–135; vol. 2, nos. 63–78. Transliteration and translation: Fuchs 1994: 189–248. English translation: Luckenbill 1927: §§53–75.

of captives (Rooms 4 and 8), hunting and feasting (Room 7), and processions of tribute (Room 10). A shorter summary text was carved at the southwest end only of Room 14, the reliefs of which showed courtiers before the king in one register.[38] Four rooms (6, 9, 11, and 12) contained reliefs in one register that bore no text at all. They showed processions of tribute (Rooms 6 and 11) and courtiers before the king (Rooms 9 and 12). Also, exterior façades L, N, n, and m, which were decorated with tribute processions in one register, were uninscribed.

A few general observations regarding which texts accompany what types of images may be drawn from the preceding. First, in rooms inscribed with the annals, the subject of the reliefs is always warfare. The converse, however, is not necessarily true: in Room 1, scenes of warfare are accompanied by the summary inscription. Second, tribute processions are usually uninscribed. The single inscribed example, from Room 10, carries the summary text. Third, scenes of punishment of rulers from foreign lands are accompanied by the display inscription. Finally, two of the rooms decorated with the king and processions of courtiers are uninscribed, while the third, Room 14, has a unique summary text.

From these observations, certain relationships between images and texts may tentatively be suggested. In general, it appears that the text selected in a given room would have been the one most appropriate to the representations in that room. For example, in those rooms decorated with the punishment of foreign rulers, we can recognize rulers from both the eastern (skin cloaks) and western (turbans) portions of the empire, brought together before the king. In these cases, the summary text, which emphasizes the geographical range and extent of the empire, is clearly more appropriate than the annals, which emphasize chronology. Likewise, in the tribute processions from Room 10, the bearers are divided into eastern and western contingents, and here also the display text would be most appropriate.

In rooms decorated with scenes of warfare, however, the emphasis appears to be on individual campaigns. Reade, following Amin, has argued that each room decorated with scenes of warfare was devoted to the events of a single campaign.[39] Thus Rooms 2, 5, 13, and 14 recorded Sargon's campaigns of 716, 720, 714, and 715 respectively. Regardless of whether the dates assigned by Reade are in all cases correct, it is clear that his basic proposal is correct: the relief decoration of each room is clearly concerned with the events in a single part of the empire, with none of the discontinuity or variety of settings that are seen in the battle reliefs of Assurnasirpal II or Tiglath-pileser III, who do mix several campaigns in a single room. Thus the most appropriate textual complement for these images that concern themselves with recording the events of a single campaign would be the annals, which share the same concern. To be sure, the images still

38. Weissbach 1918: 175–85; Fuchs 1994: 75–81. English translation: Luckenbill 1927: §§77–90.

39. El-Amin 1953 and 1954; Reade 1976.

do not "illustrate" the texts or vice versa. Indeed, only a small portion of the annals text carved in a given room would parallel the imagery in that room, since the room decoration would be devoted to only one of the fourteen campaigns recounted by the annals. Even then, the written narrative and its pictorial equivalent were parallel, not identical, versions of the same story, for the pictorial account includes only some of the episodes recorded in the text, and the epigraphs on the sculptures likewise make it clear that the visual record included episodes omitted by the text. Nonetheless, the spirit of both the war reliefs and the annals text is historical and chronological, and in this sense they are complementary and can be contrasted with the punishment/tribute scenes and summary text whose emphasis is geographical and synthetic.

It remains to consider why the war scenes in Room 1 are accompanied by the summary, instead of the annalistic, text. It appears that this divergence from the norm can be explained by reference to the size of Room 1, which was apparently a bathroom and was much smaller than the other four rooms decorated with battle scenes. In this case, space limitations were probably the factor that dictated the substitution of the summary text for the preferred, but much lengthier, annals.

Epigraphs

A considerable number of epigraphs survive from the reliefs of the northwest wing of Sargon II's palace at Dur Sharrukin (fig. 37).[40] Most of these epigraphs were inscribed on the narrative reliefs of Rooms 2, 5, 13, and 14, which were in two registers, with a band of annalistic text between (listed by room and slab number):

| Room 2[41] | 7 | "The city Harhar." |
| | 14 | "The city Kindau." |

40. The original publication of the text of Sargon II's epigraphs is Botta and Flandin 1849–50: vols. 1, 2, and 4. The epigraphs were edited and studied by el-Amin 1953 and 1954, whose conclusions were summarized and augmented by Reade 1976. Nine of the epigraphs were reedited by C. B. F. Walker in Albenda 1986: 107–12.

41. Fuchs 1994: 276–77. Individual references are to volume and page or plate number in Botta and Flandin 1849–50, el-Amin 1953, and Albenda 1986:

Harhar	Botta vol. 1: 55, vol. 4: 180; el-Amin 1953: 50–52, fig. 8; Albenda 1986: 108, pl. 112
Kindau	Botta vol. 4: 180; el-Amin 1953: 57–58, fig. 13
[T]ikrakka	Botta vol. 4: 180; el-Amin 1953: 56–57, fig. 12
Bit-Bagaia	Botta vol. 1: 76, vol. 4: 180; el-Amin 1953: 55–56, fig. 11; Albenda 1986: 109, pl. 123
Kishesim	Botta vol. 1: 68, vol. 4: 180; el-Amin 1953: 54–55, fig. 10; Albenda 1986: 109, pl. 125–26
Ganguhtu	Botta vol. 4: 180; el-Amin 1953: 52–54, fig. 9

	17	"The city [T]ikrakka."
	H1	"The city Bit-Bagaia."
	22	"The city Kishesim."
	28	"The city Ganguhtu."
Room 5[42]	5	"The city Gabbutunu."
	10	"The city ʾAmqa[r]runa."
	15	"The city Baʾil-Gazara."
	16	"The city Sinu."
Room 13[43]	Slab 4	"The city Musasir I besieged, I captured."
Room 14[44]	2	"The city P[a]zashi, a fortress of the land of Mannea on the pass to Zikirtu."
	10	"Camp of Tak[. . .]."
	12	"The city Kisheshlu I besieged, I captured."

A few epigraphs, somewhat longer than the rest, were found on the Room 8 reliefs, whose subject was a single register depicting the punishment of captives, inscribed with a summary text.

42. Fuchs 1994: 277. Individual references are to volume and page or plate number in Botta and Flandin 1849–50, and el-Amin 1953:

Gabbutunu	Botta vol. 2: 89, vol. 4: 180; el-Amin 1953: 36–37, fig. 3; Albenda 1986: 109–10, pl. 95
ʾAmqa[r]runa	Botta vol. 2: 93, vol. 4: 180; el-Amin 1953: 37–40, fig. 4; Albenda 1986: 110, pl. 98)
Baʾil-Gazara	Botta vol. 4: 180; el-Amin 1953: 41–43, fig. 5
Sinu	Botta vol. 4: 180; el-Amin 1953: 43–46, fig. 6

43. Botta and Flandin 1849–50: vol. 2, 141, and vol. 4, 180; el-Amin 1953: 225–28, fig. 19; Albenda 1986: 110–11, pl. 133; Fuchs 1994: 278.

44. Fuchs 1994: 278–79. Individual references are to volume and page or plate number in Botta and Flandin 1849–50, and el-Amin 1953:

P[a]zashi	Botta vol. 2: 145, vol. 4: 180; el-Amin 1953: 219–24, fig. 18; Albenda 1986: 112, pl. 136)
⌜tàk⌝-[. . .]	Botta vol. 2: 146, vol. 4: 180; el-Amin 1953: 216–19, fig. 16; Albenda 1986: 111, pl. 137
Kisheshlu	Botta vol. 2: 147, vol. 4: 180; el-Amin 1953: 215–16, fig. 15; Albenda 1986: 112, pl. 138

⌜tàk⌝-[. . .] was restored by Reade (1976: 98–99), following Postgate, as Taklak-ana-Bel, eponym for the year 715. Though this is possible, it should be noted that in the eponym lists the first syllable of Taklak-ana-Bel is always written *tak*, instead of *tàk* (Ungnad 1938: 427–28). A more probable value for this broken sign would be *kib*.

FIG. 37. Dur Sharrukin, Sargon's palace, Room 14, Slabs 1–2, siege of Pazashi (after Botta and Flandin 1849: vol. 2, pl. 145).

Room 8[45]   12   (illegible: blinding of a captive)

17   "[Be]l-sha[rri-us]ur of the city K[ishesi, Kiba]ba of the city [Harhar], Assur-le'u of the [land] Karal[la], reb[ellious lords], I put f[et]ters of ir[on] on th[eir] hands and feet."[46]

25   "Ilu-iabi'[di of the land Ham]a, I fla[y]ed his [sk]in."

45. Fuchs 1994: 277–78. Individual references are to volume and page or plate number in Botta and Flandin 1849–50, Albenda 1986, and el-Amin 1954:

Slab 12   Botta vol. 2: 118, vol. 4: 181; Albenda 1986: pl. 75; only a few signs are preserved and el-Amin did not suggest a restoration

Slab 17   Botta vol. 2: 119bis, vol. 4: 181; Albenda 1986: pl. 77; el-Amin 1954: 29–35; fig. 22; cf. Luckenbill 1927: §§56–57

Slab 25   Botta vol. 2: 120, vol. 4: 181; Albenda 1986: pl. 78; el-Amin 1954: 26–27, fig. 21; cf. Luckenbill 1927: §55).

46. Grant Frame warns me that the reading of the first line of this epigraph—the part before Assur-le'u—is very uncertain (personal communication, letter of 9 May 1996). See also Fuchs (1994: 278), who suggests "Paddira" instead of "Kishesi," but suggests no reading for the rest of the first line.

Epigraphs might also be expected in the similarly decorated Room 4, though none were reported, perhaps because the upper part of most of the reliefs in that room were lost. There seem to have been no epigraphs in Rooms 6, 7, 9, 10, 11, and 12, or on exterior façades L, N, n, and m, and the decoration of Rooms 1 and 3 was so poorly preserved that any epigraphs they may have contained are lost. One 2-line epigraph, "[The ci]ty Ashguru I besieged, I captured," was on a loose fragment dissociated from its original architectural context.[47] From this summary it can be seen that Sargon's epigraphs are confined to those reliefs that record his dealings with enemies of the empire. They do not occur on the procession reliefs, nor on those for which the subject is hunting.

Several apparent innovations may be seen in Sargon's use of epigraphs, when compared to the preserved examples of his predecessor. In Sargon's palace, the epigraphs in Rooms 2 and 5 each consist only of a single city name, as was the case with those of Tiglath-pileser III. In Rooms 13 and 14 and on the unlocated slab, however, the epigraphs instead consist of short sentences, two of which require two lines of text (Room 14, Slab 2, and the unlocated slab), though each still deals with only a single subject. These epigraphs are similar in form to those on the bronze doors of Assurnasirpal II and Shalmaneser III. The epigraphs of Room 8 occupy two, three, or more lines, and at least one of these includes three separate subjects (Slab 17).

It is not clear whether this shift from short to more extended epigraphs has any chronological significance. The reliefs of Rooms 2 and 5, dealing with the campaigns of 716 and 720 B.C., may have been carved earlier than those of Rooms 13 and 14, which treat the slightly later campaigns of 714 and 715.[48] The preserved captions from Room 8 also label captives from 716 and 720, and it may be that this projecting wing, which apparently served as one of the principal reception suites, was one of the earliest areas to be decorated. The inclusion of campaigns through the year 708 in the annalistic and summary texts carved on the reliefs in all these rooms indicates that at least the inscribed portion of the decoration was not added until late in the king's reign. There is, however, no reason to assume that the reliefs and the extended texts that accompany them were necessarily carved at the same time; indeed, the uninscribed space running across the center of some of Tiglath-pileser III's reliefs may indicate a significant gap between the carving of the reliefs and the texts. Since Sargon's longer epigraphs are similar to those on the bronze doors of Assurnasirpal II and Shalmaneser III, it might be suggested that the shift to longer epigraphs in the course of decorating Sargon's palace was inspired by someone taking a new look at these earlier examples.

47. Fuchs 1994: 279. Identified by Reade (1976: 97, "Unknown A"); this epigraph was directly below a section of annalistic relief text in 14 lines (Botta and Flandin 1849–50: vol. 4, 163).

48. I follow here the campaign identifications of Reade 1976.

Whatever the explanation, this increase in length of Sargon's epigraphs apparently resulted in some difficulty in fitting them comfortably onto the reliefs. In the reliefs of both Tiglath-pileser III and Sargon II, the relief carvers made no provision for the epigraphs, which in consequence appear to have been added almost as an afterthought, being fitted into whatever space was available. There seems to have been no standard location for Sargon's epigraphs: in some cases they are carved directly on the wall of the city under siege, while in others they are fitted into the background above or beside it.[49] This arrangement works well enough for very brief epigraphs, and also for the longer epigraphs that accompany the summary images on the reliefs of Room 8, where there is a considerable amount of otherwise unoccupied background area. The longer epigraphs fit less comfortably into the densely populated space of the two-register campaign narratives. The clearest example of this is the two-line epigraph recording the capture of the Mannean fortress of Pazashi (Room 14, Slab 2; see fig. 37). Here the only free space is the city wall that, stair-like, climbs the side of a hill, and the epigraph that is crowded into this space also proceeds upward in a series of steps. This problem of crowding of the epigraphs is solved in the reliefs of Sennacherib, whose designers may have included the epigraphs in their plans and left appropriate amounts of free space.

The advantage of these longer epigraphs for Sargon's campaign narratives is not clear. The only information they usually add that is not found in the shorter epigraphs is "I besieged, I captured." This information is far from inconsequential, but one would think this action is presented sufficiently clearly by the reliefs themselves, whose subject is unmistakably attack, surrender, and plunder. The only element that might not be clear from the reliefs is the "I," that is, the name of the king, who orchestrates the proceedings but is not always shown as an active participant in each scene of combat. The problem with this is that one cannot tell from the epigraph who the "I" is, and this information cannot be gathered easily from the central text register either, because there the name of the king is repeated only sporadically. Therefore, though Sargon's long epigraphs include somewhat more information than do his short epigraphs, the only really useful additional information they contain—the identity of the perpetrator of the deeds shown—is presented inadequately and is subject to misinterpretation by viewers unfamiliar with the events shown. While the king's contemporaries and immediate successors would certainly know whose deeds these were, his royal posterity might not. Since these would be the kings who would honor Sargon's memory by restoring his palace and the reliefs that commemorate his deeds, inadequate identification of the protagonist of the reliefs could cause confusion.

---

49. On wall: Room 2, Slabs 14, 17, H1, 22; Room 5, Slabs 2, 12. In background: Room 2, Slabs 7, 28(?); Room 5, Slabs 5, 15(?), 16(?); Room 13, Slab 4.

Another difference between the reliefs of Sargon II and those of Tiglath-pileser III is that, while Tiglath-pileser seems to have mixed labeled and un-labeled cities in a single relief series, in Sargon's reliefs virtually every city is labeled.[50] To be sure, the evidence is somewhat defective on both sides, due to the fragmentary nature of Tiglath-pileser's reliefs and to the damage to the sur-face of some of Sargon's, but it appears that Sargon was either striving for greater specificity or greater consistency overall than was Tiglath-pileser III.

Yet another apparent innovation in the palace reliefs of Sargon II is extend-ing the use of epigraphs to label people in more-or-less formal scenes in one reg-ister. This occurs for certain only in Room 8, but the badly damaged but very similar representations in Room 4 probably also originally carried epigraphs. In both cases, the subject was the punishment by the king of errant enemy princes captured by Sargon in both eastern and western campaigns.[51] Since the reliefs in these rooms mix captives from several campaigns and omit an identifiable geo-graphical setting, the only indications the viewer has of the identity of these cap-tives are their style of dress and the epigraphs. Here, in the absence of most of the visual indicators that aid in the identification of a narrative subject, therefore, the epigraphs alone are responsible for transforming fairly generalized subjects into highly specific ones.

As with the epigraphs of his predecessors, the epigraphs of Sargon II include place names not found in the annalistic or summary texts of his palace. Reade combined this fact with his hypothesis that the decoration of each room was de-voted to a single campaign to propose that the information in the epigraphs could be used to augment the campaign narratives in the annals.[52] Of the six place names recorded by the epigraphs in Room 2, which Reade identified as the sixth campaign of 716 B.C., Tikrakka (Shikrakki) and perhaps also Ganguhtu are not mentioned elsewhere in Sargon's texts, while Bit-Bagaia and Kindau are mentioned only in the accounts of the seventh campaign of 715.[53] The epigraphs of Room 5, whose subject Reade identified as the second campaign in 720, iden-tify four cities: Gabbutunu, ʾAmqaruna, Baʾil-Gazara, and Sinu. None of these

50. In Room 2, every well-preserved city has an epigraph except that on Slab H2; the same is true in Room 5, with the possible exception of the city on Slab 2; in Rooms 13 and 14, every preserved city has an epigraph.

51. The identifiable princes were captured during Sargon's campaign to the west of 720 B.C. and his campaign to the east of 716 (Luckenbill 1927: §§5, 10–11).

52. Reade 1976.

53. Reade 1976: 102–4. Tikrakka/Shikrakki is mentioned elsewhere only by Tiglath-pileser III (Luckenbill 1927: §§795, 811); the only other certain mention of Ganguhtu is from the time of Shamshi-Adad V (823–811 B.C.; ibid., §722), but it may also have been included in a damaged portion of Sargon II's annals for the 6th campaign, now preserved only as *ga-nu*-[. . .] (Lie 1929: 14:92), though the traces hardly seem to favor Amin's read-ing *ga-nu-u*[*n-g*]*u-uḫ*(?)-[*tu*] (1953: 52–54).

cities is to be found either in the summary texts or in the preserved annals, which, however, are quite fragmentary for this campaign.[54] In the Room 14 reliefs, identified by Reade as the seventh campaign in 715, one of the two cities mentioned in the epigraphs, Kisheshlu, also occurs in the annalistic and summary narrations of this campaign; but the other, Pazashi/Panzish, is known only from the account of the eighth campaign preserved in Sargon's letter to the god Assur.[55] All the cities recorded in the preserved epigraphs from Rooms 8 and 13 are also found in the annals and summary texts. To summarize, of a total of twelve city names preserved in epigraphs from Rooms 2, 5, and 14, seven are not found elsewhere in Sargon's preserved palace inscriptions, while two others are apparently included with the representation of a campaign different from the campaign that mentions them in the annals.[56]

Thus it appears that the epigraphs on Sargon II's narrative reliefs are not particularly closely related to the annals and summary inscriptions carved with them. This feature will be discussed more fully in the analysis of Sennacherib's epigraphs. By contrast, the preserved epigraphs from the essentially formal scenes of punishment in Room 8, if they have been restored correctly, do seem to be closely related to the accompanying summary text, which includes all of the people and places mentioned in the epigraphs.[57] This difference is probably to be explained by a difference in the sources for the formal images in Room 8 and for the historical narratives in the other rooms. Each historical narrative relief series must have been based on a detailed report of the campaign being depicted, assuming that Reade's one campaign per room hypothesis is correct and the resulting series of images is annalistic in character. The formal scenes of Room 8, however, display captives from several different campaigns and show them all together in a neutral, nonhistorical setting. The source for these summary images may well have been a summary text that likewise emphasized the breadth of the king's conquests. Such a summary text represents a synthesis, drawn from more detailed chronological sources, whose purpose is to emphasize the king's major accomplishments. Since both these summaries, the verbal and the visual, deal

---

54. Reade 1976: 99–102. Tadmor confirmed Amin's identification of Gabbutunu and ʾAmqaruna with the biblical Gibbethon and Ekron (Tadmor 1958: 83 n. 243). Baʾil-Gazara may be related to Tiglath-pileser III's Gazru (biblical Gezer). The only other occurrences of any of these names in Sargon's records is in letters: ʾAmqaruna (*Iraq* 17 [1955] 134:42; Parpola 1987: no. 110:r.13) and Sinu (Parpola 1987: nos. 93:8, 230:r.4, 231:r.1).

55. Luckenbill 1927: §150; Reade 1976: 98–99.

56. These figures are more useful for Rooms 2 and 14, which depict campaigns well preserved in the annals, than for the campaign of Room 5, whose annalistic counterpart is mostly lost.

57. It is not certain whether the nearly destroyed epigraph of Room 8, Slab 12, can be related to any portion of the summary text from that room.

with highlights of the king's reign, we would expect substantial, if not complete, agreement on what these highlights are, regardless of whether the two versions were conceived independently or together. Thus the principle of selection for the subjects of the formal reliefs of Room 8 may have been different from that employed for the narrative reliefs, and in consequence the relationship of the epigraphs to the accompanying text differs as well.

Summary: Sargon II

In Sargon II's palace at Dur Sharrukin, texts were inscribed in as wide a range of locations as they had been in Assurnasirpal's palace at Kalhu—on the backs of slabs, doorway colossi, thresholds, the face of the wall slabs, and epigraphs on the wall reliefs—and the variety of texts used in these locations was considerably greater than in Assurnasirpal's palace. As in Assurnasirpal's palace, the backs of all the wall slabs were inscribed with a single text, in this case a short summary text that focuses on Sargon's beneficence to his people. Also as in Assurnasirpal's palace, the spaces between the legs of all of Sargon's colossi displayed another summary text, this one emphasizing his conquests and the magnificence of his palace. Unlike Assurnasirpal's colossus inscriptions, though, Sargon's were all complete.

As in Assurnasirpal's palace, threshold slabs in Sargon's palace were carved with a variety of texts, in this case five different summary texts of various lengths. The choice of which of these texts would be carved on a given threshold depended in part on the size of the slab and, perhaps, in part on the function of the room in which it was inscribed. The walls of all of Sargon's state apartments were lined with stone slabs carved with narrative and formal reliefs, and most of these were inscribed with either a single long annalistic or summary text, located in the same position as in Assurnasirpal's palace. Again, the choice of text in most cases seems to have been influenced by the subjects on the reliefs that accompanied them but perhaps in a few cases also by the size of the room. Epigraphs are more common now than in Tiglath-pileser's reliefs and figure in virtually every Sargon relief series that deals with foreign enemies. Some of these epigraphs are very brief, like those of Tiglath-pileser III, but others are more extended, providing basic narrative information.

With respect to its inscribed decoration, then, the visual appearance of Sargon's palace was quite similar to that of Assurnasirpal II, and since Sargon restored and resided in Assurnasirpal's palace, it was presumably the direct source for his own. Both had inscribed doorway colossi, inscribed thresholds, and bands of inscription running across the relief slabs on the walls of the rooms. To be sure, the form of some of these inscriptions had changed: in place of Assurnasirpal's brief Standard Inscription, the wall slabs of Sargon's palace carried extended annalistic or summary texts, and Assurnasirpal's annalistic threshold inscriptions were replaced in Sargon's palace with summary inscriptions. But the overall visual effect of the placement of these inscriptions was identical in the two palaces. Even the introduction of epigraphs into the reliefs of Sargon did not notably affect this likeness, since the epigraphs were for the most part brief and inconspicuous, blending in with the other details of the relief background.

Chapter 7

Sennacherib (704–681 B.C.)

Immediately following his accession to the throne, Sennacherib moved the administrative capital of the empire from Dur Sharrukin to Nineveh, one of the oldest and most important cities of ancient Assyria. Once on the Tigris, Nineveh is now about a kilometer east of the river, directly opposite modern Mosul in northern Iraq. Surrounded by rich, well-watered farm land, Nineveh is the site of the most popular ancient Tigris ford and consequently controlled major trade routes in all directions. Sennacherib made Nineveh the largest city in the known world, building a new city wall with as many as 18 gates, a huge new palace, an arsenal, temples, roads, bridges, and canals. Sennacherib's new palace, the largest in Assyria, was built in the oldest part of the city, along the southwest side of the large citadel mound of Kuyunjik, overlooking the former junction of the Tigris and Khosr rivers (fig. 38). According to Sennacherib's texts, his new "Palace Without Rival" was on the site of an old one (probably that of Mutakkil-Nusku) in the area between the Ishtar Temple and ziggurrat and the Khosr and Tigris rivers. He says he demolished the old building and enlarged its site by constructing a new terrace 914 by 440 cubits (about 500 by 240 meters) in extent.[1]

In 1847 Austin Henry Layard began systematic excavations on Kuyunjik and had uncovered a substantial part of Sennacherib's palace, which he called the Southwest palace, by the time he left in 1851.[2] He was followed by Hormuzd Rassam (1852–1854, 1878–1882), William Loftus (1854–1855), George Smith (1873–1874), E. A. W. Budge (1889–1891), Leonard W. King (1903–1904), R. Campbell Thompson (1904–1905), Tariq Madhloom (1965–1971), and David Stronach and John Russell (1989–1990). By far the largest part was excavated by Layard, who exposed the state apartments, an area about 200 meters square at the palace's southwest end. Excavating by means of tunnels because of the thick accumulation of earth overhead, he exposed the walls of some 70 rooms, most of which were paneled with stone slabs carved in relief with Sennacherib's royal

1. Russell 1991.
2. Layard 1849a and 1853a.

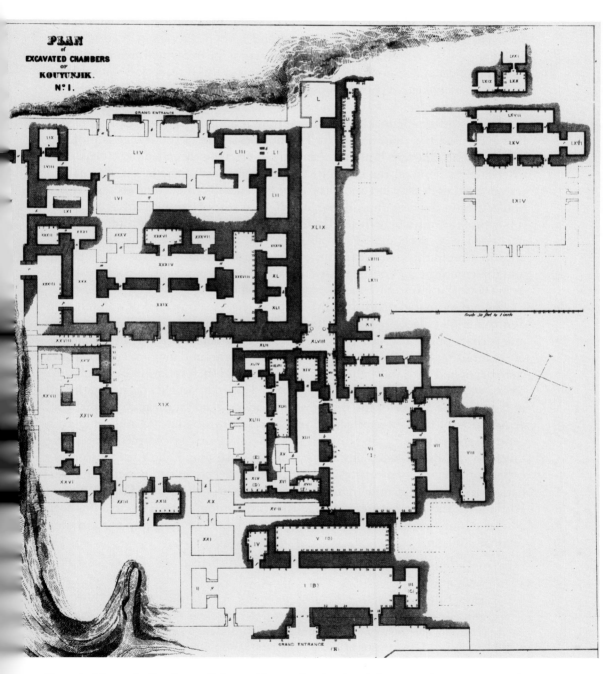

FIG. 38. Nineveh, Southwest Palace of Sennacherib, plan (after Layard 1853a: opp. 67).

exploits. The excavated area included a throne-room court (H), a throne-room suite (I–VI) of the usual plan, an inner court (VI) surrounded by typical reception suites, a second inner court (XIX)—a feature not found in earlier Assyrian palaces—also surrounded by reception suites, and a group of rooms of uncertain plan facing the southwest terrace. In the western part of the excavated area was a group of small, undecorated domestic rooms and beyond this a reception suite that an inscription carved on a pair of colossi identifies as the residence of Sennacherib's favorite queen.

It is clear from Sennacherib's description of his palace, however, that Layard had excavated less than half of it. The northeast end of the palace is probably "Sennacherib's Eastern Building" (sometimes erroneously called the *bīt nakkapti*) excavated by King on the edge of Kuyunjik southeast of the Ishtar Temple and reexcavated under my direction as part of Stronach's Nineveh project. Inscribed bull colossi in the Eastern Building identify it as part of Sennacherib's palace and it is approximately where the end of the main palace should be, according to Sennacherib's own accounts.[3] King also reported scattered traces of Sennacherib construction in the area between the state apartments and the Eastern Building, and these must be part of the palace as well. This material will be published fully in my contribution to Stronach's excavation report.

Layard estimated that he uncovered 9880 feet (3011 meters) of wall reliefs in Sennacherib's palace.[4] A few of these reliefs date to the reign of Assurbanipal and perhaps one of his successors, but most are Sennacherib's.[5] As in the palaces of Assurnasirpal II and Sargon II, only rooms in or around major reception suites were decorated with wall reliefs, but the number of such rooms in Sennacherib's palace was considerably larger. The palace had been thoroughly burned at the fall of Nineveh, and most of the reliefs were badly cracked and scarred by the heat. A selection of the better-preserved reliefs was drawn by Layard and other 19th century artists working at Nineveh.[6] A few more-or-less complete slabs were taken to the British Museum and fragments have found their way into other collections, but the vast majority are still *in situ*, deeply buried under later occupation levels. In the mid-1960s, Tariq Madhloom of the Iraq Department of Antiquities and Heritage reexcavated the throne-room suite. This area has been converted into a site museum where some 100 reliefs are now displayed in their original position.

3. Russell 1991: 78–86.
4. Layard 1853a: 589.
5. Russell 1991: 117–51.
6. The drawings are in 7 folio volumes entitled "Original Drawings," in the Departmental Archives, Department of Western Asiatic Antiquities, The British Museum. A selection was published in Layard 1849b and 1853b. For publication details of individual slabs, see Russell 1991: 279–88.

Fɪɢ. 39. Nineveh, Southwest Palace of Sennacherib, Room I, Slab 4, detail of inscription on back of wall slab (photo: author).

The Texts on the Backs of Slabs

Two texts are known to have been used on the backs of Sennacherib's colossi and wall slabs. The more common of the two is very short: "Palace of Sennacherib, great king, king of the world, king of Assyria, the almighty one, the lord of all kings" (fig. 39). Layard copied it from the backs of the bulls in Room I, Door *e*, and it is visible on the backs of relief slabs in Rooms I and V as well. It has also been reported on wall slabs from Room LI(n) and from the "Ishtar Temple Procession" in Court H, and we found one fragmentary example in fill while excavating Sennacherib's "Eastern Building," which is probably the eastern end of his palace. Finally, Rawlinson published examples on slabs from Nebi Yunus, the site of Sennacherib's arsenal, which indicates that the text was not confined solely to the main palace.[7]

It is probable that this was the text used on most of the wall slabs and colossi throughout Sennacherib's palace. In comparison with the much longer texts that appeared on the backs of slabs in the palaces of Assurnasirpal II and Sargon II, which offer abundant information about the king, his deeds, and the appearance of his palace, Sennacherib's text is little more than a tag that names the owner. Sennacherib may have felt that this was all a future king would need to know to order the restoration of the building.

The other text, which is somewhat longer, is known only from Room XXXIII. Layard copied one example from the back of Lion 1 in Room XXXIII,

---

7. Text: Layard 1851: 75:D (from Layard, Ms A, p. 300). Transliteration and translation: Russell 1991: 271. Study: Frahm 1997: 140–41, "T 71." Room I, Door *e*: Layard 1849a: vol. 2, 126; Room I wall slabs: Russell 1991: 269–70, fig. 132; Room V: Madhloom 1969: 48; Room LI(n): Paterson 1915: 4; "Ishtar Temple Procession": Gadd 1936: 94; Nebi Yunus: Rawlinson 1861: pl. 6, no. 8.A. Layard also reported Sennacherib's "name and usual titles" on the backs of slabs in Room XXXIII, but this must be the other text (see below).

Door *p*, and Rawlinson published at least two more examples on the backs of wall slabs from Room XXXIII in the British Museum. It reads: "Palace of Sennacherib, great king, powerful king, king of the world, king of Assyria: NA₄.^{d}ŠE.TIR stone, the appearance of which is like mottled barley(?), which in the time of the kings, my fathers, was valued only as a necklace stone, revealed itself to me at the foot of Mt. Nipur. I had female sphinxes made of it and had them dragged into Nineveh." This text was clearly composed to identify this special stone, which was so valued for its natural beauty that it was left unsculptured in those rooms where slabs of it lined the walls.[8]

Colossus Inscriptions

The arrangement of reliefs on the throne-room façade (H) of Sennacherib's palace was the same as on Sargon II's palace: a pair of human-headed bull colossi in each of the three exterior doors and addorsed pairs of bull colossi, between which were lion-clutching humans, on the two buttresses between the doors. The spaces between the legs of the bulls were inscribed with a variety of texts, ranging from an extended annalistic text and palace-building account on the bulls in the central door, to a historical summary and brief palace-building account on the façade buttresses bulls, to a detailed description of the size and appearance of the palace on the examples in the side door. An interesting innovation is that these colossi have only four legs, which gives them a more naturalistic appearance than that of their five-legged predecessors. A similar arrangement of colossal figures was reported for the poorly-recorded west façade of the palace, and bull colossi also occurred in a number of other major palace doorways. A well-preserved uninscribed example was found in the Nergal Gate on the north stretch of the city wall (fig. 40).

There is a considerable shift in the content and function of Sennacherib's palace bull inscriptions when compared with Sargon's. Though quite a few of these inscriptions are known, their identification and state of publication is fairly confusing, and so all of them are discussed in detail in Catalog 3. The content of the texts of Sennacherib's inscribed bulls may be summarized as follows:

Court H, Façade Bull 1   Six campaign historical summary (lost; possible fragment: Hannover Bull) plus an abridged palace-building account (part *in situ*).

8. Layard 1853a: 459. Text: Rawlinson 1861: pl. 7.E; Layard, Ms C, fol. 66 recto. Transliteration and translation: Russell 1991: 276. Study: Frahm 1997: 140–41, "T 72." The stone was left unsculptured in Rooms XXIX and XXX (Layard 1853a: 445–46) and probably in XXXIII as well, though in the latter room it was later carved by Assurbanipal. On the use of this stone in the palace, see Russell 1991: 99.

FIG. 40. Nineveh, city wall, Nergal gate, bull colossus, width ca. 4.5 m (photo: author).

Court H, Façade Bull 3   Six campaign historical summary (partially preserved, probably Smith's "Bull 2") plus an abridged palace-building account (part *in situ*; possible fragment: Papal Bull).

Court H, Façade Bull 10   Six campaign historical summary (lost; possible fragment: Hannover Bull) plus an abridged palace-building account (lost).

Court H, Façade Bull 12   Six campaign historical summary (Smith's "Bull 3") plus an abridged palace-building account (part *in situ* + Meissner and Rost, pl. 8; possible fragment: Papal Bull).

Court H, Door a	An annalistic account of the first six campaigns plus a long palace-building account (Rawlinson, IIIR 12–13).
Court H, Door c	A long palace-building account (Layard, ICC 38–42).
Room I, Door d	Five-campaign historical summary plus a long palace-building account (Layard, ICC 59–62; possibly Smith's "Bull 2").
Room I, Door e	Probably a five-campaign historical summary (lost) plus a long palace-building account (Layard, Ms A, 135–36).
Court VI, Door a	A long palace-building account (Layard, ICC 38–42 variant).
Court VI(?), Door k(?)	Uncertain, but I have tentatively attributed Layard, Ms D, fols. 24–29 (Smith's "Bull 1"; Meissner and Rost, pls. 6–7) to these bulls.
Room LX, Door a	Probably a five- or six-campaign historical summary (lost) plus an abridged palace-building account (Layard, Ms C, 56 verso–57 verso).
Court LXIV, Door a	An abridged palace-building account (Layard, Ms C, 55 verso–56 verso).

A comparison of the bull inscriptions of Sennacherib with those of his father, Sargon II reveals considerable differences in form and content, which may in turn point to a change in intended function. The most noticeable of these differences are the increased variety of types of content and the considerably greater length of Sennacherib's bull inscriptions. It will be recalled that all of Sargon's palace bulls carried the same inscription, a text consisting of a brief historical resume, arranged geographically, followed by an account of the building of Dur Sharrukin. The preserved Sennacherib bulls, on the other hand, exhibit a variety of texts that conform to three general types. The first type, seen in Court H, Door a, consists of an extended annalistic narrative, followed by a palace-building account. The second type consists of a historical resume, arranged chronologically, followed by a palace-building account. This type of text was found on Façade Bulls 1, 3, 10, and 12 in Court H, in Doors d and e of Room I, and in Door a of Room LX. The third type of text—found in Door c of Court H, Door a of Court VI, and Door a of Court LXIV—consists entirely of a palace-building account.

Though the Southwest Palace bull inscriptions seem to conform to these three general types, no two of the published texts are identical. In addition to the orthographic variants that are the rule in Assyrian palace inscriptions, these inscriptions also give differing versions of details, such as the dimensions of the palace; they exhibit varying degrees of abridgment; and they seemingly intermix passages drawn from the entire corpus of Sennacherib palace texts. The inscriptions also cover different time periods, with some recording five and others six campaigns. In the case of Room I, Door d, the historical resume covers five campaigns, but campaigns one and four, both against Babylonia, are combined, so that the order of presentation is one and four, followed by two, three, and five. This is not the pattern of geographical rotation employed in Sargon's bull inscriptions but rather a slightly modified chronological presentation. The resume of Smith's Bull 3 adds the sixth campaign, against Babylon, but rather than combining it with campaigns one and four, it is placed at the end, suggesting that the scribes updated the five-campaign resume not by rewriting it but simply by adding to it. It appears, then, that most of Sennacherib's palace bull inscriptions were compiled individually. We cannot know all of the considerations that applied when each was composed, but clearly the scribes were interested in presenting information that was up-to-date, and presumably they were also aware of the amount of space available for each inscription, tailoring them accordingly.

The question of space available for inscription raises the second major difference between the bull inscriptions of Sennacherib and Sargon II: length. As discussed earlier, Sargon's bull inscriptions occupied four rectangular panels, one under the belly and one between the hind legs of each of the two bulls in the doorway. Each of Sennacherib's inscriptions also occupied both bulls of the doorway, but in a return to the practice of Assurnasirpal II, the inscription was no longer confined to rectangular panels; it now filled the entire space under the belly and between the legs. Furthermore, Sennacherib's elimination of the spurious foreleg visible in the side view of the colossi of all of his predecessors expanded the space available for inscription under the belly. The result of this expansion was felt not in Sennacherib's smaller bulls, where the inscriptions were only slightly longer than Sargon's, but rather in the large bulls, such as those in Door *a* of Room I, where the inscription was more than two and a half times as long as Sargon's.[9]

It remains to account for this variety in the Sennacherib bull inscriptions, especially noticeable when contrasted with Sargon's use of a single text for all his colossi, regardless of size or location. It seems to me that this variety must be viewed not simply in the context of Sargon's colossus text but rather in the context of the entire corpus of Sargon's palace inscriptions. Sargon had different types of texts composed for different types of features of his palace decoration: bulls and the walls of Room 14 carried a historical resume, arranged geographically, plus a building account; thresholds were inscribed with a brief historical resume or with a resume plus building account; the inscribed band between the registers of narrative relief in Rooms 2, 5, 13, and 14 carried an annalistic account of the king's reign plus a building account; the formal scenes of tributaries in Rooms 1, 4, 7, 8, and 10, were inscribed with a lengthy historical resume, arranged roughly chronologically, plus a building account; and the narrative reliefs carried brief captions identifying the towns and peoples represented.[10]

---

9. Calculations of relative lengths of Sargon and Sennacherib bull inscriptions based on the number of pages each occupies in Luckenbill's translation (1927: §§92–94, 301–29, 407–16).

10. References to Fuchs 1994. Bulls: pp. 60–74; Room 14 summary text: pp. 75–81; thresholds: pp. 249–75; annals: pp. 82–188; other summary text: pp. 189–248. See also the chapter on Sargon II (above, pp. 99–123).

In the palace of Sennacherib, by contrast, the only visible inscriptions were the bull inscriptions, the captions on the reliefs, and brief texts on a few thresholds. If Sennacherib were to retain the variety of Sargon's inscriptions, which he apparently wished to do, then his bulls would have to carry the range of texts that formerly had been apportioned to a variety of palace locations. Thus in Sennacherib's throne room, the bulls of Door *a* had a text similar in form to Sargon's annalistic inscriptions; in Door *d* was a resume arranged chronologically, similar to Sargon's chronological resume; and in Door *c* was a text whose principal emphasis was on the building account, similar to Sargon's bull and threshold texts. To be sure, the correspondence between Sennacherib's bull texts and the corpus of Sargon's palace texts was not complete; Sennacherib, for example, was far more interested than his father in presenting a detailed and complete account of his building activities. But it is clear that when Sennacherib eliminated or modified a type of text, it was not for lack of a place to carve it but rather because he wished to express priorities different from those of his father.

Thresholds

The sculptural decoration of the threshold slabs in Sennacherib's Southwest Palace are fairly well known from descriptions and drawings of Layard's excavations. According to Layard, "the pavement slabs were not inscribed as at Nimroud; but those between the winged bulls at some of the entrances, were carved with an elaborate and very elegant pattern."[11] This observation is not quite correct. He published a drawing of only one of these thresholds, that from Room XXIV, Door *c*, whose pattern he described as "a border of alternate tulips or lotus flowers and cones, inclosing similar ornaments arranged in squares and surrounded by rosettes."[12] In his note to this engraving, Layard stated that "many of the entrances at Kuyunjik have similar pavements" and drawings of some of these were published by Albenda.[13] All of these patterns consist of various arrangements of the basic elements described by Layard for Room XXIV, Door *c*.

In Sennacherib's throne room (Room I), Layard reported that the threshold of Door *e* (formerly *a*) was "elaborately carved with figures of flowers, resembling the lotus, and with other ornaments."[14] This slab, which was cleaned in 1990, was the source for Original Drawings V, plate 56 (fig. 41; see fig. 3). Layard failed to mention that this threshold has a brief two-line inscription carved across its

---

11. Layard 1853a: 652.
12. Layard 1853b: pl. 56; 1853a: 442.
13. Layard 1853b: 7; Albenda 1978: 14–16, pls. 8–15.
14. Layard 1849a: vol. 2, 126.

FIG. 41. Nineveh, Southwest Palace of Sennacherib, Room V, Door *e*, threshold. Original Drawings V, 56 (photo: Trustees of the British Museum).

middle, and this is also omitted in the drawing, though the space that contains it is shown. The text reads: "Sennacherib, king of the world, king of Assyria: a palace without rival for ⌜his royal⌝ dwelling inside Nineveh he caused to be built anew."[15]

15. Edition: Russell 1991: 269. Study: Frahm 1997: 128, "T 60."

Madhloom's excavations revealed that Room I, Door *a*, and Room V, Door *a*, were also decorated with floral thresholds, but no inscriptions were reported, and at present these slabs are covered with earth.[16] According to a notebook of cuneiform copies by William Boutcher in the British Museum, however, the threshold of Room I, Door *a* was in fact inscribed.[17] The text is similar to that on the threshold of Room I, Door *e*. Because it is brief and has not been published, I give it in full here. It is labeled: "From centre of pavement slab between the large bulls at Grand Entrance.—Palace of Sennacherib.—Kouyunjik." The text reads:

1. [md]30-PAP.MEŠ-SU MAN GAL MAN *dan-nu* MAN ŠÚ MAN KUR *aš+šur* É.GAL
   ZAG.DI.NU.TUK.A
2. *a-na mu-šab be-lu-ti-šú qé-reb* MURUB$_4$ URU *ša* NINA.KI *eš-šiš ú-še-piš*

1. Sennacherib, great king, strong king, king of the world, king of Assyria: a palace without rival
2. for his royal dwelling in the middle of the city of Nineveh he caused to be built anew.

These are the only inscribed thresholds I know of in Sennacherib's palace, but there may be others.

In view of the expanded format and content of Sennacherib's throne room colossi, a similar phenomenon with respect to the threshold slabs associated with them might be expected. Such was not the case however; all available evidence indicates that the visible surfaces of most of Sennacherib's palace thresholds, unlike those of his predecessors, were devoid of inscriptions. The text on the two inscribed examples is very brief, stating only that Sennacherib built this palace. I will speculate on possible reasons for the reduction or elimination of the threshold as a carrier of long texts in the final chapter.

Epigraphs on the Wall Reliefs

The reliefs on the courtyard wall north of the throne-room façade showed not the tribute processions that were in this location in the palaces of Assurnasirpal II and Sargon II but rather a military campaign in Babylonia. Tribute processions, which had been the most frequent relief subject in Sargon's palace, were

16. El-Wailly 1965: 6; Albenda 1978: 14, pl. 8. There are undecorated thresholds in Room I, Doors *c* and *f* (el-Wailly 1965: Arabic section, fig. 2 following p. 9; Madhloom 1967: pl. 9).

17. British Museum, Department of Western Asiatic Antiquities, Departmental Archives, "Copies of Inscriptions discovered at Kouyunjik and Nimrud in 1854–5 by Wm. Kenneth Loftus," pp. 10–11.

entirely supplanted by scenes of military activity in Sennacherib's palace. Other Sargon relief subjects that were omitted from Sennacherib's palace decoration were punishment of captives, processions of courtiers, banquets, and hunts. Only two of his predecessor's subjects appear: military campaigns, which were the subject in all but 3 of the 38 rooms for which the subject is known, and procurement of palace building materials, in this case the quarrying and transportation overland of human-headed bull gateway colossi on two walls in Court VI (with military scenes on the other two walls) and the transportation by water of a very large piece of wood or stone in Room XLIX. Processions of attendants and horses going in and out of the palace were depicted on the walls of Room LI, a corridor that probably led to a postern gate, and deportation of captives was apparently the subject of Room XLIII.

Sennacherib began construction on his palace early in his reign, and at the time his wall reliefs were carved, his artists had only the first few campaigns to choose from as subjects. In *Sennacherib's Palace without Rival at Nineveh* (1991), I suggested that all of Sennacherib's military reliefs can be associated with his first three campaigns: the first campaign of 703 B.C. to Babylon, the second campaign of 702 B.C. to the Zagros Mountains to the east, and the third campaign of 701 B.C. to the Levant. Recently, however, Eckart Frahm has argued persuasively that an epigraph in Sennacherib's throne room probably records an event from the fifth campaign, of 697 B.C., and representations of the fourth and fifth campaigns might be expected elsewhere in the palace as well.[18] This would be consistent with the inscriptions on the bull colossi, which, as we have seen, record either five or six campaigns, and with the text on the backs of the wall slabs in Room XXXIII, which were made of stone acquired during the fifth campaign.

As far as is known, each room was decorated with a single campaign, with the exception of Court LXIV and probably the throne room (I). The evidence for determining the pattern of distribution of the military subjects is fragmentary, but it appears that in the throne-room suite and in the major reception suites around the inner court of the throne room (Court VI), a mixture of campaigns was shown in each suite. Thus, in the throne-room suite, Babylonia was shown in the outer court (H) and Room III, the Levant and probably the upper Tigris in the throne room (I), the Zagros in Room V and half of Court VI, and procurement of building materials in the other half of Court VI. The distribution of subjects in the rooms around Court XIX seems to have followed a different pattern, with the Zagros campaign in the rooms north of the court and the campaign to the Levant predominating in the rooms to the west of it.

The format of Sennacherib's wall reliefs is different from that used by his predecessors. Sennacherib's reliefs omitted the band of inscription that divided the slabs of the earlier kings into two narrow registers of relief and carved his relief

18. Frahm 1994; Frahm 1997: 124–25, "T 39."

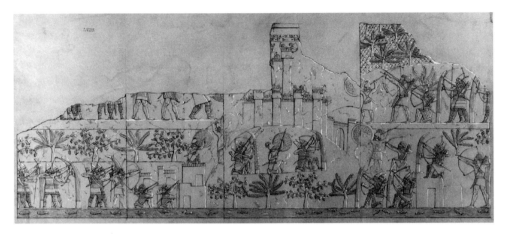

FIG. 42. Nineveh, Southwest Palace of Sennacherib, Room XIV, Slabs 8–11, siege of Alammu(?). Original Drawings IV, 58 (photo: Trustees of the British Museum).

images over the entire surface. On this expanded pictorial area, Sennacherib's artists adopted the spatial convention of a high implied viewpoint with relatively small-scale figures more-or-less freely disposed across the slab. The sense of depth is most effective for subjects depicted against a patterned background, such as mountains or water. When the subject does not permit such a setting—for example, in reliefs that show the Babylonian plain—the slab is divided into registers by multiple groundlines or by narrow uninscribed margins. The only texts that intrude on any of Sennacherib's reliefs are brief captions inscribed next to the king or the cities he encounters.

I have discussed Sennacherib's epigraphs in considerable detail elsewhere, and what follows is largely based on that study.[19] Only a few of what must once have been a large number of Sennacherib epigraphs are now known. This must be largely because, as Layard observed, the upper portion of most of Sennacherib's reliefs, the usual location for epigraphs, were destroyed.[20] The problem is clearly evident on Slab 10 of Room XIV, where the epigraph was the only part of the slab top to be preserved (fig. 42). Most epigraphs at the top of Sennacherib's single-register compositions must have been lost, as were the epigraphs in the upper register of reliefs of Sargon II, all of whose surviving epigraphs were in the lower of the two relief registers. Nevertheless, some 28 Sennacherib epigraphs are recorded from 15 different rooms of his palace. All are given here in Catalog

19. Russell 1991: 24–31, 269–78.
20. Layard 1853a: 148.

Fɪɢ. 43. Nineveh, Southwest Palace of Sennacherib, royal chariot, fragment stored in Room V (photo: author).

4, which incorporates a number of updates to the edition of the epigraphs given in *Sennacherib's Palace without Rival at Nineveh*.[21]

The increased height of Sennacherib's relief registers resulted in more space being made available for epigraphs, some of which are considerably longer than those of earlier kings. None of Sennacherib's known epigraphs are only city names like Tiglath-pileser III's and Sargon II's Room 2 and 5 epigraphs. A few are of the general form of Sargon's Room 13 and 14 epigraphs (listed by room and slab number, if known):

> "The city Bit-ib/lu . . .]." (XXXVIII:17/18)
> "The city [GN] I besieged, I captured." (I:4a)
> "Dilbat (*var.* ⌜Aranziash⌝, Alammu) I besieged, I captured, I carried off its booty." (III:8, V:35, XIV:10)
> "The city Bit-Kubatti I besieged, I captured, I carried off its booty, I burned it." (LX:2)
> "[The city GN I besieged, I captured(?)] ⌜I carried off its booty, I tore down, I⌝ demolished, ⌜I burned⌝." (XLVII:?)

The majority of the epigraphs, however, give not only the setting and action, but identify Sennacherib as well. They are often located near the image of the king. Those in front of the king in booty review scenes, for example, all begin "Sennacherib, king of the world, king of Assyria," and then continue as follows:

> "⌜the booty⌝ of the city Kasusi(?) ⌜passed in review⌝ before him." (V:11; also V:30 and XLV:?, where the place name is lost)

21. Russell 1991: 269–78, Appendix 1.

Fɪɢ. 44. Nineveh, Southwest Palace of Sennacherib, Room XLIX, Slabs 2–4, water transport of a large object. Original Drawings IV, 62 (photo: Trustees of the British Museum).

> "the booty of the marshes of the city Sahrina passed in review before him." (LXX:4)
>
> "sat in a *nēmedu*-throne and the booty of the city Lachish passed in review before him." (XXXVI:12)
>
> "the cities of [PN or GN] he goes to capture." (VI:2)
>
> "ꜙthe bootyꜙ [. . .] of the city [GN . . .]." (unknown room; fig. 43)

Sennacherib's camp and tent are also labeled:

> "Camp (*var.* tent) of Sennacherib, king of Assyria." (I:9, V:41, X:7, XXXVI:12)

One of the longest epigraphs, over a captured city, reads like an excerpt from the annals:

> "[Sennacherib], king of the world, king of Assyria: [Manija]e, [king of] ꜙthe city Ukkuꜙ, [feared] the onslaught of [my] ꜙbattleꜙ. He deserted [Ukku], his power ꜙbaseꜙ, and ꜙfledꜙ [to] ꜙdistant partsꜙ. ꜙThe soldiersꜙ [who dwelt] therein, who had flown to the summit of the [inaccessible] mountains ꜙlike birdsꜙ, ꜙI followedꜙ after them and ꜙdefeatedꜙ them at the mountain top. The city ꜙUkkuꜙ, his royal ꜙcityꜙ, ꜙI burnedꜙ." (I:1)

Epigraphs over scenes that depict the procurement of construction material are likewise very informative. Those in Court VI all begin "Sennacherib, king of the world, king of Assyria," and then continue:

> "joyfully he caused great bull colossi, which were made in the district of Balatai, to be dragged to his royal palace in Nineveh." (VI:60)
>
> "at the command of the god, white limestone had been discovered in the district of Balatai for the construction of my palace. I caused men (*var.* soldiers) from enemy towns and the inhabitants of hidden (*var.* rebel-

lious) mountain regions, conquest of my hand, to wield iron picks and masons'-picks(?), and I had them make (*var.* they carved) great bull colossi for the gates of my palace." (VI:66; variants from VI:68)

Two fragmentary epigraphs found loose in Room XLIX originally belonged to a relief series that showed a large object being transported by water (fig. 44):

"Sennacherib, king of the world, king of Assyria: I caused great columns of cedar, product of Mt. Sirara and Mt. Lebanon, to be brought up the Tigris."

"Sennacherib, king of the world, king of Assyria: I caused great columns of cedar to be brought up the Tigris. I had them loaded ⌜on⌝ a sledge/raft(?) and pulled up through the canal."

Other epigraphs are known, but were not copied by Layard (VI:62 and VII:14) or are illegible (I:24), and one text that Layard considered to be an epigraph apparently is not.[22] In addition to the epigraphs cited here, all of which were found on reliefs, Rawlinson published a tablet that seems to be a collection of Sennacherib epigraphs.[23] It begins with a long passage that describes a campaign in the mountains (lines 1–9; Campaign 2?); then follows the place name Bit-Kubat (line 10; Campaign 2); then a passage describing the flight of Merodach-Baladan (lines 11–13; Campaign 4); then the defeat of Shuzubu (lines 14–16; Campaign 4?); then the place names Sumer (line 18; Campaigns 1 or 4) and Meluhha(?) (line 19; Campaign 3). The only one of these that corresponds with the preserved epigraphs on the reliefs is Bit-Kubat, which is presumably identical with the Bit-Kubatti reported in Room LX. It is not clear whether this collection represents a preliminary draft for the Sennacherib epigraphs, a later copy made from them, or a text assembled independently of the epigraphs. The mixture of campaigns in the tablet shows that it did not derive from the decoration of one or even two rooms, and this suggests that it is a later compilation, rather than a preliminary draft, which would be expected to concentrate on a single room or campaign. Strong, who edited the text, felt it was a copy made by a student.[24] If these are epigraphs, they are unusual for their length and narrative detail, though the epigraph from Room I, Slab 1, is equally long.

It is not known whether every enemy city in Sennacherib's reliefs was labeled with an epigraph. Not only were the tops of most slabs destroyed, but in some cases the epigraph that identifies a city may not have been placed over the city itself but instead next to the image of the victorious king on a neighboring slab. These

---

22. See final entry in Catalog 4.

23. Text: Rawlinson 1870: pl. 4:4. Transliteration and translation: Luckenbill 1924: 156:xxiv. Study: Frahm 1997: 211–12.

24. S. A. Strong, "On Some Cuneiform Inscriptions of Sennacherib and Assurnasirpal," *Journal of the Royal Asiatic Society*, n.s. 23 (1891) 148.

epigraphs always commence with Sennacherib's name and titles and serve as much to identify the king as his defeated enemy. They usurp, therefore, one of the main functions of the text register on the reliefs of his predecessors, namely, the identification of the king, and because the royal name recurs so frequently in the epigraphs, they perform this function more efficiently than the texts they replaced. Sennacherib's epigraphs, then, serve a more active role in the interpretation of the images, identifying the participants on both sides and giving a descriptive summary, thereby focusing attention on the significant features of the action.[25]

Several complete editions of Sennacherib's annals are preserved. Of the cities mentioned in his epigraphs, only three—Balatai, Bit-Kubatti, and Sahrina—are definitely included in his annals. The remaining six—Lachish, Alammu, Aranziash, Dilbat, Kasusi, and Mt. Lebanon, plus one other fragmentary name—are mentioned by Sennacherib only in his epigraphs.[26] This lack of overlap between the annals and the epigraphs makes it clear that the known editions of the annals, which were intended to be buried in the palace walls or carved on the doorway bulls, could not have been the source for the campaign episodes depicted in the wall reliefs. There must have been a more detailed written source or sources on which both the verbal and visual accounts were based. This could have been detailed accounts of individual campaigns, made either while the campaign was in progress or immediately after its conclusion, or it could have been a series of booty lists augmented by personal recollection. Either of these could later have been condensed and edited into the various sorts of verbal and visual narratives and summaries with which we are familiar.[27]

There is no doubt that scribes accompanied royal campaigns; the palace reliefs of Shalmaneser III, Tiglath-pileser III, Sargon II, Sennacherib, and Assurbanipal all show them. Usually the scribes are depicted in pairs, one writing

25. Russell 1991: 25–28.
26. Balatai: Luckenbill 1924: 108:62, 121:50, 129:63, 132:74, Frahm 1997: 75:77; Bit-Kubatti: Luckenbill 1924: 26:73, 27:5, 58:25, 67:10; Sahrina: ibid., 52:38. Alammu is mentioned in a Sargon II letter (Waterman 1930: vol. 2, no. 891:5); Dilbat by Tiglath-pileser III, Sargon II, Esarhaddon, and Assurbanipal (Parpola 1970: 103); Mt. Lebanon by Assurnasirpal II, Shalmaneser III, Tiglath-pileser III, Esarhaddon, and Assurbanipal (Parpola 1970: 221–22); and Aranziash by Shalmaneser III, Tiglath-pileser III, Sargon II, and Assurbanipal (Parpola 1970: 23, 126). Kasusi, Lachish, and A-ta(?)-un(?)-[x] apparently occur in no other Neo-Assyrian sources. It is possible that the city [URU x-x-(x)-z]i-a-šu should be restored Elenzash instead of Aranziash, though it is not attested with these signs (Russell 1991: 273). In Sennacherib's annals, Elenzash is written *el-en-za-áš* (Luckenbill 1924: 28:27, 59:32, 68:15), but it is written *e-le-en-zi-* [. . .] in the broken occurrence of the name at Jerwan (Jacobsen and Lloyd 1935: 26, no. 45T; Parpola 1970: 123; Frahm 1997: 157, no. 45+). Frahm (1997: 123, 126) doubts that Aranziash and Elenzash are the same city.
27. Russell 1991: 28.

Aramaic on a scroll and the other writing Akkadian on a clay tablet or wax-covered wooden writing board, apparently recording enemy dead and captured booty.[28] Both the scroll and writing board are perishable, and to my knowledge, none of these booty lists survive. There are, however, several examples of very detailed campaign accounts that were apparently composed immediately after the conclusion of the campaign they record. The best known of these is the account of Sargon II's eighth campaign recorded in his "letter to the god Assur."[29] Examples from Sennacherib's reign are an early account of his first campaign and a fragmentary tablet that records part of his third campaign, against Judah.[30]

If the epigraphic/visual and annalistic/verbal accounts were compiled independently of one another, but drawing on the same source material, the problem remains of how to explain the differences between them. Three possible explanations come to mind. First, the visual narratives and their accompanying epigraphs could have been compiled at a different time, presumably earlier, than the written annals. It is striking, for example, that while Sargon II founded Dur Sharrukin in 717 B.C., his fifth year, and none of his preserved reliefs show events definitely after 714, the annalistic and summary texts that accompany the reliefs encompass the first fourteen years and were therefore composed after 708 and before 706, the year the new capital was inaugurated.[31] It seems unlikely that the massive job of carving the wall reliefs was also put off until after 708, for it is difficult to see how this would have allowed time for both the carving and inscribing of the reliefs. It seems far more likely, rather, that the reliefs were planned and carved throughout the time the palace was under construction, and the inscriptions only were added at the very end, thus ensuring that they would be as up-to-date as possible.

Similarly, except for the reliefs in the throne room, none of the reliefs from Sennacherib's palace can be demonstrated to show events later than his third campaign, which dates to 701 B.C., though some of the bull texts include the sixth campaign and were thus composed after 694. Finally, in the palace of Tiglath-pileser III was a relief series that provided a space for an annalistic text that was never carved, presumably because the king died before the palace was completed.[32] All of this points to the conclusion that the program of the palace

28. Russell 1991: 28–29, 292 n. 36. Concerning the opinion that the man with a scroll is an artist, Jerrold Cooper observes that drawing would have to be done on a flat surface, whereas the medium (papyrus or leather) shown in the reliefs is hanging down and so was being used for writing lines of script, not drawing (personal communication, letter of 6 May 1994).

29. Thureau-Dangin 1912.

30. First Campaign: S. Smith 1921; Frahm 1997: 42–45. Third campaign: Na'aman 1979, Frahm 1997: 229–32.

31. For the chronology, see Tadmor 1958: 94–97.

32. Reade 1979b: 72–75.

reliefs was planned considerably earlier than the time of compilation of the extended texts that were to accompany them, and thus differences in detail might be expected.

A second explanation for the differences between the epigraphic/visual and annalistic/verbal records might be to suggest that the two were compiled by different people. We do not know who was responsible for planning the visual program for the decoration of a Neo-Assyrian palace, but among the planners must have been at least one scribe to interpret the written campaign records and prepare the epigraphs. If this was not the same scribe who was also responsible for preparing the written annals, then we might attribute some differences in the two records to different opinions regarding which events were essential and which could be omitted.

A third explanation could be that the two types of records were conceived for different purposes or with different emphases. There is a certain regularity and unity in the annalistic and summary palace inscriptions; no single campaign or region is unduly emphasized at the expense of another, and the primary concern seems to be to give a balanced and complete picture of the military activities of the king. The emphasis in the visual record in the later Assyrian palaces, on the other hand, is on single campaigns, and in Sennacherib's palace at least, it appears as though the decoration of entire suites of rooms might have been devoted to a single campaign.[33] In such cases, one would expect a greater emphasis on the multiplicity of individual events comprising the campaign than would be found in the more synthetic version in the annals. For example, in its account of the campaign against Judah, Sennacherib's palace annals mention only a single city, Jerusalem, by name, adding that 46 other walled cities were taken as well.[34] While this is an adequate verbal description of the events, a visual description of the same campaign would have to show the capture of at least some of these other cities, particularly because Jerusalem itself was not captured and would thus make an uninspiring subject for a narrative relief. The result was that the visual account of the campaign to Judah added at least one event not explicitly recorded in the annals, the capture of Lachish shown in Room XXXVI.

The true explanation for the differences in the visual and verbal record must be a combination of some or all of the above three factors and perhaps others besides, which might have varied from palace to palace. For example, the details of the visual account might also have been affected by the size of the room, which could have determined the number of individual events to be shown, and by the anticipated audience, which might result in the graphic depiction of particular events aimed at that audience—events that might be passed over in the compilation of the more general annalistic and summary texts.[35]

33. Russell 1991: 171–74.
34. Luckenbill 1924: 70:28–29.
35. For the audience for Assyrian palace reliefs, see Russell 1991: 223–40.

Summary: *Sennacherib*

In comparison with Sargon II's palace, the interior of Sennacherib's palace must have appeared largely devoid of inscriptions. The colossi were still inscribed, but thresholds were decorated either exclusively or predominantly with floral patterns. The band of text that formerly divided the wall reliefs was missing as well. The information that had formerly been provided by the annalistic and summary texts carved on the wall reliefs was now confined to the colossi. The only texts that did figure in the wall reliefs were the epigraphs. Rather than distract from the image, these brief texts served, by their mere presence, to focus attention on specific elements of the representation. They also identified the king, as well as his foes, and provided a brief summary of the most important parts of the action.

This chapter built on previous work I have done on this king and presented much new material on his colossus inscriptions and epigraphs. A number of colossus inscriptions, both *in situ* at Nineveh and in manuscript copies in the British Museum, are presented in Catalog 3 for the first time. Among my most important contributions are the positive identification, finally, of the summary inscription on the throne-room façade colossi, the discovery of a manuscript copy of an inscription that may have been carved on five-legged bulls, suggested identifications for George Smith's "Bulls 1 to 3," a discussion of the unpublished colossus inscription in Room LX, and a substantial addition to the published transliteration of the inscription in Court LXIV. Full text editions of all of Sennacherib's known epigraphs are presented here in Catalog 4, including two important recently-discovered examples that describe palace construction.

Chapter 8

Esarhaddon (680–669 B.C.)

Palace inscriptions of Esarhaddon have been found in four different structures in three cities. At Nineveh, where he ruled at least for the first part of his reign, he continued his father's work on the Nineveh arsenal. Later he may have intended to move the capital back to Kalhu (Nimrud), where he restored the arsenal and began construction of a new palace. He also rebuilt the palace at Tarbisu, about 5 kilometers north of Nineveh, as a residence for the crown prince.

The Nineveh Arsenal

Esarhaddon's arsenal text states that he greatly enlarged the arsenal (*ekal māšarti*) on Nebi Yunus, the smaller mound of Nineveh, and that victories against hostile regions were commemorated there in sculpture, presumably in wall reliefs.[1] These sculptures, if they were ever completed, have not been recovered, because the state apartments of the arsenal have not been excavated. Layard excavated briefly on Nebi Yunus and reported that he found "the walls of a chamber. They were panelled with inscribed, but unsculptured, alabaster slabs. The inscriptions merely contained the name, titles, and genealogy of Esarhaddon."[2] Layard's copies of two of these inscriptions are preserved in Ms C. They are captioned "From Nebbi Yunus. Behind Slab." The first reads:

Palace of Esarhaddon, great king, powerful king, king of the world, king of Assyria, son of Sennacherib, king of Assyria, son of Sargon, king of Assyria.[3]

1. Borger 1956: 59–63, esp. 62:28–29; Luckenbill 1927: §§697–98.
2. Layard 1853a: 598.
3. The Layard copy (Ms C, fol. 66v) reads:

(1) É.GAL ᵐaš+šur-PAP-AŠ MAN GAL

(2) MAN *dan-nu* MAN ŠÚ MAN KUR aš+šur

The second is similar but briefer, omitting the phrase "great king, powerful king."[4] As with the short text on the back of the Sennacherib wall slabs, this text was apparently intended only to identify the owner of the slabs. The absence of the titles "governor of Babylon, king of Sumer and Akkad" and "king of the kings of Egypt, Paturisu, and Kush," both of which later become part of Esarhaddon's standard titulary, suggests that the slabs on which they are carved were erected early in his reign. This interpretation is reinforced by the date of 676 B.C. for Esarhaddon's earliest foundation prism, which describes work on the Nineveh arsenal and was found embedded in the arsenal's foundation platform.[5] A later edition of the building account, however, is dated to early 672 B.C., indicating that work continued on the arsenal throughout Esarhaddon's reign.[6]

Excavations in 1990 directed by Manhal Jabur of the Iraq State Organization for Antiquities and Heritage in a large courtyard of the arsenal have exposed a monumental entrance façade decorated with bull colossi, beyond which is a large room—perhaps a throne room—paneled with stone slabs, apparently unsculptured. The façade is decorated with a pair of addorsed bull colossi with a lion-clutching human between each pair, and several doorways lined with bull colossi. An interesting feature of some of these colossi is that they are composed of relatively small blocks of stone tightly fitted together prior to being carved.[7] Some are unfinished. In the spaces between the bulls were winged deities. Some of

---

(3) DUMU ^{md}30-PAP.MEŠ-SU MAN KUR AŠ

(4) A MAN-GIN MAN KUR AŠ

A close duplicate, labeled "On reverse of Slabs at Nebi Yunus," is in Rawlinson 1861: pl. 48:2. It omits MAN GAL and substitutes KUR AŠ for KUR *aš+šur*. See also Borger 1956: 69, §32.

4. The Layard copy (Ms C, fol. 66v) reads:

(1) KUR ^mAŠ-PAP-AŠ MAN KUR AŠ

(2) A ^m30-PAP.MEŠ-SU MAN KUR AŠ

(3) A ^mMAN-GIN MAN KUR AŠ-*ma*

An exact duplicate, labeled "On reverse of Slabs at Nebi Yunus," is in Rawlinson 1861: pl. 48:3. See also Borger 1956: 69, §33.

5. 22 Aiaru, eponym Banba, published by A. Heidel, "A New Hexagonal Prism of Esarhaddon," *Sumer* 12 (1956) 9–37.

6. Month Addaru, eponym Atar-ilu (Borger 1956: 64).

7. One bull was discovered in 1986: Abd al-Sattar Jabbar Musa, "The Discovery of a Colossal Winged Bull at Tell Nebi Yunis," *Sumer* 45 (1987–88) 112, and Arabic pp. 96–98; J. Black, "Excavations in Iraq, 1985–86," *Iraq* 49 (1987) 242–43, pl. 47:c; Scott and MacGinnis 1990: 71, pl. 13:a. The remainder of this façade still awaits publication, but it is evidently part of the same façade reported by Layard (1853a: 598) and Rassam (1897: 4–7).

these slabs were inscribed on the back with an Esarhaddon text. The two ex-amples I saw were near-duplicates of the first Layard example, except that one added the epithet "king of the world" to the names of both Sennacherib and Sar-gon, while the other added this epithet only to Sargon's name.

The Kalhu Arsenal

At Kalhu (Nimrud), Esarhaddon restored the arsenal (Fort Shalmaneser) and built a heavily-fortified stone postern gate and retaining wall, much of it still well-preserved, at its southwest corner (fig. 45; see fig. 20, p. 65). This wall formed the exterior face of a terrace, on top of which was a group of rooms.[8] The outer face of this new stretch of wall was the location of Esarhaddon's four longest visible palace inscriptions, the same text carved twice at each side of the gate (fig. 46). A photograph of one exemplar of the inscription has been published by Reade but, because (to my knowledge) no transliteration and translation are available, the full text of the inscription just west of the portal is given here:[9]

1. KUR ^maš+šur-PAP-AŠ MAN GAL MAN *dan-nu* MAN ŠÚ MAN KUR AŠ GÌR.NÍTA
   KÁ.DINGIR.KI
2. MAN KUR EME.GI$_7$ *u* URI.KI A ^{md}30-PAP.MEŠ-SU MAN ŠÚ MAN KUR *aš+šur*
3. DUMU ^mMAN-GIN MAN ŠÚ MAN KUR AŠ-*ma* É.GAL *ma-šar-ti šá qé-reb* URU *kàl-ḫa*
4. *šá* ^{md}SILIM.MA-*nu*-MAŠ MAN KUR AŠ DUMU ^maš+šur-PAP-A NUN *a-lik pa-ni-ia*
5. *e-pu-šú qaq-qa-ru ki-šub-ba-a ki-ma a-tar-tim-ma lu aṣ-ba-ta*
6. *ina eš-qi* NA$_4$ KUR-*e tam-la-a uš-mal-li* É.GAL
7. *a-na mul-ta-u-te be-lu-ti-*⌈*ia*⌉ *ab-ta-ni ṣe-ru-uš-šú*

1. Palace of Esarhaddon, great king, mighty king, king of the world, king of Assyria, governor of Babylon,
2. king of Sumer and Akkad, son of Sennacherib, king of the world, king of Assyria,
3. son of Sargon, king of the world, king of Assyria: For the arsenal in the city of Kalhu
4. which Shalmaneser, king of Assyria, son of Assurnasirpal, a prince who preceded me,
5. built, I took a vacant plot of land for an addition.
6. With strong mountain stone I built up a terrace. A palace
7. for my lordly leisure I built on it.

---

8. Marked "Western Mound, Tulul el-Azar" on Mallowan 1966: vol. 3, plan 8.
9. Photograph in Reade 1982: 105, fig. 78.

FIG. 45. Kalhu, Fort Shalmaneser, postern gate of Esarhaddon (photo: author).

The other three inscriptions next to the gate are duplicates of this one. From this text it is clear that this wall and the terrace it supports are the foundation of the new residence in the arsenal referred to here and described in greater detail in an Esarhaddon foundation cylinder.[10] As to the date of the text, and therefore of the work that it commemorates, the inclusion of the titles "governor of Baby-lon, king of Sumer and Akkad" suggests a later date than the Nineveh arsenal text, but the absence of any titles associated with the conquest of Egypt indicates a date before 671 B.C. This is consistent with the date of a foundation cylinder from 672 B.C. that also describes the rebuilding of the arsenal.[11]

The Southwest Palace at Kalhu

In addition to restoring the arsenal, Esarhaddon also built or rebuilt a pal-ace—Layard's "Southwest Palace," at the southwest corner of the Kalhu citadel

10. Postgate and Reade 1980: 317; Borger 1956: 34.
11. Dated to the 5th of Ab, eponym Nabu-beli-usur (Borger 1956: 32–35, "Klch. A").

FIG. 46. Kalhu, Fort Shalmaneser, postern gate of Esarhaddon, inscription on wall west

(fig. 47). This may have been a reconstruction of part of Tiglath-pileser III's palace, which Esarhaddon used freely as a source of building materials. Only a single group of rooms, covering an area of some 60 by 35 meters, was fully excavated. Their plan, as reconstructed by Turner, is atypical, consisting of two parallel long rooms with column bases in their side and end doorways, and beyond and parallel to these, a row of smaller rooms; the central of these smaller rooms seems to be the focus of the suite. The function of this suite is unknown. The palace was to have been decorated with wall reliefs, and Esarhaddon secured stone slabs for this purpose by the (in Neo-Assyrian times) unprecedented expedient of looting them from neighboring palaces at Kalhu. Layard found sculptured slabs that had been removed from the nearby palaces of Assurnasirpal II and Tiglath-pileser III and placed on the walls of the Southwest Palace in preparation for reuse, but the project was abandoned, presumably upon the death of the king, before any of these slabs were recarved.

The part of the palace Layard excavated included three monumental portals, which he designated *a*, *b*, and *c*, all on roughly the same axis. The jambs of Door *a* were formed by human-headed winged lions, while those of Doors *b* and *c* were human-headed bulls, all four-legged (fig. 48). Of the lions in Door *a*, Layard reported: "There were no inscriptions between the legs and behind the bodies of the lions." A few lines were, however, found on the back. Layard published the inscription from the back of Bull 1, Door *b*, together with variants from the backs

of gate (photo: author).

FIG. 47. Kalhu, Southwest Palace of Esarhaddon, plan (after Layard 1849a, plan 2).

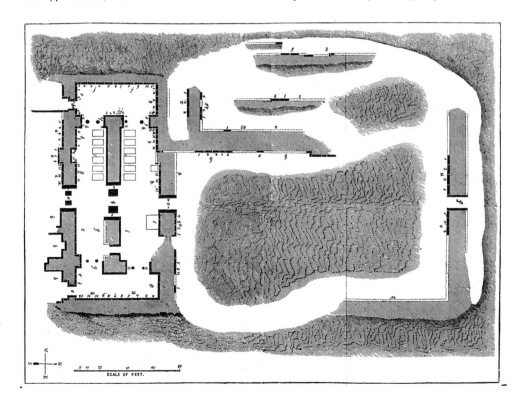

FIG. 48. Kalhu, Southwest Palace of Esarhaddon, Door *a*, colossi. Original Drawings III, S.W. I (photo: Trustees of the British Museum).

of four of the other colossi.[12] These are the only inscriptions of Esarhaddon to have been found in the Southwest Palace and so are of considerable importance for dating the structure. Layard's hand-copies of the five inscriptions are preserved in Ms A, and from these it is clear that there are three distinct texts represented here, each colossus in a pair being carved with the same text. Since Layard's published composite edition of the inscriptions is somewhat confusing and disguises the individual characteristics of each text, the texts from the three doors are given in full in Catalog 5. All three texts begin the same way:

> Palace of Esarhaddon, great king, mighty king, king of the world, king of Assyria, governor of Babylon, king of Sumer and Akkad.

The text on Bulls 1 and 2 of Door *c*, which is the shortest, then concludes:

> king of the kings of Egypt, Paturisu, and Kush, king of the four quarters.

12. Description: Layard 1849a: vol. 1, 351–52; vol. 2, 25–26, 197. Plan: Layard 1849a: vol. 1, plan II (facing p. 34); Barnett and Falkner 1962: fig. 5. Text: Layard 1851: pl. 19a. Transliteration and translation: Borger 1956: p. 36, §24.

The inscriptions on Lion 1 of Door *a* and Bulls 1 and 2 of Door *b* are longer and in most respects similar to one another. The texts in both doors continue:

> builder of the temple of Assur, restorer of Esagila and Babylon, renewer of the statues of the great gods, king of Egypt, who defeated the king of Meluhha.

The text on Lion 1 of Door *a* then concludes:

> son of Sennacherib, king of Assyria.

The inscription on Bulls 1 and 2 of Door *b*, the longest, concludes:

> king of the four quarters, son of Sennacherib, king of the world, king of Assyria, son of Sargon, king of the world, king of Assyria.

The references to Egypt, Paturisu (Upper Egypt), and Kush and Meluhha (terms for Nubia) are significant here, because they indicate that all three of these texts were composed after Esarhaddon's defeat of the Egyptian king Taharqa in 671 B.C. Since these texts were carved on the backs of the gateway colossi, they prove that the colossi could not have been erected before the last year or so of the king's reign. The cessation of work on the palace, then, must be attributed to the king's death and not to abandonment due to some other cause. The late date for the raising of the colossi also explains why the spaces between their legs were uninscribed: inscriptions had doubtless been intended for these locations, but the king died before they could be carved.

The Palace of the Crown Prince at Tarbisu

Esarhaddon rebuilt the palace at Tarbisu (modern Sherif Khan), some five kilometers north of Nineveh, as a residence for the crown prince. The site was first investigated in early 1850 by Layard, who reported finding "two inscribed limestone slabs" of Esarhaddon, and again by Rawlinson in 1852. A large part of the mound, including the palace, was excavated in 1968 by a Mosul University team under the direction of Amer Suleiman.[13] The palace plan combines traditional and novel features. The best-preserved block of rooms consists of a courtyard with reception suites of typical late Assyrian plan on its east and west sides. On its south side, however, was the unusual feature of a broad stone staircase that led up to a columned porch or vestibule. This, the only unequivocal example of a North Syrian *bīt ḫilāni* to have been excavated in an Assyrian palace, seems to have functioned as a sort of grand entrance for a third reception suite, located directly behind the porch.

13. Layard 1853a: 598–99; Curtis and Grayson 1982: 87; Suleiman 1971.

Rawlinson published two inscriptions "from slabs at Sherif Khan," probably from the two slabs found by Layard. Both commence:

> I, Esarhaddon, great king, mighty king, king of the world, king of Assyria, governor of Babylon, king of Sumer and Akkad.

The shorter inscription then concludes with a reference to the palace:

> the palace in the city Tarbisu, for the residence of Assurbanipal, I built and completed.[14]

The longer one adds one more title, followed by a slightly fuller identification of the palace:

> king of the kings of Egypt, Paturisu, and Kush: the palace in the city Tarbisu, for the residence of Assurbanipal, the crown prince of the *bīt ridûti*, my offspring, I built and completed.[15]

There is no indication in the published information of whether these were wall slabs or pavement slabs, or whether the inscriptions would originally have been visible or turned against a wall or floor. Even without such a clear context, though, they are of interest. The earliest Esarhaddon text that refers to this palace is a foundation cylinder dated 672 B.C., the same year that Assurbanipal was declared crown prince. This text, which was presumably buried in the palace foundation platform or in one of its walls, omits the title "king of the kings of Egypt, Paturisu, and Kush" but does say that the palace is intended for the crown prince, Assurbanipal.[16] This suggests that work on this palace was still at an early stage in 672 B.C. The first of the two palace inscriptions cited above also omits the king of Egypt title, while the other includes it, which probably indicates that the first slab was inscribed before the conquest of Egypt in midsummer 671 B.C. and the second one afterward. This information makes it clear that, as with the Southwest Palace at Kalhu, this palace was being worked on very late in the king's reign.

Summary: Esarhaddon

There are relatively few palace inscriptions of Esarhaddon, but the examples that are known come from four different palaces and therefore give a fair idea of the extent of this king's building activities. Since each inscription begins with a

---

14. Rawlinson 1861: pl. 48:6; Borger 1956: p. 73, §45.
15. Rawlinson 1861: pl. 48:5; Borger 1956: p. 72, §44.
16. Dated to the 18th of Aiaru, eponym Nabu-beli-usur; Borger 1956: 32–33, 71–72, "Trb. A."

different version of Esarhaddon's titulary, and since some of these titles are chronologically significant, it was possible to recover the probable order of construction of the four palaces. Other contributions in this chapter are the publication for the first time of a transliteration and translation of Esarhaddon's important Kalhu arsenal inscription, observations on inscriptions found in the Nineveh arsenal, and the sorting out of the three different texts inscribed on the backs of colossi in the Southwest Palace at Kalhu.

Chapter 9

Assurbanipal (668–631 B.C.)

Assurbanipal ruled from Nineveh, living for a time in Sennacherib's palace, which he refurbished. At least one set of wall reliefs in Sennacherib's palace is his, and perhaps others as well. He later built a new palace at Nineveh. It had no colossi in its doorways, but its major rooms were decorated with wall reliefs that are among the finest surviving examples of Assyrian sculpture. He also continued work on the Nineveh arsenal.

The Nineveh Arsenal

In a foundation prism dated 649 B.C., Assurbanipal claims, like his father and grandfather, to have restored the Nineveh arsenal (*ekal māšarti*).[1] In the course of excavations on the arsenal by the Iraq State Organization for Antiquities and Heritage under the direction of Manhal Jabur, at least one wall slab with an Assurbanipal inscription on its back was discovered.[2] The text, which is unpublished, is very brief: "Palace of Assurbanipal," followed by basic titles and a genealogy. The primary value of this inscription is that it provides concrete confirmation of the claim in his foundation cylinder.

The Palaces of Nineveh

Assurbanipal apparently restored Sennacherib's palace around 650 B.C. and decorated at least one room, XXXIII, with his own wall reliefs (see fig. 38, p. 125).[3] His major project at Nineveh, however, was the reconstruction of the crown prince's palace (*bīt ridûti*)—commonly called the North palace—to the north of

1. Month of Ab, [day lost], eponym Ahilayya. Piepkorn 1933: 86:64–72, 88:97–99.
2. I am very grateful to Mr. Jabur for sharing with me his discoveries in the arsenal.
3. Uninscribed reliefs in three more rooms apparently date to late in Assurbanipal's reign or to the reign of one of his successors (Russell 1991: 117–51).

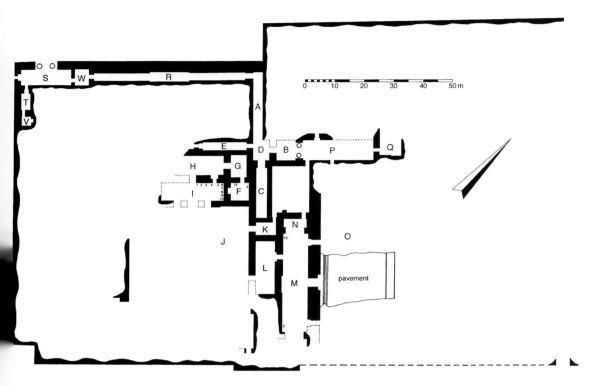

FIG. 49. Nineveh, North Palace of Assurbanipal, plan (source: author).

the Nabu Temple on Kuyunjik. Only a fraction of the palace, an area of some 135 × 120 meters, has been recovered (fig. 49). The excavations of H. Rassam (1853–1854) and W. Loftus (1854–1855) exposed its central portion: the throne-room suite with parts of its inner and outer courtyards, a few additional rooms around the inner court, and a system of hallways that communicated with the outside, all of which were lined with wall reliefs.[4]

Human-headed bull colossi were not used on the throne-room façade (O), nor did they appear anywhere else in the known part of the North Palace. Instead, the throne-room façade was decorated with plain stone slabs, and the slabs on the jambs of its center door were carved with a group of three deities. The reliefs in the throne room (M) displayed a selection of Assurbanipal's military campaigns to several different regions. The rooms behind the throne room were also decorated with military subjects, but the subject in each of these rooms was apparently only a single campaign (Rooms F, G, H, I, J, L). A group of passageways

4. For the excavation and decoration of the North Palace, see Barnett 1976.

that led from the throne-room area to the palace exterior was lined with reliefs featuring hunts: processions to and from a lion hunt (Rooms A, R); tame lions (Room E); the king hunting lions (Room C); and lions, gazelles, and wild horses (Room S). A number of reliefs had fallen into some of these passageways from an upper storey. They show lion hunts, military campaigns, and Assurbanipal and his queen dining in a garden.

In general, the military reliefs are arranged in two registers and the hunting reliefs in one, but there are exceptions. In compositions having multiple registers, the registers are separated by a narrow uninscribed band of stone. Registers are often further subdivided by continuous groundlines. The only inscriptions on the reliefs are captions placed next to the part of the image they label. In most of the North Palace compositions, figures adhere fairly firmly to the groundlines though occasionally—particularly in the hunting scenes—they are distributed more freely across the relief surface.

The Teumman-Dunanu Epigraphs

As mentioned earlier (p. 128), the wall slabs of Room XXXIII in the Southwest Palace were of an attractive fossiliferous limestone imported by Sennacherib from the mountains to the north of Assyria, and he may have left them uncarved, as were the slabs of the same stone in the neighboring Rooms XXIX and XXX. Be that as it may, Assurbanipal carved (or recarved) the slabs in Room XXXIII with scenes that are identified by epigraphs as his defeat of the Elamite king Teumman and the Gambulian king Dunanu, events that probably occurred in 653 B.C.[5] The same subject, also identified by epigraphs, was depicted on the walls of Room I in the North Palace.

Most of the epigraphs on the walls of Southwest Palace Room XXXIII and North Palace Room I, along with a great many others that deal with this Elamite campaign, are also preserved in a number of epigraph collections on clay tablets.[6] Taken together, the epigraphs provide an account of the campaign that is in many respects more detailed than that recorded in Assurbanipal's fullest annalistic account of the same event.[7] Since the epigraphs are also much more closely keyed to the sculptural representations of the campaign than are the annalistic accounts, they can assist both in reconstructing the original extent of the two re-

5. Reade 1979b: pls. 17–20.
6. Collected, transliterated, and translated in Weidner 1932–33: 175–91. Texts published in Leeper 1920: pls. 9–36, and Bauer 1933: vol. 1, pl. 20; vol. 2, pp. 91–105. New edition in Borger 1996: 299–307. Weidner (1932–33: 191–203) also published 32 epigraphs from tablets that deal with Assurbanipal's campaigns against Shamash-shum-ukin of Babylon and Tammaritu of Elam, but because only one of these epigraphs was also found on a palace relief, they are not considered here.
7. Piepkorn 1933: 60–77.

lief series and in determining the position of the surviving slabs within those series. I begin, then, with a full list of these epigraphs in translation, arranged in an
order that corresponds roughly to the chronological order of the events to which
they refer. Then follows a description of the Teumman-Dunanu relief cycles in
Southwest Palace Room XXXIII and North Palace Room I and the role of the
epigraphs in them. I conclude with some observations on the epigraph tablets
and their relationship to the reliefs.

The Epigraph Tablets: The Teumman-Dunanu Cycle

Epigraphs that record events from the campaign against Teumman of Elam
and Dunanu of Gambulu are preserved on at least nine tablets, as well as on reliefs in Room XXXIII of the Southwest Palace and in Room I of the North Palace
at Nineveh. By far the largest collection is Weidner's "Text A," a tablet on which
37 epigraphs are preserved in whole or in part.[8] This is Weidner's main text, and
he used the sequence of epigraphs in this tablet to establish the numbering system in his text edition. The epigraphs in Text A are arranged in a modified chronological order, the rationale for which will be discussed later. In the list below,
they are rearranged into what I believe to be rough chronological order, based on
comparison with the order of the same events in annals Edition B, but the sequence of the episodes that are not included in the annals is occasionally uncertain. The numeral designation of each epigraph in the list below indicates its
position in Text A.

In addition to Text A, Weidner edited a number of other epigraph tablets
from the Teumman-Dunanu series, which he designated Texts B, C, D, E, F, and
G, plus another tablet (BM 83-1-18, 442) that is closely related to the epigraphs.
Borger published an additional epigraph tablet, designated Text H by Wäfler.[9] In
the chart below, the texts in which each epigraph occurs are noted in the right

---

8. Text A: British Museum K 2674 + Sm 2010 + 81-2-4,186 + 80-7-19,102 (Leeper
1920: pls. 9–12, 32–33; Weidner 1932–33: 178–87). Though Weidner assigns 38 epigraphs to Text A, his no. 9 was restored entirely from other sources.

9. Weidner's footnote that identifies his Texts B–G is garbled (1932–33: 177 n. 9);
it was corrected by Reade (1970: 327).

Text B   British Museum Rm 2, 364; Leeper 1920: pls. 34–35; Weidner 1923–33: 186–88.
Text C   British Museum K 1914 + K 13765; Bauer 1933: vol. 1, pl. 20 + Leeper 1920: pl. 36;
         Weidner 1932–33: 186–88.
Text D   British Museum K 4527 + K 12000a; Leeper 1920: pls. 41 + 33; Weidner 1932–33:
         188.
Text E   British Museum Sm 1350; Leeper 1920: pl. 31; Weidner 1932–33: 188–89.
Text F   British Museum K 13741; Leeper 1920: pl. 29; Weidner 1932–33: 189.
Text G   British Museum K 2637; Leeper 1920: pl. 36; Weidner 1932–33: 189.
British Museum 83-1-18, 442   Leeper 1920: pl. 34; Weidner 1932–33: 191.
Text H   British Museum 81-7-27, 246; Borger 1970: 90.

column. Epigraphs from wall reliefs in Southwest Palace Room XXXIII and North Palace Room I are designated SWP:XXXIII and NP:I. Epigraphs that are not in Text A are placed in their apparent chronological position and differentiated numerically from the Text A epigraphs by the addition of "a" (episodes omitted entirely from Text A) and/or "v" (variant version of an epigraph). The English translations, which are based on Weidner (1932–33), Luckenbill (1927), Gerardi (1988), CAD, and AHw, do not claim to be definitive, but should be reasonably accurate.

Composite list of Teumman-Dunanu epigraphs, arranged chronologically by general subject [10]

The March to Hidalu

1	The army of Assurbanipal, king of Assyria, which I sent out for the conquest of Elam, accompanied by Ummanigash, son of Urtak, king of Elam, the fugitive who had submitted to me.	Text A
30	Ummanigash, son of Urtak, king of Elam, submitted to me. I sent my army with him to assist him.	Texts A, B
2	Simburu, the *nāgiru* of Elam, heard of the approach of my troops. At the mention of my name he became frightened. He came before my envoy and submitted to me.	Texts A, B, C
1a	I sent Tammaritu, [the third brother of Ummanigash(?)], with him. [. . . I established him as king over(?)] the people of Hidalu.	Text B
3	Umbakidinu, the *nāgiru* of Hidalu, carries the head of Ishtar-nandi, king of Hidalu. Zineni, his *ša pān māti*, is likewise depicted in the lower register. The might of Assur, my lord, and the fear of my majesty overwhelmed them. They cut off the heads of the nobles of Elam, who had not submitted to me, and cast them down in front of my magnates (GAL.MEŠ). They submitted to me.	Text A
3v	Fear of my majesty overwhelmed Umbakidinu, the *nāgiru* of Hidalu. He cut off the head of Ishtar-nandi, king of Hidalu, [in the presence of his army(?)], brought it here, cast it down [in front of] my magnates (GAL.MEŠ), and submitted to me.	Texts B, C
3v	[Fear] of my majesty overwhelmed [Zin]eni, the *ša pān māti*, and Ishtarta-[. . .], the *bēl pīḫati*, of Elam [. . .] moved them to submit to me [. . .] my camp.	Text C

10. Numerical designation indicates position in Text A.

The Battle of Til-Tuba

4	The line of battle that Assurbanipal, king of Assyria, drew up against Teumman, king of Elam, and with which he accomplished the defeat of Elam.	Text A
31	The line of battle of Assurbanipal, king of Assyria, which accomplished the defeat of Elam.	Texts A, E, SWP: XXXIII
32	The line of battle of Teumman, king of Elam.	Texts A, E
33	The defeat of the troops of Teumman, king of Elam. At Til-Tuba, Assurbanipal, great king, strong king, king of the world, king of Assyria, defeated countless of his warriors and threw down their corpses.	Texts A, H, SWP:XXXIII
35	I dammed up the Ulai River with the bodies of the warriors and people of Elam. For three days I made that stream flow full of bodies instead of water.	Texts A, F
5	Teumman, king of Elam, saw the defeat of his troops. To save his life he fled and tore at his beard.	Text A
6	⟨Tammaritu⟩, son of Teumman, king of Elam, who escaped from the rout, tore his garment and said to his father: "Hurry, do not delay!"	Text A
7	Teumman, king of Elam, who was wounded in fierce battle, fled and hid in a forest to save his life. The *bubūtu* (frame?) of his royal chariot broke and it fell on top of him.	Texts A, D, H
7a	Teumman, in desperation, said to his son: "Take up the bow."	Texts D, H, SWP:XXXIII
8	A wagon (pole?) pierced Teu[mman, king] of Elam, and it also pierced [Tammaritu], his son, whom he could not help.	Texts A, D, H
9	Teumman, king of Elam, was wounded in fierce battle. Tammaritu, his eldest son, took him by the hand and they fled to save their lives. They hid in the midst of a forest. With the encouragement of Assur and Ishtar, I killed them. I cut off their heads before one another.	Text D(?), SWP: XXXIII
9v	Teumman, king of Elam, was wounded in fierce battle. Tammaritu, his eldest son, took him by the hand and they fled to save their lives. They hid in the midst of a forest. With the encouragement of Assur and Ishtar, I killed them.	Texts D(?), H
9v	[. . .] rulership which [. . .] Teumman, king of Elam, [. . .] I cut off his head in the presence of [his army].	83-1-18, 442
10a	The head of Teum[man, king of Elam], which a common soldier in my army [cut off] in the midst of bat[tle]. To bring me the good ne[ws] they hastily dispatched it to Assy[ria].	SWP:XXXIII
10av	The head of Teumman, king of Elam.	Text E

The Battle of Til-Tuba

15	Mr. (*blank*), who was wounded by an arrow, but did not die, called to an Assyrian to behead him, saying: "Come, cut off my head. Take it before the king, your lord, and make a good name for yourself."	Text A, SWP: XXXIII
16	Ituni, the *šūt rēši* of so-and-so (*blank*), king of Elam, whom he insolently sent against me, saw my powerful onslaught. With his own hand he drew the iron dagger from his belt and cut his bow, the trusted companion of his arm.	Texts A, F, NP:I
17	Ummanigash, the fugitive, the servant who submitted to me. At my command, the *šūt rēši* I had sent with him brought him joyfully into Susa and Madaktu and set him on the throne of Teumman, whom I had defeated.	Text A, SWP: XXXIII
17v	[. . .] set him [on the throne . . .] Umman[igash . . .]	83-1-18, 442
17a	Land of Madaktu.	SWP:XXXIII

The Celebration in Nineveh Following the Defeat of Teumman

10	I am Assurbanipal, king of the world, king of Assyria, con-queror of his foes. Through the power of Assur, Sin, Sha-mash, Bel, Nabu, Ishtar of Nineveh, Ishtar of Arbela, Ninurta, and Nergal, the soldiers who won my victory cut off the head of Teumman, king of Elam, brought it quickly, and threw it down in front of my chariot-wheels before the "Long live the viceroy of Assur" Gate.[a]	Texts A, E
10v	I am Assurbanipal, king of Assyria. The gods Assur and Kish[ar . . .] before the "Long [live the vice]roy of Assur!" Gate [. . .] caused to stand. My chariot-wheels, which the h[ead of Teumman . . .]	83-1-18, 442
11	[The head of Teumman, king of Elam(?)]. With a knife [I cut(?)] the tendons of his face and spat upon it.	Text A
12	Nabu-damiq and Umbadara, nobles who Teumman, [king of Elam], had sent [monthly(?)] with insolent [messages]. Filled with anger against their lord, I detained them [in my presence. They saw in front of me the head of Teumman, their lord], which had been brought to me. [Umbadara] tore at his beard, [Nabu-damiq] stabbed himself with the iron dagger at his belt.	Texts A, E

The Celebration in Nineveh Following the Defeat of Teumman

13	[I], Assurbanipal, king of Assyria, entered joyfully into Nineveh with the severed head of Teumman, [king of] Elam, who I defeated with the help of Assur.	Text A
14	I, Assurbanipal, king of Assyria, I presented the head of Teumman, king of Elam, like an offering in front of the gate inside the city. As it had been said of old by the oracle, "You will cut off the heads of your enemies, you will pour wine over them, [. . .]!", accordingly the gods Shamash and Adad granted this in my time: [. . .] I cut off the heads of my [enemies], I poured wine [over them, . . .].	Text A[b]

a. The "Gate of Assur of the city of Assur," in the south wall of Nineveh (Luckenbill 1924: 112:74).

b. Elnathan Weissert (personal communication, conversation of 9 January 1996) pointed out the similarity between this epigraph and an epigraph on a lion hunt relief that shows the king pouring wine over lions he has slain. Wine-pouring occurs in this epigraph also and suggests my translation here of *muḫḫuriš* as 'like an offering'. This differs slightly from AHw 651b, *mi/uḫḫuriš* ('als Opfergabe') and differs completely from CAD M/1 68, *maḫāru* 7c ('to expose').

The Campaign Against the Gambulians

18	I directed my troops, who had undertaken the campaign against Elam and had not yet rested from their exertions, toward Sha-pi-Bel, the city of Dunanu. They set up camp outside that city, blockaded it, and blocked its escape routes.	Text A
19	Terror overcame Dunanu, [son of] Bel-iqisha, the Gambulian, and he abandoned his city. He came before my envoys and submitted to me.	Text A
36	[I am] Assurbanipal, king of Assyria, who with the help of Assur, my lord, defeats my enemies and attains the desires of my heart. I built up a ramp against Sha-pi-Bel, fortress of the Gambulians. The brilliance of my majesty overwhelmed Dunanu, son of Bel-iqisha, and he broke his bow. [He and] his magnates (GAL.MEŠ), [came before] my envoy with fervent entreaties and they submitted to me.	Text A
37	I captured [Dunan]u, son of Bel-iqisha, alive with my hands. My warriors bound him with iron fetters and sent him quickly to me [at Ni]neveh.	Texts A, C, G

The Campaign Against the Gambulians

38	[I am Assurbanipal, king] of Assyria, who at the command of the great gods, his lords, [goes unopposed(?) and] attains the desires of his heart. [I carried off to Assyria Dunanu, son] of Bel-iqisha, Samgunu, [younger brother of Dunanu], Nabu-na'id and Bel-etir, [sons of Nabu-shuma-eresh], the governor of Nippur, [. . .] his brothers, [. . .] the people of Gambu[lu . . .].	Text A

Assurbanipal Receives Dunanu in Milqia[a]

20	I, Assurbanipal, ⌜king⌝ of Assyria, offered abundant sacrifices in Milqia and observed the feast of the goddess Shatri (Ishtar of Arbela). At that time Dunanu, bound hand and foot with iron fetters, was brought before me.	Text A
21	[After] I had completed [the rite of the *bīt akī*]*ti*, I threw Dunanu, son of Bel-iqisha, [the Gambulian], down onto his stomach and held up a [bow] over him.	Texts A, G[b]

a. Milqia is the location of the *bīt akīti* of Arbela (Pongratz-Leisten 1994: 79–80). Assurbanipal restored this structure (Streck 1916: vol. 2, 248).

b. Elnathan Weissert (personal communication, conversation of 9 January 1996) pointed out the similarity between this epigraph and an epigraph on a lion hunt relief that shows the king holding a bow over lions he has slain. Weissert also suggested the excellent restoration of the first line of the epigraph.

The Victory Celebration in Arbela

34	I am Assurbanipal, king of Assyria. After I had offered sacrifices to the goddess Shatri and had celebrated the *akītu* festival, and after I had seized the reigns of the chariot of Ishtar, I entered Arbela amidst rejoicing with Dunanu, Samgunu, Aplaya, and the severed head of Teumman, king of Elam, which Ishtar my lady delivered into my hands.	Texts A, E, G[a]
33a	Joyfully I took the road to Arbela with the severed head of Teumman, king of Elam.	Texts B, E
22	[Dunanu, son of Bel-iqi]sha, the Gambulian, [. . . hand a]nd foot to the city of ⌜Assur⌝ (?, URU ŠÀ.⌜URU⌝-a) [. . . before(?)] me [. . .].	Text A[b]
	GAP OF SOME 8 LINES BETWEEN 22 AND 23	
23	[. . .] inside [. . .] Ap[lai(?) . . .]	Text A

The Victory Celebration in Arbela

24	Du[nanu, . . .] the ladies [. . .]	Text A
25	[I hung] the head [of Teumman around the neck of Dunanu(?)] and the he[ad of Ishtar-nandi around the neck of Samgunu(?). . . .] the 「crown」 prince(?) [. . .]	Text A
26	I chained Dunanu, Samgunu, and Aplaya, together with a bear, to the Gate of the Rising and Setting of the Sun for display to my people.	Texts A, E[c]
27	The city [Arbela(?) . . .], which [. . .]	Text A
28a	「The city Arbela.」	NP:I
	GAP OF SOME 25 LINES BETWEEN 27 AND 28	
27a	I am Assurbanipal, king of the world, king of Assyria. Ursa, king of Urartu, sent his nobles to ask about my health. I made Nabu-damiq and Umbadara, nobles of Elam, stand before them with the writing boards containing the insolent messages. Opposite them (are) Mannu-ki-ahhe, Dunanu's *šanû* (deputy), and Nabu-usalli, his *ša muḫḫi āli* (city overseer). I tore out their tongues and flayed them.	Text E
27av	I am Assurbanipal, king of the world, king of Assyria, who with the encouragement of Assur and Ishtar my lords, conquered my enemies and attained the desires of my heart. Rusa, king of Urartu, heard of the strength of Assur, my lord, and fear of my kingship overwhelmed him. He sent his nobles to ask about my health. In the center of Arbela, I made Nabu-damiq and Umbadara, nobles of Elam, stand before them with the writing boards containing the insolent messages.	SWP:XXXIII
28	[Mannu-ki-ahhe and Nabu-usalli] spoke great insults against Assur, the god, my creator. I tore out their tongues and flayed them.	Text A, SWP: XXXIII
28v	[I tore out the tongues] of Na[bu-usalli and Mannu-ki-ahhe] and flayed them.	Text B

a. Elnathan Weissert (personal communication, conversation of 9 January 1996) suggested this translation.

b. Weidner's (1932–33: 182) restoration of the city name Ruʾa in Epigraph 22 fits the traces, but makes no sense in the context. Assur fits the traces equally well (URU šÀ.「URU」-a), and in Cylinder B, Assurbanipal says he displayed Dunanu in Assur and Arbela (Piepkorn 1933: 74:81). It is clear from Epigraph 34, however, that Assurbanipal went directly from Milqia to Arbela, and the events that follow in Epigraphs 25–28 also take place in Arbela, so it appears that Assur would be out of place here.

c. This is presumably the name of one of the gates of Arbela. To my knowledge, no full list of Arbela gate names is known.

	The Celebration in Nineveh Following the Defeat of Dunanu	
29	[Duna]nu, son [of Bel-iqi]sha, the Gambulian, who had disrupted the exercise of my kingship. I slaughtered him on a slaughter bench like a sheep and dismembered him.	Text A

	Epigraphs of Uncertain Chronological Position	
?	[I am Assurbanipal, king of the world, king of Assyria. Through the power of Assur, Sin], Shamash, Bel, [Nabu, Ishtar of Nineveh], Ishtar of Arbela, [Ninurta, and Nergal . . . I have defeated] my enemies [and achieved the desires of my heart].	Text B
?	I am Assurbanipal, [king of Assyria, who Assur and Ishtar] placed in power and [strength over his opponents and who attained the desires of his heart . . .] king of Elam [. . .].	Text B
?	[. . .] which in Elam [. . .] mighty deeds [. . .] ⌜Elam⌝ [. . .]	Text F

It is interesting to compare this account of the Teumman-Dunanu campaign assembled from epigraphs on tablets and reliefs with the accounts compiled for the royal annals. The earliest and longest annalistic account of the campaign is Edition B, dated 649 B.C., which is the prism that describes work on the Nineveh arsenal (see above, p. 154).[11] This account begins with a very lengthy justification for Assurbanipal's decision to make war on Teumman. Among the factors cited by the text as influencing his decision are Teumman's insolent messages, his boasting, his evil plots, a lunar eclipse that foretold Teumman's downfall, a seizure inflicted on Teumman by the gods as a warning, and Teumman's declaration of war on Assurbanipal. Assurbanipal, who was in Arbela at the time, sought advice from Ishtar, who assured him of her support and counseled him to remain in Arbela while she fought Teumman. None of this prologue is included in the epigraphic account.

After all this buildup, the account of the campaign itself in annals Edition B is anticlimactic and receives only a few sentences: the Assyrian and Elamite armies met by the Ulai River, Teumman's army was defeated and Elamite corpses blocked the Ulai, Teumman was beheaded "in the presence of his army," Ummanigash was placed on Teumman's throne, Tammaritu was made king of Hidalu, and the booty was distributed among the Assyrian soldiers. An additional detail,

11. Piepkorn 1933: 61–77. An excellent analysis of the campaign accounts is provided by Gerardi (1987: 135–57).

that Teumman was beheaded by a common Assyrian soldier, is buried in the account of the subsequent campaign against Ummanigash, and this is repeated in Epigraph 10a.[12] There is much additional information in the epigraphic account, which includes details of the march through Hidalu, the pursuit and death of Teumman and Tammaritu, and the fates of Urtak (Epigraph 15) and Ituni.

In annals Edition B, the account of the campaign against Dunanu follows immediately. Only very brief justification is given for this campaign, and the account of the battle is likewise brief—the siege of Sha-pi-Bel is dealt with in a sentence. Again, the epigraphic account of these events gives information not in the annals, including the weariness of the Assyrian army, the use of a blockade and siege ramp, and the details of Dunanu's surrender. In the annalistic version, there follows an extensive list of booty and a brief description of the leveling of the city, the latter not mentioned in the epigraphs.

The remainder of the annalistic account is concerned with the victory celebrations in Nineveh, Assur, and Arbela. The treatment accorded important captives and trophies of the campaign—Teumman's head, Dunanu, Samgunu, Umbadara, Nabu-damiq, Aplaya, Mannu-ki-ahhe, Nabu-usalli, Nabu-na'id, Bel-etir, and the bones of Nabu-shuma-eresh—are described in some detail. A number of these passages are repeated verbatim in the epigraphs, but some of the epigraphs add new information, such as Assurbanipal's presence in Milqia, his triumphal entry into Arbela in the chariot of Ishtar, and the display of captives with a bear. The epigraphic account also usually makes it clear where each event in the celebrations took place, information that is much less clear in the annals.

The Edition B account remained the standard recension of the Teumman-Dunanu campaign until 645 B.C., though the slightly later Edition K, from about 646 B.C., added a report of emissaries sent to Assurbanipal by Rusa, king of Urartu, an event recorded also in Epigraphs 27a and 27av.[13] Annals Edition F, dated to 646 or 645 B.C., presented a new recension of the Teumman-Dunanu campaign, and this version was repeated in Edition A, which probably dates to 643 B.C.[14] Both of these editions record the construction of the North Palace, and two exemplars of Edition A were found *in situ* in the walls of that palace.[15] Edition A, therefore, is apparently the annalistic version of the campaign that was current at the time the wall reliefs were being designed. The account of the Teumman-Dunanu campaign in Edition A is very brief and includes little information that was not already in Edition B.[16] In Edition A, the lengthy prologue and the account of the victory celebrations were omitted and the description of

12. Piepkorn 1933: 78:61.
13. Piepkorn 1933: 103; Cogan and Tadmor 1981: 238–39.
14. Gerardi 1987: 68–69, 72.
15. Barnett 1976: 23 n. 11
16. Streck 1916: vol. 2, 26–29.

FIG. 50. Nineveh, Southwest Palace, relief of Assurbanipal, Room XXXIII, Slabs 1–3,

the defeat of Teumman and Dunanu was reduced to a few sentences. The epigraphs owe little or nothing to this account.

The epigraph collections thus seem to represent a different textual tradition than do the annalistic accounts. Though the epigraph tablets must have been compiled at about the same time that Edition A of the annals was current, the two are completely dissimilar. Some of the epigraphs are similar to passages in the earlier annalistic edition of the campaign, Edition B, but many have no equivalent in either annalistic version and must be based on other sources.

Epigraphs on Reliefs in Room XXXIII of the Southwest Palace

Having looked at the entire surviving repertory of epigraphs that deal with the Teumman-Dunanu story, we may now see which ones were used in the pictorial version of the same events on the walls of Room XXXIII. Six wall slabs in

the battle of Til-Tuba, width 546 cm. British Museum, WA 124801 (photo: author).

Room XXXIII are largely intact, three to either side of Door *p*.[17] All were divided horizontally across the center into two discrete registers, each with its own subject, and each of these registers was further subdivided to suit the requirements of the narrative. There are a total of eight epigraphs on the six intact slabs, and two more on fragments. According to the epigraphs, the slabs to the west of the entrance record Assurbanipal's victory at Til-Tuba in Elam, while those to the east show a procession before the king at the city of Arbela (modern Erbil) on the upper half, and a scene of homage outside the moated city of Madaktu in Elam on the lower half (figs. 50, 61 [p. 177]).

With this relief series, the epigraph as a formal narrative device has truly come of age. These epigraphs come in a variety of lengths and forms, which seem largely to be determined by their functional roles in the composition. Of the slabs that were originally to the left of the surviving Slab 1, only fragments are

17. Layard (1853a: 446) reported that the remainder of the wall slabs in the room "had been purposely destroyed and the fragments used for the foundations of a building raised over the Assyrian ruins."

FIG. 51. Nineveh, Southwest Palace, relief of Assurbanipal, Room XXXIII, fragment of Slab o, Epigraph 33, width 38 cm. British Museum, WA 135122 (photo: author).

preserved.[18] These show Assyrian chariots and cavalry galloping rightward, mowing down fleeing Elamites. Two of the fragments carry epigraphs. One of these, consisting of a few signs above the head of an Assyrian soldier, is evidently the same as Text A, no. 31:

> [The line of battle of Assurbanipal, king of As]syria, which accomplished the def[eat of Elam].[19]

The other is more completely preserved, though the scene it labels is not preserved on the fragment (Text A, no. 33; fig. 51):

> The defeat of the troops of Teumman, king [of Elam]. At Til-Tuba, Assurbanipal, [great king, strong king], king of the world, king of Assyria, [defeated] countless [of his warriors] and threw down their corpses.[20]

18. A number of these fragments are in the British Museum, Istanbul, and in a number of smaller collections (listed in Bleibtreu, Turner, and Barnett 1998; the largest pieces are British Museum WA 124804 and 124808.

19. Istanbul, Eski Sark Eserleri Müzesi, no. 6332 (published in M. Kalaç, "A Fragment from a Relief of Asurbanipal," *Istanbul, Arkeoloji Muzeleri, Yilligi* 5 [1952] 64–67; M. Kalaç, "Son Asur çagina ait on kabartma parçasi," *Türk Tarih Kurumu, Belleten* 18 [1954] 35–50; M. Falkner, "Die Reliefs der assyrischen Könige," *Archiv für Orientforschung*, 17 [1954–56] 415–16, Abb. 9:2). The fragmentary text is restored from Weidner 1932–33: 184, no. 31: [si-id-ru ša ᵐAN.ŠÁR-DÙ-A MAN KUR] ⌈AN⌉.ŠÁR.KI šá-kin ⌈BAD₅⌉.[BAD₅ KUR ELAM.MA.KI].

20. British Museum, WA 135122. The text was published by Gerardi (1988: 34) from an inaccurate copy by Bezold. The correct text is:

1. BAD₅.BAD₅ ÉRIN.ḪI.A.MEŠ ᵐte-um-man LUGAL [KUR ELAM.MA.KI]

FIG. 52. Nineveh, Southwest Palace, relief of Assurbanipal, Room XXXIII, detail of Slab 3, "take up the bow!" British Museum, WA 124801 (photo: author).

Only a small part of the upper register of Slabs 1–3 survives, without captions, but the lower register is almost complete (fig. 50). The action in the lower register flows generally from left to right, with the Assyrian army descending a mountainside that fills the entire height of the register at the far left, driving the Elamites before them. The remainder of Slab 1 and the left part of Slab 2 are subdivided into three narrow subregisters. The Assyrian command post is in the upper of these, while in the lower two the battle rages on, with the Assyrians continuing to push the Elamites to the right. In the right half of Slab 2 and all of Slab 3, the battle degenerates into a rout, and the system of subregisters gradually gives way to a mass of dead and dying enemy soldiers scattered chaotically across the relief surface.

Even at a glance, the general drift of the action here is readily apparent and there can be no doubt who are the victors and who the vanquished; but within

---

2. *ša qé-reb tíl*-URU.*tu-ú-bu* ^mAN.ŠÁR-DÙ-A [MAN GAL MAN *dan-nu*]
3. MAN SÚ MAN KUR AN.ŠÁR.KI *ina la me-i-*⸢*ni*⸣ [*iš-ku-nu*]
4. *id-du-*⸢*ú*⸣ ⸢LÚ⸣.ÚŠ.MEŠ [*qu-ra-di-šú*]

Note that this is not a "plaque," but rather a fragment of relief slab.

FIG. 53. Nineveh, Southwest Palace, relief of Assurbanipal, Room XXXIII, detail of Slab 3, beheading of Teumman. British Museum, WA 124801 (photo: author).

this image of general rout, there are several very specific stories being told, and the composition is so dense and the action so chaotic that no viewer could be expected to single them out and follow them unaided. This is where the epigraphs play their role, for throughout this series, but especially where the fighting is fiercest, they arrest and focus the viewer's attention. For literate viewers, furthermore, they explain why this particular bit of the action is significant. Three of the epigraphs deal with the most important of these "hidden" stories, the fate of the Elamite king Teumman. The first of these, chronologically, is on Slab 3, above the images of Teumman and his son, Tammaritu, beset by Assyrian soldiers (fig. 52; omitted from Text A; see no. 7a above):

Teumman, in desperation, said to his son: "Take up the bow."[21]

The next epigraph labels the group to the immediate right of the preceding (fig. 53; Text A, no. 9):

Teumman, king of Elam, was wounded in fierce battle. Tammaritu, his eldest son, took him by the hand and they fled to save their lives. They hid

21. Gerardi 1988: 30.

FIG. 54. Nineveh, Southwest Palace, relief of Assurbanipal, Room XXXIII, detail of Slab 1, cart with the head of Teumman. British Museum, WA 124801 (photo: author).

in the midst of a forest. With the encouragement of Assur and Ishtar, I killed them. I cut off their heads before one another."[22]

The third epigraph in the Teumman story is in the upper subregister of Slab 1, above a cart (fig. 54; omitted from Text A; see no. 10a above):

Head of Teum[man, king of Elam], which a common soldier in my army [cut off] in the midst of bat[tle]. To bring me the good ne[ws] they hastily dispatched it to Assy[ria].[23]

Once Teumman, with his distinctive feathered crown, has been identified, uncaptioned images of him seem to jump out of the clutter. Such uncaptioned episodes can usually be matched with epigraphs known from tablets, but they are not inscribed on the reliefs. At the top of Slab 2, for example, Tammaritu and an arrow-pierced Teumman are dumped from their wrecked chariot (fig. 55). This evidently corresponds with the second part of Text A, no. 7:

The *bubūtu* (frame?) of his royal chariot broke and it fell on top of him.

22. Gerardi 1988: 31.
23. Gerardi 1988: 29.

Fig. 55. Nineveh, Southwest Palace, relief of Assurbanipal, Room XXXIII, detail of Slab 2, wreck of Teumman's chariot. British Museum, WA 124801 (photo: author).

Slightly below and to the right, Tammaritu holds his father's hand as they flee (fig. 56). This filial gesture is described further to the right in the epigraph, already quoted, that accompanies the scene of their execution. Similarly, below and to the left of the captioned image of Teumman's beheading, a soldier holding a head races leftward, and further to the left is another soldier carrying a head, presumably the heads of Teumman and Tammaritu (fig. 57). This action is referred to in the epigraph on Slab 1, already quoted, that labels the chariot carrying Teumman's head. These unlabeled episodes do not really require separate captions; they are either specified or alluded to in the existing captions, but it takes some looking to search them out.

Another epigraph in this part of the composition, on Slab 2, tells the story of one of Teumman's relatives (fig. 58; Text A, no. 15):

Urtak, in-law of Teumman, who was wounded by an arrow, but did not die, called to an Assyrian to behead him, saying: "Come, cut off my head. Take it before the king, your lord, and make a good name for yourself."[24]

24. Gerardi 1988: 30, with slight changes in translation.

FIG. 56. Nineveh, Southwest Palace, relief of Assurbanipal, Room XXXIII, detail of Slab 2, Tammaritu leading Teumman by the hand. British Museum, WA 124801 (photo: author).

An unlabeled group to the right, where Slabs 2 and 3 join, consists of an Assyrian threatening an Elamite, shown in the act of cutting his bow (fig. 57). On the basis of its similarity to a labeled image of the same event in Room I of the North Palace, Reade identified this as Ituni (fig. 59; Text A, no. 16):

> Ituni, the *šūt rēši* of Teumman, king of Elam, whom he insolently sent against me, saw my powerful onslaught. With his own hand he drew the iron dagger from his belt and cut his bow, the trusted companion of his arm.[25]

It is interesting that these last two episodes, which in the epigraph tablets stand as isolated and essentially unexplained cases of despair among Teumman's followers, are arranged in the reliefs in a way that makes the relationship between Teumman's fate and his followers' actions visually explicit, for between Urtak and Ituni runs the soldier with the head of Teumman. As Durand observed, their

25. Reade 1964: 6; Gerardi 1988: 22–23, with slight changes in translation.

Fig. 57. Nineveh, Southwest Palace, relief of Assurbanipal, Room XXXIII, detail of Slabs 2–3, soldier with the head of Teumman and the surrender of Ituni. British Museum, WA 124801 (photo: author).

desperate acts are thereby shown to be responses to the sight of the head of their lord being carried by the Assyrian, stark proof of the finality of their defeat.[26]

Most of the upper register of Slabs 1–3 is lost, but its subject was different than that of the lower register. On the largest preserved section, at the top of Slab 3, two files of Elamite or Gambulian captives—men, women, and children—are shown being driven toward the left by mace-wielding Assyrian soldiers. On the other preserved part of the upper register, at the left end of Slab 1, kneeling captives are shown grinding something up (fig. 60). No epigraph is preserved on the relief here, nor is an appropriate epigraph to be found among those in Text A, which is broken at this point, though no. 38 is evidently related to it. This subject is, however, described in annals Edition B:

> Nabu-na'id and Bel-etir, sons of Nabu-shuma-eresh, the governor of Nippur, whose father had incited Urtak to fight against Assyria—the bones of Nabu-shuma-eresh, which they had brought from Gambulu to

26. Durand 1979–80: 17.

Fig. 58. Nineveh, Southwest Palace, relief of Assurbanipal, Room XXXIII, detail of Slab 2, surrender of Urtak. British Museum, WA 124801 (photo: author).

Assyria—these bones before the gate in the middle of Nineveh I had his sons crush.[27]

This establishes the subject of this part of the upper register as the victory celebration in Nineveh that followed the defeat of Gambulu.

Both the lower and upper registers of Slabs 4 to 6, to the east of Door *p*, are substantially preserved (fig. 61). In the lower register, an Assyrian soldier leads an Elamite by the hand into the presence of a large group of bowing Elamites outside a walled, moated city (fig. 62). Above the pair is an epigraph (Text A, no. 17):

[Umman]igash the fugitive, the servant who submitted to me. At my command, the *šūt rēši* I had sent with him brought him joyfully into Susa and Madaktu and set him on the throne of Teumman, whom I had defeated.[28]

27. Piepkorn 1933: 75–77.
28. Gerardi 1988: 32, with slight changes in translation.

FIG. 59. Nineveh, North Palace of Assurbanipal, Room I, fragment of Slab 2(?), surrender of Ituni, width 84 cm. British Museum, WA 124941 (photo: author).

The city is labeled (fig. 63; not in Text A; see no. 17a):

> Land of Madaktu.[29]

The river that runs beneath this scene is choked with the victims of the Til-Tuba battle. Though not captioned on the relief, the river is described by an epigraph in Text A (no. 35):

> I dammed up the Ulai River with the bodies of the warriors and people of Elam. For three days I made that stream flow full of bodies instead of water.

In the upper register is a royal review. At right, at the top of Slab 6, is Assurbanipal in his chariot facing left (fig. 64). Above him is a long caption (Text A is broken at this point; see no. 27av):

29. Gerardi 1988: 33.

FIG. 60. Nineveh, Southwest Palace, relief of Assurbanipal, Room XXXIII, detail of Slab 1, grinding bones. British Museum, WA 124801 (photo: author).

FIG. 61. Nineveh, Southwest Palace, relief of Assurbanipal, Room XXXIII, Slabs 4–6, victory celebration in Arbela (above) and the installation of Ummanigash in Madaktu (below), width 449 cm. British Museum, WA 124802 (photo: author).

Fig. 62. Nineveh,
Southwest Palace, relief of
Assurbanipal, Room
XXXIII, detail of Slab 5,
Ummanigash. British
Museum, WA 124802
(photo: author).

> I am Assurbanipal, king of the world, king of Assyria, who with the en-
> couragement of Assur and Ishtar my lords, conquered my enemies and at-
> tained the desires of my heart. Rusa, king of Urartu, heard of the strength
> of Assur, my lord, and fear of my kingship overwhelmed him. He sent his
> nobles to ask about my health. In the center of Arbela, I made Nabu-
> damiq and Umbadara, nobles of Elam, stand before them with the writ-
> ing boards containing the insolent messages.[30]

The Urartian ambassadors, short fellows with floppy-topped caps, stand before
the king's chariot. They are shown two more times to the left, on Slabs 4 and 5,
witnessing the punishment of captives from the campaign against Elam and
Gambulu. One pair of captives is shown twice at the right side of Slab 4: having

30. Gerardi 1988: 32–33, with slight changes in translation.

Fig. 63. Nineveh, Southwest Palace, relief of Assurbanipal, Room XXXIII, detail of Slab 6, Madaktu. British Museum, WA 124802 (photo: author).

Fig. 64. Nineveh, Southwest Palace, relief of Assurbanipal, Room XXXIII, detail of Slab 6, royal chariot. British Museum, WA 124802 (photo: author).

FIG. 65. Nineveh, Southwest Palace, relief of Assurbanipal, Room XXXIII, detail of Slab 4, tongue pulling and flaying. British Museum, WA 124802 (photo: author).

their tongues pulled out in the third subregister and being flayed directly above in the second subregister (fig. 65). Above them is the caption (Text A, no. 28):

> Mr. (*blank*) and Mr. (*blank*) spoke great insults against Assur, the god, my creator. Their tongues I tore out, their skins I flayed.[31]

In other texts these two omitted names are given as Mannu-ki-ahhe and Nabu-usalli (see no. 27a).[32] Two uncaptioned Gambulians just to the right are shown with heads hanging from their necks (fig. 66). They are probably Dunanu and Samgunu, who are described this way in the annals and possibly in a badly damaged epigraph in Text A (no. 25), which I have restored as follows:[33]

> [I hung] the head [of Teumman around the neck of Dunanu(?)] and the he[ad of Ishtar-nandi around the neck of Samgunu(?). . . .] the ⌈crown⌉ prince(?) [. . .]

31. Gerardi 1988: 31, with slight changes in translation.
32. See also annals Edition B, col. vi:83–87 (Piepkorn 1933: 75). It is uncertain whether these names were left blank in Text A, which is broken at this point (Leeper 1920: pl. 11: rev. 2)
33. Piepkorn 1933: 73.

FIG. 66. Nineveh, Southwest Palace, relief of Assurbanipal, Room XXXIII, detail of Slab 5, heads hanging from necks of captives, spitting. British Museum, WA 124802 (photo: author).

The lower of these two figures is apparently being struck and spat upon by a third Gambulian, presumably an Assyrian collaborator.

Epigraphs on Reliefs in Room I of the North Palace

Ten slabs from the Teumman-Dunanu relief cycle in Room I are shown in Boutcher's plans of the North Palace: Slabs 1–4 to the left and 5–6 to the right of Door *a* on the northwest wall and Slabs 6–10 on the northeast wall. Of these, Slabs 1–4 and 8 are unrecorded except for a fragment of Slab 1 or 2 in the British Museum (WA 124941); drawings exist of Slabs 5–7 and 9–10, and a fragment of Slab 9 is in the Louvre (AO 19914).[34] Both fragments include epigraphs. The

34. Barnett 1976: text-plates 6–8, pls. 24–26.

format of the Teumman-Dunanu reliefs in Room I is similar to that of the reliefs in Room XXXIII: two main registers, each devoted to a different subject and each subdivided as necessary into subregisters. Three epigraphs, only two of which are published, were reported on the Room I slabs.

Hormuzd Rassam referred to two of these epigraphs in a letter to Layard that apparently describes the lower register of Slabs 1–4:

> In [Room I] were found two slabs with some inscriptions on them. The first have three long lines inscribed over a tent in which there are some persons and human heads with a scribe holding a clay tablet in his hand. The other epigraph contains four lines in a better preservation than the first. These are inscribed over a man (apparently of some dignity) who is in the act of being beheaded by an Assyrian officer![35]

Concerning the first of these epigraphs, Lobdell added:

> Above the tent are inscribed three lines about two feet in length, doubtless making mention of the victor and the victory.[36]

Rassam apparently did not copy this epigraph, and so its content is unknown. The epigraph in approximately the same position on Slab 1 in Room XXXIII is no. 10a, which reports the dispatching of Teumman's head to Assyria. Both Rassam and Lobdell agreed in locating the Room I epigraph "over the tent," however, while epigraph no. 10a is actually over the cart next to the tent. Also, both Rassam and Lobdell reported that the epigraph over the tent had relatively long lines. Epigraph no. 10a seems hardly long enough to fill three lines two feet long, unless the signs were spaced out: the nearby Ituni epigraph (see below), which is 61 signs in length, fills four lines, each about one foot in length, while epigraph no. 10a is only 46 signs long and therefore should have required only half the space that the epigraph over the tent in Room I was reported to occupy. It appears likely, therefore, that the epigraph over the tent was not no. 10a but rather one that was considerably longer. Since none of the epigraphs that deal specifically with the Til-Tuba battle on the tablets seem sufficiently long, this may have been a variant epigraph composed or compiled especially for the relief in Room I.

The second epigraph reported by Rassam, on a large fragment now in the British Museum (see fig. 59, p. 176; WA 124941; Text A, no. 16), is clearly the one that records the surrender of Ituni:

> Ituni, the *šūt rēši* of Teumman, king of Elam, whom he insolently sent against me, saw my powerful onslaught. With his own hand he drew the iron dagger from his belt and cut his bow, the sign of his strength.[37]

---

35. Letter of 30 January 1854, from Mosul; British Library, Manuscripts Division, Layard Papers, vol. 51, Add. Ms 38981 (quoted in Barnett 1976: 42).
36. Lobdell 1854: 480.
37. Gerardi 1988: 22–23, with slight changes in translation.

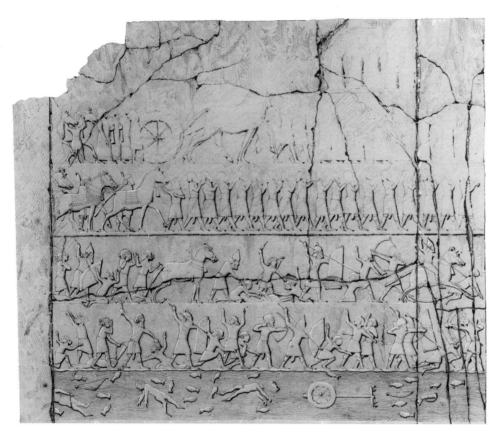

Fig. 67. Nineveh, North Palace of Assurbanipal, Room I, Slabs 5–6, procession to Arbela (above) and battle of Til-Tuba (below). Original Drawings VII, 11 (photo: Trustees of the British Museum).

It is uncertain whether this fragment belonged originally to Slab 1 or 2; in his first plan of the North Palace, Boutcher showed it as Slab 1, but in his final plan it is Slab 2.[38] If the arrangement of episodes of the Til-Tuba battle here was similar to that in Room XXXIII of the Southwest Palace, then we would expect to find the Assyrian headquarters tent on Slab 1 and Ituni on Slab 2 or 3.

There seems to be no record of the subject of the upper register of Slabs 1–4. The subjects of Slabs 5–10, known for the most part only from Boutcher's drawings, are the conclusion of the Til-Tuba battle (fig. 67) and entry into Madaktu or Susa in the lower register, and the entry into Arbela in the upper. No epigraphs

38. Barnett 1976: text-plates 6 and 8.

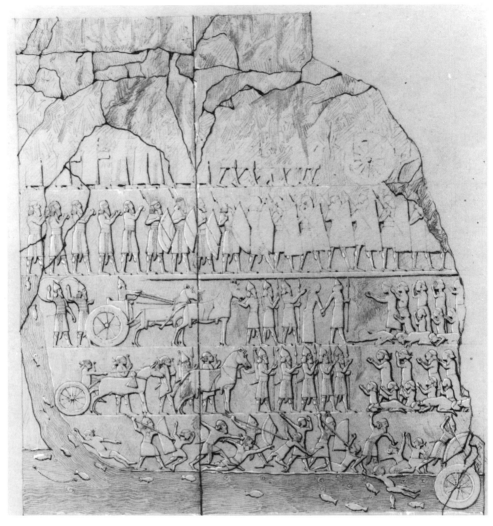

FIG. 68. Nineveh, North Palace of Assurbanipal, Room I, Slabs 6–7, procession to Arbela (above) and the installation of Ummanigash in Susa (below). Original Drawings VII, 12 (photo: Trustees of the British Museum).

were reported or drawn in the lower register, but the image of Ummanigash being led into an Elamite city by Assurbanipal's officer is very close to its counterpart in Southwest Palace Room XXXIII (fig. 68). Unlike the representation in Room XXXIII, however, the figure of Ummanigash in Room I was apparently never labeled; according to the drawing, the relief was fairly well-preserved here, and there is no room for an epigraph. The city they enter is not identified on the pre-

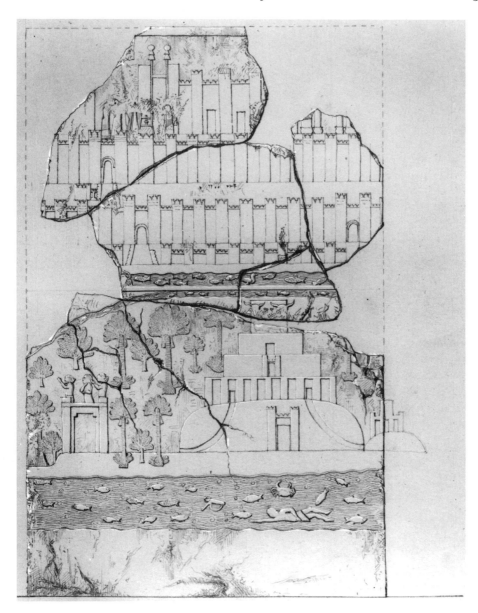

FIG. 69. Nineveh, North Palace of Assurbanipal, Room I, Slab 9, Arbela (above) and Susa (below). Original Drawings V, 1 (photo: Trustees of the British Museum).

served part of the Room I relief (but may have been on the missing Slab 8). On the basis of the Room XXXIII parallel, we would expect Madaktu, but the city in Room I is characterized by a horned ziggurrat, which Reade observed is consistent with the description of Susa in Assurbanipal's annals (fig. 69).[39] The epigraph in Room XXXIII, it will be recalled, specified that Ummanigash entered both Susa and Madaktu (Text A, no. 17). Gerardi observes that the first text that recounts the sack of Susa is Edition F, dated 646/645 B.C. This text also describes the reconstruction of the *bīt ridûti*, or North Palace, and it was presumably composed as a foundation document for that building. The availability for the first time of a detailed account of the sack of Susa, which may not have been accessible to the planners of the Room XXXIII decoration, may well have influenced the choice of the city represented in Room I of the North Palace.[40]

The single epigraph preserved in the upper register of Slabs 5–10 is a brief label on a multi-walled city on Slab 8 (fig. 69; not in Text A; see no. 28a):

⌜The city Arbela.⌝[41]

In the highest part of the city, outside a towered gate flanked by standards, a figure, apparently Assurbanipal, with the head of Teumman at his feet, holds his bow and makes an offering before an incense stand and table. No appropriate epigraph is preserved either on the relief or in the tablets, but this scene may be the subject of one of the lost epigraphs between numbers 27 and 28.

The upper register of Slabs 5–7 is poorly preserved but shows a procession of Assyrians walking rightward toward Arbela in the lowest subregister, and in the middle subregister another file marching to the right that consists of a large chariot at left, a group of walking Assyrians(?), and another large chariot at right (figs. 67, 68). The upper subregister seems also to have shown figures marching to the right. No epigraphs are preserved here, but the upper part of these slabs is badly damaged and any epigraphs may have been destroyed. It is probable that one or both of the large chariots in the middle subregister belong to Assurbanipal; the subject depicted would then seem to be that described by epigraph no. 34 in Text A:

> I am Assurbanipal, king of Assyria. After I had offered sacrifices to the goddess Shatri and had celebrated the *akītu* festival, and after I had seized the reigns of the chariot of Ishtar, I entered Arbela amidst rejoicing with Dunanu, Samgunu, Aplaya, and the severed head of Teumman, king of Elam, which Ishtar my lady delivered into my hands.

39. Reade 1979b: 97–98; Luckenbill 1927: §810.
40. Pamela Gerardi, personal communication, letter of 15 November 1995.
41. The city name has been read as Dêr and Babylon, but neither reading fits the surviving signs, and Unger's reading of Arbela is certainly correct ("Arbailu," in *Reallexikon der Assyriologie*, vol. 1 [Berlin, 1928] 142).

General Observations: The Teumman-Dunanu Reliefs and Epigraphs

It is apparent from the plans of Southwest Palace Room XXXIII and North Palace Room I that only a fraction of the reliefs survived in each room. Based on Layard's plan of Room XXXIII and assuming that all of its walls were originally sculptured, the six slabs that survive account for only about one-fifth of the total wall space. Similarly, in the case of Room I, Slabs 1–10 fill about one-third of the total wall space shown in Boutcher's third plan. The subjects of the missing reliefs may be identified by comparing the reliefs in the two rooms both with one another and with the epigraph tablets. Two of the subjects present in Room XXXIII (the Dunanu victory celebrations in Nineveh and the victory celebration in Arbela) are missing from Room I, and one of the Room I subjects (the procession to Arbela) does not survive in Room XXXIII. In addition, several subjects included in the epigraph tablets are not preserved in reliefs from either room: the march to Hidalu, the celebration in Nineveh following the victory over Teumman, the campaign against Dunanu of Gambulu, and the celebrations in Milqia and Assur.

We can get an idea of the appearance of some of these missing subjects from the descriptions in the epigraph tablets, some of which seem to correspond in a general way to unlabeled reliefs in Room H, which was adjacent to Room I. On a group of reliefs in that room, as Reade observed, are depicted the advance of the Elamite army in the lower register and the city of Nineveh in the upper (fig. 70).[42] These subjects recall the epigraphs from the tablets that refer to the battle line of Teumman (Text A, no. 32) and to victory celebrations in Nineveh (Text A, nos. 10–14, 29, 37–38). Whether the subject of the Room H reliefs was also the Teumman–Dunanu campaign or another Elamite campaign, the epigraph tablets provide a general narrative framework within which to locate images that otherwise, as in the case of the Room H reliefs, are difficult to interpret.

This raises the interesting question of the sequence of epigraphs in Text A. In a very useful study of the Teumman–Dunanu epigraph tablets and their relationship to the palace reliefs, Reade observed that though the order of the epigraphs in Text A is essentially chronological, there are nonchronological variations of two types.[43] First, Epigraphs 30–38 cover the same ground as 1–29, that is, they are two distinct versions of the Teumman–Dunanu narrative. Second, Epigraphs 10–14 (Nineveh celebration of the victory over Teumman) and Epigraph 34 (triumphal entry into Arbela after the victory over Dunanu) are out of sequence, because they are followed by some of the epigraphs that deal with the chronologically earlier Til-Tuba battle.

42. Reade 1979b: 104, 107.
43. Reade 1979b: 99–100.

FIG. 70. Nineveh, North Palace of Assurbanipal, Room H, Slab ?, Nineveh (above) and advancing Elamites (below), width 118 cm. British Museum, WA 124938 (photo: author).

Reade suggested that both of these chronological anomalies could be accounted for by assuming that the scribe who compiled Text A was working directly from the reliefs, an assumption that seems to be supported by the reference to "the lower register" in Epigraph 3. According to this explanation, the scribe started at the beginning of the relief cycle and moved through it, recording Epigraphs 1 to 29, shifting between registers as necessary to maintain chronological order. After completing the cycle once, he went through it again from beginning to end and added Epigraphs 30–38. Epigraphs 10–14 and 34 are out of sequence, Reade suggested, because at these points, part way through his recording of the Til-Tuba battle in the lower register, the scribe shifted to the Nineveh and Arbela celebrations in the upper register, and then returned to the lower to continue the Til-Tuba account. Reade outlined his proposed scheme for relating Text A to the wall reliefs in the following two diagrams, the first by caption subject, the second by caption number:[44]

Nineveh review (Teumman)	Nineveh march	Arbela march	Arbela review	Nineveh review (Dunanu)	
Hidalu	Victory of Til-Tuba	Susa/Madaktu installation	Sha-pi-Bel siege	Milqia	
10–12	13–14	34, 25–26	28	29	
1–3, 30	4–9, 15–16, 31–33, 35	17	18–19, 36–38	20–21	

Reade then compared the compositional sequence implied by these diagrams with the actual sequences found in Southwest Palace Room XXXIII and North Palace Room I:

ROOM XXXIII: Nineveh review (Dunanu) (29 etc.) door Arbela review (28)

             Til-Tuba battle (4–9 etc.) Susa/Madaktu (17)

ROOM I: . . . ? . . . door Arbela march (34, 25–26)

             Til-Tuba battle (4–9 etc.) Susa (17)

On the basis of this comparison, he observed that the compositional sequence in Room I was consistent with, and the sequence in Room XXXIII inconsistent with, the sequence implied in Text A. He concluded, "this text may therefore describe the Room I series."[45]

44. Reade, 1979b: 100–101, with slight adjustments to the caption numbers that deal with the Arbela march and Sha-pi-Bel siege to reflect my understanding of their chronological sequence.

45. Reade, 1979b: 101.

Reade's demonstration that Text A seems to "describe" the reliefs in Room I is original and ingenious, but it leaves open the important question of the nature of the actual relationship between the text on the tablet and the epigraphs and images on the reliefs. The simplest of the possible such relationships are:

1. The tablet served, as Durand argued, as the "program" for the decoration of Room I, drawn up before the reliefs were carved.[46]
2. The tablet served as a collection of draft epigraphs, compiled either before or after the Room I reliefs were carved, to be drawn upon as necessary in captioning the reliefs.
3. The tablet is a description of the Room I reliefs, compiled from the images after they had already been carved on the walls.
4. The tablet was compiled after Room I had been completed and is a copy of epigraphs actually on the walls.

More complex possible relationships that take into account the Room XXXIII reliefs and the additional Teumman-Dunanu epigraph tablets are:

5. Text A is a description of the Room XXXIII reliefs and was compiled for use as the program for the reliefs in Room I.
6. Text A was a preliminary draft of epigraphs for the Room I Teumman-Dunanu relief cycle and was later used as a source in compiling later drafts or the final program, perhaps represented by one or more of Texts B–H.
7. One or more of Texts B–H were compiled from images and/or epigraphs in Room XXXIII or Room I, and these texts in turn served as source material for Text A.

And so on.

In order to begin to sort the possibilities from the probabilities, it is necessary first to look closely at the various sources with the goal of determining their structural and chronological relationships to one another. One type of evidence that could prove useful here is colophons on the tablets. In Text A, for example, the colophon reads, "copy of a writing board that was read before the king." The preserved part of the colophon of Text B reads "[. . . in the cen]ter of Nineveh," presumably referring to a palace or other building.[47] Unfortunately, colophons are not preserved on any of the other tablets that record epigraphs from the Teumman-Dunanu cycle, but colophons are present on five epigraph tablets that deal with the campaigns against Shamash-shum-ukin of Babylon and Tammaritu of Elam.[48] Three begin, "that which is on the walls of the *bīt ridûti* [. . .]," that is, the North Palace at Nineveh, and two of these continue "[. . .] of the south

---

46. Durand 1979–80: 16.
47. Rm 2,364, left edge (Leeper 1920: pl. 35).
48. Weidner 1932–33: 191–203.

house," which may refer to a suite of rooms.[49] The fourth reads "the east house, on the walls," and the fifth, "from the palace (or temple) of Nin[eveh]."[50] It appears from these colophons that these latter five tablets record epigraphs that were already on, or were intended for, wall reliefs in one or more palaces, and such may well have been the case for some of the Teumman-Dunanu epigraph tablets for which the colophons are missing. The colophon of Text A, however, does little to clarify the connection between that text and the wall reliefs.

The internal characteristics of each text also provide clues to the relationship between tablets and reliefs. There are eleven different collections of Teumman-Dunanu epigraphs—nine on tablets and two on relief series. In the discussion that follows, each is considered in turn for such evidence.

Text A

K 2674 + Sm 2010 + 81-2-4, 186 + 80-7-19, 102 was Weidner's main text for the Teumman-Dunanu cycle of epigraphs. The tablet is in four columns, two on the obverse and two on the reverse. Substantial parts of each column are preserved, but a number of epigraphs are fragmentary and there is a gap in the middle of each column: about 10 lines are missing from Column i, 8 from Column ii, 25 from Column iii, and 15 from Column iv. The colophon, which is completely preserved, reads, "copy of a writing board that was read before the king." Though Weidner's edition purports to be of this text, he made liberal use of epigraphs on other tablets and reliefs to restore missing passages, and these restorations are not always clearly indicated. The most notable cases are his Epigraph 9, which is completely lost in Text A, and Epigraph 10, for which only 9 signs are preserved in Text A.

Text A is by far the most fully preserved of the Teumman-Dunanu epigraph collections. Though Reade considered this collection possibly to be based on the relief series in Room I, the connection is actually far from clear. In Epigraph 16, which is the only caption that appears both in Text A and in Room I, the scribe of the tablet evidently could not remember Teumman's name—or could not spell it—and so called him 'so-and-so' (*annanna*), followed by a blank space. In the

---

49. K3096, r.10 (Leeper 1920: pl. 21); K2642, rev. ii.9–10 (Leeper 1920: pl. 22); K4457 + Rm 2,305 + 80-7-19,133, rev. 23–24 (Leeper 1920: pl. 15).

50. Rm 2,120, rev.(!)6 (Leeper 1920: pl. 23); Rm 40, left edge (Leeper 1920: pl. 17). The reverse of Rm 40 bears an incantation with a separate colophon: "in front of the images of *apkallus*" (Leeper 1920: pl. 18:12). An *apkallu* is a type of apotropaic figure, in this case probably a human figure with his hair styled in six curls, since this was the only type reported in Assurbanipal's palace (Russell 1991: 180–84). One of the epigraphs on the obverse is duplicated with minor variants on Slab 13 in Room M of the North Palace (Gerardi 1988: 23–24), and this incantation may have been engraved on or near an *apkallu* relief in the same palace.

version of this epigraph in Room I, however, the name of Teumman appears correctly. This suggests that if the two versions of the epigraph are related at all, the one in Text A precedes that in Room I. The case of Epigraph 15, which occurs both in Text A and in Room XXXIII, is similar. In the version in Text A, the name of the subject, Urtak, is omitted; in its place is the masculine determinative followed by a blank space. The Room XXXIII version, in contrast, begins: "Urtak, in-law of Teumman." Again, if there is a connection, then Text A seems to precede Room XXXIII.

There are at least three other general difficulties with proposing a direct relationship between Text A and the reliefs in either Room XXXIII or Room I. The first is that subjects that are described by epigraphs in Text A may appear without any caption on the reliefs. In Room XXXIII, for example, the image of Ituni cutting his bow is readily identifiable on the basis of its similarity to its captioned counterpart in Room I, but in Room XXXIII the appropriate caption, Text A, no. 16, is omitted. Similarly, because the scene that shows the entrance of Ummanigash into Madaktu in Room XXXIII is captioned, there is no mistaking the identity of the same scene when it reappears in Room I where, however, the expected caption, Text A, no. 17, is absent.

The second difficulty is apparent only in Room XXXIII, because too few epigraphs are preserved in Room I on which to base a comparison. Of the ten epigraphs preserved in Room XXXIII, four are not found in Text A. Admittedly, one of these, "Land of Madaktu" (no. 17a), may be too brief and obvious to require duplication on a tablet, while another, no. 27av, may be lost in the gap between Epigraphs 27 and 28. The other two, however, Epigraphs 7a and 10a, are certainly significant enough to be included in Text A if it were copied from or the direct source for the reliefs, and no. 7a in fact appears both in Texts D and H.

The final difficulty is that the sequence of captioned episodes in Text A is different from that in Room XXXIII and apparently also in Room I. In Room XXXIII, the order of the identifiable episodes in the lower register, captioned and uncaptioned (with uncaptioned episodes in brackets), from left to right is:

> $31 \rightarrow 33$ (or $33 \rightarrow 31$) $\rightarrow$ 10a $\rightarrow$ [7] $\rightarrow$ 15 $\rightarrow$ [16] $\rightarrow$ 7a $\rightarrow$ 9 $\rightarrow$ [35] $\rightarrow$ 17 $\rightarrow$ 17a.

In Text A, the order of the same episodes is:

> $7 \rightarrow 9 \rightarrow 15 \rightarrow 16 \rightarrow 17 \rightarrow 31 \rightarrow 33 \rightarrow 35.$

Similarly, in the upper register the order of identifiable episodes from left to right is $28 \rightarrow [25(?)] \rightarrow$ 27av, while the order in Text A is $25 \rightarrow 28$. On the basis of these comparisons, it seems clear that the order of epigraphs in Text A cannot derive solely from either their left-to-right or right-to-left order on the Room XXXIII reliefs, an observation that would still hold true whether the scribe compiled the list in the course of one or two hypothetical circuits of the room. In

Room I the left-to-right order of the identifiable episodes in both registers (lower: 16 → [35] → [17] → [17a]; upper: [34(?)] → 28a) does seem consistent with their order in Text A, but the number of these episodes is too small to allow such a generalization to be made with confidence.

These various considerations suggest that, Reade's observations on sequence notwithstanding, Text A was not copied directly from the reliefs in Rooms I or XXXIII, nor, despite the reference to the "lower register" in Epigraph 3, was Text A the direct source for the epigraphs on those reliefs. Once some distance has been placed between Text A and the reliefs, other explanations for the sequence of epigraphs in Text A begin to suggest themselves. Taken on its own, it reads very much the way a draft program for a relief series might be expected to read. That is to say, it presents a number of separate stories, each of which is told in a sequence of word pictures (the "epigraphs") and each of which is worked through to its conclusion before another story is begun. The result is that stories or episodes that may actually overlap chronologically are ordered in a way that makes them appear consecutive.

This becomes clear from looking at the tablet itself. Epigraphs 1 to 3 set the stage, introducing the protagonists (Assurbanipal, the Assyrian army, Ummanigash) and chronicling the march to Elam. Epigraph 4 introduces Assurbanipal's opponent, Teumman of Elam, and the succeeding epigraphs, 5 to 14, focus exclusively on Teumman's story: his flight and capture, the execution of him and his heir, and the adventures of his head in Assyria. Once Teumman's story is told, we return briefly to Til-Tuba (Epigraphs 15–17) for the story of the contrasting fates of Assurbanipal's enemies (Urtak, Ituni) and friends (Ummanigash). In contrast to the extensive visual record of the Til-Tuba battle on the reliefs in Southwest Palace Room XXXIII and North Palace Room I, there is very little emphasis on the spectacle of battle in Text A, which deals instead with the fates of individuals, particularly Teumman. Epigraph 18 introduces a new story, the campaign against Dunanu of Gambulu, and his story—his surrender, public display, and execution—is the subject of Epigraphs 19 to 29. As with the Teumman story, the battle receives only passing mention (Epigraph 18). Again, it is the fate of Assyria's enemies—personified especially by Dunanu, but also by his lieutenants Samgunu, Aplaya, Mannu-ki-ahhe, and Nabu-usalli—that is the focus of the story.

It may have been at this point that, as the colophon reports, the writing board that contained the original version of Text A "was read before the king." In any event, someone evidently reviewed the text at this point and nine epigraphs were added to the end. The primary purpose of this additional group of epigraphs seems to have been to tell two additional stories. The first of these, Epigraphs 30 to 35, is the Til-Tuba battle itself, which had been neglected in the first group of captions. This sequence is introduced by Epigraph 30, a variant version of Epigraph 1, and continued in Epigraph 31, a variant version of Epigraph 4 that differs from 4 in its shift of emphasis from the person of Teumman to the soon-to-be-defeated Elamite army. Despite appearances, Epigraph 34 is not really out of place in this context, since it relates another of the indignities suffered by Teumman's head and therefore is a sort of postscript to the story of the head told in Epigraphs 10 to 14. Similarly, Epigraphs 36 to 38 recount the remainder of the story, begun in Epigraph 18, of the siege of Sha-pi-Bel. Again, the first epigraph in the sequence, no. 36, is a variant of Epigraph 19, but with increased emphasis on the successful outcome of the siege.

The preliminary nature of this collection, the absence of some epigraphs that appear on the reliefs, and the colophon all suggest that Text A is, as Durand suggested, an outline of the program for a relief cycle. The "epigraphs" here seem to have been composed, for the most part, not primarily as texts to be engraved on the reliefs, but rather as descriptions of the episodes to be included in such a cycle. If this is the case, then the colophon would indicate that the king played some role, perhaps a substantial one, in the planning of the relief decoration of his palace.

Text B

Rm 2, 364 is a fragment from the left side of a tablet. Both the top and bottom are missing. On the obverse are five fragmentary epigraphs: 28v, 33a, 1a, 2, and 3v; on the reverse are two epigraphs that seem not to be variants of any of the Text A examples; and on the left edge are Epigraph 30 and the fragmentary colophon, "[. . . in the cen]ter of Nineveh." The colophon suggests that these epigraphs were either prepared for or copied from reliefs in some building, presumably one of the palaces.

Only two (2, 30) of the eight epigraphs in the preserved part of Text B are found in the same form in Text A, two more (3v, 28v) are variants of Text A examples, and the other four seem to have no equivalent in Text A. This lack of overlap between the two texts suggests that they are based on different sources. Text B seems also to bear little relationship to the epigraphs in Room XXXIII. None of the epigraphs on Text B are duplicated in Room XXXIII. The only example of overlap is Epigraph 28v, which not only appears in a different form in Room XXXIII but also includes the difficult foreign names that were left blank in the version in Room XXXIII. Two other features of Text B are also striking: the apparently nonchronological—indeed, essentially reverse chronological—order of the epigraphs, noted by Reade, and the jump from Arbela, at the end of the Teumman-Dunanu narrative, to Hidalu, at its beginning, without intervening text.[51] The internal evidence of Text B, therefore, seems consistent with the colophon in supporting the probability that these epigraphs were either copied directly from palace reliefs without regard for sequence, presumably in the North Palace, or were prepared as final drafts of epigraphs for that palace, possibly as guides for the mason carving the epigraphs on the reliefs.

51. Reade 1979b: 101.

Text C

K 1914 + K 13765 are two fragments from the bottom of a tablet. They contain a total of four consecutive epigraphs, two on the obverse (2, 3v) and two on the reverse (a different 3v, 37). No colophon is preserved. The two epigraphs on the obverse of Text C duplicate the last two before the break on the obverse of Text B, and therefore Weidner considered the two texts to be probable duplicates.[52] Text C shares other features with B. Like B, it does not seem particularly close to Text A—only two of its four epigraphs duplicate examples in A. Also like B, it skips around, in this case from Hidalu to Gambulu with no transition. It seems probable, then, that Text C bears the same relationship as does Text B to the wall reliefs and to Text A.

Text D

K 4527 + K 12000a are two fragments from the middle of a tablet. The preserved epigraphs are all on the obverse: the last line of an unidentified epigraph of which only the word "sons" is preserved, followed by Epigraphs 7, 7a, 8, and 9 or 9v. The colophon is apparently not preserved. The surviving part of this text suggests that it is fairly closely related both to Text A and to the reliefs in Room XXXIII. The order is chronological and appears to follow that of Text A. Furthermore, at least two of its epigraphs—three if Weidner's restoration of Epigraph 9 in Text A is correct—duplicate examples in Text A. At the same time, two of the Text D epigraphs (7a, 9) are duplicates, or near-duplicates, of epigraphs in Room XXXIII, though the other two were certainly not carved there. This suggests that Text D may represent either a more advanced stage of the program for Room XXXIII or Room I than does Text A, or that Text D was copied from epigraphs in Room I or some other North Palace reliefs, now lost. The first possibility seems the more likely of the two, since the second would require a considerably greater density of epigraphs than was found on the surviving Room I reliefs.

Text E

Sm 1350 is the top part of a tablet. The first five epigraphs on the obverse (31, 32, 10av, 10, 12) and the last four on the reverse (34, 26, 33a, 27a) are preserved. This fragment has no colophon, but there are numerals on the left edge. The epigraphs seem to be in chronological order and the tablet must originally have covered the entire Teumman-Dunanu cycle. The epigraphs on the obverse, which recount the first part of the Teumman-Dunanu campaign, deal briefly with the Til-Tuba battle (31, 32, 10av) and at greater length with the reception of Teumman's head in Nineveh (10, 12). Those on the reverse are from the end of the campaign and describe the victory celebration in Arbela. The selection of epigraphs in the preserved part of the tablet would seem to be good choices for captions on reliefs,

---

52. Weidner 1932–33: 186.

because they are primarily concerned with identifying the king ("I, Assurbanipal") and the foes he has singled out for especially interesting punishment. Indeed, one of these epigraphs (31) was actually on a relief in Room XXXIII and two others (10av, 27a) appeared in variant form in three more epigraphs in the same room. Further evidence that these epigraphs were descriptions of specific images is the phrase 'opposite them' (*ina tarṣīšun*) in Epigraph 27a, which in this context seems to be a visual location reference.

This tablet is unlikely to have served as a guide for, or to have been copied from, the decoration of Room XXXIII, both because of the variants noted and because the names of Mannu-ki-ahhe and Nabu-usalli (misspelled Ninurta-usalli here), which had been left blank in the epigraph in Room XXXIII (28), are spelled out fully in Text E, as are all of the other difficult foreign names. These features of Text E make it seem likely that it was copied directly to or from reliefs in Room I or some other North Palace room.

A unique feature of this tablet is the placement of numerals on the left edge beside some, but not all, of the epigraphs. The first three short epigraphs are unnumbered, Epigraph 10 is numbered 1, and 12 is numbered 2. No number is preserved by Epigraph 34, but its top part, where any number would have been, is broken away. Epigraph 26 is numbered 27, while the last two, 33a and 27a, are unnumbered. The absence of numbers in five out of eight cases where they could have been preserved seems to indicate that the epigraphs in Text E were not intended to be numbered continuously. Weidner suggested that some epigraphs were numbered to facilitate their correct placement in large or complex compositions.[53] It is also possible that they refer to slab or scene numbers.

Text F

K 13741 is a small fragment from one side of a tablet. Three epigraphs—16, 35, and an otherwise unattested epigraph—are preserved in a very fragmentary state. All three deal with the campaign against Elam and, so far as can be ascertained, appear to be in chronological order. Based on its position in the text, the unattested epigraph may deal with the conclusion of the Elamite campaign or the enthronement of Ummanigash. Epigraph 16, which describes Ituni cutting his bow, is known not to have been inscribed on the Room XXXIII reliefs; it did appear on a relief in Room I but, if the trace at the end of line 2 can be trusted, in the variant form found in Text A.[54] Text F was not, therefore, copied directly from reliefs in either Room XXXIII or, apparently, Room I. It may have served as

53. Weidner 1923–33: 189.
54. The trace at the end of line 2 supports the reading t[uk-lat] ("trusted one"), which is the variant from Text A, rather than *si-mat* ("sign of, that which befits"), the variant from Room I (Leeper 1920: pl. 29).

a program description for one of these rooms or as a source for the scribe preparing epigraphs for Room I.

Text G

K 2637 is a fragment from the right side of a tablet. The top, bottom, and any colophon the tablet may have carried are missing. Parts of three epigraphs are preserved: 21, 37, and 34. All are present in Text A, though in a different order and with small variants. They seem to be listed here neither in chronological order (which would probably be 37, 21, 34) nor in the order used in Text A (21, 34, 37). None of these epigraphs were reported on reliefs in Room XXXIII or Room I, but this is presumably because the reliefs that showed these subjects were not recovered. The preserved part of Epigraph 37 is identical in orthography and lineation to the example in Text C but different in lineation from the example in Text A. Because of the orthographic differences from Text A, and because of the non-chronological order of the epigraphs, it is possible that these epigraphs were copied directly from reliefs in Room XXXIII or the North Palace.

Text H

BM 81-7-27, 246 is a fragment from the middle of one face of a tablet. Parts of five epigraphs are preserved: 7, 7a, 8, 9v, 33. The order of the epigraphs is purely chronological. The preserved part of the text seems to be a close duplicate of Text D, though the two do not join. Text H is less closely related to Text A (Epigraph 7a is not in Text A and Epigraph 33 is in its correct chronological position in Text H) than it is to the reliefs in Room XXXIII—Epigraphs 7a, 33, and a close variant of 9v are all on the Room XXXIII reliefs. As in Text D, however, Epigraphs 7 and 8 were definitely not carved on the Room XXXIII reliefs, so Text H cannot have been copied from Room XXXIII. Like D, Text H is probably either an advanced stage of the program for Room XXXIII or Room I, or it was copied from lost epigraphs in the North Palace.

BM 83-1-18, 442

This is a fragment from the middle of a tablet. On the obverse are three fragmentary epigraphs(?) from the Teumman story: 9v (not the one in Text H), 10v, and 17v. On the reverse are two epigraphs that are not attested elsewhere: the first refers to a battle and the second to a campaign against the Medes. These brief texts read like epigraphs but are not closely related to any of the epigraphs on the other tablets or on the wall reliefs. Of the epigraphs on the obverse, 9v is similar to a passage in the annals, and the other two are very free variants of epigraphs in Text A.[55] The order, which places the arrival of Teumman's head in

---

55. Piepkorn 1933: 70:1–3.

Nineveh before the enthronement of Ummanigash, is like that of Text A, however, and it may be that this text is a preliminary compilation of some of the
material that would later be used in composing Text A.

Summary: *The Teumman-Dunanu Reliefs and Epigraphs*

Having now considered all of the epigraph tablets in turn, it may be of some
interest to arrange them in a way that may reflect both the order in which they
were composed and their relationship to the epigraphs on the reliefs in Southwest Palace Room XXXIII and North Palace Room I. The very tentative sequence that I suggest is as follows:

1. BM 83-1-18, 442 may be the earliest of the epigraph collections. None of
   its epigraphs are close duplicates of those in the other texts, though they
   cover the same subjects.
2. Text A is probably an early full version of the program for the reliefs in
   Room XXXIII. Some of the Room XXXIII epigraphs appear here, but
   others are omitted.
3. Texts D and H probably represent an advanced stage of the program for
   Room XXXIII. All of the episodes described in these two texts are identifiable in Room XXXIII and the majority of their epigraphs were carved on
   the reliefs there. The fact that these texts are close duplicates suggests that
   multiple copies of the program were made just prior to the execution of
   the reliefs.
4. Room XXXIII: The reliefs and epigraphs in this room were apparently
   carved shortly after Texts D and H were compiled.
5. Text F may have served as a program description for North Palace Room I
   or as a source for the scribe preparing epigraphs for that room. The episodes described here seem closer to the episodes emphasized in Room I
   than in Room XXXIII.
6. Text E seems to be an advanced stage of the program for a room in the
   North Palace (maybe Room I) or to have been a guide for the scribes who
   placed the epigraphs on the reliefs in that room. The numerals in the left
   margin may have aided this process.
7. Room I: The reliefs and epigraphs in this room may have been carved
   around the time that Texts E and F were compiled.
8. Texts B and C may have been copied directly from palace reliefs in the
   North Palace. This interpretation is supported by the nonchronological
   order of the epigraphs, which suggests that their copyist was not working
   from a chronological master text, and perhaps by the fragmentary colophon on Text B.

9. Text G may also have been copied from reliefs in the North Palace. Its nonchronological order of presentation recalls that of Texts B and C and its fragment of Epigraph 37 is identical to the example on C.

This sequence is probably incorrect in detail and very possibly even in its main points. Nevertheless, the method used to determine the sequence serves to highlight the differences between these similar-looking epigraph collections and to indicate possible ways of interpreting these differences in the context of the process by which palace reliefs were designed and executed.

When the Til-Tuba battle reliefs were in New York in 1995 for the "Art and Empire" exhibition at the Metropolitan Museum of Art, I had the good fortune to view the sculptures in the company of the film director Martin Scorcese. We traced the visual narrative and studied the epigraphs on the reliefs. I told him about the "epigraphs" in Text A that were not carved on the slabs. Scorcese observed that the relationship between the tablet and sculpture seems clear. Text A, he suggested, was the verbal script for the visual narrative. In constructing a visual narrative from a verbal one, he explained, a film-maker first tries to express as much of the script as possible in purely visual terms. Only then is dialogue introduced to convey the parts of the narrative that cannot be expressed visually. For the teller of visual narratives, in other words, pictures come first and words are added later and only when absolutely necessary.[56]

In Assurbanipal's Teumman-Dunanu sculptures, most of the script of Text A has been presented purely pictorially. In a few places, however, the verbal script accompanies the picture, primarily in order to identify the most crucial participants and actions and to convey speech. Indeed, two of the four epigraphs on the intact slabs of the Til-Tuba battle relief are direct quotations: "Take up the bow!" and "Come, cut off my head. . . ." In contrast, there are direct quotations in only three (nos. 6, 14, 15) of the 38 preserved epigraphs in Text A, and one of these is an oracle. This suggests that, while the emphasis of the "epigraphs" in Text A was primarily on description, those on the reliefs themselves played the nondescriptive roles of identification and quotation.

Other Assurbanipal Epigraphs

Most of the epigraphs on reliefs in the North Palace do not appear in any of the collections on tablets. In an important study of Assurbanipal's epigraphs, Gerardi (1988) observed that for purposes of analysis, all of that king's epigraphs may be grouped into three categories. She designated the first of these categories "labels." These include single words, sentence fragments, and brief declarative

56. Personal communication, conversation on 31 July 1995.

sentences composed in the first person.[57] The only two single-word labels have already been discussed (listed here by palace, room, and slab; epigraphs from the Teumman-Dunanu cycle are cross-referenced to the list at the beginning of the chapter):[58]

> "Land of Madaktu." (SWP:XXXIII:6 = Epigraph 17a)

> "City of Arbela." (NP:I:9 = Epigraph 28a)

Seven examples are in the form of declarative sentences:

> "City of [Bit]-Bunakki, [royal] city of [. . .]" (NP:misc. fragment 1)

> "Hamanu, royal city of Elam, I surrounded, I conquered, I carried off its plunder." (NP:F:2)

> "[City X], royal city of Elam, [I surrounded(?)] I conquered(?), I carried off its plunder." (NP:S¹:A:middle)

> "Hamanu, royal city of Elam, I surrounded, I conquered, I carried off its plunder, I destroyed utterly, I burned with fire." (NP:S¹:A)

> "[. . .], city of [Elam, I surrounded, I conquered, I destroyed utter]ly, I burned with fire." (NP:misc. fragment 2)

> SWP:XXXIII:0 = Epigraph 31
> SWP:XXXIII:4 = Epigraph 28

Gerardi termed her second category of epigraph "*anāku*," that is, 'I', so named because they all begin "I, Assurbanipal, king of the world, king of Assyria." This type is always located before or above the image of the king, and all but one example are in the first person. In reliefs that show military campaigns, they identify tribute, prisoners, and booty; in the hunting reliefs, they describe the action.[59] Eleven *anāku* epigraphs are preserved on palace reliefs. Six of these deal with the outcome of campaigns:[60]

> "I, Assurbanipal, king of the world, king of Assyria, who, [at the command of Assur and] Ninlil, attained the desires of his heart. The city of Din-[Sharri(?)], city of Elam, I besie[ged], I conquer[ed. Char]iots, carts, horses, [mules I brought out], I counted as booty." (NP:V¹/T¹:A)

---

57. Gerardi 1988: 7. Translations of all epigraphs here are from Gerardi 1988: 22–35, "Appendix B," with alterations suggested by Elnathan Weissert (personal communication, conversation of 9 January 1996). See also Borger 1996: 297–99.

58. A fragment of what is apparently another single-word Assurbanipal epigraph was reported on a relief fragment found by R. C. Thompson in secondary context in the vicinity of the Nabu Temple at Nineveh. According to Falkner, the preserved text reads: URU *qi-bi/gab*-[. . .] (Falkner 1952–53: 249–51).

59. Gerardi 1988: 7–8, 14–15.

60. Translations of all epigraphs are from Gerardi 1988: 22–35, "Appendix B."

"[I, Assurban]ipal, king of the world, king of Assyria, [who with the encouragement of Assur and Ishtar] conquered his enemies [. . .] Bit-Luppi [I besieged, I conquered]. The people who dwell therein, [chariots, carts,] horses, mules, I brought out, I counted as booty." (NP:F(?):15(?) = "Plaque A")

"I, Assurbanipal, king of the world, king of Assyria who, at the command of the great gods, attained the desires of his heart. Clothing, jewelry, royal insignia of Shamash-shum-ukin, faithless brother, his harem, his *šūt rēšis*, his battle troops, his state chariot, his lordly vehicle, whatever equipment of his palace, as much as there is, people, male and female, young and old, they made pass before me." (NP:M:13)

"⸢I⸣, [Assurbanipal . . .] As[sur . . .] Ela[m . . .]" (NP:S¹:A:top)

"⸢I⸣, [Assurbanipal . . .] who at the [command . . .] the enemy [. . .] who [. . .] I plun[dered . . .]." (NP:V¹/T¹:F)

SWP:XXXIII:6 = Epigraph 27av

The other five *anāku* epigraphs are on hunting reliefs. As Gerardi observed, the hunting *anāku* epigraphs are more descriptive in character than are the campaign epigraphs, but unlike descriptive epigraphs (see below), they are all in the first person:[61]

"I, Assurbanipal, king of the world, king of Assyria, for whom Assur, king of the gods, and Ishtar, lady of battle, decreed a heroic destiny [. . .]. Nergal who goes in front, caused me to hunt nobly. Upon the plain, as if for pleasure, [. . .] I went out. In the plain, a wide expanse, raging lions, a fierce mountain breed, attacked [me and] surrounded the chariot, my royal vehicle. At the command of Assur and Ishtar, the great gods, my lords, with a single team [harnes]sed to my yoke, I scattered the pack of these lions. [Ummana]pp[a, son of U]rtaki, king of Elam, who fled and submitted [to me . . .] a lion sprang upon him [. . .] he feared, and he implored my lordship (for aid)." (NP:S¹:A-B; fig. 71)[62]

"I, Assurbanipal, king of the world, king of Assyria, for my great sport, an angry lion of the plain from a cage they brought out. On foot, three times I pierced him with an arrow, (but) he did not die. At the command of Nergal, king of the plain, who granted me strength and manliness, afterward, with the iron dagger from my belt, I stabbed him (and) he died." (NP:S¹:C:top; fig. 72)[63]

61. Gerardi 1988: 14–15, with revisions.
62. Part of this translation is from E. Weissert, "Royal Hunt and Royal Triumph in a Prism Fragment of Ashurbanipal (85-5-22, 2)," in *Assyria 1995*, ed. S. Parpola and R. M. Whiting (Helsinki, 1997) 341–45.
63. The text was collated by Postgate (1969: 103).

FIG. 71. Nineveh, North Palace of Assurbanipal, Room S¹, Slabs A-B, lion hunt. Original Drawings V, 3 (photo: Trustees of the British Museum).

"I, Assurbanipal, king of the world, king of Assyria, for my pleasure, on foot, a fierce lion of the plain, I seized by its ears. With the encouragement of Assur and Ishtar, lady of battle, with my spear I pierced its body." (NP:S¹:C:middle; fig. 72)

"I, Assurbanipal, king of the world, king of Assyria, for my princely sport, a lion of the plain I seized by the tail. At the command of Ninurta and Nergal, the gods, my trust, with my mace I smashed its skull." (NP:S¹:D: middle; fig. 73)

"I, Assurbanipal, king of the world, king of Assyria, whom Assur and Mullissu have granted exalted strength. The lions that I killed: I held the fierce bow of Ishtar, lady of battle, over them, I set up an offering over them, (and) I made a libation over them." (NP:S¹:D:bottom; fig. 73)

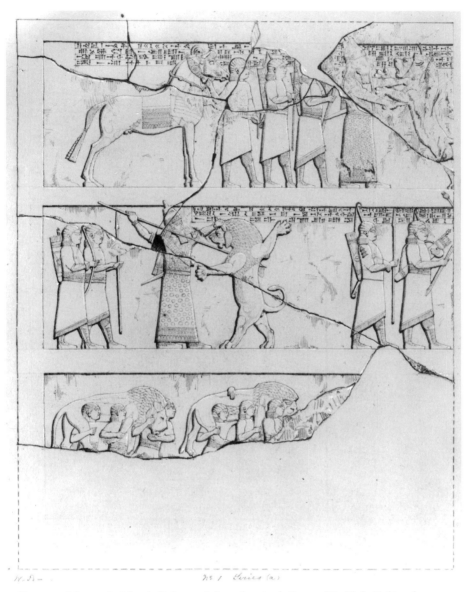

FIG. 72. Nineveh, North Palace of Assurbanipal, Room S¹, Slab C, lion hunt. Original Drawings V, 4 (photo: Trustees of the British Museum).

Gerardi calls her third category of Assurbanipal epigraphs "descriptive." These do not begin with the name and titles of the king and they are not associated with his image. Their function is usually to identify the king's opponents and to describe their actions. Often they provide background information that is

FIG. 73. Nineveh, North Palace of Assurbanipal, Room S/1, Slabs D-E, lion hunt, width 267 cm. British Museum, WA 124886, 124887 (photo: author).

not readily apparent from the relief or focus attention on a single moment in the story. They are narrated from the point of view of the Assyrian king but are usually composed in the third person. Gerardi identified a total of 10 descriptive epigraphs on Assurbanipal palace reliefs. The type was plentiful in Room XXXIII of the Southwest Palace (6 examples) but relatively scarce in the North Palace (4 examples), which suggests that their dense use in Room XXXIII was an experiment that may not have caught on. I will return to this question shortly.[64]

"[. . .] his good (deeds?) they love, all the princes of the wor[ld . . .] kings of Elam, whom, with the encouragement of Assur and Ninlil, my hands conquered [. . .] they stood(?), their royal meal they prepared with their own hands and they brought (it) [before me]." (NP:S¹:A)

64. Gerardi 1988: 8–10. Translations are from Gerardi 1988: 22–35, "Appendix B."

"[. . .] weapon of Assur, my lord, [. . .] from the mountain, place of his refuge, [. . . x] of Murubisi [. . . x] of Assur, my lord, [. . .] Ummanaldash, he seized and [. . .] he brought him before me." (NP:M:2?)

"[. . . who previously Assur and(?)] Ishtar conquered, he prepared for battle. At the beginning of his fight, in the city [. . . Assur and Ishtar] who encourage me, a few soldiers, the defeat of [his] troops [accomplished . . .] their x, the rest of them who fled in battle [. . .]. Thus they spoke: "Fear not!" Assur [. . .]." (NP(?):Loftus's notebook)

NP:I:1 = Epigraph 16

SWP:XXXIII:1 = Epigraph 10a
SWP:XXXIII:2 = Epigraph 15
SWP:XXXIII:3 = Epigraph 7a
SWP:XXXIII:3 = Epigraph 9
SWP:XXXIII:5 = Epigraph 17
SWP:XXXIII:0 = Epigraph 33

Assurbanipal's Epigraphs: General Observations and Conclusions

To conclude, it may be of interest to compare the relative frequency of Gerardi's three types of epigraphs on the palace reliefs with their frequency in epigraph Text A. First, though, the Text A epigraphs must be sorted into Gerardi's categories, and this turns out to be no simple matter. The main problem is that nearly every epigraph in Text A is to a considerable degree descriptive and in many cases it is difficult to decide whether an epigraph should be categorized as a label or as descriptive. The most useful criteria in deciding these cases are person and length. The *anāku* epigraphs in Text A are likewise descriptive in character and sometimes mix first- and third-person narrative, but since by definition they begin with *anāku*, they are easier to classify. The result of this classification of the epigraphs in Text A is as follows:

LABELS	1, 4, 11, 25, 26, 27, 28, 29, 30, 31, 32
anāku	10, 13, 14, 20, 34, 36, 38
DESCRIPTIVE	2, 3, 5, 6, 7, 8, 9, 12, 15, 16, 17, 18, 19, 21, 22, 33, 35, 37
UNCERTAIN	23, 24

In Table 9.1, this result is compared with the types of epigraphs found on the wall reliefs.

Table 9.1. Total Numbers of Epigraphs of Gerardi's Three Types

Source	Labels	*anāku*	*Descriptive*	*Total*
Text A	11	7	18	36
Room XXXIII	3	1	6	10
North Palace	6	10	4	20

In Table 9.2, the same data are expressed in percentages.

Table 9.2. Percentages of Epigraphs of Gerardi's Three Types

Source	Labels	*anāku*	*Descriptive*	*Total*
Text A	30%	20%	50%	100%
Room XXXIII	30%	10%	60%	100%
North Palace	30%	50%	20%	100%

These tables indicate a remarkable consistency in the proportion of each type of epigraph between Text A and Room XXXIII, compared with a substantially greater incidence of *anāku* epigraphs at the expense of descriptive epigraphs in the North Palace. There are at least two ways that could be suggested to account for the shift in the types of epigraphs reported from Room XXXIII to the North Palace. The first possibility is that the different proportions reflect a change of preference that occurred between the times the two palaces were decorated, with descriptive epigraphs becoming less fashionable and *anāku* epigraphs becoming more so. The other possibility is that some other variable is creating the appearance of a shift in types favored. The most probable such variable would be a change in the frequency with which epigraphs of any type occur. The frequency of epigraphs in North Palace and Southwest Palace rooms decorated by Assurbanipal, without respect to epigraph type, are given in Table 9.3.

Table 9.4 summarizes the total number and frequency of epigraphs in the North Palace with the equivalent figures for Southwest Palace Room XXXIII. Since rooms in which no epigraphs were found may not have been completed, they are omitted from Table 9.4.

Tables 9.3 and 9.4 show that the overall frequency of epigraphs in the North Palace was significantly less than that in Southwest Palace Room XXXIII. In

Table 9.3. Number and Frequency of Epigraphs in Assurbanipal Rooms[a]

Room	Total epigraphs	Published slabs	Epigraphs per slab
North Palace			
F	3	12	0.25
I	3	7	0.4
M	2	8	0.25
G	0	3	0
H	0	4	0
J	0	11	0
L	0	12	0
S	0	17	0
upper rooms			
hunt	5	5	1
banquet	1	5	0.2
military	5	12	0.4
Southwest Palace			
XXXIII	10	7	1.4
XIX	0	22	0
XXVIII	0	13	0

a. The reliefs in Southwest Palace Rooms XIX and XXVIII probably date to the end of Assurbanipal's reign.

Table 9.4. Number and Frequency of Epigraphs in North Palace vs. Room XXXIII

Palace	Total epigraphs	Published slabs	Epigraphs per slab
North Palace	19[a]	49	0.4
Room XXXIII	10	7	1.4

a. This number differs from the North Palace total given in Table 9.1 because only epigraphs that can be assigned to a clear context are included in Table 9.4. Three epigraphs on loose fragments are omitted from Table 9.4 and two examples reported by Rassam but never published (in Rooms F and I) are included.

Table 9.5. Frequency of individual types of epigraphs in the North Palace vs. Room XXXIII

Palace	Labels per slab	anāku per slab	Descriptive per slab
North Palace	0.12	0.20	0.08
Room XXXIII	0.43	0.14	0.86

Table 9.5, data from Tables 9.1 and 9.4 are combined to give the frequency of individual types of epigraphs in the North Palace and Southwest Palace Room XXXIII.

Table 9.5 indicates that the overall lower frequency of epigraphs in the North Palace seen in Table 9.4 was distributed unevenly among the three types of epigraphs. Even though the frequency of labels and descriptive epigraphs is much lower in the North Palace than in Room XXXIII, the incidence of *anāku* epigraphs is actually higher. Even if only one of the five *anāku* epigraphs on the North Palace lion hunt slabs is counted, the frequency of *anāku* epigraphs in the North Palace would be about the same as that in Room XXXIII. The explanation for this would seem to be that on the palace reliefs, every image of the king should ideally be captioned, and only the *anāku*-type epigraph is used for this purpose. In both the North Palace and Room XXXIII, the image of the king occurs once on every five to ten slabs, and so the frequency of *anāku* epigraphs should remain relatively constant from room to room.

A clear difference between the North Palace and Room XXXIII, however, at least on the basis of the available evidence, is the frequency of labels and, especially, descriptive epigraphs. A foundation prism from the wall of North Palace Room I is usually dated to 643 B.C., and so the wall reliefs in the central part of the palace cannot have been erected and carved until sometime after that date.[65] The presence of uncarved slabs on the walls of some North Palace rooms (N, O, P, Q, T, V) and the absence of epigraphs on reliefs in several rooms in which we would expect to find them (see Table 9.3) both suggest that the palace decoration was incomplete at the time of Assurbanipal's death in 631 B.C.[66] In other words, the relief carving could have been finished in some rooms, but the king died before epigraphs had been added to these reliefs. In the case of North Palace rooms that do contain epigraphs, the apparent reduction in the use of labels and descriptive epigraphs in comparison with Room XXXIII may suggest that the dense captioning of Room XXXIII had gone out of fashion.

65. Gerardi 1988: 2 n. 4.
66. Naʾaman 1991.

Summary: Assurbanipal

Epigraphs were the only type of palace inscription visible in Assurbanipal's palace at Nineveh. A few of these epigraphs, along with some others on Assurbanipal reliefs in Room XXXIII of the Southwest Palace, are found also on clay tablets that seem to be collections of epigraphs, including numerous examples that do not occur on the preserved reliefs. In an effort to determine the ways in which the epigraphs on the tablets are related to the reliefs and epigraphs on the palace walls, the corpus of material that deals with Assurbanipal's campaign against Teumman of Elam was here assembled, translated, and subjected to a much closer analysis than it had heretofore received. I concluded that some of the epigraph tablets are best understood as drafts of the program of a relief cycle, others may have served as guides for the relief carvers, and still others may have been copied directly from epigraphs on existing wall reliefs. This analysis resulted in a much clearer picture both of the process by which a narrative relief cycle may have been planned and executed and of the role of epigraphs in that process. Among the potentially useful contributions in this chapter were English translations of all epigraphs that deal with the Teumman campaign, a fully illustrated analysis of the way epigraphs function in the narrative reliefs that show this campaign, a thorough discussion of each tablet that includes Teumman cycle epigraphs, and a typological classification and comparative analysis of Assurbanipal's epigraphs on both reliefs and tablets.

Chapter 10

Conclusions

My goal in this study has been to navigate back to their source the too-often diverging streams of philology and archaeology as they apply to the cuneiform inscriptions that were inscribed in prominent locations in Neo-Assyrian palaces. The character, quantity, and state of publication of these inscriptions varies considerably from king to king, and this variability largely has determined the nature of the questions I have been able to ask of the materials ascribed to each king; it has also affected the answers I have been able to suggest.

Though the focus of this book has been on the work of individual kings, it is worth drawing attention to several chronological patterns that have emerged. The locations and types of inscriptions in Assyrian palaces are summarized in the following table:

Table 10.1. Locations and Types of Assyrian Palace Inscriptions[a]

King	Slab Backs	Thresholds	Text Register on Wall Reliefs	Colossi	Epigraphs on Wall Reliefs
Assurnasirpal II	summary	annals/ summary	summary	summary	no
Shalmaneser III		summary		summary	
Adad-nirari III		genealogy			
Tiglath-pileser III	no		annals		label
Sargon II	summary	summary	annals/ summary	summary	label/caption
Sennacherib	label	label	no	annals/ summary	caption/ annalistic-type
Esarhaddon	label				
Assurbanipal	label	no	no	no	caption/ annalistic-type

a. Adapted and enlarged from Russell 1991: 32; entries with insufficient information are left blank.

Several trends and patterns may be discerned from this table. Let us begin with the columns, which highlight what types of texts were used in specific locations, and how these types changed over time.

Inscriptions on the Backs of the Slabs

In the case of the texts on the backs of the wall slabs, the only type of "hidden" text analyzed in this study, there is a shift from comparatively long summary texts at the beginning of the sequence to brief labels at the end. In every case, the purpose of this text seems primarily to have been to identify the king who erected the wall slabs. In the case of Assurnasirpal II, this process of identification required a relatively lengthy text that included his titulary, a resume of his conquests, and a brief building account. These same elements figure in all of Assurnasirpal's texts, however, and the formulation in the slab back text, which I suggest is one of the earlier Kalhu texts, is among his shortest.

We have no wall slabs of Shalmaneser III or Adad-nirari III. A pair of bull colossi of Shalmaneser III was found at Kalhu, inscribed on their backs with a long annalistic text, but we do not know whether they originally belonged to a palace or a temple. Surprisingly, no text is reported on the reverse of the numerous wall reliefs of Tiglath-pileser III. Layard, who made careful records of inscriptions he found on the backs of wall slabs, found dozens of Tiglath-pileser wall reliefs during his first campaign at Kalhu but reported only one occurrence of Tiglath-pileser's name, and this on a pavement slab.[1] Since Assyrian royal names were one thing for which Layard was specifically looking, it seems almost certain that Tiglath-pileser's slabs carried no inscription on their reverse. We might speculate that Tiglath-pileser may not have known that wall slabs could be inscribed on the back. Unless he had removed any Assurnasirpal II examples in the course of repairs to the Northwest Palace, he would not have been aware that such inscriptions were present. The omission of such inscriptions in his own palace, therefore, may have been due simply to ignorance.

This was not the case for Sargon II, who restored Assurnasirpal's palace around the same time that he was embarking on his own major building campaign at Dur Sharrukin. As with all of the palace inscriptions at Dur Sharrukin, the appearance and length of the text on the back of the wall slabs is modeled closely on that in Assurnasirpal's palace at Kalhu. In Sargon's text, however, Assurnasirpal's lengthy resume of conquests was replaced by a brief summary of the favors the king had granted to the cities of his realm, followed by a lengthy building account. The apparent "all-purpose" character of the Assurnasirpal text,

1. Layard 1849a: vol. 2, 196–97.

therefore, has been replaced here by a text that emphasizes Sargon's urban activities, culminating in his founding of a great new metropolis of his own. Sargon has retained the form of Assurnasirpal's model while transforming its substance into something more specifically appropriate to its context.

Sargon's successors retained the convention of placing a text on the back of each wall slab, but their brief texts are essentially labels. For whatever reason, Sennacherib no longer used this location to convey any message more than ownership and, as far as we can tell from the limited evidence, Esarhaddon and Assurbanipal followed suit. One exception is the text from the backs of colossi and wall slabs in Room XXXIII of Sennacherib's palace, which briefly identify the stone and its source after giving the name of the king. This is essentially a label for the stone, however—not a general characterization of royal deeds, as were the earlier examples. Perhaps Sennacherib realized that inscriptions on the backs of the slabs would be seen by no living soul and therefore that an extensive inscription in this location would provide only a poor return on the effort required to produce it. This presupposes some knowledge on our part of the purpose of these inscriptions, however, and this we lack. None of the inscriptions on the backs of the wall slabs of any king are addressed to any particular reader, nor do they make any requests of the reader. Under these circumstances, we may speculate that they were intended for future kings or the gods, or that they simply identify the owner of the slabs to no one in particular. Whatever their audience, these hidden texts assert the legitimacy of the king by associating his name with the splendid royal works on which they are inscribed.

Thresholds

In the case of the texts carved on thresholds, we begin with a variety of long texts under Assurnasirpal II and, by the time of Assurbanipal, there are no texts in this location at all. There is a greater range of texts on Assurnasirpal's thresholds than in any other location in his palace, from the brief text that was also found inscribed on stone tablets in the palace walls to long annalistic texts that occur nowhere else in the palace. The majority of these slabs, however, were carved with the throne-base text, always truncated, which is the same text that appears on the colossi that lined some of these doorways. We cannot recover the criteria that governed the selection of a particular text for a given location, but it is noteworthy that in general long texts tend to be carved on large slabs and short texts on small ones.

The thresholds of Shalmaneser III were inscribed with summary texts, as were most of Assurnasirpal's threshold texts, but Shalmaneser's were evidently tailored for each location, where they appear in their entirety. The Shalmaneser texts were apparently compiled shortly after 843 B.C., the date of the last event they recount, and the next known palace threshold text appears in Adad-nirari III's addition to Assurnasirpal's palace, sometime between 810 and 783 B.C. This text is unique among Assyrian palace inscriptions, consisting solely of an extended genealogy. While the visual effect of these thresholds is very similar to that of their models in the older part of the palace, their content is very different in its overwhelming insistence on legitimacy through lineage. As with the texts on the Assurnasirpal thresholds, however, two of the three exemplars were truncated, perhaps reflecting a lack of practice and resultant loss of scribal expertise in palace decoration during the decades that elapsed between the decoration of Fort Shalmaneser and Adad-nirari's palace.

As with the texts on the backs of slabs, the threshold texts of Sargon II look very much like their models in Assurnasirpal's palace and, like most of the Assurnasirpal examples, they are summary texts. Also like Assurnasirpal's threshold texts, there are several different Sargon threshold texts, of various lengths, comprising the royal name and titles, some form of territorial resume, and usually a building account. Unlike the Assurnasirpal examples, however, the Sargon examples are selected with an eye to the space available and are always carved in their entirety. Purely floral threshold decoration was introduced on some buildings at Dur Sharrukin, though not in the palace, where the will to imitate the traditional forms of Assurnasirpal's palace seems to have dictated the appearance, if not the content, of the inscribed and sculptured decoration. This tradition had no hold on Sennacherib, however, who freely introduced floral thresholds throughout his palace, with brief labels on a few slabs in major doorways as his only apparent concession to tradition. Likewise, Assurbanipal's thresholds are all decorated with a floral pattern, and none carries an inscription.

The Text Register on Wall Slabs

In Assurnasirpal II's palace, every wall slab, whether sculptured or not, carried a register of text running across its face. While the visual effect is of a single long text running from slab to slab, in fact each slab carries a separate inscription. With a few exceptions, this text is always the so-called Standard Inscription, consisting of a titulary, geographical summary, and palace-building account. This text is carved in its entirety once on each slab, except that on narrower-than-usual slabs it may be truncated to fit the available space. Even though this text is carved beside or across every sculptured slab in the palace, its content has nothing to do with the visual imagery. Rather, its generalized, universalized image of the king, insistently reinforced through endless repetition, exists as a parallel to the more concrete images expressed in the sculptures.

Tiglath-pileser III may not have been aware of what was carved on the backs of Assurnasirpal's palace relief slabs, but he clearly was familiar with what they looked like from the front, and the long inscription on his palace reliefs retains the general look of its Assurnasirpal model. It differs strikingly in content, however, being now in fact what the Assurnasirpal examples only appeared to be, namely, a long annalistic or summary text that runs continuously from slab to slab. These inscriptions still do not refer directly to the subjects depicted on the slabs with them, but in the case of the historical reliefs at least, the annalistic text and the pictures are now telling the same general story, which they both present using the conventions of historical narrative. Sargon II's inscribed wall slabs also mimic the appearance of Assurnasirpal's but changed the content of the texts. In his case, rooms decorated with reliefs of military campaigns tended to be inscribed with annals, while non-military narrative subjects carry long summary texts. Finally, as with all the other text types, Sennacherib here broke with tradition, completely eliminating long texts from his wall reliefs, and Assurbanipal followed suit.

Colossus Texts

As with most of his other palace inscriptions, the text inscribed on Assurnasirpal II's gateway colossi is a standard text, truncated as necessary to fit the space at hand. This text, an expanded version of the Standard Inscription, was evidently originally compiled for the throne base in Room B, which it fits quite nicely. The throne base is the only place, however, where this text appears in its entirety, and it seems that, as with other standardized Assurnasirpal texts, this text was used more-or-less indiscriminately whenever the space to be filled required something longer than the Standard Inscription. As with the inscriptions on the wall slabs, it appears that the main concern was that a text be displayed in every possible location, not that it be complete or tailored to the space at hand.

The summary text on the front of the Shalmaneser colossi from Kalhu, by contrast, was evidently compiled with this or a similar-sized space in mind. The annalistic text on their backs was a standard text that seems to have been a bit long for its intended space, but instead of being truncated to fit, passages were omitted from its middle, a less brutal and obvious form of abridgment.

Sargon II again imitated Assurnasirpal's example. All of his colossi are inscribed with a single summary text, which, however, always appears in its entirety. The fitting of this inscription to its intended location was facilitated by the practice of ruling off rectangular panels under the belly and between the hind legs of each bull and carrying each inscription across both colossi in a doorway. The creation of four uniform panels must have made the transfer of the text from the master to the stone a much more predictable process than formerly, a process that would have grown easier with each repetition.

Sennacherib continued his father's practice of beginning a text on one bull in a doorway and concluding it on the other. He expanded the range of text types carved on the bulls, however. Instead of a single standard text, Sennacherib's colossi bear three general types of text—annalistic plus building account, historical summary plus building account, and building account alone—and no two of his colossus inscriptions seem to be identical. He also expanded the space carved with text, both by returning to Assurnasirpal's practice of filling the entire space under the belly and between the legs and by eliminating the fifth leg on his colossi, creating a much larger space under the body than previously, with the result that his longest colossus texts are much longer than Sargon's. Whereas Sargon's annals and long summary texts had occupied the surface of the wall slabs, in Sennacherib's palace these types of texts had been moved to the colossi. Esarhaddon's Southwest Palace colossi had no inscription on their obverse, and Assurbanipal's North Palace had no colossi at all.

Epigraphs

Both Assurnasirpal II and Shalmaneser III placed epigraphs on their bronze door reliefs. I refer to these as "captions" because they consist of complete sentences that identify the geographical location and the action depicted and, in the case of Assurnasirpal, identify the figure of the king as well. Epigraphs do not appear, however, on the wall reliefs of Assurnasirpal. It is not clear whether this is a deliberate omission or whether their inclusion was never even considered to be an option. The fact that no distracting text is present on the relief surface greatly enhances the purely visual impact of the images, but at the expense of the historical specificity that the images were evidently intended to convey.

Tiglath-pileser III was the first king known to have included epigraphs on his palace wall reliefs. Perhaps in keeping with his evident intent to imitate the visual qualities of Assurnasirpal's reliefs, these epigraphs—which are so brief that, following Gerardi, I refer to them as "labels"—are kept very inconspicuous. They are less informative than the bronze door epigraphs of his predecessors, giving only the name of the foreign city that is depicted, without a verb or any further information. These city names, however, are the single bit of crucial historical information that cannot be gathered from context, and so Tiglath-pileser's brief labels provide exactly what is necessary—no more and no less—to enable the reliefs to function as historical records.

Though Sargon II's palace decoration was also patterned closely on that of Assurnasirpal II, he did follow Tiglath-pileser in including epigraphs on his wall reliefs. A number of these are city-name labels, as on the reliefs of Tiglath-pileser, but others are complete sentences similar to those found on the bronze doors of Assurnasirpal and Shalmaneser. In another shift from tradition, in one room these longer epigraphs were used to identify enemy kings and describe their punishment. It has already been noted that Tiglath-pileser deviated from the practice of Assurnasirpal by juxtaposing narrative texts (the annals) with narrative images (the historical reliefs) on his wall slabs, and that Sargon followed suit. With Sargon's epigraphs, we see a further development of this process, as narrative text and image are now placed together within the picture field. Whereas the annals and historical reliefs coexist as independent, though juxtaposed, narratives of the story of Sargon, the brief narratives of the epigraphs are thoroughly dependent upon and subordinated to the narratives of the images.

In Sennacherib's palace, this process is carried a dramatic step further. Now the annals were to be found only on the bulls in the main door of the throne room, and other types of long summary and narrative texts were likewise confined to the colossi. The only narrative visible to someone inside one of Sennacherib's rooms was the visual narrative of the wall reliefs. These images are now complemented by narrative epigraphs that identify people, places, and actions, sometimes in so much detail that they read like annalistic excerpts. Once again, these inscriptions are visually subordinated to the images they label, but some of them provide so much information that they can stand on their own as well—little verbal stories lurking among the visual ones.

Finally, in the palace of Assurbanipal, epigraphs assume an unprecedented importance, not only because they are prominently displayed on the wall reliefs but also because they are the *only* inscription that would have been visible at all. The seeker of Assurbanipal's written annals would evidently have been thwarted. Only the pictures tell the king's story, but with the help of extensive narrative epigraphs on conspicuous text panels that regularly punctuate the visual field. On the one hand, it is tempting to say that pictures have finally triumphed over text, and it is true that the visible texts now seem slavishly to follow the story of the pictures. On the other hand, one cannot help but notice that, in a relief series such as the small lion hunt from the upper rooms, five epigraphs on five successive slabs present a several-hundred-word narrative of the events depicted, a narrative that easily stands on its own. In other words, as in the earlier palaces, we again have a long text juxtaposed with the pictures, but now it is embedded in the image rather than running along beside. Furthermore, a close look at some of the so-called epigraph tablets suggests that the "epigraphs" may have preceded the images and indeed may have served as the master text, or script, from which the images were drawn. Therefore, while a walk through the palace would have left no doubt that pictures had triumphed over words as the dominant mode of public expression, every one of these pictures probably began as a text, a genesis whose fossil remains are visible on the relief surface in the form of the epigraphs.

General Patterns in Locations and Types of Palace Inscriptions

The most striking pattern shown in Table 10.1 is the decrease in the number of palace inscriptions from the palace of Assurnasirpal II, where almost every stone surface carried some sort of text, to the palace of Assurbanipal, where the only visible inscriptions were captions on the wall reliefs. Concurrent with this is a change in the locations favored for inscriptions, from Assurnasirpal's palace, where inscriptions appeared almost everywhere *except* on the carved wall relief surface, to Assurbanipal, where this was the *only* place that inscriptions were carved. The palaces of both Assurnasirpal II and Sargon II displayed inscriptions on doorway colossi, thresholds, and across the middle of the wall slabs, and Sargon's reliefs also carried epigraphs. This pattern began to change with Sennacherib's palace, however, where the only visible inscriptions were long texts on the colossi, brief texts on a few thresholds, and epigraphs. In Assurbanipal's palace, there were no colossi and, as far as is known, no inscribed thresholds.

Another feature that varies through time is the length and type of inscriptions in particular locations. The text on the middle of the wall slabs increased, from a relatively condensed standard summary in the palace of Assurnasirpal, to very lengthy annals in the palaces of Tiglath-pileser III and Sargon, and then did not appear at all in the palaces of Sennacherib and Assurbanipal. The texts on colossi expanded similarly, from a short standard summary in Assurnasirpal's palace, to a much longer one in Sargon's, and finally to a variety of lengthy annalistic, summary, and construction accounts under Sennacherib. Epigraphic texts also expanded, at least on the wall reliefs, from labels consisting of single place names under Tiglath-pileser, to brief explanatory captions under Sargon, and then to a mixture of captions and annalistic excerpts under Sennacherib and Assurbanipal. Relatively long epigraphs had appeared in Assyrian palaces before Tiglath-pileser as well, but only on bronze doors and the throne base of Shalmaneser. Threshold texts, by contrast, began as lengthy annalistic excerpts and standard summaries in the palace of Assurnasirpal, continued as a series of standard summaries of various lengths under Sargon, and then were reduced to brief labels under Sennacherib.

One of the most interesting aspects of Table 10.1 is that it highlights the shift in location of annalistic texts, which occur in some form in each palace but in greatly differing contexts. As presented in the table, this shift appears as a diagonal trend from upper left to lower right. In Assurnasirpal's palace, annals occurred on several major thresholds, though none of these seem to have displayed the records of more than a single year, nor was a single year repeated in more than one location. It is not clear whether a complete annals series was represented over a series of thresholds, or whether only selections were presented, but in either case, there is no evidence for more than one annals series being displayed in the palace. In the palaces of Tiglath-pileser and Sargon, the annals were moved to the text register on the wall reliefs in some rooms. Each annals series seems to have been presented in its entirety in every room where it was inscribed, so that each of these palaces displayed several complete copies of the annals text.

In Sennacherib's palace, the annals were again moved, this time to the colossi in the main door of the throne room, and this is the only location where an annalistic text is known to have been displayed. Sennacherib's apparent restriction of his full annalistic text to this single location may be linked to one of the most important innovations of his reign, namely the introduction of foundation documents in the form of cylinders and prisms of baked clay that were inscribed with his annals and a building account (see fig. 4). Such prisms had been used in the Middle Assyrian period by Tiglath-pileser I, who buried a number of them in the foundations of the Anu-Adad Temple at Assur. This type of object does not appear to have been used again in Assyria until Sargon II placed them in the walls of the temple complex beside his palace at Dur Sharrukin. The Sargon examples were devoted primarily to an account of the founding and construction of Dur Sharrukin and included only a brief historical summary.

Sennacherib, who was closely involved with the construction of Dur Sharrukin, continued the use of clay cylinders as foundation documents after he moved his capital to Nineveh in his first year. From the very beginning, he inscribed his cylinders with annals plus a building account, and the length of this text grew over the years as the number of his campaigns and building projects mounted. Four such cylinders were found in the walls of Sennacherib's palace by Hormuzd Rassam, and hundreds of additional fragments attest to Sennacherib's widespread use of these objects.[2] In Sennacherib's palace, therefore, the annals had by and large moved out of sight. With the exception of the example in his throne-room door, the primary function of these long historical texts had become to identify Sennacherib not for his contemporaries but rather for distant posterity. Esarhaddon and Assurbanipal continued this practice of placing their annals on foundation cylinders and prisms; to my knowledge, no annalistic text of either of these kings has been found inscribed on stone. The annalistic-type excerpts of Assurbanipal's epigraphs, therefore, were the closest thing to an annalistic text that is known to have been visible in his palace.

A final feature that varies from king to king is the practice of truncating a standard text to fit a surface. This is common in Assurnasirpal's palace, occurring on all the colossi and some of the thresholds and wall slabs. Its only later occurrence, however, seems to be on thresholds in the Upper Chambers of Adad-nirari III. This would seem to be evidence for increasing professionalism on the part of scribes who, with practice, became adept at fitting texts to various-sized spaces.

2. Russell 1991: 41–42.

In conclusion, perhaps the clearest lesson that can be drawn from this study is that more palace inscriptions must be published; there are reports of inscriptions in nearly every Assyrian palace that have not yet been made available for study. I have suggested here that a great deal of information on building sequence, chronology, scribal practices, and royal expression is fossilized in the Assyrian palace inscriptions, but we must have a statistically significant sample and a clear knowledge of architectural context in order to draw this information out. Publishing all known palace inscriptions will be a big job, but doing so is the only possible justification for disinterring them in the first place.

Chapter 11

Further Reflections

Let us step back a bit for a final look at the palace inscriptions and the buildings they adorn, in their historical context. At the beginning of this study, I suggested that "in attempting to determine the meaning of an Assyrian palace inscription, we are faced with two general challenges: reconstructing its physical context, and experiencing the thought patterns of those who wrote it and those who perceived it." This book has mostly focused on the former challenge, in the belief that understanding the physical context must precede any attempt to reconstruct mental context. The latter challenge can be the topic of further studies, but it is tempting here to offer some preliminary observations on how the material covered in this book may contribute to such studies.

A basic assumption in this book has been that the Assyrians gave some thought to the decoration of their palaces and that the finished product is the result of a series of choices. In making this assumption, I essentially follow Marcus in ascribing "an active intelligence to artisans and patrons of antiquity, granting them the same abilities and intentions that we would credit to ourselves as sentient social beings," though I would caution that such abilities and intentions may find unfamiliar (to us) expression in such a remote context.[1] Nevertheless, our own social sensibilities are the only ones we truly have access to; as I suggested in the introduction, all we can do is reconstruct the ancient context as carefully as we can and hope that our modern interpretation of the result is good enough, "hope that the inevitable deficiencies in our results will be a matter only of resonance, and not fundamental misunderstanding."

This approach can certainly yield interesting and plausible results when applied to the Assyrians, one of the best-documented peoples of antiquity. Of particular relevance in the present context is Porter's important study of the royal inscriptions of Esarhaddon, in which the content of texts displayed in Babylonia was contrasted with that of texts intended for Assyrian audiences.[2] She con-

1. Marcus 1995: 2487.
2. Porter 1993.

cluded that these texts were often composed with audience in mind, and this emphasis on the importance of *social* context as a determinant of content parallels my own argument for the similar importance of *physical* context. The remainder of this chapter, then, will consider larger contexts.

The reign of Assurnasirpal II establishes the pattern for Assyrian territorial expansion and royal construction for the remainder of the imperial period. We have far more documentation for this king than for any of his predecessors, but virtually all of these documents are royal building inscriptions. In other words, we have only Assurnasirpal's version of the events of his reign, and while it is a highly plausible account, it nevertheless represents a single unverifiable viewpoint. Fortunately, in addition to his words, we also have the archaeological proof of one of his major accomplishments, namely the new Assyrian capital city of Kalhu.

The foundation of a new capital in the Assyrian heartland was not a traditional event. The only clear precedent was the foundation of Kar Tukulti-Ninurta by Tukulti-Ninurta I, soon after 1232 B.C. While this certainly represents an abandonment of Assur as the primary administrative city of the realm, the new city was only three kilometers to the north, and therefore the idea of Assur as the geographical heart of Assyria had not changed. Nevertheless, Tukulti-Ninurta I and his father Shalmaneser I both acknowledged the strategic and economic importance of northern Assyria, as evidenced by both kings' work on the temple of Ishtar of Nineveh. In addition, according to Assurnasirpal II, Shalmaneser I built, or rebuilt, the city of Kalhu, on the Tigris just north of its confluence with the Greater Zab, two days journey north of Assur and one day south of Nineveh. The few Middle Assyrian texts that mention Kalhu suggest that it was a city of some importance, probably a provincial capital.[3] We do not know why Shalmaneser was interested in Kalhu, but he may well have valued its central location.

A century later, Tiglath-pileser I became the first Assyrian king to take his army all the way to the Mediterranean, where he received the tribute of local kings and hunted some type of sea creature with a harpoon. His grandfather, Mutakkil-Nusku, had built a palace at Nineveh and his father, Assur-resh-ishi I, had added a second palace, restored the Ishtar Temple, and restored the *bīt kutalli*, or 'back house'. In Neo-Assyrian times, the *bīt kutalli* was the term for the arsenal, and it may have been a military headquarters in the Middle Assyrian period as well. Tiglath-pileser likewise acknowledged the importance of a northern Assyrian staging point for campaigns to the north and west by restoring the Ishtar Temple at Nineveh and completing two palaces there. This was balanced, however, by extensive construction in Assur, including restoration work on the major temples and the palace. The palaces in both cities were decorated with basalt images of

3. Postgate and Reade 1980: 320.

exotic animals in their entrances, evidently representing the fauna at the furthest extremities of the realm, and in one of the Nineveh palaces the king's "victory and might" were depicted, possibly in narrative pictures.[4] In this period, then, Assyria had essentially two main centers: the traditional cult and administrative center of Assur in the south and the newly-renovated, strategically-located commercial and military center of Nineveh in the north.

Early in the ninth century, at the beginning of another period of Assyrian expansion, Tukulti-Ninurta II likewise divided his attention between Assur and Nineveh. At Assur, he restored the city wall, the Assur Temple, and a palace, which was evidently decorated with glazed terracotta orthostats painted with military scenes and a standard titulary. He apparently had great plans for Nineveh as well: a large stone slab from there bears an inscription from the palace of Tukulti-Ninurta in the city Nemed-Tukulti-Ninurta ("Abode of Tukulti-Ninurta"). This, along with palace bricks, from the site suggest that he not only built at Nineveh but that he also considered the city to be so important that he renamed it after himself.[5] This is the general backdrop against which we must view the remarkable, but not wholly unprecedented, building activities of Tukulti-Ninurta II's son, Assurnasirpal II.

Assurnasirpal was clearly anxious to make both of the traditional Assyrian centers fit for a king: at Assur he completely rebuilt the palace and the temple of Sin and Shamash, and at Nineveh he completely rebuilt the Ishtar Temple and worked on a palace. Nineveh seems to have been more important than ever. Its location at the intersection of the best north-south and east-west routes in northern Mesopotamia and its fertile hinterland made it an ideal garrison city and staging point for royal campaigns. According to Assurnasirpal's annals, three of his first five royal campaigns originated from Nineveh, and the other two probably also started there. Foreign tribute was delivered to him at Nineveh as well.

In the annals of the campaign of his fourth year, Assurnasirpal states that the Zamuans who submitted to him were made to perform corvée work in Kalhu, indicating that the restoration of the city was underway by then. The Nimrud Monolith, inscribed sometime after Assurnasirpal's fifth year, gives the first account of the reconstruction of Kalhu, reporting that the king dug a canal, planted orchards, and built a city wall and a palace. Every subsequent campaign, beginning with the sixth year, originated from Kalhu. It is clear, therefore, that from this time forward Kalhu was Assurnasirpal's chief administrative city.

Assurnasirpal's preserved texts do not articulate the reasons for this elevation of Kalhu, but it is tempting to speculate. It seems likely that the king needed a new city somewhere in the Assyrian heartland to accommodate a steady stream of deportees. The annals of his first years contain frequent mention of the depor-

4. Grayson 1991a: 55.
5. Grayson 1991a: 179–80; Reade 1981: 145.

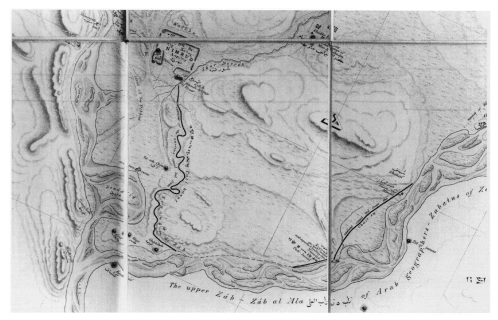

FIG. 74. Kalhu and environs, with the Greater Zab River to the south (after F. Jones, *Vestiges of Assyria*, 1852, sheet 3).

tation of enemy populations to Assyria, and his later texts confirm that many of these people, including those from Suhu, Laqu, Sirqu, Zamua, Bit-Adini, Hatti, and Patina, were settled in Kalhu.[6] Many of these people were deported to Assyria during Assurnasirpal's early campaigns, and we may wonder if the resources of the existing metropolises began to be overtaxed by their numbers.

Certainly Assur, on the southern fringe of the rainfed agricultural zone and already having a large population, could not substantially increase its population without also increasing food imports, nor did the surrounding topography lend itself to a major expansion of the city area. In addition, it appears that a plentiful source of irrigation water was an important consideration in the expansion of Assyrian royal cities, and it is very difficult to bring irrigation water into the city of Assur. Nineveh can support a large population and has a superb location, but it too must already have had a substantial existing population. Furthermore, if Nineveh was, as I suspect, the primary garrison city for the Assyrian army, then a

6. This list is from the Standard Inscription and is repeated throughout the palace. The Banquet Stele adds Kaprabu, Bit-Zamani, and Shubru, and omits Bit-Adini (Grayson 1991a: 276, 289–90).

Fig. 75. Kalhu, view to southeast from ziggurrat in the direction of Assurnasirpal II's canal and the Greater Zab River (photo: author).

significant portion of its agricultural resources would already have been committed to the military. Again, a substantial influx of new population would presumably have necessitated a concomitant increase in food imports. Nineveh is also difficult to irrigate, because the Tigris valley is too low and the Khosr River carries an insufficient volume of water during much of the year. Arbela can also support a large population but is not centrally located.

Kalhu, by contrast, is located on the Tigris at a point roughly one third of the distance from Nineveh to Assur, very near the center of the Assyrian heartland and no more than a two-day march from all of the major Assyrian cities. It is situated well within the Assyrian rainfed agricultural zone and is surrounded by rich farmland and therefore had the open spaces and agricultural resources to support a large population. Assurnasirpal claims that before he restored the city, it had been neglected and apparently largely abandoned. This suggests that the agricultural resources of its environs were not being fully exploited and could be used to support the large influx of Assyrians and foreigners that the establishment of the capital would bring.

Another of Kalhu's attractions is that it is perhaps the easiest Assyrian city to irrigate, because the nearby Greater Zab carries a large volume of water year-round and its river bed is at a high-enough elevation to be tapped not too far from the city (figs. 74, 75, 76). This irrigation would not have dramatically increased

FIG. 76. View of the Greater Zab River near Kalhu (photo: author).

the population the city could support, but it would have allowed the city itself to become a garden spot.[7] It is surely significant that on the Nimrud Monolith, Assurnasirpal's earliest account of the building of Kalhu, the very first project mentioned, before the walls or buildings, is a canal: "I dug out a canal from the Upper Zab and called it Bābelat-ḫegalli ('Bearer of Abundance'). I planted orchards with all kinds of fruit trees in its environs." A later text lists more than forty different types of trees, imported from the lands through which he marched, that were planted in these orchards. "The canal cascades from above into the gardens. . . . Streams of water as numerous as the stars of heaven flow in the pleasure garden."[8] The emphasis on this canal in most of the Kalhu building accounts shows that it was viewed as a major part of the city's appeal.

Once the selection of Kalhu had been made, the rapidly-expanding population of deportees was prevailed upon to provide the labor to support the construction of the new city. The Nimrud Monolith, apparently composed shortly after Assurnasirpal's fifth year, commemorates the initial stages of Kalhu's construction (fig. 77). This remarkable monument, which was found in the courtyard of the Ninurta Temple adjacent to the palace, is in the form of a large stele, sculptured with a colossal image of the king. It is inscribed with a long text that begins

7. Oates (1968: 44–49) discusses the agricultural carrying capacity of rainfed and irrigated land around Kalhu.

8. Grayson 1991a: 252, 290.

FIG. 77. Kalhu, Ninurta Temple
courtyard, stele of Assurnasirpal II
("Nimrud Monolith"), height 294 cm.
British Museum, WA 118805 (photo:
Trustees of the British Museum).

with an extensive titulary, continues with an annalistic account of the king's first
five years, and concludes with a building account. Grayson observed that the
large number of scribal errors in the inscription, especially toward the end, suggest that it was completed hastily to meet a deadline.[9] The omission of the campaign of the sixth year strongly argues that the text was composed immediately
after the campaign of the fifth year, and the monument itself was presumably
rushed to completion shortly thereafter.

The primary focus of the building account here is the new palace, which is
described briefly:

> I founded therein a palace as my royal residence (and) for my lordly lei-
> sure for eternity. I decorated it in a splendid fashion. I surrounded it with

9. Grayson 1991a: 238.

knobbed nails of bronze. I made high doors of fir, fastened them with bronze bands, and hung them in its doorway. I took and put therein thrones of ebony and boxwood, dishes decorated with ivory, silver, gold, tin, bronze, iron, booty from the lands over which I gained dominion.[10]

This is followed by a very long list of blessings and curses addressed to future kings who restore or destroy the palace, including an injunction against using the palace as a storehouse, already cited in the chapter on Sargon II. The focus of the text makes it clear that this stele was erected to commemorate the construction of the new palace. The sketchy description of the building itself together with the extensive curse formula suggests that it is a foundation document. Cifarelli observes that such stele were traditionally erected at the periphery of the realm to commemorate the annexation of new territory and suggests that its placement in the new capital served a similar ideological function: Kalhu, an Assyrian royal city that had become "dilapidated, . . . dormant and had turned into ruin hills" was thereby reclaimed from the forces of disorder.[11]

There is no way to tell how far the construction of the palace had advanced at the time this document was composed. The building account is sketchy and formulaic, suggesting that construction was still underway, or even just beginning, but the fact that Assurnasirpal departed from Kalhu on his campaign of the very next year seems to indicate that there was some sort of royal residence there. The difference between the rather mundane palace described in the Nimrud Monolith, whose only notable features were its knobbed nails and fir doors, and the magnificent palace known from archaeological discovery led de Filippi to suggest that these are two distinct buildings and that the plainer palace was later replaced by the finer palace. As evidence, she cites the fir wood used in the doors in the early account, which could have been obtained fairly close to Assyria. This was replaced in the later accounts by cedar and other exotic woods that seem to have come from a distance, far to the west, areas that Assurnasirpal did not have access to when the first building account was written.[12] An alternative hypothesis, as Cifarelli suggests, is that these accounts represent the palace at several stages in its construction history, from simple beginning to elaborate culmination.[13] Logical as this latter explanation seems, it appears that it can only be true if the decorated state apartments were added to the palace several years after the Nimrud Monolith was inscribed, as we will shortly see.

In his sixth year, Assurnasirpal and his army departed from Kalhu on the greatest expedition of his reign. The second, final edition of Assurnasirpal's annals, which covers five campaigns from years six through eighteen, was inscribed

10. Grayson 1991a: 252.
11. Cifarelli 1995: 153.
12. de Filippi 1977: 37–39.
13. Cifarelli 1995: 369.

on pavement and wall slabs in the Ninurta Temple. The most puzzling feature of the text is that the campaigns of the sixth and eighteenth years are dated, but the intervening three campaigns are identified only by the month, not the year, in which they began. This has led to much speculation on the chronology of this portion of Assurnasirpal's reign, and the mystery has only recently been solved by Cifarelli. She proposes that the three undated campaigns took place in close succession, probably in years seven, eight, and nine, and that they are not dated because Assurnasirpal considered them to be a continuation of the campaign begun in the sixth year.[14]

The objective of this extended campaign was the Mediterranean coast, which no Assyrian king had reached since the time of Tiglath-pileser I. In years six through eight, Assurnasirpal established his control, successively, over the Habur valley, and then the middle Euphrates from the borders of Suhu in the south to the border of Carchemish, capital of the powerful state of Hatti in the north. Then, in his ninth year, Assurnasirpal crossed the Euphrates near Carchemish, received rich tribute and hostages from Sangara, king of Hatti, and proceeded virtually unopposed to Lebanon and the Mediterranean coast, collecting tribute along the way. He also cut great timbers of cedar and other western wood and sent them back to Assyria for the roofs of the temples of the gods Assur and Sin-Shamash in the city of Assur and Ishtar in Nineveh. In effect, this expedition was a massive shopping trip—Assurnasirpal's emphasis on the acquisition of luxury goods and building timber in his account of this campaign led Cifarelli to suggest that its primary purpose was to procure materials necessary for the construction and embellishment of his grand building projects at home, foremost among them the new capital at Kalhu.[15] In the course of this extended campaign, Assurnasirpal also established Assyrian colonies on both sides of the Euphrates and on the Orontes, thereby ensuring continued Assyrian access to this source of essential raw materials. Possibly as early as 875 B.C., therefore, Assurnasirpal had opened a corridor to virtually unlimited natural resources. As we have seen, he commemorated this success by inscribing annalistic accounts of his visits to Carchemish and the Mediterranean on the throne base and gateway colossi in his palace. Furthermore, most, if not all, of the narrative reliefs in the throne room may be associated with the campaign of years six to nine as well.[16]

Assurnasirpal's palace at Kalhu as we know it postdates the campaign to the Mediterranean. Every inscription in the palace, from the tablets immured in its foundations to the text inscribed on the throne base, contains a reference to this campaign. Whatever the palace of the Nimrud Monolith may be, it is not the palace we know with its familiar wall reliefs, for these walls were evidently

14. Cifarelli 1995: 161.
15. Cifarelli 1995: 161.
16. Cifarelli 1995: 276–80.

erected after the Mediterranean campaign. As we have seen, every wall slab in the palace has a reference to this campaign carved on its back, and this text concludes with a description of the gateway colossi in the new palace at Kalhu, reminding us that the first time Assurnasirpal had seen sculptured orthostats and gateway colossi was on his visit to Carchemish.

It is surely no coincidence, therefore, that sculptured wall slabs first appear in Assyrian buildings immediately following Assurnasirpal's return from Carchemish. While the imagery of Assurnasirpal's palace reliefs has precedents in Middle Assyrian wall paintings and cylinder seals, in the White Obelisk, and in the glazed orthostat tiles of Tukulti-Ninurta II, the application of this imagery to sculptured wall reliefs is apparently entirely new, a concept with a direct source in the architecture of Carchemish. Indeed, with its gateway colossi and sculptured wall slabs, Assurnasirpal's palace was the first Assyrian palace in the style that later kings would describe as "like a palace of the land Hatti," an architectural similarity that nicely complements the inscribed textual references to the extent of Assurnasirpal's realm. Later Assyrian kings, starting with Tiglath-pileser III, would consciously emulate North Syrian palaces by building *bīt ḫilāni*s "like a palace of the land Hatti" in their palaces in Assyria.

The greatest innovation in Assurnasirpal's palace decoration, however, is arguably not the wall reliefs, for which the indigenous and external sources seem fairly clear, but rather the tremendous mass of palace inscriptions, a feature that is unprecedented and has no known source. This mandate created the likewise massive and unprecedented challenge of producing a text for, and then presenting it on, every stone slab in the palace. In meeting this challenge, the evidence gathered together in this book suggests that, initially, texts were selected to fit the space at hand. As the realities of the size of the project became evident, however, an expedient compromise was adopted, whereby on standard-sized slabs a standard-sized space was reserved so that a standard text could be reproduced in its entirety. On non-standard slabs—narrow wall slabs, colossi, and thresholds—the standard text was simply truncated.

The reason for this great mass of inscription, which seems to far surpass any practical purpose of mere labeling or recording, remains unclear. I can think of several interrelated possible explanations. First, these texts unequivocally mark the ownership of every valuable, permanent fitting in the palace. In this sense, they may be seen not as labels on the palace as a whole but as labels for the individual stones, each of which represented a considerable expenditure of resources. This was a very expensive palace, incorporating far more decorative stonework than any previous Assyrian palace, and one could argue that Assurnasirpal wished to take credit for every bit of it. Second, the palace inscriptions serve as decoration. On the bulls, thresholds, and two-register wall reliefs, they fill what would otherwise be empty space. On single-register slabs, they provide a visual counterpoint to the imagery—pictures of powerful words juxtaposed over pictures of powerful beings. On plain wall slabs, they transform dull structural fittings into active royal monuments.

This leads directly into a third explanation: the inscriptions imbue everything they cover with the aura of royalty. Royal inscriptions are the physical images of the royal word and are therefore a form of royal imagery—in fact, the most fundamental and widespread form of royal imagery. According to this hypothesis, the carving of inscriptions is not a matter of choice but rather an imperative: royal monuments *must* carry royal inscriptions. Just as royal stele have an extensive text carved directly across the image of the king, so too every image and every slab in the palace carries a royal inscription, simply because it is a royal monument. Assurnasirpal palace reliefs display royal words and deeds, and their juxtaposition emphasizes that the two are inseparable aspects of a single identity. Viewed in this light, the concealment, endless repetition, and frequent truncation of Assurnasirpal's palace inscriptions become less problematic. We make the modern mistake of trying to imagine an audience for the *content* of these inscriptions when in fact what seems to have been of greater importance is their presence as visual icons of kingship; to Assyrian eyes, sculptures and palace inscriptions are both "pictures" of the king.

Similarly, we see a problem in the lack of correspondence between Assurnasirpal's palace reliefs and palace inscriptions, but again this is because we expect pictures to illustrate text or vice versa and because we expect this correspondence to occur at the level of content. In fact, Assyrian eyes were accustomed to the sort of juxtaposition of text and image that is seen on the Nimrud Monolith, where a visual "portrait" of the way a king looks is juxtaposed with a verbal "portrait," in the form of a royal inscription, of the things the king does. To our literal minds, these seem quite different concepts, but to the Assyrians these two "portraits" may have seemed to be essentially indistinguishable aspects of a single truth. In the decorative program of Assurnasirpal's palace, image and text both have important jobs to do, so important that neither is subordinated to the other. In the same vein, the texts on the sculptures give the images a voice. This relationship is clearest on steles, such as the Nimrud Monolith, where the text is the voice of the image of the king, in effect enlivening the image. The same relationship occurs on the palace reliefs: through their inscribed texts, all of these images speak the praises of the king.

To summarize, it appears that Assurnasirpal's palace was initially conceived as a more-or-less traditional royal residence for the new capital of Kalhu. In its final form, however, it became both symbol and manifestation of Assyria's central place in a world that had in the meantime grown much larger and richer than before. The primary event that effected this transformation seems to have been the campaign to Carchemish and the Mediterranean, which confirmed the supremacy of Assyrian power—as evidenced by the ready acquiescence of foreign kings to the Assyrian army—and opened the way to tremendous wealth through unmediated access to the goods and natural resources of North Syria and the Mediterranean. The decoration of the palace both evokes and records this triumph, the former through its display of gateway figures, wall reliefs, and huge roofing timbers, and the latter through the content of the reliefs and palace inscriptions. Assurnasirpal's status as the richest, most powerful monarch in the world is likewise affirmed through texts and images that record the obeisance and gifts of his rivals and through the palace itself, by far the most splendid in the world. The palace inscriptions—images and records of royal power—play a pivotal role in this rhetoric.

Assurnasirpal's successors lived in, added to, and restored his palace over the next 150 years, and in their own palace building projects they generally followed the pattern of palace inscription usage established in Assurnasirpal's palace at Kalhu. We don't know what city Shalmaneser III considered to be his residential capital at the beginning of his reign, but most of the military campaigns of his first twelve years departed from Nineveh (thereafter, the point of origin is not mentioned at all). This confirms that Nineveh was still considered to be the most strategically-sited city in Assyria and suggests that it was again the principal garrison city of Assyria; perhaps it had remained so even after Assurnasirpal's move to Kalhu.

Shalmaneser III continued the reconstruction of Kalhu, most notably with the addition of a huge new palace, later called an arsenal, at the southeast corner of the city. The principal throne base in this palace was apparently inscribed soon after Shalmaneser's thirteenth year, the year after the last campaign listed as starting from Nineveh, and it is likely that the palace was in use by that time. The walls of the state apartments of this building were apparently painted but were not covered with stone slabs, nor were there colossi in its doorways, and so the number of locations suitable for palace inscriptions was much more restricted than in Assurnasirpal's palace. Perhaps because there were relatively few spaces to inscribe and perhaps because the scribes now had considerable experience with architectural inscriptions, Shalmaneser's texts appear to be composed to fit the space at hand and are never truncated.

Shalmaneser continued his father's practice of inscribing thresholds and throne bases. On the few well-preserved published examples, the text is a very selective geographical summary, which focuses primarily on the extent of the king's control, as evidenced by citation of the location of his victories and the erection of his steles. In the case of his principal throne base, there is an apparent divergence in the message of the relief decoration, which shows an alliance with a Babylonian king and the peaceful delivery of tribute from the west and south, and the text, which emphasizes military conquests. The later Black Obelisk shows precisely the same disjunction between its reliefs and inscription. We may see here an acknowledgment of different roles for text and image, with the images presenting models for the behavior of non-Assyrians toward their Assyrian overlords, while the texts record the actions that brought these foreigners into tributary relationship with Assyria. This presentation is consistent with Shalmaneser's policy of campaigning actively in the areas opened up by his father in order to transform an Assyrian presence into outright Assyrian control of trade and resources.

Shalmaneser's reign ended in chaos, because one of his sons, Assur-da'in-apla, led most of the major Assyrian cities in a revolt that began in 826 and was not completely put down until 820, when another son, Shamshi-Adad V, emerged victorious. His reign was relatively short and was marked by little recorded building activity. His son, Adad-nirari III, inherited a stable, if shaken, realm and proved to be a strong, vigorous king who campaigned actively in all directions. He also continued work at Kalhu, building a great new Nabu Temple as well as an addition to the south side of Assurnasirpal's palace. Again, the walls were painted and there were no wall slabs or colossi, so the only inscriptions were on three thresholds in its doorways. All three thresholds carry the same text, though on two of them it is somewhat truncated. This unusual text consists solely of an extended genealogy that traces Adad-nirari's royal line back to the first kings of Assyria.

It is difficult to know what to make of this text. Adad-nirari's reign is sometimes portrayed as a period of decline for the Assyrian monarchy, a decline in part brought on by the consolidation of too much wealth and power in the hands of strong, semi-independent provincial administrators.[17] This may be true, but the historical record is very flawed; the most obvious decline is in the number of royal records from the reign of Adad-nirari, for whom we lack even a single annalistic text. Most of the little that we know of his military activity comes from records composed in his name by his provincial administrators, so it is no surprise that these officers appear to be playing a prominent role in shaping events. It is very likely that annals composed for the capital would present a different perspective.

Given the lack of comparative texts, then, it seems risky to venture an interpretation of the reason for placing a genealogy, rather than a more traditional type of text, on the thresholds of the new addition to the palace. Nevertheless, it is difficult to avoid the speculation that the insurrection of 826 and the rise of very powerful nonroyal individuals must have made Assyria appear to be a quite different type of political environment than it was under Shalmaneser. In a state where sons could vie violently for the throne and powerful officials wielded quasiroyal authority, the question of what sets a king apart from a non-king must have seemed unusually pressing. The traditional answer to this question, of course, is legitimacy, a legitimacy that derives both from lawful succession and from royal descent. It may be no coincidence, therefore, that one of the very few

17. Grayson 1982: 271–76.

known inscriptions of Adad-nirari III deals not with his exploits but with the foundations of his rule and, by extension, the foundations of kingship itself.

The reigns of the next three kings were characterized by rebellion and territorial losses in the west, the continued prominence of provincial officials, uprisings in the Assyrian heartland, and virtually no known building activity. Apart from the chronicles, the only historical texts are on stele erected by provincial governors that record their own deeds. The next king, Tiglath-pileser III, who campaigned in all but one of the years of his reign, reestablished Assyrian control in the west to the Mediterranean coast and increased the number of Assyrian provinces in that region, expanded and consolidated Assyria's frontiers to the north and east and conquered Babylonia, becoming the first Neo-Assyrian king to be recognized as king of Babylonia. His major building project was the construction of a new palace at Kalhu. Assurnasirpal's palace must have been getting rather shabby by this time, and instead of restoring that old palace, Tiglath-pileser reports that he built a new palace facing the Tigris. The palace architecture has not been located, but wall slabs from it were found in the center of the Kalhu citadel and in Esarhaddon's Southwest Palace, which suggests that Tiglath-pileser's palace was probably a further addition to the south end of Assurnasirpal's palace. According to his inscriptions, Tiglath-pileser's was the first Assyrian palace to include a *bīt ḫilāni* "like a Hittite palace," an appropriation of a desirable North Syrian architectural form that mirrors the king's appropriation of the territory in which it originated.

It is clear from Tiglath-pileser's building accounts and from the surviving wall slabs that his new palace was meant to be patterned directly on Assurnasirpal's palace, though in the absence of architectural remains it is not possible to see how this in fact worked out. Certainly the idea of wall reliefs is copied directly from Assurnasirpal's palace, because these had not been used in the intervening palaces of either Shalmaneser III or Adad-nirari III at Kalhu. Tiglath-pileser also carried over the idea that these reliefs should be inscribed, but with two important modifications. First, instead of a standard text repeated over and over, the major inscription on Tiglath-pileser's reliefs is a long annalistic text that proceeds from slab to slab down the wall. The reason for this switch is unknown, but it may have to do with a perception that a purely historical text was better suited than a summary text to accompany the historical narrative reliefs. It may also reflect an increased appreciation for the importance of annalistic texts, a form, as we have seen, that had previously received little exposure in Assyrian palace decoration.

The principal difference between summary and annalistic texts is that the purpose of the former is to define the king in terms such as his titles and territorial claims, while the purpose of the latter is to record his deeds. It may be that for such an active and militarily successful king, the modern truism "actions speak louder than words" would have held in ancient times as well and that a text that detailed each of the king's conquests would have held greater appeal than one that simply listed them. Or, it may be that the king wanted to insure that a record of his deeds would continue to be available for posterity. In the present or the future, the annals serve essentially as a formal demonstration of, rather than a mere assertion of, the power and authority of the king. However this may be, the focus on the details—names, dates, and places—of the king's triumphs in the annals, seems appropriate to the similar specificity of the narrative reliefs and also to the sustained, systematic approach the king followed in his campaigns.

Tiglath-pileser's other modification of the model derived from Assurnasirpal was his introduction of brief captions onto the surface of his reliefs. As already suggested, this small addition gives the images a degree of documentary specificity that was previously missing. It is now possible for the reliefs to be related directly to the accompanying annals because, ideally at least, every city name that occurs on the reliefs should appear somewhere in the annalistic inscription in the same room, if not on the same slab or wall. This introduces a previously unavailable level of reading to the decoration of each room so that, in theory, the epigraphs permit the reliefs to serve as direct illustrations of the annalistic text and permit the text to serve as the explanation of the reliefs. Visually, then, Tiglath-pileser's reliefs are essentially identical to Assurnasirpal's, but the narrative content of text and image is now much more closely related, and for the first time on the wall reliefs we have a type of inscription—epigraphs—that is fully subordinated to the image it labels.

We have no palace inscriptions from the brief reign of Shalmaneser V, but his successor, Sargon II, was the greatest Assyrian builder since Assurnasirpal II. In addition to sponsoring restoration work at Nineveh, Kalhu, and Assur, Sargon founded an entirely new capital city, Dur Sharrukin, some 20 km. northeast of Nineveh. The reason for this move is unclear, because Dur Sharrukin's location is inferior to Kalhu and Nineveh both strategically and for ease of communication. Sargon's texts say nothing about his reasons for building a new capital except that he did it at the decree of the gods and because he wished to do so. Furthermore, he does not go into much detail about the virtues of the new site. He reports that it was built in the vicinity of the city of Magganubba, on the springs at the foot of Mt. Musri (the modern Jebel Bashiqa and Jebel Maklub), in the hinterlands above Nineveh. He also claims that none of the 350 Assyrian kings who preceded him had recognized the possibilities of the site. Like Assurnasirpal, Sargon says he dug a canal for the city, and the building accounts in his colossus text and in the summary text in Room 14 both begin with a description of the royal pleasure garden, "a replica of Mt. Amanus," planted with all kinds of trees from Hatti.[18] This garden is apparently also depicted in the wall reliefs from

18. Fuchs 1994: 38–39, 66–67, 78, 293, 304, 309–10.

FIG. 78. Dur Sharrukin, Sargon's palace, Room 7, Slabs 12–13, view of Sargon's pleasure garden (after Botta and Flandin 1849, vol. 2, pl. 114).

Room 7, which is part of the suite of rooms that overlooks the probable site of the garden, just north of the city (figs. 78, 79).[19]

19. Winter 1982: 362; Stronach 1990a: 172.

FIG. 79. Dur Sharrukin, view of probable site of Sargon's pleasure garden, north of the citadel (photo: author).

FIG. 80. Dur Sharrukin and environs, with the Jebel Bashiqa to the east and Nineveh to the southwest (after F. Jones, Vestiges of Assyria, 1852, sheet 3).

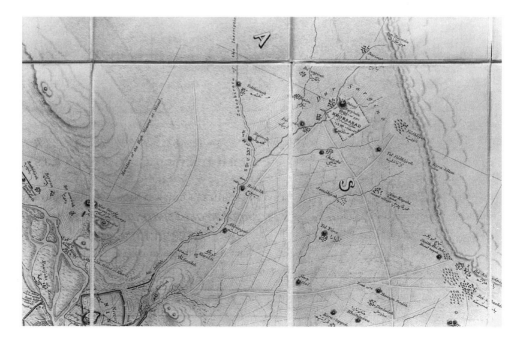

FIG. 81. Dur Sharrukin, view from the citadel toward Jebel Bashiqa, with City Gate 1 in the middle ground and orchards at the foot of the mountain in the background (photo: author).

FIG. 82. Dur Sharrukin, view from northwest towards the citadel, with the Naʾur stream in the foreground (after Botta and Flandin 1849, vol. 1, pl. 1).

Though Sargon's statements here give us little sense of his motives for building a new capital, they do provide ample fuel for speculation concerning his choice of a site. Sargon's references to the springs, canal, and pleasure garden make it clear that, as with Assurnasirpal at Kalhu, a plentiful supply of irrigation water was essential. Dur Sharrukin, on the fertile plain between the Jebel Bashiqa and the Khosr River, benefits from two perennial springfed streams, the Naʾur and the Fadla, both of which originate at the foot of the Jebel Bashiqa (figs. 80,

81, 82). The Naʾur runs past the northwest stretch of the city wall before joining the Khosr River to the west. Both Botta and Place observed that it had sufficient water to run a number of mills and to irrigate the fields and orchards around it. The Fadla passes the city just south of the city walls. Though not as large as the Naʾur, it nevertheless provides ample water for the irrigation of orchards. Botta and Place both attribute Sargon's selection of this site at least partially to its abundant water supply.

Botta cited the Arab geographer Yaqut (1179–1229), who described the area in his geographical dictionary *Mujam al-Buldan:* "One finds there an abundance of water and gardens irrigated by the plentiful flow of the Ras el-Naʾur, called Zarat. In the vicinity is an ancient ruined village called Saroʾun," clearly a corrupt form of Sharrukin.[20] To which Botta added that the flatness of the terrain and the great quantity of water that converges there give the residents ample opportunity to irrigate their farms and orchards, which explains the "freshness of this little district in the midst of the general aridity."[21] The land is very fertile and because it is further to the north than Kalhu, it receives more rainfall. Place observed that despite the primitive agricultural techniques of its nineteenth-century inhabitants, the earth produced such an abundance of grain that there was a surplus to export to Baghdad. The land can produce two crops annually with irrigation, so that in Place's day it was called "the plain with two spring-times."[22]

The water from the two springs is sulfurous, and Place said that the locals attributed curative powers to it. He reported that people who reside throughout the entire length of the Tigris valley were afflicted by a malady called "Aleppo boils." The people of Khorsabad village were not affected, however, and if a sufferer came to this area, the malady was cured within a few weeks, instead of running its usual course of a year. Place suggested that this water may have been thought similarly beneficial in antiquity, and he felt that this might have been an important consideration for a site that was intended to hold a large population.[23] Though it seems improbable that Dur Sharrukin was built as a spa, its healthy waters may have contributed to the site's appeal.

Equally important, apparently, was the site's proximity to Nineveh. Though this was not quite a move to Nineveh, it was nearly so, as Sargon's earliest account of the site locates it in the hinterland (*rebītu*) of Nineveh. The distance between the two cities is not great; the good road that connected the cities could have been traversed in four hours on foot, two hours by cart, and an hour by fast horse. Botta observed that with a spyglass he could see the palace mound of Dur Sharru-

20. Botta 1850: vol. 5, 18–19.
21. Botta 1850: vol. 5, 21–22.
22. Place 1867–70: vol. 1, 14.
23. Place 1867–70: vol. 1, 14.

kin from the highest houses in Mosul, so communication by signal could have been accomplished very quickly.[24] This gives the site something of the character of a suburban estate, located in one of the richest farming areas in the vicinity of Nineveh. Dur Sharrukin itself commands magnificent vistas, with the mountainous Jebel Maklub to the east and expansive fertile plains everywhere else.

Loud observed that the platforms for Sargon's palace and Palace F (the arsenal) seemed to be built on existing mounds on the otherwise flat terrain. He suggested that the precise siting of the city may have been influenced by the presence of two suitably-spaced natural mounds around which the remainder of the city could be built.[25] One of these mounds may be the location of Magganubba, which Sargon gives as the name of the existing town at the site and describes as rising "like a tower."

Though in hindsight the location Sargon chose for his new city has ample virtues, his reasons for wanting to build a new capital anywhere still remain unclear. Perhaps his own explanation, that he built a new capital because he wanted to, is sufficient, but still this was not a project to be undertaken lightly, and one wonders if there was more to it. Sargon's emphasis on the newness of the site, which none of his 350 predecessors had thought to build, indicates that he considered this to be a virtue, and it is certainly true that Assyrian kings placed high value on being the first to accomplish some great deed, a feature of Assyrian kingship that Liverani has called "heroic priority."[26] In these terms, Sargon's accomplishment was indeed unique, for of the two possible precedents, Kar Tukulti-Ninurta was built on a new site but very close to the previous capital, while Kalhu was built far from the previous capital but on an existing site. Nevertheless, one feels that in a case such as this, heroic priority is more likely to be invoked as a retrospective justification rather than being the initial motivation.

It is quite possible that Sargon simply wanted his own city. He may have felt that the existing structures that covered much of the Kalhu citadel precluded the possibility of building as he wished. That these structures may also have been inadequate for his administrative needs is suggested by the fact that the palace he built at Dur Sharrukin is apparently much larger than the one at Kalhu, and the subsidiary palaces, or "residences," at Dur Sharrukin are likewise larger and more numerous than those known from Kalhu. Grayson has suggested that fear may have motivated Sargon, a usurper, to place some distance between himself and the entrenched nobility of Kalhu.[27] While this is possible, the fact that Sargon did not found Dur Sharrukin until his fifth year suggests that he was well able to cope with his subjects without running away. In any case, there is no reason to

24. Botta 1850: vol. 5, 18.
25. Loud and Altman 1938: 54.
26. Liverani 1979: 308–9.
27. Grayson 1991b: 88.

think that the established nobility would have been any worse off under Sargon, unless he had taken steps against them.

Nevertheless, Sargon would have been quite familiar with the recent history of the Assyrian succession: of the last eight Assyrian kings, at least three—Shamshi-Adad V, Tiglath-pileser III, and Sargon himself—had come to the throne as the result of insurrection. In all three cases, the uprising was centered in one or more of the major Assyrian cities. Shamshi-Adad came to the throne following a general uprising in every major Assyrian city except Kalhu, Tiglath-pileser because of an uprising in Kalhu, and Sargon probably as the result of an uprising in Assur. The specific causes of the unrest in the first two cases are unknown, but in Sargon's case it was precipitated by the ill-advised action of his predecessor, Shalmaneser V, in revoking the privilege of exemption from corvée duty of the citizens of Assur and perhaps also Harran.

This was one type of special privilege (others were land grants and exemption from taxation) that was granted by Assyrian kings to those whose support the kings required. Since such grants were understood to be perpetual, over time this practice severely restricted both the revenue and land available for the king's use, particularly in royal cities where such favors were most numerous. While the maintenance of these privileges presumably helped to ensure the support of the cities, it also constrained the king's ability to increase revenue or build new projects in these cities. The foundation of a new capital would allow the king to build to his heart's content on a site where the only privileges would be those he himself granted.

The population of this new city, by Sargon's own account mainly deportees, would have fulfilled their corvée obligation through construction of the city and then would have settled there as law-abiding, tax-paying Assyrian citizens. Indeed, one could suggest that the new city was founded to provide a home for the masses of deportees generated by the campaigns of Tiglath-pileser III and Sargon, as may have been the case with Assurnasirpal's move to Kalhu. By the later part of the eighth century, however, deportees were being moved from one part of the empire to another, rather than being concentrated in the heartland, and they would presumably only be brought to a new capital if Sargon needed them there.

Saggs suggested that one of Sargon's motivations in founding Dur Sharrukin was strategic.[28] By 717, the only real threat to Assyria's borders was Urartu, whose sphere of influence began in the Taurus foothills some 50 km. north of Nineveh. Dur Sharrukin stands in the Khosr valley, astride the northern approach to Nineveh. That it may have been founded primarily as a fortress is suggested by its very name, "Fort Sargon." One would think, however, that there would be no need to move the entire central government into such a fortress and that if there was any real perception of danger, the king would not jeopardize the

28. Saggs 1984: 98.

administration of his realm by placing it directly in the path of a potential invading army. Sargon may, however, have considered this to be a more convenient staging point for campaigns to the north and west than was Kalhu.

I wonder if one of Sargon's reasons for founding Dur Sharrukin was the same as the stimulus that has been proposed for the sculptural decoration of Assurnasirpal's palace at Kalhu, namely Carchemish, which fell to Sargon's army in 717 B.C., the same year that Dur Sharrukin was founded.[29] Certainly, Sargon's new palace had a larger number of self-consciously "Hittite" features than did any previous Assyrian palace: a *bīt ḫilāni* "like a Hittite palace" (Monument x) decorated with sculptured basalt slabs, which was the stone of choice for North Syrian sculpture but does not occur in Assyria, a royal pleasure garden "like Mt. Amanus" that was planted with trees from Hatti, and large stone column bases of North Syrian form. Furthermore, the location of the city itself, at the foot of the first large mountain east of Nineveh, evokes the hills of the Upper Euphrates and the mountains of Lebanon. With the fall of Carchemish, Assyria was for the first time the uncontested master of all the land from the Tigris to the Euphrates. Sargon may well have wanted to express the breadth of this newly-consolidated realm by building a new capital that blended traditional Assyrian forms together with the most desirable features of western capitals.

Whatever his reasons for founding a new capital, the city that Sargon actually built was virtually a copy of Kalhu. Though the plan of Dur Sharrukin was more geometrically regular than that of Kalhu, it retained Kalhu's square shape and enclosed nearly the same area of land. Both cities had the citadel on the northwest wall and the arsenal on the southwest wall, and the citadels of the two cities were the same size. Adjacent to Sargon's palace was a temple complex and ziggurat, while the remainder of the space on the citadel was occupied by a large Nabu Temple and palatial residences for royal officials, just as at Kalhu. Sargon's palace seems to have been considerably larger than Assurnasirpal's (though the latter is incompletely excavated), but the plan of its state apartments was modeled closely on those of Assurnasirpal's palace and Fort Shalmaneser. The decoration of Sargon's state apartments—gateway colossi, sculptured wall slabs, and royal inscriptions carved on every surface—was likewise copied from Assurnasirpal's palace. Despite the apparent boldness of his break with tradition in moving the capital to a site where none had been before, the city he built there was in most respects as traditional as could be. In its replication of Kalhu, the new capital affirmed the power of the traditions embodied in the old one.

In Sargon's palace, inscriptions appeared in the same places as in Assurnasirpal's palace, namely on colossi, thresholds, and the backs and fronts of wall slabs, and so the visual effect of the inscriptions in the two palaces was quite similar. The number of different texts composed for Sargon's palace, however, was

29. Tadmor 1958: 94.

greater: one for the backs of slabs, another for colossi, five different texts for thresholds, and two different summary texts and an annalistic text for wall reliefs—a total of ten different "standard" texts, compared with only five (palace wall foundation text, slab back text, Standard Inscription, throne-base text, and annals) in Assurnasirpal's palace. Furthermore, each of Sargon's palace texts seems to have been composed with a certain amount of space in mind, and each seems to have been presented in its entirety without truncation.

Sargon followed Tiglath-pileser III's practice of inscribing an annalistic text between his narrative reliefs and placing epigraphs on the sculptures themselves. The epigraphs in Rooms 2 and 5 were simple labels, like those of Tiglath-pileser, and functioned in the same way, as nominal links between the annalistic text and narrative reliefs. The epigraphs in Rooms 8, 13, and 14, however, were in the form of full sentences, which presented a direct textual commentary on the scenes they accompanied. Such epigraphs had already occurred on the bronze doors of Assurnasirpal II and Shalmaneser III, but this was the first time they had appeared on the palace reliefs. In effect, the epigraphs here were taking on a life of their own as narrative texts that provided a third version of the events recorded in the long texts and pictures, though their content and placement tied them much more closely to the pictures than to the annalistic or summary texts. This trend would continue into the reigns of Sargon's successors.

I have already noted how similar the decoration of Sargon's palace was to Assurnasirpal's of a century and a half earlier, and I have attributed this to a desire on Sargon's part to copy time-honored forms. This apparent conservatism may, however, have more complex causes than mere adherence to visual tradition. The Assyrian empire under Sargon was a much bigger and more diverse place than it had been under Assurnasirpal. When, following his excursion to Carchemish and the Mediterranean, Assurnasirpal chose to commemorate his kingship with texts carved all over his palace, there can have been no question that these texts would be written in Akkadian. Sargon, in contrast, inherited an empire where Akkadian speakers were outnumbered by speakers of Aramaic. The Assyrian expansion had been so successful that the traditional identity of Assyria itself was in danger of being lost. The situation is dramatically illustrated in a letter from Sargon to an officer in Ur:

> As to what you wrote: "If it is acceptable [to the k]ing, let me write down and send (my messages) to the king in Aramaic on letter-scrolls," why would you not write and send (your messages) in Akkadian on clay-despatches? Really, the despatch(es) which you write must be drawn up like this very (royal) order![30]

Clearly, as far as Sargon was concerned, the official language of Assyria was Akkadian, even if most of his subjects, including his officials, were more comfort-

30. Parpola 1987: xvi.

able with Aramaic. We get the sense that the purpose of this letter was not so much to ensure bureaucratic consistency as to insist on the preservation of national identity. In this light, Sargon's decision to cover nearly every stone surface in his palace with an Akkadian inscription betokened not only a nod to tradition but also a reaffirmation of the very essence of what it meant to be Assyrian. He would be the last king to use palace inscriptions in this way.

With Sennacherib, we come to a king whose approach to rule appears so pragmatic that his motivations seem, from our perspective, refreshingly transparent. A case in point was his very sensible decision to move the principal Assyrian administrative center to Nineveh, which has always been the true geographical and commercial center of northern Mesopotamia. The most puzzling question concerning this move is not "why did Sennacherib do it?" but rather, "why hadn't it been done long before?" Sargon's death on the battlefield may have served as a sufficient omen to justify Sennacherib's abandonment of his father's capital; one imagines that nearly any argument would have sufficed. Dur Sharrukin may have been a lovely place to live, but its peripheral location would have made it an inconvenient place from which to rule.

Sennacherib's approach to the reconstruction of Nineveh was as practical as his father's approach to Dur Sharrukin had been idealized. The city walls were laid out to enclose the largest possible area within the limits imposed by the topography, without concern for geometrical regularity in their plan. The city area that resulted was double that of Kalhu. There was no preconceived number of gates per wall as at Dur Sharrukin. Instead, gates were placed as needed, on the lines of principal roads or to provide access to major structures inside and outside the walls. Two existing tells, known today as Kuyunjik and Nebi Yunus, were incorporated into the western stretch of the city wall as the sites for the palace and arsenal respectively. The challenge of ensuring an adequate supply of irrigation water was met through an aggressive program of canal construction that continued throughout the king's reign.

This apparent pragmatism extended to the layout and decoration of Sennacherib's palace as well. To be sure, we find in Sennacherib's palace the traditional throne-room suite with its inner court and subsidiary reception suites, seen also in Assurnasirpal's and Sargon's palaces. The plan of the remainder of Sennacherib's state apartments is novel, however, with additional courtyards and reception suites, some having a unique plan. Sennacherib's state apartments still have bull colossi in their doors and reliefs on their walls, but the subject of these reliefs is now overwhelmingly scenes of conquest. The ideal of voluntary delivery of tribute that was the subject of many of Sargon's reliefs has been replaced with the more sobering reality of the consequences of non-delivery.

One of the most striking differences was the tremendous reduction in the number of palace inscriptions in Sennacherib's palace. Of the three most prominent locations for extended palace inscriptions in the palaces of Assurnasirpal and Sargon—wall slabs, thresholds, and colossi—only the colossi in Sennacherib's palace were inscribed, and the text on the backs of his wall slabs was reduced to a mere label. Only one of Sennacherib's known colossus inscriptions was an annalistic text; the remainder were either palace-building accounts or building accounts prefaced by a historical summary. Sennacherib's annals were for the most part confined to cylinders and prisms immured in the palace walls, placed there for the eyes of future royal scribes, who, it had become clear, were the only people who would be able to read them anyway. For Greater Assyria, cuneiform palace inscriptions had ceased to be a viable medium of public communication, virtually supplanted by the more universally comprehensible medium of relief sculpture. The exception to this trend is the epigraphs, which now all have the form of brief to medium-length narrative texts. These texts can be quite detailed, but as with their simpler predecessors, they refer only to the events depicted on the reliefs they accompany. From Assurnasirpal's palace reliefs, where the texts tell us nothing about the pictures, we are approaching a scheme where the texts tell only about the pictures.

It is not easy to draw many general conclusions from Esarhaddon's palace inscriptions, apart from the fact that the surviving examples are all short, straightforward texts that name the king and identify the building. In three cases—the Nineveh arsenal, the palace on the Kalhu citadel, and probably Tarbisu—the text was on the backs of wall slabs or colossi, invisible to contemporaries. The fourth text, on the Kalhu arsenal wall, was likewise brief and to the point, identifying Esarhaddon by his most important titles, followed by three sentences that describe the building. Our evidence for this reign is defective, because some of these structures were never completed, but the surviving remains suggest that, as with Sennacherib, foundation cylinders had replaced palace inscriptions as the mode of choice for communicating the king's historical records.

With Assurbanipal, the trend initiated by Sennacherib of eliminating visible palace inscriptions reached its culmination. Assurbanipal omitted doorway colossi from his palace at Nineveh, and with them went the last of the locations established by Assurnasirpal for palace inscriptions. The only remaining visible texts were the epigraphs, which are now sometimes so detailed that, like the annals they replaced, they go well beyond the picture they accompany. This may be because in Assurbanipal's reign, the epigraphs may actually have served as the original source or program for the pictures they ostensibly labeled.

Assurbanipal's elimination of visible inscriptions from his palace seems ironic, because he is the Assyrian king credited with doing the most to preserve Akkadian literature by collecting large numbers of copies and originals of Akkadian texts for his library at Nineveh. He is also the only Assyrian king who claims to have been literate in both Akkadian and Sumerian. It may be, however, that Assurbanipal's nearly inscriptionless palace and his apparent passion for Assyrian texts are symptoms of the same phenomenon. Parpola has suggested that Sargon's successors yielded to the pressure to administer the empire in Aramaic and that this explains the virtual absence of preserved royal correspondence from their reigns.[31] If, as I have suggested above, Sennacherib's drastic curtailment of the use of Akkadian texts in his palace reflects an ongoing abandonment of Akkadian as the major language of the empire, then the absence of long Akkadian inscriptions in Assurbanipal's palace may reflect the reality that Akkadian was a dying language, inadequate for contemporary communication. The king's "literary" interest in Akkadian texts may therefore have been an effort to preserve scholarly knowledge of this dying language in which the entire history of Assyria and Babylonia was recorded.

31. Parpola 1987: xvi.

Catalog 1

Assurnasirpal II
Colossus Inscriptions

I know of sixteen colossi that survive today from Assurnasirpal's Northwest Palace, and two more are documented by a Layard drawing and text copies (the two examples in Berlin are plaster casts of originals in London). These are listed here according to their original location in the palace. In each case, the amount of the 62-line Throne-Base Text that was actually inscribed on each example is indicated; line numbers and translations are from Grayson's edition of the text (1991a: 224–28). Following the convention used by Meuszynski, each colossus is listed by its room, door, and slab designation on the plan (fig. 7), the three being separated by hyphens.

B-*a*-1 (Room B, Door *a*, Slab 1): London, British Museum WA 118801 (formerly no. 809), a human-headed lion facing right. The inscription terminates with *a-na* KUR *lab-na-na* ('to Mt. Lebanon'), in line 26 of the Throne-Base Text. This is the middle of the sentence introducing the Mediterranean campaign.

> Bibliography: Meuszynski 1981: 25; Paley and Sobolewski 1992: 30. Edition and bibliography: Grayson 1991a: 223–28 and microfiche 372–93, "Ex. 6." Photograph: Budge 1914: pl. 4. Note that this plate is incorrectly labeled "No. 841," though the correct number, "809," can be seen on the base of the colossus in the photo. Grayson (1991a: 223) repeated this error, interchanging "No. 841" with "No. 809." Layard's original list of variants from this colossus is Ms A, p. 72. LeGac's "E. 2" is Column iii of this inscription (1907: xviii).

B-*a*-2: London, British Museum WA 118802 (formerly no. 841), a human-headed lion facing left. The inscription is two words shorter than its counterpart, B-*a*-1, ending with ᵈ*nin-urta* ÁGA SANGA-*ti-ia* ('the god Ninurta who loves my priesthood'), in line 26 of the Throne-Base Text. Again, this is the middle of the sentence that introduces the Mediterranean campaign.

Bibliography: Meuszynski 1981: 25; Paley and Sobolewski 1992: 30. Edition and bibliography: Grayson 1991a: 223–28 and microfiche 372–93, "Ex. 7." Photograph: British Museum, *Guide to the Babylonian and Assyrian Antiquities* (3d ed.; London, 1922) pl. 7. Layard's original list of variants from this colossus is Ms A, p. 72. LeGac's "E. 91" is Column iv of this inscription (1907: xviii).

B-b-1: Baghdad, Iraq Museum 26472, a human-headed bull facing right. The area behind the tail is uninscribed, the inscription beginning instead between the hind legs. It concludes with *a-di* KUR *gíl-za-n[i]* 'to the land Gilzanu' about two-thirds of the way through the geographical summary of the king's conquests. This corresponds to the end of line 13 in the Throne-Base Text, but because the text to this point is also identical to the Standard Inscription, it is not possible to say which text was used here.

Bibliography: Meuszynski 1981: 25; Paley and Sobolewski 1992: 31. Photograph: P. Amiet, *Art of the Ancient Near East* (New York, 1980) fig. 595 (inscription partially legible). Inscription unpublished and not copied by Layard; my observations are based on notes made from the original.

B-b-2: Baghdad, Iraq Museum 26473, a human-headed bull facing left. The inscription concludes with ⌜KUR⌝ *za-ban* TA URU.DU₆ 'the land Zaban, from the city Til-(sha-Zabdani/Abtani)'. The inscription here is not damaged; it simply stops in the middle of this place name, slightly further into the geographical summary than in B-b-1. This is the end of line 14 in the Throne-Base Text, but as with B-b-1, the text to this point is also identical to the Standard Inscription. The area behind the tail is uninscribed.

Bibliography: Meuszynski 1981: 25; Paley and Sobolewski 1992: 30–31. Photograph: Nara Prefectural Museum of Art, *The Silk Road: The Oasis and Steppe Routes* (exhibition catalog for "The Grand Exhibition of Silk Road Civilizations," 24 April to 23 October, 1988), Nara, Japan, 1988, pp. 35, 186 (inscription legible). Layard's original copy of this inscription is Ms A, pp. 88–89. It is uncertain whether the truncated place name is to be restored Til-sha-Zabdani or Til-sha-Abtani; either can occur in this position on Assurnasirpal II colossi (King and Budge 1902: 194 n. 7).

B-c-1: In situ, a lion centaur facing left (fig. 83). The inscription ends *né-me-qi šá* ᵈ*é-a* 'the wisdom that the god Ea' in line 23 of the Throne-Base Text. This is the first part of one of the epithets that precedes the account of the campaign to the Mediterranean.

Bibliography: Meuszynski 1981: 32, 34; Paley and Sobolewski 1992: 24, fig. 3. Photograph: Shukri 1956: figs. 3–6. Inscription unpublished; my observations are based on my photographs of the inscription. Layard's original copy of this inscription is Ms A, pp. 78–80. LeGac's "E. 79" is Column iv of this inscription (1907: xviii).

B-c-2: In situ, a lion centaur facing right (fig. 84). The inscription on this colossus is not the Throne-Base Text but rather the Standard Inscription. The text is truncated, concluding with *a-di* UGU A.MEŠ *lu ú-šá-píl* 'I dug down to water level', which is line 17 of the Standard Inscription, roughly halfway through the palace-building account that concludes the text.

> Bibliography: Meuszynski 1981: 32, 34; Paley and Sobolewski 1992: 23, fig. 4. Photograph: Shukri 1956: figs. 3–6. Inscription unpublished; my observations are based on my photographs of the inscription. Layard's original copy of this inscription is Ms A, pp. 78–80. For the Standard Inscription, see Grayson 1991a: 268–76.

B-d-1: In situ, a lion centaur facing left (fig. 85). The inscription concludes with *ina* GIŠ *pu-aš-ḫi a-duk* 'with the spear I killed', which is the end of line 42 in the Throne-Base Text. This inscription terminates exactly at the end of the hunting account.

> Bibliography: Meuszynski 1981: 32–33; Paley and Sobolewski 1992: 15–16, fig. 1. Photograph: Shukri 1956: figs. 9–11. Inscription unpublished; my observations are based on my photographs of the inscription. Layard's original list of variants from this colossus is Ms A, pp. 121–22.

B-d-2: In situ, a lion centaur facing right (fig. 86). The inscription ends *ad-di-šú-nu* 'I caged them', near the end of line 34 in the Throne-Base Text. This is the middle of the hunting account.

> Bibliography: Meuszynski 1981: 32–33; Paley and Sobolewski 1992: 15, fig. 2. Photograph: Shukri 1956: figs. 9–11. Inscription unpublished; my observations are based on my photographs of the inscription. Layard's original list of variants from this colossus is Ms A, p. 122.

D-0 (unnumbered colossus on façade east of Door *d*): In situ, a human-headed bull facing right (fig. 87). Most of the inscription is destroyed, but the end is preserved: *ina šub-ti a-duk* 'I killed from an ambush pit', in line 41 of the Throne-Base Text. This is near the end of the hunting account.

> Bibliography: Meuszynski 1981: 31; Paley and Sobolewski 1992: 17, fig. 7. Photograph: Shukri 1956: fig. 11. Inscription unpublished; my observations are based on my photographs of the inscription.

E-6 (unnumbered colossus on façade west of Door *c*): In situ, a human-headed bull facing left (fig. 88). The inscription ends between the hind legs with *ana* KUR *lab-na-na lu-ú a-lik* 'to Mt. Lebanon I marched', in line 26 of the Throne-Base Text. This is the beginning of the account of the campaign to the Mediterranean. The inscription is not continued behind the tail. Near this colossal bull was found the forepaw of a colossal lion of similar scale. Paley and Sobolewski suggested that this originally belonged to one of the figures flanking the central portal.

Bibliography: Meuszynski 1981: 32; Paley and Sobolewski 1992: 22, fig. 6. Photograph: W. Orthmann, *Der Alte Orient* (Propyläean Kunstgeschichte 14; Berlin, 1975) pl. 175 (inscription partially legible). Inscription unpublished; my observations are based on my photographs of the inscription. Colossal lion: Paley and Sobolewski 1992: 17, fig. 11, pl. 4.

F-*f*-1: In situ, a human-headed bull facing right (fig. 89). As with B-*d*-2, this inscription ends *ad-di-šú-nu* 'I caged them', near the end of line 34 in the Throne-Base Text. This is the middle of the hunting account.

> Bibliography: Meuszynski 1981: 36, 39; Paley and Sobolewski 1992: 38, fig. 8. Inscription unpublished; my observations are based on my photographs of the inscription.

F-*f*-2: In situ, a human-headed bull facing left (fig. 90). Column i, between the front legs, is mostly defaced, but the remainder are preserved. Column iv, behind the tail, ends *ina pa-an aš+šur* ZI *ši-i* TI 'before Assur may these creature(s) live', the end of line 39 of the Throne-Base Text. Since this is the concluding sentence of the account of the wild animals put on display for the people of Kalhu, it is a good place to break the text. To make the inscription end at this point, however, the signs in the last two lines are very small and crowded. It is clear that here the scribe was trying hard to reach a good stopping place before breaking off. This is the only colossus where this seems to have mattered.

> Bibliography: Meuszynski 1981: 36, 39; Paley and Sobolewski 1992: 38–39, fig. 9. Inscription unpublished; my observations are based on my photographs of the inscription. LeGac's "E. 85" is Column iii of this inscription (1907: xviii).

G-*b*-1: New York, Metropolitan Museum of Art 32.143.2, a human-headed lion facing left. The inscription concludes *e-piš ba-ʾu-ri iq-bu-ni* 'they commanded me to hunt', in line 40 of the Throne-Base Text. This sentence should introduce a list of elephants, bulls, and lions hunted by the king, but instead the inscription abruptly terminates.

> Bibliography: Meuszynski 1981: 49; Paley and Sobolewski 1992: 37. Edition and bibliography: Grayson 1991a: 223–28 and microfiche 372–93, "Ex. 3." Photograph: Winlock 1933: 17. Layard's original list of variants from this colossus is Ms A, pp. 123–24.

G-*b*-2: London, British Museum WA 118873 (formerly no. 77), a human-headed lion facing right (fig. 91). The arrangement of the text on this colossus is atypical, beginning between the hind legs, continuing under the belly and between the front legs, and then concluding behind the tail. King observed that this inscription also omits lines 23 (*ú-sa-pu-ú* EN-*ti* 'they prayed to my lordship') to 25 (through *a-gi-iš ú-ma-ʾi-ru-ni* 'sternly they commanded me'), the last group of epithets before the description of the campaign to the Mediterranean. The inscription terminates with *ina* GIŠ.GIGIR.MEŠ-*ia pa-tu-te* 'from my hunting(?) chariot', in line 41 of the Throne-Base Text. Again, this is the middle of a sentence, this time from the hunting account.

> Bibliography: Meuszynski 1981: 49; Paley and Sobolewski 1992: 37. Edition and bibliography: Grayson 1991a: 223–28 and microfiche 372–93, "Ex. 2." I do not know of a published photo of the original. A photo of the cast in Berlin is in H. Schäfer and W. Andrae, *Die Kunst des Alten Orients* (Berlin, 1925) 508. Layard's original copy of this inscription is Ms A, pp. 82–84.

S-*e*-1: London, British Museum WA 118872 (formerly no. 76), a human-headed bull facing left. The inscription ends with *ma-da-ti-šú-nu am-ḫur-šu-nu* ('their tribute I received from them'), in line 31 of the Throne-Base Text. This verb concludes the account of the Mediterranean campaign and the next sentence introduces a new subject, the breeding and hunting of animals. This inscription, therefore, ends at a natural break in the text.

> Bibliography: Meuszynski 1981: 49; Paley and Sobolewski 1992: 42. Edition and bibliography: Grayson 1991a: 223–28 and microfiche 372–93, "Ex. 5." Photograph: Budge 1914: pl. 5. LeGac's "E. 396" is Column iv of this inscription (1907: xviii).

S-*e*-2: New York, Metropolitan Museum of Art 32.143.1, a human-headed bull facing right. The inscription ends with *mu-ra-ni-šu-nu a-na ma-a'-diš ú-šá-li-di* 'I bred their cubs in great numbers', in line 35 of the Throne-Base Text. This inscription breaks at the end of a sentence, roughly halfway through the passage describing the hunting and breeding of wild animals.

> Bibliography: Meuszynski 1981: 49; Paley and Sobolewski 1992: 42. Edition and bibliography: Grayson 1991a: 223–28 and microfiche 372–93, "Ex. 4." Photograph: Winlock 1933: 19. Layard's original list of variants from this colossus is Ms A, p. 132. LeGac's "E. 23" and "E. 386" are Columns iii and iv respectively of this inscription (1907: xviii).

BB-*a*-1: Possibly in situ, a human-headed lion facing right. Layard copied the full inscription on this colossus but did not publish it except as unlabeled variants to his edition of the Throne-Base Text. The top part of Column i, behind the tail, is lost; the preserved part begins [GIŠ.TUKUL-*šú la*] ⌜*pa*⌝-*da a*-⌜*na*⌝ [*i-da-at* EN-*ti-ia*] *lu-ú it-muḫ* ÉRIN.ḪI.A.MEŠ ('[his] ⌜merciless⌝ [weapon] in [my lordly arms] he placed, the troops') in line 8 of the Throne-Base Text. The remainder of the inscription is well-preserved. It concludes between the forelegs with URU *ar-ma-da šá* MURUB₄ *tam-di* ('the city Arvad, which is in the sea') in line 29 of the Throne-Base Text. This is the end of a sentence, but the middle of a section; the tribute list that should follow has been omitted. Reade published an unlabeled Layard drawing that he suggested should be identified with this lion but did not offer conclusive proof (fig. 92). Layard's copy of the inscription confirms this identification, however. Layard's drawing shows the first few signs in each column of the inscription on the lion, and these match the first signs in each column as given in his copy of the text: the first signs of Column i in the drawing, A.ḪI.A, are a rough copy of ÉRIN.ḪI.A, the first full line in the copy of the inscription. The beginnings of the other three columns are identical in the drawing and inscription copy. This colossus and its companion (BB-*a*-2) may be preserved in situ, but I have not seen this part of the palace.

> Bibliography: Paley and Sobolewski 1987: 67; Paley and Sobolewski 1992: 46. Text: Layard, Ms A, 63–64. Drawing: Reade 1985: 209, pl. 38. The drawing is Original Drawings, vol. 4, Misc. 4. Reade's observation that the lion in the drawing is only 6 feet long, smaller than the BB lions as shown in Layard's plan (1849a: vol. 1, facing p. 62), is based on his misreading of Layard's handwriting on the drawing. Layard's note actually gives the length as 8 feet (he writes "6" with the "tail" pointing up), and the proportions of the figure as drawn require a length of about 8 feet to be consistent with the noted height of 4 feet 4 inches.

BB-*a*-2: Possibly in situ, a human-headed lion facing left. As with its companion, Layard copied the full inscription on this colossus but published it only as unlabeled variants to his edition of the Throne-Base Text. The inscription, which is fairly well preserved, begins between the front legs and is distributed in the usual manner. It concludes behind the tail with *ub-la-ši-na* ('I brought them') in line 31 of the Throne-Base Text. This sentence serves as the transition between the account of tribute from Mediterranean cities and the passage that describes the breeding of exotic animals and is a reasonable place to break the text. Part of one sentence was omitted in the transition between Columns ii and iii: *ina re-ṣu-te* ('with the help') to *ra-ḫi-ṣi* ('the devastator'), lines 10–11 of the Throne-Base Text. From the pattern of preservation of the inscription, it appears that much of this figure above the legs was lost or damaged. A number of lines are missing from the beginning of Column iv, behind the tail, due to damage: from [*a-di* KUR *ḫaš-mar* . . .] ('[to Mt. Hashmar . . .]') to [. . . SANGA]-*ti-˹ia˺* (' . . . my [priesthood]'), equivalent to lines 16–26 of the Throne-Base Text. Much of the left part of the first 4 lines under the belly was lost, which suggests that the sculpture above this area was damaged also. I know of no drawing or photograph of this colossus, though like its companion, it may still be in situ.

> Bibliography: Layard, Ms A, 64–66.

Catalog 2

Assurnasirpal II
Threshold Inscriptions

All of the thresholds in situ are shown by Paley and Sobolewski (1987: plan 2), but they give no indication whether individual examples are inscribed, and only four of the thresholds are published in any form. Most of my observations are based on photographs I took in 1990. I am grateful to Samuel Paley for going over these photos with me and helping to identify numerous indistinct signs. The responsibility for any deficient readings of the texts is entirely my own.

Room A, Door *a*: Layard found an inscribed stone threshold in this doorway and copied its inscription, which is the Palace Wall Foundation Text (Layard, Ms A, 12; Grayson 1991a: 300, no. 34.). The inscription, which gives the full text and is very well-preserved, is in 11 lines.

Room B, Door *a*: There is no stone threshold slab in this doorway. Layard observed that the threshold of Door *a* consisted not of a large alabaster slab but rather of "common sun-dried brick" augmented at the center by "a few square stones carefully placed" (Layard 1849a: vol. 1, 116). He expected protective figurines to be under these stones but found nothing. Perhaps an alabaster threshold originally did exist in this doorway but was removed for reuse elsewhere by one of Assurnasirpal's successors.

Room B, Door *b*: No threshold slab is visible today in this doorway, but Layard found one there and copied it (Layard, Ms A, 86–88). The inscription, which is unpublished, is the truncated Standard Inscription in 40 lines. Layard does not indicate whether the inscription was oriented toward Room B or F. Most of the lines are fairly well preserved, though there is a pattern of wear that runs diagonally from upper left to lower right, presumably indicating the flow of traffic through this door. The last preserved words in line 40 are *a-di e-reb* ^d[*šam-ši*] ('to the setting of [the sun]' (Grayson 1991a: 276:14), and there is room for an additional 10 or so signs at the end of the line. Therefore, the inscription probably concluded just before the description of the rebuilding of Kalhu. The genealogy is abridged in the third generation in line 3. Line 24 ends "to the land Urartu."

Room B, Door c: Layard published the inscription from only one threshold, that in Door c of Room B. The text was originally on at least two slabs. The only part still in situ is a large slab that completely fills the space between the two lion colossi (fig. 93). Layard published the first 36 lines of the inscription on this slab as ICC 48–49 (Layard 1851: pls. 48–49). The inscription begins at the southeast corner of the slab, with its lines running from east to west across the threshold; it is intended to be read from outside the door, looking into the throne room. The first two lines give the version of the genealogy that is found in the Palace Wall Foundation Text (Grayson 1991a: 234–35), a variant of which occurs by itself on some other stone door fittings in the palace (see "Unknown 1" below). The remainder of the text is a fairly close duplicate of a passage from Assurnasirpal's annals, as preserved in inscriptions on the Nimrud Monolith and from the Ninurta Temple, recording the first part of the campaign in the king's fifth year. The annalistic part begins at the beginning of the campaign, *ina* ITI.SIG$_4$ ('In the month of Simanu'), and proceeds through [ANŠE.KUR.RA].MEŠ ('horses'; Grayson 1991a: 208:ii:86–210:ii:101, 234–35, no. 10). The only noteworthy difference between Layard's publication (1851: 48–49) and the Ninurta Temple annals is the omission by Layard (48:4) of "I consecrated a palace in the city of Til-uli" (Grayson 1991a: 208:ii:87).

This inscription is now mostly worn away, but it is clear from the surviving traces that line 36 is only about two-thirds of the way down the slab and that Layard's edition ends where it does only because beyond this point the inscription is almost entirely illegible. The beginnings of several more lines are preserved and it seems probable that the inscription continued for some 20 more lines, covering the remainder of the slab.

Layard published a second inscription, ICC 84 (Layard 1851: pl. 84 bottom), that he also said was from the threshold in Room B, Door c, and Grayson (1991a: 236) identified the original as a slab now in the British Museum (fig. 94). This inscription, which has only 19 lines, duplicates another portion of the annalistic account of the campaign in the fifth year, beginning with URU *ku-ú-ku-nu* ('The city of Kukunu') and concluding with ŠE.AM.MEŠ ('barley'; Grayson 1991a: 210:ii: 110–211:ii:117, 236, no. 14). LeGac apparently used a squeeze of this inscription (E. 72$^{a–b}$) in compiling his comparative text of the annals (1907: xiii, and 83:ii: 110 to 86:ii:117).

Since the large slab on which ICC 48–49 was carved apparently originally had about 20 additional lines, and because ICC 84 begins about 20 lines after ICC 49 breaks off, it seems probable that ICC 84 was the continuation of the text on the large slab.[1] The inscription is very well preserved and it is clear from the photograph that it did not originally continue beyond the part Layard published. As with the majority of Assurnasirpal's bull inscriptions, therefore, this text also apparently broke off in the middle of a sentence, unless it was continued on yet other, unpreserved, adjacent slabs. The socket for the latching pole in the middle of line 1 indicates that the slab was inside Room B, adjacent to the south side of the ICC 48–49 slab and oriented in the doorway so as to be read from inside Room B. Indeed, Layard's plan, though it omits most thresholds, does seem to show a slab here (Layard 1849a: vol. 1, plan 3, facing p. 62). Thus the first line of ICC 48–49, facing outward, and the first line of ICC 84, facing inward, were originally adjacent to one another.

Room B, Door *d*: The large threshold slab between the lion colossi in this doorway is inscribed with the "throne base/colossus text" (fig. 95). Traces of 38 lines survive at the east edge of the slab. As in Room B, Door *c*, the inscription begins at the southeast corner of the slab, with its lines running from east to west. The first two lines are completely worn away. The preserved part begins with (Adad-nirari) 'king of the universe' (MAN šú) and ends around line 25 of the "throne-base text" (Grayson 1991a: 224:2–226:25). Line 16′ of this threshold inscription begins with 'the land U[rartu]' (KUR ú-[ra-ar-ṭí]). The preserved text reaches about three-quarters of the length of the slab, and so this slab must originally have carried some 50 lines of inscription. In addition, there is a narrow threshold slab abutting the north side of the large central slab (see fig. 7). This slab is now worn smooth, but if it was originally inscribed, it could have continued the text on the central slab for another 10 or so lines. These 60 lines would have been equivalent to roughly the first 40 lines of the "throne-base text," which is about the same amount that was included in the longest colossus inscriptions, Y-b-1 and Y-b-2. Unless the concluding 20 or so lines of the "throne-base text" were carved on another slab—for example, a doorsill—this is another example of a text breaking off when space ran out. Many of the preserved signs are filled with a material that appears to be copper (fig. 96). Botta noted the same feature at Dur Sharrukin, where he explained the presence of copper on the thresholds as the result of door fittings being melted in the fire that destroyed the palace (Botta and Flandin 1849–50: vol. 5, 68). I cannot say whether that is also the case at Kalhu, where, however, there is no evidence of intense heat, or whether the signs in this slab were deliberately inlaid, presumably to reduce wear.

1. The lines of the threshold inscription are slightly less than half as long as those of the Ninurta Temple annals. The threshold is missing 9 lines of the Ninurta Temple text (Grayson 1991a: 210:ii:101–110), equivalent to roughly 20 lines in the threshold text.

Room B, Door *e*: Though the large threshold slab that was presumably originally in this doorway is apparently lost, three smaller slabs survive from the south side of the doorway: the doorsill, the west doorpost seat, and a fragment of the east doorpost seat (Paley and Sobolewski 1992: 21). Paley and Sobolewski have generously shared with me the notes on these slabs made during the Polish excavations. The inscriptions on two of them can be read from photographs published by Sobolewski (1982c: 241–43). On the west doorpost seat was the beginning of the Standard Inscription, in 13 or 14 lines, its titulary slightly abridged in the third generation. The text is preserved through *i-[pe-lu-ma]* ('gained dominion over'), but it originally continued for at least a few more signs (Sobolewski 1982c: fig. 5; Paley and Sobolewski 1992: 21; Grayson 1991a: 275: 1–5). The inscription was oriented to be read from inside the room. The text apparently broke off when the space was filled. According to the excavation notes, the surface of the fragment of the east doorpost seat was badly eroded and any inscription had disappeared.

Of the doorsill, only the eastern three-fifths was preserved. It was inscribed with a text in 2 columns, which were separated in the center of the slab by the rectangular door-latch socket. The inscription was oriented so as to be read from inside the room. Only 4 or 5 fragmentary signs survive from Column i, at the end of the first 2 lines—not enough for me to establish the original text inscribed there. The first 7 lines of Column ii are preserved. The text was from near the end of the annalistic account of the campaign in the fourth year, from ⌜UGU⌝-*šú-*⌜*nu*⌝ GAR ('upon them I imposed') through GEŠTIN.MEŠ ('wine'; Sobolewski, 1982c: fig. 4; Paley and Sobolewski 1992: 21; Grayson 1991a: 208:ii:79–81). In the photo there appear to be traces of at least four more lines, with space for 3 more beyond this, giving the inscription a total length of between 11 and 14 lines. This is not sufficient space for the remainder of the account of the fourth campaign, which therefore presumably broke off uncompleted. It seems reasonably likely that the large threshold slab(s), now lost, that were originally between the colossi in this door carried the first part of the annalistic account of the fourth year.

Room C, Doors *b*, *c*: There are no threshold slabs in these doorways.

Room F, Door *f*: Truncated "throne-base/colossus inscription" in 47(+?) lines (fig. 97). The inscription begins at the northwest corner of the slab; it is oriented to be read from Court Y, looking toward Room F. The final lines of the inscription are very worn: the last line I can read with certainty is 45, which begins KUR *a-mur-ra-a-a* ('the land Amurru'; Grayson 1991a: 226:28), but traces of lines 46 and 47 are visible, which would be equivalent to some part of line 29 of the throne-base text (Grayson 1991a: 226:29). The threshold has space for another 5 lines or so between line 47 and its south edge, but I can see no traces of signs beyond line 47.

Room G, Door *a*: Truncated Standard Inscription in 18 lines (fig. 98). The inscription ends with *it-muḫ* ('placed'; Grayson 1991a: 275:6). The titulary is abridged in the third generation.

Room G, Door *b*: There is no threshold slab in this doorway.

Room G, Door *c*: The inscription on this slab is almost wholly obliterated. Traces of signs are visible at the beginnings of at least three lines, but there is not enough for me to establish which text was used. The slab is relatively small and the vertical spacing of the traces suggests that the inscription originally occupied about 18 lines. Careful cleaning and lighting of this slab might reveal more traces of the inscription.

Room G, Door *d*: There is no threshold slab in this doorway.

Room H, Door *b*: Truncated Standard Inscription in 37 lines (fig. 99). The inscription seems to end with DINGIR.MEŠ GAL.MEŠ ('the great gods'; Grayson 1991a: 276:12). Line 27 begins "to the land Urartu." The titulary for the third generation in line 4 is badly worn but seems to be abridged.

Room H, Door *c*: Truncated Standard Inscription in 25 lines. The inscription stops with *ur-du-ti ú-pu-šú* ('they performed servitude'; Grayson 1991a: 276:12). Because this is the final word in the historical summary, this inscription ends at a natural break in the text. In line 3 the titulary is abridged in the third generation, and line 19 ends with "to the land Urartu."

Room H, Doors *d*, *e*: The threshold slabs in these doorways are uninscribed.

Room J, Door *a*: This threshold carries the Palace Wall Foundation Text (Grayson 1991a: 300, no. 34). The inscription, which gives the full text and is well-preserved, is in 13 lines.

Room J, niche in south wall: The inscribed slab on the floor here is not a threshold, because this is not a doorway but rather a niche pierced completely through the mudbrick wall and sealed off at the back by the wall slabs in Room H. The inscription, in 13 lines, is the Palace Wall Foundation Text (Grayson 1991a: 300, no. 34). The full text is carved on the slab.

Room M, Door *a*: This threshold carried the full Standard Inscription in 25 lines (fig. 100). The titulary of the third generation is given in full in line 2. In lines 10–11 it has the variant EN KUR *ni-rib*(!) (11) *šá bi-ta-ni* ('to the interior of the land Nirib') instead of "to the land Urartu" (Grayson 1991a: 275, note to line 9).

Room M, niche in north wall: The slab on the floor in this deep niche is inscribed with the full Standard Inscription in 32 lines (fig. 101). The titulary of the third generation is given in full in line 2. At the end of line 12 is EN KUR *ni-rib šá bi-ta-ni* ('to the interior of the land Nirib') instead of "to the land Urartu" (Grayson 1991a: 275, note to line 9).

Room N, door to Room P: Truncated Standard Inscription in 34 lines (fig. 102). The inscription ends with *ṣa-lu-lu* UB.MEŠ ('protection of the (four) quarters'; Grayson 1991a: 276:13). The titulary of the third generation is abridged in line 3. Line 21 ends "to the land Urartu."

Room O, Door *a*: This threshold displays the Palace Wall Foundation Text (Grayson 1991a: 300, no. 34). The inscription has the complete text in 13 lines. Only the beginnings and ends of the lines are well-preserved.

Room R, Door *a*: The text on this threshold is the Palace Wall Foundation Text (Grayson 1991a: 300, no. 34). The inscription, which gives the full text and is very well-preserved, is in 12 lines (fig. 103).

Room S, Door *a*: Truncated Standard Inscription in 46(+?) lines (fig. 104). The titulary of the third generation is abridged in line 4. Line 37 should contain the reference to "Urartu" or "the interior of the land Nirib," but the slab has a large crack here and I cannot make out any traces from the photograph. The last words I can make out are [*ana*] *mi-[iṣ]-ri* [KUR-*a*] *ú-ter* ('I brought within the boundaries of my land'; Grayson 1991a: 275:11) in line 46. This may be the end of the inscription, because I do not see any further lines. Paley and Sobolewski (1987: 36) give the dimensions of the slab as 2.53 × 0.91 meters.

Room S, Door *b*: Truncated(?) Standard Inscription in 21+ lines. The latter half of the inscription is very eroded. The last word I can read with confidence is *mul-tar-[ḫi]* ('the rebellious'; Grayson 1991a: 275:4) at the end of line 11, but there are traces of signs for at least another 10 lines. The titulary for the third generation in line 4 seems to be abridged, but I cannot be certain. Cleaning and controlled lighting might show more of the inscription. Paley and Sobolewski (1987: 36) give the dimensions of the slab as 1.39 × 1.74 meters.

Room S, Doors *c*, *d*, *e*: There are no threshold slabs in these doorways.

Room T, Door *a*: Truncated Standard Inscription in 24 lines (fig. 105), concluding with UN.MEŠ ('people'; Grayson 1991a: 276:11). In line 3 the titulary is abridged in the third generation. Line 19 begins "to the land Urartu."

Room U, Door *a*: This threshold displays the Palace Wall Foundation Text (Grayson 1991a: 300, no. 34). The inscription has the complete text in 12 lines. The plan of Paley and Sobolewski shows a doorsill with a cutout for a single doorpost adjacent to the north side of this threshold (fig. 7). There is no indication whether this sill is inscribed.

Room V, Door *a*: Layard did not copy the full inscription on this threshold or give the number of lines. He did identify it as a duplicate of the Standard Inscription on Slab 1 of Room I and noted that it ended with KUR *la-qe-e* ('the land Laqû') in line 8 of that text (Layard, Ms A, p. 131; Grayson 1991a: 275:8). In addition, he listed a single variant from the Room I text, apparently either a scribal or copyist's error. The inscription evidently had an abridged genealogy in the third generation and concluded well before the Nirib/Urartu reference.

Room W(?), Door b(?): See "Unknown 2" below.

Room Z, door to Court Y: The threshold slab in this door is uninscribed, being carved instead with a floral pattern. In its present form it presumably dates to the time of Sargon II's restorations in this area (Paley and Sobolewski 1987: 59).

Room BB(WK), Door *f*: A large inscribed slab was found in front of Door *f* in Room BB(WK). According to Paley and Sobolewski, it was inscribed with the first two-thirds of the annalistic account of Assurnasirpal II's first year, from the beginning of the account through *ú-še-rib* 'I caused to enter', probably preceded by the very short titulary found also on the threshold of Room B, Door *c* (Paley and Sobolewski 1987: 72; Grayson 1991a: 196:i:43 through 199:i:83). The slab seems to be in secondary context: not only is it wider than Door *f* and slightly off-center, but the inscription is not oriented in the usual way relative to the doorway, because it begins at the northeast corner of the slab, with its lines running from north to south. According to the plan of Meuszynski and Sobolewski, the slab measures approximately 4.1 × 2.6 meters (fig. 7). If it is a threshold slab, then it is the second-to-largest one known in the palace; only the slab (now lost) originally in Room B, Door *e* could have been bigger. Considering its size and present location, the most likely original location for this slab would have been in the hypothetical Door *e* in Room BB(WK), which was apparently the central doorway in a monumental exterior façade similar in appearance to the Room B façade.

West Wing, other thresholds: I have not visited the West Wing and so have no records of inscribed thresholds in that area. Paley and Sobolewski (1987: 65, 71; fig. 7) reported thresholds in situ in Doors *a* and *d* of Room WH and in Door *a* of Room A. The latter threshold had a sill with cutouts for two doorposts adjacent to its west side. In addition, a slab that may be part of a doorsill was found just inside Door *g* of Room WG. Paley and Sobolewski do not say whether any of these slabs were inscribed.

Unknown 1: Paley (1989) published three inscribed slabs—two doorpost seats, between which was a narrow doorsill—all apparently from the same doorway, though their original location is unknown. Each slab was inscribed on both its obverse and reverse. The reverse of all three slabs carried a brief inscription giving the genealogy of Assurnasirpal, and the seats add the statement that these slabs were for the "second house" (É 2–*e*; Paley 1989: 138–39:A–C; Grayson 1991a: 356, no. 103; 358, no. 106. Grayson's statement that no. 106 was on the "obverse" is incorrect.). The obverse of all the slabs was carved with the beginning of the Standard Inscription, concluding with the genealogy (abridged titles in the third generation) on the seats and running slightly further, through 'peoples' (UN.MEŠ) on the sill (Paley 1989: 139–40:D–F; Grayson 1991a: 275:3, 356–57, no. 104). On the basis of the combined width of the three slabs, Paley suggested that the ensemble was the right size for Door *f* in Room F but added that they could also have originated in any other doorway of similar size and suggested S-*e*, WG-*g*, WK-*c*, and WH-*a* as possibilities (Paley 1989: 137).[2]

Unknown 2: A photo I took in 1989 shows a narrow inscribed Assurnasirpal palace threshold that I did not rephotograph in 1990 (fig. 106). Unfortunately, I did not note the location at the time, but it is among photos taken in the environs of Room S, so by a process of elimination it seems likely that it is from Room W, Door *b*, which apparently has a stone threshold (fig. 7). The text is a truncated Standard Inscription. My photograph shows only the final 15 lines, but from the line length it appears that the total number of lines is about 27. The inscription ends with *áš-gu-um* ('I thundered'; Grayson 1991: 275:8).

Unknown 3: Layard found at least one inscribed Assurnasirpal II threshold reused as a wall slab in the Southwest Palace at Kalhu (Layard 1849a: vol. 1, 35; vol. 2, 33). He copied but did not publish the inscription, which covered the whole slab (Layard, Ms A, 29–30). Its text is the truncated Standard Inscription in 34 lines, concluding with [. . . *aš*]+˹*šur*˺-[PAB-A] NUN-*ú* ('Ashur[nasirpal],

---

2. A doorpost seat is currently in situ at the south end of the east bull in doorway F-*f* (Agha and al-Iraqi 1976: fig. 14). This seems to be an unlikely original arrangement, however, since the doorpost would block the front of the colossus. This seat is not visible in the excavation photograph of the door (ibid., fig. 13), nor is it shown on the plan by Paley and Sobolewski (1987: plan 2), and it may have been moved to this position for display in the course of the modern restoration. Whether there could originally have been a sill and doorpost seats at the north side of this door, where there is now a stairway, seems to me uncertain.

prince'; Grayson 1991a: 276:12). Layard noted that there were an additional 5 or 6 lines that he did not copy because they were illegible. The inscription seems to have been in generally good condition, and the slab was apparently not trimmed at the sides, because the beginnings and ends of most lines are preserved. The titulary in the third generation is abridged in line 4. Line 25 ends "to the land Ura[rtu]."

Catalog 3

Sennacherib
Colossus Inscriptions

Inscriptions for which the location is known with some degree of certainty are listed by room and door or slab number, followed by a list of inscriptions for which the context is uncertain. All room, door, and slab designations are taken from Layard's second plan of Sennacherib's palace. Because the bull texts have not for the most part been adequately edited and because these accounts may provide evidence for the date that the bulls were inscribed, significant variants are listed here.

Court H, Door c

Three Sennacherib bull inscriptions were published by Layard in *Inscriptions in the Cuneiform Character* (1851; hereafter ICC), which went to press in 1850 while Layard was absent on his second campaign in Assyria (Layard 1851: "foreword"). Therefore, none of the inscriptions Layard found during his second campaign could have been included in the book, and the bull inscriptions published therein must derive from doors discovered during the first campaign: Court H, Door c; Room I, Doors d and e; and Court VI, Door a.[1]

The heading of ICC 38–42, the best preserved of Sennacherib's colossus inscriptions, gives its original location as "Entrance c, Chamber B" (later Room I, Door c; Galter, Levine, and Reade 1986: 30, no. 5). These bulls are still in situ, though more fragmentary than in Layard's day, and it is clear from their remains that Layard's identification of this inscription is correct (fig. 107). It is devoted entirely to an account of the building of the Southwest Palace. Layard's original copy is British Museum, Western Asiatic Antiquities, Ms A, 141–48. The text is

---

1. First designated Room B, Doors *a*, *b*, and *c*, and Room C, Door *b* (Layard 1849a: vol. 2, opp. 124). Layard's original copies, on which the ICC publication is based, are preserved in Layard, Ms A.

transliterated and translated as "Il" in Luckenbill (1924: 21, 117–25) and analyzed by Frahm (1997: 118, "T 30"). The inscription consisted of 106 lines distributed as follows:

Column i:	29 lines under belly of bull 1	(ICC 38–39)
Column ii:	24 lines between hind legs of bull 1	(ICC 39–40)
Column iii:	24 lines between hind legs of bull 2	(ICC 40–41)
Column iv:	29 lines under belly of bull 2	(ICC 41–42)

Apart from the unusual introduction (lines 1–6), the most significant difference between this text and that of ICC 59–62 (from Room I, Door *d*; see below) is in the lengths given for the palace extension, 454 cubits (bull 1, line 16); and the entire palace, 914 cubits (bull 1, line 19). Frahm (1997: 118, 271–72) has suggested that "454" here should be emended to "554," as in Bull 12 from the Court H façade (see below), sensibly observing that 554 added to 360, the length of the old palace, results in the total length of 914 cubits claimed for the new palace.[2] These dimensions are found in what are apparently the later bull inscriptions from the Southwest Palace, notably in the inscriptions from Court H, Door *a*— which contains an account of the first six campaigns plus a very similar building account—and the Court H Façade Bulls (see below).

Court H, Door *a*

A single bull inscription from the Southwest Palace was published in Rawlinson's *Cuneiform Inscriptions of Western Asia*, vol. III, plates 12–13 (1870; hereafter IIIR, 12–13; Galter, Levine, and Reade 1986: 28, no. 1). The inscription consists of an annalistic account of Sennacherib's first six campaigns, followed by a palace-building account. The text is transliterated and translated as "F1" by Luckenbill (1924: 21, 66–76, 117–25), where the historical portion is presented in full, while the building account is given only as variants of "Il" (Court H, Door *c*). It is analyzed by Frahm (1997: 116–18, "T 29"). The slabs bearing the original inscription are now in the British Museum (fig. 108). In IIIR, 12–13, this inscription is allotted 162 lines, but it actually occupied 164 lines, distributed as follows:[3]

Slab 1 (WA 118815a and b): 46 lines under belly of bull facing left
(2.86 m. wide)

---

2. Layard's hand copy (Ms A, 142:16) clearly reads "454." In my oblique photograph of this bull from 1989, the signs in question are well preserved and appear to read "454." This should be collated on-site if the bull hasn't been destroyed.

3. Dimensions from Bezold 1890: vol. 2, 81 n. 1. IIIR, 13, omits two fragmentary lines at the bottom of Slab 3. The true length of this portion of the inscription was noted by Paterson (1915: 2).

Slab 2 (WA 118821):   39 lines between hind legs of same
                            (1.67 m. wide)
Slab 3 (WA 118819):   34 (+2 missing) lines between hind legs of
                            bull facing right (1.71 m. wide)
Slab 4 (WA 118817):   43 lines under belly of same (2.92 m. wide)

Layard (1853a: 138) mentioned two distinct bull texts that record the first six campaigns plus building activity: the pair of bulls in the central portal of the throne room and those on the two pairs of bulls on the façade to either side of this door. The remains in situ prove that the text on the façade bulls was not IIIR, 12–13. The heading of IIIR, 12 assigns the inscription merely to "the Kouyunjik Bulls" but a letter from Rawlinson is more specific, saying it derived from "the large bulls at the grand entrance," while an original British Museum inventory describes the inscribed slabs WA 118815/17/19/21 as "from Bull on E. side of Grand Entrance to South Palace" and "Do. Do. from Bull on W. side."[4] These descriptions can refer only to what Layard (1853a: 138) called "the great bulls forming the centre portal of the grand entrance," that is, the bulls of Room I, Door *a*. Layard stated here that the bulls in this door carried an inscription of 152 lines, but this figure may be a misprint for 162, the length of the IIIR, 12–13 inscription as published. The bases of these two bulls, from which the British Museum inscribed panels were sawn, are still in situ. The base of the bull facing left, which is preserved to its full length, measures 652 cm. The combined length of WA 118815 plus 118821, which came from this bull, is 453 cm. This represents the length only of the inscribed portion. To it must be added the length of the uninscribed portion (three legs and the tail), which would give a total length consistent with that of the preserved base. A comparison of text and lineation shows that George Smith's "Bull 4" is the same inscription as IIIR, 12–13 (G. Smith 1878: 3–4, 32–34, 51, 53, 65–67, 77–78, 84–85, 89–98).

The historical section of this bull inscription is the only published example from the Southwest Palace in annalistic form, instead of the more common historical resume. As the only surviving copy of the edition of the annals compiled during the sixth campaign, it is of considerable historiographic importance. Levine (1982: 41–48) pointed out that the IIIR, 12–13 inscription recounts only the first phase of the sixth campaign as it is known from later editions of the annals and argues that this text must therefore have been composed while the sixth campaign was still in progress (probably in mid-to-late 694 B.C.). He also observed that at this point in the narrative of the sixth campaign the Nebi Yunus inscription shifts from the first-person singular (Sennacherib) to third person plural (Assyrian army), suggesting that Sennacherib was no longer with his army.

---

4. Rawlinson, letter of December 1, 1854, now in the British Museum, Department of Western Asiatic Antiquities. Both the letter and the inventory were brought to my attention by Dr. Julian Reade (personal communication, letter of August 2, 1983).

Perhaps the king's return to Nineveh, if he did return at this time, was the stimulus for the composition of this new edition of the annals.[5]

The building section is largely the same as that of ICC 38–42 (Court H, Door c), with the following important variants (page and line numbers from Luckenbill 1924, in parenthesis):

IIIR, 13, Slab 3:21: The introduction of ICC 38–42 is omitted. The conclusion of the historical section is followed by *i-na u₄-me-šú-ma* ('at that time . . .') and then commences with É.GAL MURUB₄ URU *ša* NINA.KI ('the palace inside the city of Nineveh'; 117:7).

IIIR, 13, Slab 3:32–Slab 4:1: The inscription is fragmentary here, but it is clear from the surviving signs that this passage varies significantly from ICC 38–42. Beginning in the middle of line 32, the surviving signs are as follows: *ša* ÍD *te-bil-ti* [ca. 20 signs missing] *ú-še-šir mu-ṣu-*[ca. 20 signs missing]-*ma* GI.MEŠ *a-*[ca. 70 signs missing] *a-na si-ḫi-ir-ti-šu i-na* 190 *ti-ib-ki ul-la-a re-ši-šu*. These signs and spaces do not fit the passage in the same position in ICC 38–42 (118:15–119:17). They do, however, fit the more detailed description of the same subject, the palace terrace extension, in the building description found on Sennacherib foundation prisms recording the first five campaigns (105:85–106:6; Heidel 1953: 156:22–34). The dimensions of the terrace extension are unfortunately lost, but they should be 554 by 289 cubits, as in Façade Bull 12 (see below), since further along in Slab 4, line 1, the total length of the palace is given as 914 cubits.

IIIR, 13, Slab 4:1: The inscription here omits the passage from *ana la-ba-riš* (119:18) to *šu-pu-uk-šú* (119:19), which describes the limestone facing wall built to protect the terrace foundation.

IIIR, 13, Slab 4:2–4: The passage here describing the materials used in building the palace is not taken from the edition of ICC 38–42, which reads: É.GAL NA₄.DÚR.MI.NA.BÀN.DA . . . GIŠ *e-lam-ma-ku* . . . *ab-ni-ma*: 'A palace of breccia, (numerous other materials), and *elammakku*-wood . . . I built (119:20–22).' Rather, it is the more comprehensive list that appears in the building account preserved on foundation prisms recording the first five campaigns: É.GAL.MEŠ KÙ.GI KÙ.BABBAR ZABAR NA₄.AN.ZA.GUL.ME NA₄.DÚR.MI.NA.BÀN.DA . . . GIŠ *e-lam-ma-ku* GIŠ *si-in-da-a* . . . *ab-ni-ma* 'Palaces of gold, silver, copper, carnelian(?), breccia . . . , *elammakku*-wood, and *sindu*-wood . . . I built' (106:14–20; Heidel 1953: 158:42–46).

5. Cf. Luckenbill 1924: 38:46, 76:101, 87:31. Two fragments apparently of this edition are British Museum, Department of Western Asiatic Antiquities, 1902-5-10,2 and Sm 2093 (Borger 1979: vol. 1, 65).

IIIR, 13, Slab 4:4: The structure in the form of a Hittite palace is referred to here not as a É *ap-pa-a-ti*, as in ICC 38–42 (119:22), but rather as a É *mu-ter-re-te*, as in accounts included with annals of the first five campaigns (106:20; Heidel 1953: 158:47).

Based on its inclusion of six campaigns and the total length of 914 cubits given for the palace, this inscription—like that on the bulls in Court H, Door *c* and Façade Bull 12—appears to be one of the latest accounts of the building of Sennacherib's palace. Despite this, the beginning of the building account, from IIIR, 13, Slab 3:21 to Slab 4:4, corresponds not to the text of Court H, Door *c* but rather to the somewhat different and more extended version found in foundation prisms recording only the first five campaigns. The remainder of the inscription, however, from Slab 4:4 to the end, does correspond to the Court H, Door *c* text, which diverges in several places from that of the five-campaign account.

Court H, Façade Bulls 1, 3, 10, 12

Layard (1853a: 138) reported: "On the four bulls of the façade were two in-scriptions, one inscription being carried over each pair, and the two being of pre-cisely the same import" (fig. 109, 110). This statement, which is incorrect, has caused much confusion (Russell 1985: 29–33, 36–40; Galter, Levine, and Reade 1986: 28–30). In fact, my examination of the remains of the inscriptions on Bulls 1, 3, and 12 showed that the same text was repeated on each of the four bulls.[6] Though the preserved remains are very fragmentary, enough has survived to en-able me to reconstruct a composite of the complete text, which begins with a brief historical summary of campaigns one through six (Luckenbill 1924: "F2", 76–78) and concludes with a palace-building account (unpublished). The build-ing account is similar to that in Court H, Door *c*, but it omits the descriptions of the transport of bull colossi from Tastiate, bronze casting, and the royal garden and dedication of the palace, and there are a number of variant passages (Luck-enbill 1924: 117:8–118:13, 122:14–26, 124:40–125:52), some of which are noted below.

Court H, Façade Bull 12
Column i, between the hind legs

In his *History of Sennacherib* (1878), George Smith published the historical portion of four Sennacherib bull inscriptions, which he designated "Bulls 1, 2, 3, and 4."[7] (It is important to distinguish Layard's designation of the façade bulls as Slabs 1, 3, 10, and 12, as in his final plan of the palace, from Smith's designations "Bulls 1, 2, 3, and 4," which bear no relationship to the slab numbers on Layard's

6. My preliminary transliterations of the surviving text on these three bulls is pub-lished in Russell 1998: 243–44.
7. Study: Frahm 1997: 113–16, "T 25–27."

plan. In the text that follows, I always place Smith's bull numbers in quotation marks and preface them with his name where necessary.)

Smith's "Bulls 1, 2, and 3" had differing amounts of the same text, while "Bull 4" contained a different, more comprehensive text. Unfortunately, Smith did not give the original location of any of these inscriptions, and only "Bulls 1 and 4" can be placed with certainty (see "Court H, Door *a*" above and "Ms D, Folios 24–29" below). "Bulls 2 and 3" were presented in a combined edition that uses the lineation (32 lines) and text of "Bull 3," with "Bull 2" indicated only as variants, without lineation.[8] As published by G. Smith (1878: 3, 30–31, 51–52, 67–68, 86, 88–89), this text consists of a summary account of the first six royal campaigns plus the two eponymous campaigns led by Sennacherib's generals. Smith's transliteration and translation were updated by Luckenbill (1924: 76–78) as text "F2." There is no indication of the state of preservation of either exemplar, so it is not possible to know if damaged passages in the text of "Bull 3" were restored from "Bull 2." Consequently, for "Bulls 2 and 3," the location and original state of the text are somewhat conjectural.

The original location of the "Bull 3" inscription may be deduced with reasonable certainty.[9] This historical summary is attested only on the façade bulls and under the belly of the west bull in Room I, Door *d*. The short lines in Smith's "Bull 3" inscription (10 to 15 signs/line in lines 1–10; 20–25 signs/line in lines 11–31) indicate that it was inscribed in the narrow triangular space between the hind legs of a bull.[10] Assuming that it is from one of the known bulls, it can only have come from Façade Bulls 3 or 12, where the inscription commenced between the hind legs. Part of the historical summary on Façade Bull 3 is preserved in situ, and its lineation differs slightly from that of Smith's "Bull 3," which by a process of elimination should therefore belong to Façade Bull 12. This assignment is consistent with Layard's drawing of the façade, which shows the beginning of the Façade Bull 12 inscription as intact (see fig. 110).[11] Façade Bull 3 as visible today, by contrast, is very fragmentary, and the fact that Layard did not draw this part of the façade suggests that it may always have been so (see fig. 109).

8. An examination of Smith's text for "Bulls 1 to 3" shows that, with the exception of the introductory passage, the lineation of "Bull 3" was used throughout. This is clear from comparison of the end of the "fifth" campaign (actually the second eponymous campaign) in line 25 and the beginning of the sixth campaign, also in line 25 (G. Smith 1878: 86, 88).

9. Study: Frahm 1997: 116, "T 27."

10. The brevity of line 32 (11 signs) shows that Smith gave only its historical portion (G. Smith 1878: 89). This would have been followed in the rest of the line by the first words of the building account, which continued at the top of Column ii.

11. Façade Bulls 10 and 12 have apparently been almost completely lost since Layard drew them. Of their inscriptions, none of that on 10 and only a small part of the the inscription on 12 are visible in situ today.

The lines at the beginning of Smith's "Bulls 1 and 3" seem to be about the same length, but the space allotted for the titulary on "Bull 3" is only six lines (the historical summary begins with line 7), while the "Bull 1" titulary required ten lines (G. Smith 1878: 3:1–10, 30:7). This suggests that the first four lines of the "Bull 3" titulary were completely lost and that Smith began numbering only with the preserved part.[12] Such extensive damage at the beginning of "Bull 3" would account for Smith's use of a different exemplar for the first ten lines. Since the building account in Façade Bulls 3 and 12 began in the last line of Column i, the original length of this column, including the four missing lines at the top, would have been 36 lines.

Column ii, under the belly

In *Die Bauinschriften Sanheribs* (1893: 3, pls. 6–8), Meissner and Rost published two fragmentary bull inscriptions, copied from paper casts in the British Museum, which they designated "Unnumbered Casts Nos. 1 and 2." Meissner and Rost provided no information on the dimensions or original location of these inscriptions, apart from stating that each was from the third slab of a bull inscription. In both cases, this is incorrect. The casts themselves were destroyed by Sidney Smith, who felt they had "outlived their usefulness" (Galter, Levine, and Reade 1986: 27).

The final 2–3 signs from each of the first 15 lines of Column ii survive in situ on a fragment of Façade Bull 12 (Russell 1998: 244, pl. 207). This fragment joins to the right side of Meissner and Rost's "Unnumbered Cast No. 2" (their pl. 8, hereafter MR 8; transliteration and translation: Russell 1985: 509–12; study: Frahm 1997: 119–20, "T 34") and gives the ends of its first 15 lines. The 17 partially preserved lines in this joined text are from an abridged version of the account of the building of the Southwest Palace. They parallel ICC 38:7–40:42 (Luckenbill 1924: 117:7 to 120:42), though the MR 8 text is somewhat abridged and entirely omits the description of bull transport from Tastiate (Luckenbill 1924: 118:9–13). Comparison with the lineation of the inscription on the other façade bulls suggests that Column ii of Façade Bull 12 was originally about 42 lines long. Passages of special interest in the MR 8 fragment are as follows:

> MR 8:2–3: All other preserved accounts of the building of the Southwest Palace reverse the order of these two passages, placing the reference to the previous kings *before* that to the destruction wrought by the Tebiltu River (Luckenbill 1924: 95:73–74; 99:45–46; 104:61 to 105:83; 117:8 to 118:14). The reference to the Tebiltu in line 2 uses the same wording as that of the earliest building account, written after Sennacherib's first campaign, which differs from all later accounts (Luckenbill 1924: 96:74).

12. This is further supported by the fact that no variants are listed for the first six lines of the "Bull 1" titulary (G. Smith 1878: 3:1–6).

MR 8:4: The broken *ul-[tu qa]-ʿbal*ʾ*-ti* URU at the end of this line indicates that the passage that follows, describing the rechanneling of the Tebiltu, is the version found in the building account that accompanies annals written soon after the fifth campaign (Luckenbill 1924: 105:86–87; Heidel 1953: 156:23–24).

MR 8:5: The adjective *katimti* ('hidden') occurs in this context only in building accounts dating to the time of the third campaign and earlier (Luckenbill 1924: 96:76 and 99:49). The text of line 5 has apparently been mistranslated by Luckenbill (1924: 99:48–49, 118:15) and the CAD (A/2 [1968] 349–50 s.v. *asurrakku*; E [1958] 357 s.v. *ešēru*; M/2 [1977] 249 s.v. *mūṣû* A), who associate the phrase *qereb katimti asurrakkīša* 'in its hidden depths' with the sentence that precedes it.[13] In fact, examination of building accounts written after the first and fifth campaigns shows that the phrase belongs with the sentence that follows (Luckenbill 1924: 96:75–76 and 105:87–88).

MR 8:6: The dimension of 554 cubits given here as the length of the palace platform extension is evidently the correct writing of the number written erroneously as 454 in the account from Court H, Door *c* (Frahm 1997: 118, 271–72).

MR 8:8: The total length of the palace given here, 914 cubits, is the dimension given also on the bulls in Court H, Doors *a* and *c*).

MR 8:9–10: The list of materials here is from the edition of the building account that usually accompanies annals recording five campaigns, found also in Court H, Door *a* (Luckenbill 1924: 106:14–18; Heidel 1953: 158:42–45).

MR 8:11: The "likeness of a Hittite palace" is here referred to as a *bīt muterrēti*, a term found only in accounts accompanying annals for the first five campaigns and in Court H, Door *a* (Luckenbill 1924: 106:20; Heidel 1953: 158:47).

MR 8:14–17: These lines duplicate, with some abridgments, the building accounts that accompany annals recording five and six campaigns (Luckenbill 1924: 107:40–53 and 120:28–42).

To summarize: this part of the Façade Bull 12 building account differs considerably from those on the other colossi in the throne room area. The dimensions given for the palace terrace and total length of the palace place this text in the latest group of bull inscriptions from the Southwest Palace, but the text intermixes passages both from the earliest and latest editions of the building account. Apparently all of these earlier versions were available to the Façade Bull text's compiler, who chose freely among them.

---

13. The passage seems to be translated correctly in CAD K [1971] 306 s.v. *katimtu*, though out of context.

Court H, Façade Bull 3

Parts of the last 19 lines of Column i, between the hind legs, and parts of the last 21 lines of Column ii, under the belly, survive in situ (see fig. 109; Russell 1998: 243–44, pls. 204–6). Column i, lines 1′–18a′ duplicate Smith's "Bull 3," lines 15–32, except that lines 8′–15′ are distributed slightly differently than their counterparts in Smith. Column i lines 18b′–19′ and Column ii lines 1′–21′ are parts of the abridged palace-building account that appeared also on the other façade bulls.

Façade Bull 3 seems to me to be a good candidate for George Smith's "Bull 2" (G. Smith 1878: 79, 86, 88; Frahm 1997: 115–16, "T 26"). According to Smith, "Bull 2" was a "fragment" that included at least parts of the titulary, the first five campaigns, and the two eponymous campaigns but omitted the sixth campaign. On Façade Bull 3, the part of Column i that is preserved in situ is broken off just above the sixth campaign, though it also includes the fragmentary beginnings of 11 lines recording the third and fifth campaigns. Therefore, if Façade Bull 3 is Smith's "Bull 2," the historical summary must have been taken from the part that is now broken away, which should have included the summary of the first five campaigns now missing from the remains in situ. Smith's omission of the sixth campaign from his "Bull 2" text could then be explained by assuming that he had no record of the remains in situ and so used only the now-missing fragment that contained only the part of the inscription preceding the sixth campaign. If this is the case, then the fragment itself, or a copy or cast of it, must have been available to Smith in the British Museum.

Though less likely, it is also possible that the bull inscription in Room I, Door *d*, which included the titulary and five campaigns and was definitely available to Smith, was his "Bull 2." The evidence for this possible identification is outlined under "Room I, Door *d*" below. If the Room I, Door *d* inscription was Smith's "Bull 2," then Façade Bull 3 would not have been utilized by Smith at all. Other possibilities for Smith's "Bull 2" are Façade Bulls 1 and 10. According to Layard's drawing, however, the sixth campaign should have been preserved on Façade Bull 10, which would be inconsistent with Smith's "Bull 2." Nothing is known about the inscription on Façade Bull 1, apart from my observations under that heading.

Court H, Façade Bull 1

Parts of the last 8 lines of Column i, under the belly, and parts of the first 6 and last 8 lines of Column ii, between the hind legs, survive in situ (see fig. 109; Russell 1998: 243, pls. 202–3). All belong to the abridged palace-building account that appeared also on the other façade bulls. An inscribed fragment in Hannover (see below) is probably either from this bull or from Façade Bull 10.

Court H, Façade Bull 10

Not a single fragment of the inscription from this bull is visible in situ today and no copy is known to exist. Layard's drawing of the bull shows the inscription as generally well-preserved but with the beginnings of the first twenty or so lines, presumably including the historical summary, lost (see fig. 110). This is a possible candidate, therefore, for Smith's "Bull 2," which is listed once as a "fragment" (G. Smith 1878: 79). If, however, the Façade Bull 10 inscription included six campaigns, as Layard reported and as was actually the case at least for Façade Bulls 3 and (apparently) 12, then according to Layard's drawing, at least part of the sixth campaign should have been preserved. Thus Façade Bull 10 should not be Smith's "Bull 2," which omits the sixth campaign entirely. An inscribed fragment in Hannover (see below) is probably either from this bull or from Façade Bull 1.

Room I, Door *d*

Layard's original copy of the inscription on the bulls in this door is British Museum, Department of Western Asiatic Antiquities, Ms A, 136–41 (studies: Galter, Levine, and Reade 1986: 30, no. 6; Frahm 1997: 115, "T 25"). It consists of a resume of Sennacherib's first five campaigns, followed by an account of the building of the Southwest Palace. Most of this text was published as ICC 59–62, which omitted 14 lines that are in the manuscript.[14] Luckenbill (1924: 20, 76–77, 117–24) listed only variants from this text, which he designated "E2." His edition contains several errors and does not indicate which parts of the text are missing. For a complete transliteration of ICC 59–62, see Russell (1985: 499–504).

Both Ms A, 136 and ICC 59 give its original location as "Entrance b, Chamber B" (later Room I, Door *d*). The same identification is supplied for an entirely different inscription, a variant of ICC 38–42, but that ascription is clearly erroneous (see Court VI, Door *a* below). There is good evidence, however, that the label on ICC 59–62 is correct. Concerning Room I, Door *d*, Layard says that "a considerable portion [of its inscription] remained entire" (Layard 1849a: vol. 2, 128), and the remains of Bull 2 from this door, as seen in King's photograph, seem consistent with ICC 59–62 (fig. 111). There seems to be no reason, therefore, to doubt Layard's assignment of ICC 59–62 to Room I, Door *d*. Unfortunately, these bulls have vanished completely since King's day.

The inscription apparently originally consisted of some 112 lines distributed over four panels, beginning under the belly of Bull 1 (ICC 61–62; 31 lines), then continuing between the hind legs of Bull 1 (ca. 25 lines; entirely lost), then between the hind legs of Bull 2 (ICC 59; 25 lines), and concluding under the belly

---

14. Layard's publisher omitted Layard, Ms A, 139, line 12 (from GIŠ *dup-ra-ni* to *ul-ziz-ma ša* ⌜*kúm*⌝*-me*; cf. Luckenbill 1924: 123:35–36), which should have been between ICC 60:36 and 37, and also the last 13 lines (Layard, Ms A, 140:19 to 141:31, from *šum-*⌜*mu*⌝*-ḫi* to the end; cf. Luckenbill 1924: 124:41–125:53).

of Bull 2 (ICC 60; 17 lines, plus 14 unpublished lines). Orthographic variants aside, ICC 59–62 differs from Court H, Door *c* as follows:

ICC 61:1–12: These lines, which consist of a short titulary and a resume of campaigns one to five, duplicate George Smith's "Bulls 2 and 3" (Luckenbill 1924: 76:1 to 77:23).

ICC 61:12: The historical resume apparently ends here, with the conclusion of the account of the fifth campaign, against Tumurra and Ukku. Then probably came *i-na u₄-me-šu-ma* 'at that time . . .'), followed by the building account.

ICC 62:23: The length of the extension added to the palace platform is given here as 340 cubits, instead of 554 cubits. This number added to 360, the length of the old palace, gives a total length of 700 cubits

ICC 62:27: The total length of the palace is given here as 7[oo] cubits, instead of 914 cubits.

It appears that this inscription is among the earlier bull inscriptions in the Southwest Palace. Its historical resume extends only through the fifth campaign, as compared with other examples that record six campaigns. Likewise, the palace measurements given correspond with those in Sennacherib foundation prisms that record five campaigns and are smaller than those given in bulls recording six campaigns (Luckenbill 1924: 105:91 and 106:11; Heidel 1953: 156:28 and 158:39).

Since George Smith's "Bulls 1 to 4" were based on slabs, casts, and copies in the British Museum, we would expect the five-campaign historical summary of ICC 59–62 to have been incorporated into his edition of "Bulls 1 to 3." ICC 59–62 could be the same as Smith's "Bull 2," which according to Smith included the first four royal campaigns and at least part of the fifth (G. Smith 1878: 3, 30–31, 51–52, 67–68, 86; Luckenbill 1924: 76:1 to 77:25).[15] His heading to the account of the fifth campaign refers to the "Bull 2" inscription as a "fragment" and ICC 61, which contains the portion of the text presented by Smith, is fragmentary (G. Smith 1878: 79).

Apart from this coincidence of length, the key to identifying this text would seem to be three variants from "Bull 2" that are listed in the transliteration of his primary exemplar, "Bull 3." If my identification of Ms D, fols. 24–29 as Smith's "Bull 1" is correct, then these variants ought to derive from his "Bull 2," unless he used additional—unacknowledged—inscriptions. All of the variants are near the beginning of the text, in the combined account of the first and fourth campaigns. Two of them—*ina ta-mir-ti kiš*.KI 'in the plain of Kish' (line 7) and *tar-bit*

---

15. Olmstead (1916: 45 n. 3) apparently considered the two to be the same inscription.

bir-ki-ia 'offspring of my loins' (line 11)—also occur in ICC 59–62. The other—
e-la-me-e 'Elam' (line 10)—does not (G. Smith 1878: 30–31). This discrepancy
seems to disqualify ICC 59–62 from being Smith's "Bull 2," unless we accept either that Smith here listed the variant as the primary exemplar and vice versa (a
supposition that is now unprovable) or that he introduced a variant from yet another text. Neither explanation seems consistent with Smith's apparent practice
elsewhere in this text edition, and so I am inclined to reject the identification of
ICC 59–62 with Smith's "Bull 2."

     If ICC 59–62 *is* Smith's "Bull 2," then his omission of a significant variant
must also be accounted for. This falls at the end of the Hezekiah episode. Smith's
"Bulls 2 and 3" end *ú-šak-niš še-pu-ú-a* ('I made him bow down at my feet'), while
ICC 59–62 has *še-pu-u-a ú-šak-niš-ma i-šá-ṭa ab-šá-a-[ni]* ('at my feet I made him
bow down, and he pulled my yoke'; G. Smith 1878: 68:21–22; Layard 1851: 61:
11). The absence of this variant from Smith's edition of "Bulls 2 and 3," however,
does not necessarily mean that ICC 59–62 cannot be "Bull 2." The very small
number of variants listed in Smith's edition of this text suggests that he was not
striving for a full listing of variants but rather included only those that give additional historical information. Despite this omission, therefore, it still seems possible that Smith's "Bull 2" could be ICC 59–62, though I prefer to identify it with
Façade Bull 3 and to suggest that he did not use ICC 59–62 at all in the compilation of his edition of "Bulls 1 to 3."

Room I, Door *e*

     Layard (1849a: vol. 2, 126) said that the bull inscription on Room I, Door *e*
"was so much defaced, that I was only able to copy a few lines of it." Layard's copy
is British Museum, Western Asiatic Antiquities, Ms A, 135–36 (unpublished).
The inscription evidently began under the belly of the south bull, continued between its hind legs, then between the hind legs of the north bull, and concluded
under its belly. Layard copied parts of the north bull only: the first three fragmentary lines of Column iii (followed by the notation "27 lines illegible—between
hind legs") and all of Column iv except for lines 13–15 and the last line, 33. The
portion he copied was from the long palace-building account. With the exception of minor orthographic variants, it duplicates the text on the bulls in Court
H, Door *c* and Room I, Door *d*. Indeed, each of the two preserved columns begins
and ends at exactly the same point as in Columns iii and iv of the bull in Room
I, Door *d* (ICC 59–60), though the lineation within Column iv is slightly different.[16] This close correspondence in the second halves of the two bull inscriptions
suggests that there should have been a similar correspondence in the first halves,

     16. Column iii, lines 1–3 parallel Luckenbill 1924: 121:49–50; iv, 1–32 parallel
idem, 122:23–52. The statement by Galter, Levine, and Reade (1986: 30) that "the line
numbering corresponds exactly to [the Room I, Door *d* bull]" is not quite correct.

in which case the Room I, Door *e* inscription would have begun with the same historical summary of the first five campaigns that was in Room I, Door *d* (ICC 61). Of the south bull, only the feet are preserved today (fig. 112). On the north bull both inscribed panels are still intact but are so badly worn that the inscription is largely illegible.

Court VI, Door *a*

This inscription, a near-duplicate of Court H, Door *c*, is devoted entirely to the building of the Southwest Palace (Galter, Levine, and Reade 1986: 30–31, no. 8; Frahm 1997: 118–19, "T 31"). Layard's original copy, which is British Museum, Western Asiatic Antiquities, Ms A, 148–51, provides a good example of Layard's method of copying duplicate texts. He began in the middle of the inscription, which he could not read, with Column iii, between the hind legs of his Bull 1, and copied all 22 lines in full. Layard's unusual numbering of the bulls in reverse order here follows the clockwise slab numbering pattern of Room C (later V). He then continued with Column iv, under the belly of the same bull, and copied the first 12 lines and part of line 13. At that point he apparently realized that this was a duplicate of the inscription in Court H, Door *c*, which he had just copied on the previous pages (Ms A, 141–48) and the full copy breaks off with the note: "rest compared with previous inscription—variants & restored passages noted beneath." Then he went back to p. 147, line 15 of the copy of Court H, Door *c* and began listing beneath each line the variants from Court VI, Door *a*. For lines 14 through 23(?) he listed only variants. He recommenced copying the full text near the end of line 24 (?; identified only as line 27 of Court H, Door *c*) and copied the next two lines (25–26?) in full, concluding this column with the note "last line [27?] destroyed."[17] He then turned to Column i (29? lines) on Bull 2, which was done entirely as a list of variants to Column i of the Court H, Door *c* inscription (pp. 141–44), and finally to Column ii (number of lines not known), which was listed the same way (pp. 144–45), except that the last four lines are given in full on p. 151.[18]

The text is published only as variants given as footnotes to ICC 38–42, and most of these variants are also listed in parenthesis by Luckenbill (1924: 117–25)

17. The lineation of Column iv after line 13 is not entirely certain since in the variant list Layard indicated line divisions for lines 14–21 but not 22–25. His full copy of the last lines does not give their line numbers but only says that it begins in line 27 of Court H, Door *c*. The pattern of line lengths, however, suggests that this would be line 24 in Court VI, Door *a*. Furthermore, since Column iii of Court VI, Door *a* is 2 lines shorter than its equivalent in Court H, Door *c*, the same could also well have been the case for Column iv, which would then have totaled 27 lines in Court VI, Door *a*.

18. The variant from line 7 given separately on p. 151 was also noted on the copy of Court H, Door *c* (p. 142).

in his transliteration and translation of ICC 38–42.[19] ICC 38–42 gives no indication of the lineation of the variant inscription. Layard's original copy only gives the lineation of Columns iii and iv, and these are the only parts of the inscription visible in situ today. Since the bull with Columns i and ii seems to have vanished completely, the number and distribution of lines in those columns may never be known. Though the texts of ICC 38–42 and its variant are in most respects the same, there are many orthographic variants, as well as three substantial differences. These latter are as follows:

> ICC 38, notes 14 and 15: The variant gives the length of the extension of the palace platform as 340 cubits, instead of 554.[20]

> ICC 39, note 4: The variant gives the total length of the palace as 900 cubits, instead of 914, and this is confirmed by Layard's manuscript copy. This needs to be collated against the original inscription because the expected value here would be 700 cubits.

> ICC 41, note 13: The variant omits the passage *áš-šu . . . uš-ziz* (ICC 41, lines 37–39) that describes well fittings.[21]

The measurements 340 and 700(?) cubits given here are of particular interest, because they are the ones found in building accounts that accompany the records of the first five campaigns and suggest that this inscription, like that in Room I, Door *d* is among the earlier bull inscriptions in the Southwest Palace.

The footnotes to ICC 38–42 state that the variant is from "Bulls at Entrance *b*, Chamber B," and Layard's original manuscript has the same heading. However, ICC 59–62 is also assigned by Layard to this location, apparently correctly so.

---

19. Variants listed in ICC 38–42 that are omitted by Luckenbill are (by page and line number in Luckenbill):

117:7:	*i-na* for *ina*
118:12:	*qí* for *qi*
118:16:	350 for 554
119:19:	900 for 914
119:21:	*ere$_4$-íni* for ERIN
121:52:	^{d}ALAD for ^{d}ÁLAD
124:37–39:	omits *áš-šú . . . uš-ziz*
124:39:	*ḫi-ir* for *ḫir*

In addition to these variants and those given in Luckenbill, there are 31 instances where the form of the sign was sufficiently different in the two inscriptions that Layard listed them as variants, though they were only variant forms of the same sign.

20. ICC 38, nn. 14 and 15 actually read "350," but Layard's manuscript has "340" (Ms A, 143:16).

21. In ICC 41:37, restore *ú-šá-[lik áš-šu u$_4$-me-šam-ma* A].MEŠ (Luckenbill 1924: 110:44 and 124:37) in the damaged area.

The inscription on the southeast bull from Room I, Door *b* (later Court VI, Door *a*) is still intact today, and comparison between it and Layard's manuscript for the ICC 38–42 variant shows that they are one and the same (fig. 113).

Room LX, Door *a*

Layard's only published comment on this doorway was that it contained "a pair of winged bulls" (Layard 1853a: 460). His copy of the inscription on the north bull is British Museum, Western Asiatic Antiquities, Ms C, 56 verso–57 verso (unpublished; Galter, Levine, and Reade 1986: 31, no. 22; Frahm 1997: 120–21, "T 35"). There seems to be no record of the inscription on the south bull. The inscription was apparently distributed in the usual way, beginning under the belly of the south bull, continuing between its hind legs, then continuing between the hind legs of the north bull, and concluding under its belly. Layard's copy gives the last 19 lines of column iii, between the hind legs, from [*tab*]-*ra-a-ti* to *bur-zi-gal-li*, and the last 13 lines of column iv, under the belly, from ⟨d⟩ÀLAD.dLAMMA.MEŠ to *i-da-a-šá*, the end of the inscription (though not a duplicate of Luckenbill 1924: "I1", the equivalent passages are 120:27–121:47, 123:31–125:53.). As far as it is preserved, this inscription is a close duplicate of the text on the Court H façade bulls (see above). Since the part Layard copied is equivalent to about half of the Court H façade text, it is probable that the first half of that text, including its historical summary, was on the south bull.

Court LXIV, Door *a*

Of this doorway, Layard reported only that it was "formed by winged lions" (Layard 1853a: 584). His copy of its inscription, which gives parts of Columns i and ii and all of iii and iv, is British Museum, Western Asiatic Antiquities, Ms C, 55 verso–56 verso (study: Frahm 1997: 121, "T 36"). The inscription began under the belly of the south lion (10 fragmentary lines, upper part lost), continued between its hind legs (12 lines, upper part lost), continued between the hind legs of the north lion (all 17 lines preserved), and concluded under its belly (all 21 lines preserved). Most of the text was published in transliteration by Borger, though the 8 lines at the top of Ms C 56 verso were omitted.[22] Galter, Levine, and Reade

---

22. Borger 1988: 9–10. The omitted lines are as follows:

5″. LÚ.SANGA-*ti-ia na-bu-ú* MU-*ia giš-maḫ-ḫi*
6″. GIŠ *ere₄-íni ša ul-tu* UD.MEŠ *ru-qu-ú-ti*
7″. *i-ši-ḫu-ma ik-bi-ru ma-gal qé-reb* KUR *si-ra-ra*
8″. *šad-di-i i-na pu-uz-ri na-an-zu-zu*
9″. *ú-šak-li-mu-in-ni ṣi-⌈i⌉-su-un*
10″. *ša* NA₄.GIŠ.NU₁₁.GAL *ša ina tar-ṣi* LUGAL.MEŠ
11″. AD.MEŠ-*ia a-na kar-ri nam-ṣa-ri šu-qu-ru*
12″. *sa-pan* KUR *am-ma-na-na ú-šap-tú-ni pa-⌈ni⌉-[šu]*

(1986: 32) published a translation of the unique concluding passage, which identifies this part of the palace as the residence of Sennacherib's beloved queen,
Tashmetum-sharrat. The preserved part of the text, which contains most of the
building account, roughly parallels the text of Court H, Door *c* but omits the descriptions of bronze casting, the royal garden, and the dedication of the palace,
and many of the remaining passages are abridged or rearranged.[23] Assuming that
Columns i and iv were roughly the same length, the 11 or so lines missing from
the beginning of the inscription could only have held a short titulary and the beginning of the building account. There is no room for a historical summary.

Sennacherib's "Eastern Building"

Thompson published two large fragments from a bull colossus in the "Eastern
Building," which was probably part of the eastern end of Sennacherib's palace.[24]
The fragments, which join, contain part of the palace-building account, specifically a unique list of the palace building stones and their beneficial properties. I
excavated seven further fragments of this inscription at Nineveh in 1989, and
nine more exist in copies by King and Thompson in the British Museum archives. These will be published in the Nineveh excavations final report.

Colossus Inscriptions of Uncertain Provenience
Ms D, Folios 24–29

British Museum, Department of Western Asiatic Antiquities, Departmental
Archives, Ms D, is a box that contains 44 loose sheets, mostly hand copies of cuneiform inscriptions, many of them apparently in Layard's hand. Folios 24–29 are
unbound copies of one complete Sennacherib bull inscription and part of another.
With the exception of fols. 26–27 and the first ten lines of fol. 24, they are unpublished. The copies are numbered "1" to "4" and the first sheet (fol. 24) is labeled
"From Kouyunjik (copied from paper impression sent by C[?] N. Williams)."[25]

---

23. The preserved part begins with [*ul*]-*la-a re-ši-šu* ('I raised its top'; cf. Luckenbill
1924: 119:18).

24. Location: Russell 1991: 82–86. Text: Thompson and Hutchinson 1929b: pl. LII,
nos. 122, M+N. Edition: J. M. Russell, "Sennacherib's Palace without Rival Revisited:
Excavations at Nineveh and in the British Museum Archives," in *Assyria 1995*, ed.
S. Parpola and R. M. Whiting (Helsinki, 1997) 299–301. Study: Frahm 1997: 121–22,
"T 37." Note that the end of the translation in my edition should be emended to read:
"*girimḫilibû* stone, the color of which is like that of the pomegranate, beautiful and a
pleasure to behold. . . ."

25. The American missionary W. F. Williams was in the area from 1851–71 and
sent sculptures from Nimrud to America in the early 1850s, but I cannot reconcile his
initials with those on Ms D, fols. 23 and 24 (Stearns 1961: 8–16).

The original location of the inscriptions is not given, but Meissner and Rost identified it as from a bull (see below). The handwriting and form of the cuneiform signs appear to be Layard's.

Folios 24–28 give the full text of an inscription in three columns. Column i (24 lines; fols. 24–25, both numbered "1") begins "Palace of Sennacherib." There follows a brief titulary and the beginning of Sennacherib's palace-building account. The lines are short, averaging 5 signs/line in the first five lines, 8 signs/line in the next five, and 10–11 signs/line in the remainder. It is clear from the short lines, especially those at the beginning of the column, that this part of the text was originally carved in the roughly triangular space between the legs of the colossus.

Column ii (30 lines; fols. 26–27, both numbered "2") is the continuation of the palace-building account. Its lines are longer than those of Column i, averaging 20 signs/line, and the lines are roughly the same length throughout. The greater number of lines and their greater length, when compared with Column i, indicate that this part of the text was carved in the space under the belly of the colossus. Near the ends of the first two lines is a gap, inside which is the notation: "sculpture?" Because no signs are missing, I assume that this is the point where the penis of the figure penetrates the inscription, and so I am inclined to accept Meissner and Rost's (1893: 3) identification of this colossus as a bull. Column ii is the only part of this inscription that has been published; the cast from which this copy was made is the "Unnumbered Cast No. 1" of Meissner and Rost (1893: pls. 6 and 7; Galter, Levine, and Reade 1986: 32; transliteration and translation: Russell 1985: 505–8). There are a few very minor differences between the text as copied in Layard, Ms D, 26–27 and in Meissner and Rost 1893: pls. 6–7. All of these are apparently errors made by one or the other of the modern copyists.

Column iii (23 lines; fol. 28r and v, 28r numbered "3") gives the conclusion of the building account. Its line lengths follow the pattern of Column i but are somewhat longer, averaging 6 signs/line in the first five lines, 14 signs/line in the next five, and 17 signs/line for the remainder. As with Column i, the pattern of line lengths in Column iii indicates that it was carved in the triangular space between the legs of the colossus, but in this case the space was evidently somewhat wider.

The inscription is an abridged account of the building of Sennacherib's palace at Nineveh. This text contains the same basic information and much of the same wording that is found in the Court H, Door c bull but, because it omits numerous subsidiary clauses and the descriptions of the transport of bull colossi from Tastiate, bronze casting, and the royal garden and dedication of the palace, it occupies considerably less space (Luckenbill 1924: 117:8–118:13, 122:14–26, 124:40–125:52). Passages of particular interest in the portion published by Meissner and Rost are:

Lines 3–4: The dimensions of the new palace given here are 700 by 440 great cubits and correspond to those given in building accounts accompanying annals for the first five campaigns (Luckenbill 1924: 105:91 and 106:11; Heidel 1953: 156:28 and 158:39).

Lines 23–24: "Bull colossi and sphinxes of alabaster, and slabs of alabaster, together with slabs of excellent breccia—both (types of) stone I quarried from their mountain." This passage clearly indicates the identity of the two stones that were quarried. The meaning of the equivalent passage on the bulls in Court H, Door *c* is rendered unclear by its convoluted structure.[26]

The titulary, in 10 well-preserved lines, is identical in text and lineation to George Smith's "Bull 1," and since these sheets were copied from casts in the British Museum, there can be little doubt that this cast was indeed Smith's "Bull 1" (G. Smith 1878: 3:1–10; Luckenbill 1924: 76:1–6). The absence of a historical summary in this inscription explains why Smith referred to it only for the titulary and did not mention it thereafter.

Ms D, folio 29 (numbered "4") is a fragment from Column iii(?) of another, apparently very similar colossus inscription. Both the beginning and end of the column are missing in the fragment. Parts of 15 lines are preserved, most of them nearly complete. Lines 2′–5′ average 8 signs/line (most of 1′ is lost), while the remainder average 12 signs/line. Except for different lineation and four minor orthographic variants, the fragment is an exact duplicate of Ms D, fol. 28, lines 12–21. Assuming consistent line lengths, this column would have needed four more lines to accommodate the conclusion of the text. The length and pattern of distribution of the lines in this fragment are very similar to that of Ms D, fols. 24–25, and I therefore suggest that this text was carved in a space of similar size and shape between the legs of a colossus. If so, then there must originally have been about five very short lines of text before the preserved part.

These two colossus inscriptions raise some interesting problems. The distribution of the text across three panels is unique for Sennacherib colossi, the known examples of which either have the text carved in two panels on a single colossus or in four panels distributed between a pair of colossi. The fact that the two panels from between the legs were apparently of significantly different widths, as evidenced by the greatly different line lengths between the two, is also unusual, because in other Sennacherib inscriptions carved across a pair of colossi, the spaces between the rear legs of two colossi in a pair are the same size. Further-

---

26. ^{d}ÀLAD.^{d}LAMMA.MEŠ MUNUS.ÁB.ZA.ZA-*a-ti* NA$_4$.GIŠ.NU$_{11}$.GAL *ù* KUN$_4$.MEŠ NA$_4$.GIŠ.NU$_{11}$.GAL *a-di* KUN$_4$.MEŠ NA$_4$.DÚR.MI.NA.BÀN.DA *ṣi-ra-a-ti ab-ni ki-lal-la-an ina šad-di-šú-un ab-tuq-ma*. The translation in Luckenbill—'Great slabs of breccia I fashioned and cut free on both sides, in their mountain'—is incorrect (1924: 121:i:51 to ii:8). CAD K [1971] 354, s.v. *kilallān* a, 1′, e′ translates: "I cut out both stones in their quarry," and the MR 6–7 text confirms this reading.

more, if this inscription were carved on a pair of colossi, its arrangement would have been unique, beginning between the hind legs on one colossus, continuing under the belly of one of them while the space under the belly of the other was left blank, and concluding between the hind legs of the other. Finally, the very great similarity in size and content between Column iii of the complete inscription and the fragment of Ms D, fol. 29, as well as the labels and numbers on the sheets, which seem to indicate that they belong together, suggest to me that the two separate inscriptions derive from a single pair of colossi.

To me, the only way to account for all of this is to suggest that the two inscriptions were carved on a pair of five-legged colossi. Though no such creatures have been reported in Sennacherib's palace, this does not rule out the possibility that one or more pairs were present; many of the colossi shown on Layard's plan were not even mentioned in his texts, let alone described. In this case, the complete inscription of Ms D, fols. 24–28 would have commenced in the narrow triangular panel between the front legs of a bull facing left, continued in the rectangular space under its belly, and concluded in the somewhat broader triangular space between its hind legs. The missing first two columns of the other inscription would have begun between the hind legs of the other colossus, which faced right, continued under its belly, and the third column—partially preserved as Ms D, fol. 29—would have concluded between its front legs.

In the absence of any published information on the original location of this bull text, no final determination is possible. There is some evidence, all of it circumstantial, that may permit the suggestion of a tentative location. Layard's final plan of Sennacherib's palace shows many colossi in addition to those in the area of the throne room, and most or all of these were presumably inscribed, but his published works mention only two of these inscriptions. One, on a pair of lion colossi in Court XIX, Door *a*, was "nearly illegible," however, and in any case, Ms D, fols. 24–28 seems to have been on a bull, not a lion (Layard 1853a: 230). The other inscribed bulls were in Court VI, Door *k*, and according to Layard (1853a: 71), their inscription was "nearly entire." There is no other published record of this inscription, but it could well be the one preserved in Ms D, fols. 24–29. The other bull inscription known to be from Court VI, that in Door *a*, also gives the palace length as 700 cubits, in contrast to the 914 cubits given on the colossi of the throne room façade. This hardly constitutes proof, however, particularly in light of Layard's failure to mention in print at least two other bull inscriptions, those from Room LX and Court LXIV. In addition, Layard's final plan shows that he excavated at least eleven additional pairs of colossi, besides those discussed here.[27] The inscriptions of Ms D, Fols. 24–29 could presumably

27. Eleven further pairs of colossi: Court VI, Doors *d* and *g*; Court XIX, Doors *a*, *h*, and *l*; Room XXIV, Door *c*; Room XXXIII, Door *p*; Room XXXIV, Doors *b* and *l*; West Façade, two pairs of façade bulls (Layard 1853a: opp. 67).

have been associated with any of these. Until further evidence comes to light, then, the original location of these unusual inscriptions must remain conjectural.

The Hannover Bull

A fragment of a Sennacherib bull inscription containing parts of nine lines is in the Kestner Museum, Hannover (no. 1891; photograph: Unger 1926: Taf. 61b). The preserved text includes parts of the first/fourth, second, third, fifth, and sixth campaigns (transliteration: Russell 1985: 513; cf. Luckenbill 1924: 77:14 to 78:28; Frahm 1997: 116, "T 28"), and is an exact duplicate of Smith's "Bull 3" (Court H, Façade Bull 12). The fragment appears to have been trimmed on three sides, evidently to highlight the name of Hezekiah of Judah. The lines of the Hannover bull inscription are relatively long, averaging 40 characters per line. The entire historical portion of the inscription can therefore have occupied no more than fourteen and a half lines of Column i, under the belly of a bull that faced left. The remainder of the inscription was presumably devoted to a building account.

This fragment almost certainly comes from Court H, Façade Bull 1 or 10, on both of which the historical summary began under the belly. Its lines are much longer than on other bulls known or believed to have carried a historical summary (Room I, Door *d*, and Room LX, Door *a*) and are only slightly shorter than those of the largest bulls (Court H, Door *a*), suggesting that this was one of the larger bulls in the palace. The inclusion of six campaigns in the historical summary is also consistent with an attribution to the Court H façade bulls. On Façade Bulls 1 and 10 the inscription is now preserved only at the bottom of Façade Bull 1, where the line length averages 40 signs per line, the same as the Hannover fragment. Façade Bull 10, which was apparently well-preserved when Layard drew it but now seems to be completely lost, must have had lineation similar to that on Façade Bull 1. Perhaps its destruction created the fragment that is now in Hannover. According to Galter, Levine, and Reade (1986: 32), the fragment was presented to the Kestner Museum in 1860. If it does derive from Façade Bull 10, this date would give a terminus for its destruction.

The Papal Bull

Three fragments of Sennacherib bull inscriptions were part of a group of relief and inscription fragments presented to Pope Pius IX by Giovanni Bennhi in 1855 and now in the Vatican Museum.[28] The text is part of the abridged building account that appeared on the façade bulls of Court H. Two of these fragments join, and insofar as they are preserved, roughly duplicate the sign forms and line

---

28. Photos: *Dai Palazzi Assiri: Imagini di potere da Assurnasirpal II ad Assurbanipal (IX-VII sec. a. C.)*, ed. R. Dolce and M. N. Santi (Rome, 1995) nos. 68–69, 71. Edition: Pohl 1942–43: 250:16; Pohl 1947: 463, pl. 32. Study: Frahm 1997: 120.

distribution of MR 8 (Court H, Façade Bull 12), lines 10 to 17, except for the variant *ú* instead of *u* in line 16. The third very small fragment apparently duplicates lines 6 to 9 of MR 8 and probably originates from the same bull as the others. The long lines indicate that they come from the space under the belly of a bull; this text occurred in that location on all of the façade bulls in Court H and on the north bull in Room LX, Door *a*. The lines of this inscription seem too long for the bull in Room LX, but they are just right for the façade bulls. The question of which of the façade bulls these fragments derive from hinges on how much faith one places in the hand copy of MR 8. The breaks at the right side and bottom of the Vatican fragments roughly match the breaks at the lower right corner of MR 8. The vertical alignment of signs in the Vatican fragments varies somewhat from that of MR 8. The major difference is the sign variant in line 16. Because of the rough appearance of the MR 8 copy, I am inclined to suggest that the Vatican fragments and MR 8 are from the same bull, namely Façade Bull 12, and to explain the single variant as a copying error in MR 8.[29] If one accepts the MR 8 copy as accurate, however, then the nearly identical Vatican fragments most probably derive from one of the other façade bulls.

The Austrian Bull

Galter and Scholz published a Sennacherib fragment, apparently from a colossus, now in an Austrian private collection.[30] The fragment gives a few signs from seven lines of a Sennacherib building account. Based on the surviving bit, the lines were slightly shorter than those under the belly of Façade Bull 12 (MR 8). An unusual variant (*nukkulu*) in line 5' does not occur in the known Sennacherib bull texts, so I cannot suggest an original location for this piece.

Loose Fragment in Room V

An irregular piece of stone now stored in Room V of Sennacherib's palace may derive from one of his colossi (fig. 114). The inscribed surface measures 22 × 40 cm. and contains parts of six lines, three of which evidently begin at the left margin. The preserved text is as follows:

1'. ⌜LÚ⌝.KÚR *ag-*⌜*ṣi*⌝ [. . .]
2'. LUGAL URU *ṣi-du-un-*⌜*ni*⌝ [. . .]
3'. *ki-ma nu-ú-ni ip-*[*par-šid-ma* . . .]

29. In Sennacherib's bull inscriptions, the word in question here, *nabû* ('to name'), appears as *na-bu-ú* in ICC 39:37 and Layard Ms C, 56 verso, line 5, as well as in the Papal bull, and *na-bu* in IIIR, 13, Slab 4, line 10. The form *na-bu-u* appears only in MR 8: 16, though it should be noted that in the inscriptions of Sennacherib's predecessors, *na-bu-u* is occasionally substituted for the more common *na-bu-ú* (AHw [1972] 699b).

30. H. D. Galter and B. Scholz, "Altvorderasiatisches in österreichischen Sammlungen," *Archiv für Orientforschung* 35 (1988) 35; Frahm 1997: 119, "T 32."

4'. *i-na ra-šub-*⌐*bat*⌐ [. . .]
5'. [LUGAL-*ti*]-*šú ú*-[*še-šib-ma* . . .]
6'. [*ú-šal*]-⌐*pit rap*⌐-[*šú* . . .]

The fragment gives the end of the second and beginning of the third campaign. The text duplicates Smith's "Bulls 2 and 3" except for line 3', which has
the variant "like a fish he fled," otherwise unattested in this context in Sennacherib colossus inscriptions. The lineation is almost the same as that of Smith's
"Bull 3" (Court H, Façade Bull 12).[31] If this fragment *is* from a bull, therefore, it
must be from Column i of an inscription that begins between the hind legs. The
only known candidates are Court H, Façade Bulls 3 and 12. If Façade Bull 12 is
Smith's "Bull 3," as argued above, then this fragment, which has slightly different
lineation, cannot be from that bull. Unfortunately for attribution, it also cannot
be from Façade Bull 3, because this very passage is still preserved in situ on that
bull. For now, therefore, the context of this fragment remains a mystery. Perhaps
it was not part of a colossus inscription at all, or perhaps it derives from an unrecorded colossus, such as one of the bulls on the palace's west façade, about
which almost nothing is known but which could have been inscribed in the same
manner as those on the Court H façade.

31. Lines 1', 4', and 5' of the fragment begin in the same places as lines 16, 19, and
20 of Smith's "Bull 3" (Luckenbill 1924: 77). The remaining lines begin only slightly
earlier or later.

Catalog 4

Sennacherib Epigraphs

This catalog is an updated version, with additions, of the edition of Sennacherib's epigraphs in Russell 1991: 269–78, "Appendix 1."

ROOM I (B)

Slab 1: Epigraph, "almost illegible," still visible in situ at the upper right above the city (Layard 1849a: vol. 2, 125–26; Russell 1991: fig. 133). The preservation is very poor. A version of this epigraph was published in Russell 1991: 270–71. I presented a revised version in a poster at the 39th Rencontre Assyriologique Internationale, Heidelberg, 6–10 July 1992, which incorporated my further thoughts as well as valuable improvements suggested by William R. Gallagher, University of Vienna, to the restoration of lines 3, 4, 5, and 6 (personal communications, letters of September 1991 and 13 May 1992), but the king and city names still remained uncertain. The poster was used by Eckart Frahm as the basis for a further-improved version, in which he suggested that the enemy king is Manijae of Ukku, whom Sennacherib defeated in his fifth campaign (Frahm 1994; Frahm 1997: 124–25, "T 39"). In the edition below, signs marked * are restored from Layard's two manuscript copies: Ms A, p. 300 (Layard's field copy), and British Library, Manuscript Division, Layard Papers, Add. Ms 39079, fol. 160 (probably the copy made for the printer, which was published as Layard 1851: 85:b).

1. [ᵐᵈ30-PAP.MEŠ-SU] ⌜MAN⌝ šú MAN KUR aš+[šur ᵐma-ni-ia]-e
2. [MAN] ⌜URU uk-ki⌝ ti-⌜ib⌝ ta-ḫa-[zi-ia e-dúr]-ma
3. [URU uk-ku(?)] ⌜URU⌝ tuk-la-te-šú e-zib-[ma ana ru]-⌜qé⌝-te
4. ⌜in-na⌝-bit ba-ḫu-la-[te a-šib] ŠÀ-šú
5. ⌜ša⌝ a-na zuq-ti KUR-i ⌜mar-ṣi⌝ [iṣ-ṣu]-riš
6. ip-par-šú ar-ki-šú-[un ar-de*]-ma
7. i-na zuq-ti KUR-i [áš-ta*]-kan
8. ⌜taḫ⌝-ta-šú-un URU ⌜uk*-ki⌝
9. ⌜URU⌝ LUGAL-ti-šú i-na ᵈ⌜GIŠ*⌝.[BAR* aq-mu]

1. [Sennacherib], king of the world, king of Assyria: [Manija]e,
2. [king of] ⌜the city Ukku⌝, [feared] the onslaught of [my] ⌜battle⌝.
3–6. He deserted [Ukku], his power ⌜base⌝, and ⌜fled⌝ [to] ⌜distant parts⌝.
      ⌜The soldiers⌝ [who dwelt] therein, who had flown to the summit
      of the [inaccessible] mountains ⌜like birds⌝, ⌜I followed⌝ after
      them and
7–9. ⌜defeated⌝ them at the mountain top. The city ⌜Ukku⌝, his royal
      ⌜city⌝, ⌜I burned⌝.

Slab 4a: Fragmentary epigraph still preserved on the first slab to the north
of Door e, apparently not recorded by Layard (Russell 1991: 271; Frahm 1997:
125, "T 40"). This transliteration was made from the original, which is very badly
worn:

1. URU a-ta(?)-un(?)-[. . .]   The city of [GN]
2. al-me KUR-[ud]   I besieged, I conquered.

Slab 9: Epigraph over the head of the king enthroned in his fortified camp
(Layard 1849b: 77; Russell 1991: 271; Frahm 1997: 125, "T 41"):

uš-man-nu šá ᵐᵈ30-PAP.MEŠ-su MAN KUR aš+šur

Camp of Sennacherib, king of Assyria.

Slab 24: Epigraph on very badly damaged slab, subject uncertain (Russell
1991: 272; Frahm 1997: 125, "T 42"). This rough transliteration was made from
the original:

1. me-re-⌜x⌝-[. . .]
2. ma-ra-[. . .]-⌜x-x-x⌝
3. un-⌜x⌝-[. . .]-⌜x⌝-un
4. ana ᵐ⌜ni⌝-[. . .]-ir

Room III (G)

Slab 8: Epigraph (Layard 1851: 82:A; Russell 1991: 272; Frahm 1997: 126,
"T 43"):

1. dil-bat-KI al-me KUR-ud   Dilbat I besieged, I conquered,
2. áš-lu-la šal-la-su   I carried off its spoil.

Room V (C)

Slab 11: Epigraph "over the king in a chariot" (Russell 1991: 272; Layard
1851: 75:E; Frahm 1997: 126, "T 44"). In 1991 (Russell 1991: 307 n. 12), I spec-
ulated on how this slab, which is certainly No. 11 in Room V (formerly C), came
to be identified by Layard (1851: 75:E) as No. 2 in Room III (formerly G). I have
since confirmed that this epigraph is correctly labeled "No. 11 Chamber C" in

Layard's field copy (Layard, Ms A, p. 300). This was miscopied as "No. 11 Chamber G" in the copy Layard prepared for the printer (Layard, Ms B, fol. 29). This then became "No. 2 Chamber G" in the printed version. This transliteration was made from the original, except for the PAP.MEŠ in line 1, which is now missing from the original but is preserved in Layard's copy (1851: 75:E:1):

1. ^{md}30-PAP.MEŠ-SU MAN [šú] Sennacherib, king of [the world]
2. MAN KUR aš+šur-KI ⌜šal-la-at⌝ king of Assyria, ⌜the booty⌝
3. URU ka-su-⌜ṣi⌝ of Kasusi(?)
4. ma-ḫar-šu ⌜e⌝-[ti]-⌜iq⌝ ⌜passed in review⌝ before him.

Slab 30:   Above the king was an epigraph that Layard said "had been entirely defaced" (Layard 1849a: vol. 2, 133; Russell 1991: 273; Frahm 1997: 126, "T 45"). This transliteration was made from the original:

1. [^m]^d[30-PAP].⌜MEŠ⌝-[SU MAN šú] S[ennacherib, king of the world]
2. MAN KUR [aš+šur-KI šal]-⌜la⌝-[at] king of [Assyria, the boo]ty
3. ⌜URU⌝ [x-x-x-(x)]-⌜bu-x⌝ of [GN]
4. [ma-ḫar-šu e]-ti-iq passed in rev[iew before him].

Slab 35:   Fragmentary epigraph, still visible on the slab in situ (Layard 1851: 81:B; Russell 1991: 273; Frahm 1997: 126, "T 46"):

1. [URU a-ra-an-z]i-a-šu [The city of Aranz]iash
2. [al-me KUR]-ud [I besieged, I conqu]ered,
3. [aš-lu-la šal]-la-su [I carried off its sp]oil.

Note: The broken first sign in line 1 may be either *nam* or *zi*, followed by *-a-šu*. The only city name known to end this way is Aranziash/Erinziash. Elenzash is also possible, though it is not attested with these signs; in Sennacerib's annals, Elenzash is written *el-en-za-áš* (Luckenbill 1924: 28:27, 59:32, 68:15), but it is written *e-le-en-zi-* [. . .] in the broken occurrence of the name at Jerwan (Jacobsen and Lloyd 1935: 26, no. 45T; Parpola 1970: 23, 123, 126).

Slab 41:   Fragmentary epigraph across the center of the Assyrian fortified camp, still visible on the slab in situ (Russell 1998: Catalogue, Room V, Slab 43):

⌜uš⌝-[man-nu šá ^m] ⌜d⌝30-PAP.MEŠ-SU MAN ⌜KUR⌝ [aš+šur]

[Camp of] Sennacherib, king [of Assyria].

COURT VI (I)
Slab 2:   Fragmentary epigraph from "bas-relief representing Siege." In Layard 1851: 75:C this epigraph was erroneously assigned to Slab 2 in Court H

(Russell 1991: 269; Frahm 1997: 124, "T 38"). The correct location is given in Layard's original manuscript (Layard, Ms A, p. 134).

1. [. . .] MAN ŠÚ MAN ⟨KUR⟩ aš+šur URU.MEŠ
2. [. . .]-ti a-na ka-šá-di il-la[k]

1. [Sennacherib], king of the world, king of Assyria, the cities of
2. [PN or GN] he goes to conquer.

Slab 60: Epigraph (G. Smith 1878: 160–61; copy in Meissner and Rost 1893: 43, pl. 10:1; original visible in Paterson 1915: pl. 29; Russell 1991: 274; Frahm 1997: 126, "T 47"). Layard's manuscript copy of this epigraph (Ms C, fol. 66v) is labeled "Over king superintending removal of bull. No. 62 Ch. I [i.e., Court VI] (Kouyunjik)." Slab 62 did have two unrecorded 4–line epigraphs, and they could well have had this same text, but neither was over the king. Since this copy is identical to the epigraph now visible over the king on Slab 60 (British Museum, WA 124824), I believe Layard misnumbered the slab in his label on the manuscript copy (see also Russell 1991: 295 n. 45).

1. md30-PAP.MEŠ-su MAN ŠÚ MAN KUR aš+šur dÀLAD.dLAMMA.MEŠ
2. GAL.MEŠ ša i-na er-ṣe-et URU ba-la-ṭa-a-a
3. ib-ba-nu-ú a-na É.GAL be-lu-ti-šú
4. ša qé-reb NINA.KI ḫa-di-iš ú-šal-da-da

1. Sennacherib, king of the world, king of Assyria: great bull colossi,
2. which were made in the district of Balatai,
3. to his lordly palace,
4. which is in Nineveh, joyfully he had them dragged.

Slab 62: Two 4–line epigraphs, illegible in the drawing, perhaps duplicates of the epigraph on Slab 60 (Layard 1853b: 17; Russell 1991: 274).

Slab 66: Epigraph (Meissner and Rost 1893: 43, pl. 10:2; Russell 1991: 275; Frahm 1997: 126, "T 48"):

1. md30-PAP.MEŠ-su MAN ŠÚ MAN KUR aš+šur NA$_4$ pi-i-lu pe-ṣu-ú
2. ša ki-i ṭè-im DINGIR-ma a-na šip-ri É.GAL-ia ina er-ṣe-[et]
3. URU ba-la-ṭa-a-a in-nam-ru UN.MEŠ da-ád-me
4. na-ki-ri ù ÉRIN.MEŠ ḫur-šá-a-ni pa-az-ru-ti KUR-ti šu^{II}-ia [ina]
5. qul-me-e ù ak-kul-la-ti AN.BAR ú-šá-áš-[šu-nu-ti]
6. dÀLAD.dLAMMA.MEŠ GAL.MEŠ a-na KÁ.MEŠ É.GAL-ia ú-še-e-[piš]

1. Sennacherib, king of the world, king of Assyria: white limestone
2. which, at the command of the god, for the construction of my palace
   had been discovered

3. in the district of Balatai; I had men from enemy towns
4. and the inhabitants of hidden mountain regions, conquest of my hand,
5. wield iron picks and mason's-picks(?),
6. and I had great bull colossi made for the gates of my palace.

Slab 68:   6–line epigraph (visible in Paterson 1915: pl. 36; transliterated in V. Scheil, *Recueil de travaux* XV [1893] 149; Russell 1991: 275; Frahm 1997: 127, "T 48"); duplicate of Slab 66, with the following variants:

line 3:   *ba-ḫu-la-ti* (soldiers), instead of UN.MEŠ (men)
line 4:   *la kan-šu-ti* (rebellious), instead of *pa-az-ru-ti* (hidden)
line 6:   *ib-tu-[qu]* (they carved), instead of *ú-še-e-[piš]* (I had made)

ROOM VII
Slab 14:   Illegible unpublished epigraph in front of the king in his chariot (Layard 1853b: 29; Russell 1991: 275).

ROOM X
Slab 7:   Fragmentary epigraph (Layard 1853b: 50; Russell 1991: 275):

uš-man-nu ša ᵐᵈ30-[. . .]   Camp of Senn[acherib . . .]

ROOM XIV
Slab 10:   Epigraph (see fig. 42; S. Smith 1938: pl. 63; Russell 1991: 275; Frahm 1997: 127, "T 49"):

1. [URU] *al-am-mu al-me* [KUR-*ud*]
2. [*aš*]-*lu-la šal-l*[*a-su*]

1. [The city of] Alammu I besieged, [I conquered,]
2. [I] carried off ⌜its spoil⌝.

ROOM XXXIII
Slabs 1–6:   Eight epigraphs, all dating to the reign of Assurbanipal (Gerardi 1988). These post-date Sennacherib and therefore are not included here; translations are given in Chapter 9.

ROOM XXXVI
Slab 12:   Epigraph in front of enthroned king (Russell 1991: 276; Frahm 1997: 127, "T 50"):

1. ᵐᵈ30-PAP.MEŠ-SU MAN ŠÚ MAN KUR *aš+šur*
2. *ina* GIŠ.GU.ZA *né-me-di ú-šib-ma*
3. *šal-la-at* URU *la-ki-su*
4. *ma-ḫa-ar-šu e-ti-iq*

1. Sennacherib, king of the world, king of Assyria,
2. sat in a *nēmedu*-throne and
3. the booty of Lachish
4. passed in review before him.

Epigraph over the tent (Russell 1991: 276; Frahm 1997: 127, "T 51"):

1. *za-ra-tum*	Tent
2. *šá* ^{md}30-PAP.MEŠ-SU	of Sennacherib
3. LUGAL KUR *aš+šur*	king of Assyria.

Room XXXVIII

In one of Layard's notebooks (British Library, Department of Manuscripts, Layard Papers, Add. Ms 39077, fol. 77v), under "Room V" ("vee," i.e., XXXVIII), he wrote: "on a fragment (no. 17 or 18) was the name of the city or country subdued. Only the first letters URU É ^m*ib* or *lu* remain" (my transliteration of Layard's cuneiform copy). The relief with this epigraph is depicted in an Original Drawing (vol. 6, 25b), which shows that it had two lines, though the second line was completely illegible (Russell 1991: 64, 277, fig. 36; Frahm 1997: 127, "T 52"). On the basis of these two sources, the text can be reconstructed as:

1. URU É ^m*ib* or *lu* -[. . .]	The city Bit-ib/lu-[. . .]
2. [. . .]	[. . .]

Room XLV

Mostly defaced epigraph shown in slab drawing (Russell 1991: 277; Frahm 1997: 127, "T 53"):

1. [. . .]	[. . .]
2. [. . .]	[. . .]
3. *šal-la-*[*at* . . .]	the booty [of GN]
4. *ma-ḫa-*ʿ*ar*ʾ*-*[*šu e-ti-iq*]	[passed in review] before him.

Room XLVII

In one of Layard's notebooks (British Library, Department of Manuscripts, Layard Papers, Add. Ms 39077, fol. 78v), under "Room JJ" (i.e., XLVII), he wrote: "South side a line of prisoners leaving a castle captured by Assyrians over which inscription nearly destroyed. Following letters of last line remain: *aq-*ʿ*qur*ʾ *ina* ^dGIŠ.ʿBARʾ *aq-mu*" (my transliteration of Layard's cuneiform copy). The relief with this epigraph is depicted in an Original Drawing (vol. 6, 2b; Russell 1991: 277, fig. 38; Frahm 1997: 127, "T 54"), where the epigraph appears as follows:

1′. [*aš-lu*]*-*ʿ*la šal-la*ʾ*-*[*su*] ʿ*ap-pul*ʾ
2′. ʿ*aq*(!)ʾ*-qur ina* ^dGIŠ.ʿBARʾ [*aq*]*-*ʿ*mu*ʾ

On the basis of these two sources, the text can be reconstructed as:

1. [. . .]
2. [aš-lu]-˹la šal-la˺-[su] ˹ap-pul˺
3. aq-qur ina ᵈGIŠ.˹BAR˺ aq-mu

1. [The city GN I besieged, I captured(?)]
2. ˹I carried off its spoil, I tore (it) down,˺
3. I demolished (it), with fire I burned (it).

Hall XLIX

Three fragmentary epigraphs found loose in Room XLIX originally belonged to a relief series that showed a large object being transported by water (fig. 44; Russell 1991: 277; Frahm 1997: 127–28, "T 55–57"). These epigraphs have until now been known only from Hincks's provisional translations, as published by Layard (1853a: 118):

"Sennacherib, king of Assyria . . . (some object, the nature not ascertained) of wood, which from the Tigris I caused to be brought up (*through?*) the Kharri, or Khasri, on sledges (or boats), I caused to be carried (or to mount)."

"Some objects also of wood 'brought from Mount Lebanon, and taken up (to the top of the mound) from the Tigris.'"

"Similar objects are described as coming from or up the same Kharri or Khasri."

The notes Layard used in preparing these versions of the translations are preserved in one of his notebooks (British Library, Department of Manuscripts, Layard Papers, Add. Ms 39077, fols. 48–49) [my comments are in brackets]:

"Fragments from Chamber O" [XLIX]

"? the transport of an object of wood(?) from the river Khari."

"f.[?] from mount Lebanon *lab-na-na* I brought <u>up</u> (the high mound) from the Tigris." [*lab-na-na* is written here with the cuneiform signs.]

"king & objects of wood [illegible] from the Tigris I caused to be brought up (through) the Kauser (Kasr) I caused to be carried"

Hincks gave a transliteration and another translation of two of these epigraphs in a report he submitted to the British Museum (British Library, Department of Manuscripts, Add. Ms 22097, "Readings of Inscriptions on the Nineveh Marbles by Dr. Hincks. Part 1. Received at the British Museum on the 6th of May 1854," fols. 11v–12r.). He underlined parts that were uncertain; all brackets and parentheses are Hincks's:

"[Tsinakhirib] sar <u>kinshati</u>, sar mat Assura dimmi ʾirni [ipshit] Tsirara Lib-
nana [ultu] Bartiggar yusillâ."

"Tsinakhirib, king of <u>the provinces</u>, king of Assyria, brings up from the Tigris
images of ʾirin wood (perhaps, cedar) [the work of] Tsirara and Lebanon."
(fol. 11v)

"Tsinakhirib sar <u>kinshati</u>, sar Mat-Assura dimmi ʾirni [rabuti], sha ultu kirib
Bartiggar yusiʾlâ, [ ] yanutsi yusharkibma, ultu kirib Kharri yushaldida."

"Tsinakhirib, king of <u>the provinces</u>, king of Assyria, mounted upon a _____
<u>sledge</u> [great] images of ʾirin wood, which he brought up from the Tigris, and
transported them from the Kharru." (fol. 11v-12r)

From Hincks's transliterations, I have identified previously unrecognized Layard
copies of two of these epigraphs (Layard, Ms D, fol. 17):

No. 1

1. ^{md}30-PAP.MEŠ-SU MAN ŠÚ MAN KUR *aš+šur* GIŠ *tim-me ere*$_4$-*ni*
2. [GAL.MEŠ *bi-ib-lat* KUR *si*]-*ra-ra* KUR *lab-na-na*
3. [*ul-tu qé-reb* íD].⌈IDIGNA⌉ *ú-še-el-la-a*

Sennacherib, king of the world, king of Assyria: I caused great columns
of cedar, product of Mt. Sirara and Mt. Lebanon, to be brought up the
Tigris.

Note to line 2: *bi-nu-ut* and *tar-bit* are attested with the same meaning in the
same context in Sennacherib inscriptions, and either would do as well here as
bi-ib-lat (Luckenbill 1924: 123:32, 119:23, 129:vi:59).

No. 2

1. ^{md}30-PAP.MEŠ-SU MAN ŠÚ MAN KUR *aš+šur* GIŠ *tim-me ere*$_4$-*ni*
2. [GAL].⌈MEŠ⌉ *ša* ⌈*ul*(!)⌉-*tu qé-reb* íD.IDIGNA *ú-še-la-a*
3. [*ṣe*-]-⌈*er*⌉ GIŠ *ia-nu-si ú-šar-kib-ma*
4. ⌈*ul*⌉-*tu qé-reb* íD *ḫar-ri ú-šal-da-da*

Sennacherib, king of the world, king of Assyria: I caused great columns
of cedar to be brought up the Tigris. I had them loaded ⌈on⌉ a sledge/
raft(?) and pulled up through the canal.

Note to line 3: This word, which is very clearly written in the copy, seems not to
be in the dictionaries, unless it is related to *ia-an-nu-si*: CAD I/J (1960) 322 s.v.
jannussu ("fetters?"); AHw (1965) 411 ("ein Gegenstand?"). It is presumably the
name for the sledge or raft illustrated on the wall reliefs in the same room
(fig. 44).

These two epigraphs are clearly the ones transliterated by Hincks in his report for the British Museum, and the two are also recognizable among the three cited by Layard. I have been unable to locate a cuneiform copy or transliteration of the third Layard epigraph ("similar objects are described as coming from or up the same Kharri or Khasri"), and it is possible that his second and third epigraphs are actually the beginning and end of the one I list here as "No. 2."

A footnote to No. 2 at the bottom of Layard, Ms D, fol. 17 reads: "(1) This character restored from another fragment." The character to which it refers, in line 4 of No. 2, has been crossed out. There is also a third cuneiform copy on the same sheet, but I can make nothing of it. I have not been able to make out the label (Layard's private handwriting can be difficult to decipher), which may say something like "first[?] line[?] wanting." The text is evidently a fragment and is perhaps to be read:

1. *a* [
2. *si šá* [(x?)] *i* [

I can see no connection between this fragment and the other copies on this sheet, but because the sheet is otherwise devoted entirely to epigraphs from Room XLIX, this one may derive from there as well.

Room LX

Slab 2: Epigraph "over one of the castles captured and destroyed by the Assyrians" (Layard 1853a: 460; G. Smith 1878: 52; location given in Layard's ms. copy—British Museum, WAA, Ms A, 57 verso; Russell 1991: 278; Frahm 1997: 128, "T 58"):

1. URU É-*mku-bat-ti al-me* KUR-*ud*
2. *áš-lu-la šal-la-su ina* ^dGIŠ.BAR *aq-mu*

1. Bit-Kubatti I besieged, I conquered,
2. I carried off its spoil, with fire I burned.

Room LXX

Slab 4: Epigraph in front of Sennacherib in his chariot (Russell 1991: 278; Frahm 1997: 128, "T 59"):

1. ^{md}30-PAP.MEŠ-SU MAN ŠÚ MAN KUR *aš+šur*
2. *šal-la-at* ÍD *a-gam-me*
3. *ša* URU *sa-aḫ-ri-na*
4. *ma-ḫa-ar-šu e-ti-iq*

1. Sennacherib, king of the world, king of Assyria:
2. the booty of the marshes
3. of Sahrina
4. passed in review before him.

Unknown Room

A fragmentary epigraph before the king in his chariot is on a slab fragment that is now stored in Room V of Sennacherib's palace; it probably originated elsewhere (see fig. 43). The text reads:

1. ᵐᵈ30.PAP.[MEŠ-SU MAN ŠÚ MAN KUR *aš+šur*]
2. *šal-la-*[*at* . . .]
3. URU [. . .]
4. ⌜x⌝ [. . .]

Sennach[erib, king of the world, king of Assyria] ⌜the booty⌝ [. . .] of the city [GN . . .].

The broken sign at the beginning of Line 4 begins with a vertical wedge and so cannot be the first sign of *ma-ḫar-šu* or *e-ti-iq* ('passed in review before him'). Lines 3 and/or 4 must therefore have included more or different information than is in the last lines of the other booty review epigraphs.

Probably not an Epigraph

Layard (1851: pl. 75B) identified this fragment from Kuyunjik as "probably from a bas-relief representing the siege of a city." The text reads:

1. [ᵐᵈ30-PAP.ME]*š-eri₄-b*[*a* . . .]
2. [. . . m]*i-gir* DINGIR(!).MEŠ GAL.MEŠ [. . .]
3. [*u-šat-li-mu-in*]-*ni-ma ana ul-tu ṣi-*[*tan*] *a-di* [*šil-la-an* . . .]
4. [*še-pu-u-a u-šak*]-*niš-ma i-šu-ṭu*(!) *a*[*b-ša*]-*a-ni i-*[*na u₄-me-šu-ma* . . .]
5. [*a-li-kut maḫ-ri*] AD.MEŠ-*ia ú-še-pi-šu-*[*ma*(?) . . .]
6. [. . .] *e-piš-taš ù ul-tu* [. . .]

The text is similar to portions of Sennacherib building accounts (Luckenbill 1924: 152:xvii:1–13; 103:34–35, 45; 155:xx:5–6) and can be restored as follows:

Sennacherib, [(various titles)], favorite of the great gods: [Assur and Ishtar have given] me [an invincible weapon]. From east to [west . . . I made all princes] bow down [at my feet] and they pulled my yoke. A[t that time (some structure)—which the kings who preceded me], my ancestors, had built—[. . . I completed (or restored, or beautified)] its workmanship, and [rebuilt it(?)] from [its foundations to its walls].

Though the name of the structure is lost, this is clearly a commemorative building inscription. It could have been an epigraph as well, labeling an image of the structure in question, but there is no reason to suppose this. Considering the uncertainty of Layard's identification of this inscription's original location, it seems best not to consider it to be an epigraph.

Catalog 5
Esarhaddon Colossi

The following texts are from the reverse side of colossi in the Southwest Palace at Kalhu.

Door c
Bull 1
Captioned "Inscription on Bull No. 1, Entrce. c, Pl. 2. (opposite previous)" (Layard, Ms A, p. 101):

1. É.GAL ᵐaš+šur-PAP-AŠ MAN GAL MAN *dan-nu* MAN ŠÚ MAN KUR AŠ
2. GÌR.NÍTA KÁ.DINGIR.KI MAN KUR EME.GI₇ *u* URI.KI ⌜LUGAL⌝ LUGAL
3. KUR *mu-ṣur*(!) *pa-⟨tu⟩-ri-su* KUR *ku-*⌜*si*⌝ MAN *kib-*⌜*rat*⌝ 4-*ti*

Bull 2
Captioned "Fragment on back of Bull No. 2, Entrce. c, Pl. 2." (Layard, Ms A, p. 101):

1. [É.GAL ᵐaš+šur-PAP-AŠ] MAN GAL MAN *dan-nu*
2. [MAN ŠÚ MAN KUR AŠ] GÌR.NÍTA KÁ.DINGIR.RA.KI
3. [MAN KUR EME].⌜GI₇⌝ *u* URI.KI LUGAL MAN.MEŠ KUR *mu-ṣur*(!)
4. [*pa-tu*]-⌜*ri*⌝-*si* KUR *ku-si* MAN *kib-rat*.MEŠ 4-*ti*

Door c, translation

Palace of Esarhaddon, great king, mighty king, king of the world, king of Assyria, governor of Babylon, king of Sumer and Akkad, king of the kings of Egypt, Paturisu, and Kush, king of the four quarters.

Door a
Lion 1
Captioned "Behind Bull [sic] No. 1, Entrce. a, Pl. 2" (Layard, Ms A, p. 129):

1. [É.GAL ᵐaš+šur-PAP-AŠ MAN GAL MAN *dan-nu*]
2. [MAN ŠÚ MAN] ⌜KUR⌝ AŠ GÌR.⌜NÍTA⌝ [KÁ.DINGIR.KI]

3. [MAN] ⌈KUR⌉ EME.GI₇ *u* URI.⌈KI⌉ [*ba-nu-u*]
4. ⌈É⌉ *aš+šur e-piš* ⟨É⟩.SAG.GÍL *u* ⌈KÁ⌉.[DINGIR.KI]
5. *mu-⌈ud⌉-diš ṣa-lam* DINGIR.MEŠ GAL.MEŠ
6. MAN KUR *mu-ṣur ka-mu-u* MAN KUR *me-lu-ḫi*
7. A ᵐ30-PAP.⌈MEŠ⌉-SU MAN KUR AŠ

Translation

Palace of Esarhaddon, great king, mighty king, king of the world, king of Assyria, governor of Babylon, king of Sumer and Akkad, builder of the temple of Assur, restorer of Esagila and Babylon, renewer of the statues of the great gods, king of Egypt, who defeated the king of Meluhha, son of Sennacherib, king of Assyria.

Door b
Bull 1
Captioned "On back of Bull No. 1, same entrce." (Layard, Ms A, p. 131):

1. É.GAL ᵐ*aš+šur*-PAP-AŠ MAN GAL MAN *dan-nu*
2. MAN ŠÚ MAN KUR AŠ GÌR.NÍTA KÁ.DINGIR.KI MAN KUR
3. EME.GI₇ *u* URI.KI *ba-nu-u* É *aš+šur e-piš*
4. É.SAG.GÍL *u* KÁ.DINGIR.KI *mu-ud-diš ṣa-⟨lam⟩* DINGIR.MEŠ
5. GAL.MEŠ MAN KUR *mu-ṣur ka-mu-u* MAN KUR *me-luḫ*
6. MAN *kib-rat* 4-*ti* A ᵐᵈ30-PAP.MEŠ-SU
7. MAN ŠÚ MAN KUR *aš+šur* A ᵐMAN-GIN MAN ŠÚ MAN KUR AŠ-*ma*

Bull 2
Captioned "Behind Bull No. 2, Entrce. b, Plan 2" (Layard, Ms A, pp. 130–31):

1. É.GAL ᵐ*aš+šur*-PAP-AŠ MAN GAL MAN *dan*-[*nu* MAN ŠÚ]
2. MAN KUR *aš+šur* GÌR.NÍTA KÁ.DINGIR.KI [MAN] KUR ⌈EME⌉.[GI₇ *u* URI.KI]
3. *ba-nu* É *aš+šur é-piš* ⌈É⌉.[SAG.GÍL *u* KÁ.DINGIR.KI]
4. *mu-ud-diš ṣa-lam* DINGIR.MEŠ GAL.[MEŠ MAN KUR *mu-ṣur*]
5. *ka-mu-u* MAN KUR *me-luḫ* MAN *kib-rat* ⌈4⌉-[*ti*]
6. A ᵐᵈ30-PAP.MEŠ-SU MAN ŠÚ MAN [KUR *aš+šur*]
7. A ᵐMAN-GIN MAN ŠÚ [MAN KUR AŠ-*ma*]

Door b, translation

Palace of Esarhaddon, great king, mighty king, king of the world, king of Assyria, governor of Babylon, king of Sumer and Akkad, builder of the temple of Assur, restorer of Esagila and Babylon, renewer of the statues of the great gods, king of Egypt, who defeated the king of Meluhha, king of the four quarters, son of Sennacherib, king of the world, king of Assyria, son of Sargon, king of the world, king of Assyria.

Bibliography

Abel, L.

1889   "Inschriften Rammân-nirâri's III." In E. Schrader, *Keilinschriftliche Biblio-thek*, vol. 1, pp. 188–93. Berlin.

Agha, A. A., and M. S. al-Iraqi

1976   *Nimrud "Calah."* Baghdad.

AHw   see von Soden 1965–81

Albenda, P.

1978   "Assyrian Carpets in Stone." *Journal of the Ancient Near Eastern Society* 10: 1–34.

1986   *The Palace of Sargon, King of Assyria: Monumental Wall Reliefs at Dur-Sharrukin, from Original Drawings Made at the Time of Their Discovery in 1843–1844 by Botta and Flandin.* Éditions Recherche sur les Civilizations. Synthèse, 22. Paris.

el-Amin, M.

1953   "Die Reliefs mit Beischriften von Sargon II. in Dur-Sharrukin." *Sumer* 9: 35–59, 214–28.

1954   "Die Reliefs mit Beischriften von Sargon II. in Dur-Sharrukin." *Sumer* 10: 23–42.

Barnett, R. D.

1957   *A Catalogue of the Nimrud Ivories with other Examples of Ancient Near Eastern Ivories in the British Museum.* London.

1973   "More Balawat Gates: A Preliminary Report." In *Symbolae Biblicae et Mesopotamicae Francisco Maria Theodoro de Liagre Böhl Dedicatae*, ed. M. A. Beek et al., pp. 19–22, pls. 1–4. Leiden.

1976   *Sculptures from the North Palace of Ashurbanipal at Nineveh.* London.

Barnett, R. D., and M. Falkner

1962   *The Sculptures of Assur-nasir-apli II (883–859 B.C.), Tiglath-pileser III (745–727 B.C.), Esarhaddon (681–669 B.C.) from the Central and South-west Palaces at Nimrud.* London.

Barthes, R.

1977   "Rhetoric of the Image." In *Image. Music. Text*, pp. 32–51. New York. (Originally published as "Rhétorique de l'image." *Communications* 4, 1964).

Bauer, T.
 1933 *Das Inschriftenwerk Assurbanipals.* 2 vols. Leipzig.

Bezold, C.
 1890 "Inschriften Sanherib's." In E. Schrader, *Keilinschriftliche Bibliothek,* vol. 2, pp. 80–119. Berlin.
 1889–99 *Catalogue of the cuneiform tablets in the Kouyunjik Collection.* 5 vols. London.

Bleibtreu, E., R. D. Barnett, and G. Turner
 1998 *Sculptures from the Southwest Palace of Sennacherib at Nineveh.* London.

Boissier, A.
 1896 "Bas-reliefs de Tiglat-pileser III." *Proceedings of the Society for Biblical Archaeology* 18: 158–60.

Borger, R.
 1956 *Die Inschriften Asarhaddons, Königs von Assyrien.* Archiv für Orientforschung Beiheft, 9. Graz.
 1961 *Einleitung in die Assyrischen Königsinschriften, Erster Teil: Das zweite Jahrtausend vor Chr.* Handbuch der Orientalistik. Abt. 1: Der Nahe und der Mittlere Osten, Ergänzungsband 5: Keilschrifturkunden: Abschnitt 1, Teil 1. Leiden.
 1967–75 *Handbuch der Keilschriftliteratur.* 3 vols. Berlin.
 1970 "Reliefbeischriften Assurbanipals." *Archiv für Orientforschung* 23: 90.
 1979 *Babylonisch-Assyrische Lesestücke.* Analecta Orientalia 54. 2d ed. 2 vols. Rome (1st ed.: 1963).
 1988 "König Sanheribs Eheglück." *Annual Review of the Royal Inscriptions of Mesopotamia Project* 6: 5–11.
 1996 *Beiträge zum Inschriftenwerk Assurbanipals.* Wiesbaden.

Börker-Klähn, J.
 1982 *Altvorderasiatische Bildstelen und vergleichbare Felsreliefs.* Baghdader Forschungen 4. 2 vols. Mainz am Rhein.

Botta, P. E., and E. Flandin
 1849–50 *Monument de Ninive.* 5 vols. Paris.

Brandes, M. A.
 1970 "La salle dite 'G' du palais d'Assurnasirpal II à Kalakh, lieu de cérémonie rituelle." In *Actes de la XVIIe Rencontre Assyriologique Internationale,* pp. 147–54. Gembloux.

Brinkman, J. A.
 1968 *A Political History of Post-Kassite Babylonia, 1158–722* B.C. Analecta Orientalia 43. Rome.

Budge, E. A. W.
 1914 *Assyrian Sculptures in the British Museum: Reign of Ashur-nasir-pal, 885–860* B.C. London.
 1920 *By Nile and Tigris.* 2 vols. London.

CAD
 1956– *The Assyrian Dictionary of the Oriental Institute of the University of Chicago.* Chicago.

Cameron, G.

1950 "The Annals of Shalmaneser III, King of Assyria." *Sumer* 6: 6–26.

Cifarelli, M.

1995 *Enmity, Alienation and Assyrianization: The Role of Cultural Difference in the Visual and Verbal Expression of Assyrian Ideology in the Reign of Aššurnasir-pal II (883–859 B.C.).* Ph.D. diss., Columbia University, New York.

Cogan, M., and H. Tadmor

1981 "Ashurbanipal's Conquest of Babylon: The First Official Report—Prism K." *Orientalia* n.s. 50: 229–40.

Curtis, J., and A. K. Grayson

1982 "Some Inscribed Objects from Sherif Khan in the British Museum." *Iraq* 44: 87–94.

Delitzsch, F.

1908 "Die Inschriften auf den beiden Stierkolossen Salmanassars II." *Beiträge zur Assyriologie* 6, no. 1: 144–51.

Durand, J.-M.

1979 "Texte & image à l'époque néo-assyrienne." *34–44* (Cahiers de recherche de S.T.D., Université Paris 7), No. 6: *Dire, Voir, Écrire: Le texte et l'image,* autumn 1979: 15–22.

Ellis, R. S.

1968 *Foundation Deposits in Ancient Mesopotamia.* New Haven.

Falkner, M.

1952–53 "Die Reliefs der assyrischen Könige, Zweite Reihe: Zwei assyrische Reliefs in Durham." *Archiv für Orientforschung* 16: 246–51.

Filippi, W. de

1977 "The Royal Inscriptions of Assur-Nāṣir-Apli II (883–859 B.C.): A Study of the Chronology of the Calah Inscriptions Together with an Edition of Two of These Texts." *Assur* 1, No. 7: 123–69.

Frahm, E.

1994 "Die Bilder in Sanherib's Thronsaal." *N.A.B.U.* 1994, no. 3, pp. 48–50.

1997 *Einleitung in die Sanherib-Inschriften.* Archiv für Orientforschung Beiheft 26. Wien.

Fuchs, A.

1994 *Die Inschriften Sargons II. aus Khorsabad.* Göttingen.

Gadd, C. J.

1936 *The Stones of Assyria.* London.

Galter, H. D., Levine, L. D., and Reade, J. E.

1986 "The Colossi of Sennacherib's Palace and their Inscriptions." *Annual Review of the Royal Inscriptions of Mesopotamia Project* 4: 27–32.

Gerardi, P.

1987 *Assurbanipal's Elamite Campaigns: A Literary and Political Study.* Ph.D diss., University of Pennsylvania, Philadelphia.

1988 "Epigraphs and Assyrian Palace Reliefs: The Development of the Epigraphic Text." *Journal of Cuneiform Studies* 40: 1–35.

Grayson, A. K.

　1982　　　"Assyria: Ashur-dan II to Ashur-Nirari V (934–745 B.C.)." In *Cambridge Ancient History* (2d ed.) 3/1: 238–81. Cambridge.

　1987　　　*Assyrian Rulers of the Third and Second Millennia* B.C. Royal Inscriptions of Mesopotamia, Assyrian Periods 1. Toronto.

　1991a　　*Assyrian Rulers of the Early First Millennium* B.C. I (1114–859 B.C.). Royal Inscriptions of Mesopotamia, Assyrian Periods 2. Toronto.

　1991b　　"Assyria: Tiglath-pileser III to Sargon II (744–705 B.C.)." In *Cambridge Ancient History* (2d ed.) 3/2: 71–102. Cambridge.

　1996　　　*Assyrian Rulers of the Early First Millennium* B.C. II (858–745 B.C.). Royal Inscriptions of Mesopotamia, Assyrian Periods 3. Toronto.

Güterbock, H. G.

　1957　　　"Narration in Anatolian, Syrian, and Assyrian Art." *American Journal of Archaeology* 61: 62–71.

Harper, R. F.

　1892–1914　*Assyrian and Babylonian letters belonging to the Kouyunjik Collection of the British Museum.* 14 vols. London and Chicago.

Heidel, A.

　1953　　　"The Octagonal Sennacherib Prism in the Iraq Museum." *Sumer* 9: 117–88.

Heinrich, E.

　1984　　　*Die Paläste im Alten Mesopotamien.* Deutsches Archäologisches Institut, Denkmäler Antiker Architektur 15. Berlin.

Hincks, E.

　1853　　　"On the Assyrio-Babylonian Phonetic Characters." *Transactions of the Royal Irish Academy* 22, part 4, pp. 293–370.

Hulin, P.

　1963　　　"The Inscriptions on the Carved Throne-Base of Shalmaneser III." *Iraq* 25: 48–69 and pl. 10.

ICC　　　　see Layard 1851

IIIR　　　　see Rawlinson 1870

Jacobsen, T., and S. Lloyd

　1935　　　*Sennacherib's Acqueduct at Jerwan.* Oriental Institute Publications 24. Chicago.

King, L. W.

　1909　　　*Cuneiform Texts from Babylonian Tablets in the British Museum,* vol. 26. London.

　1915　　　*The Bronze Reliefs from the Gates of Shalmaneser, King of Assyria,* B.C. 860–825. London.

King, L. W., and Budge, E. A. W.

　1902　　　*Annals of the Kings of Assyria,* vol. 1. London.

Lackenbacher, S.

　1982　　　*Le Roi Bâtisseur. Les récits de construction assyriens des origines à Teglatphalasar III.* Paris.

　1990　　　*Le palais sans rival. Le récit de construction en assyrie.* Paris.

Laessøe, J.

1959   "Building Inscriptions from Fort Shalmaneser, Nimrud." *Iraq* 21: 38–41
           and pl. 9.

Larsen, M. T.

1976   *The Old Assyrian City-State and Its Colonies.* Mesopotamia 4. Copenhagen.

Layard, A. H.

1849a   *Nineveh and Its Remains.* 2 vols. London.

1849b   *Monuments of Nineveh from Drawings Made on the Spot.* London.

1851   *Inscriptions in the Cuneiform Character from Assyrian Monuments.* London.

1853a   *Discoveries in the Ruins of Nineveh and Babylon.* London.

1853b   *A Second Series of the Monuments of Nineveh.* London.

no date   Ms A, [1845–47]. London, British Museum, Department of Western Asi-
           atic Antiquities, Departmental Archives.

no date   Ms B, [1849?]. London, British Museum, Department of Western Asiatic
           Antiquities, Departmental Archives.

no date   Ms C, [1849–51]. London, British Museum, Department of Western Asi-
           atic Antiquities, Departmental Archives.

Layard, A. H. et al.

no date   Ms D, [1849–53?]. London, British Museum, Department of Western Asi-
           atic Antiquities, Departmental Archives.

Leeper, A.

1920   *Cuneiform Texts from Babylonian Tablets, &c., in the British Museum,* vol. 35.
           London.

LeGac, Y.

1907   *Les Inscriptions d'Assur-naṣir-aplu III.* Paris.

Levine, L.

1982   "Sennacherib's Southern Front: 704–689 B.C." *Journal of Cuneiform Studies*
           34: 28–58.

Lie, A. G.

1929   *The Inscriptions of Sargon II, King of Assyria, Part I: The Annals.* Paris.

Liverani, M.

1979   "The Ideology of the Assyrian Empire." In *Power and Propaganda,* ed. M. T
           Larsen, pp. 297–317. Copenhagen.

Lobdell, J.

1854   "Respecting some recent discoveries at Koyunjik." *Journal of the American
           Oriental Society* 4: 472–80.

Loftus, W. K.

1854   "Report of the Assyrian Excavation Fund, April 28th, 1854." In Barnett
           1976: 71–75.

1855   "Report to the Assyrian Excavation Fund, February 20, 1855." In Gadd
           1936, appendix.

Longpérier, A. de

1854   *Notice des antiquités assyriennes, babyloniennes, perses, hébraïques, exposées
           dans les galeries du Musée du Louvre.* 3d ed. Paris.

Loud, G., H. Frankfort, and T. Jacobsen
  1936   *Khorsabad, Part I: Excavations in the Palace and at a City Gate*. Oriental In-
          stitute Publications 38. Chicago.

Loud, G. and, C. B. Altman
  1938   *Khorsabad, Part II: The Citadel and the Town*. Oriental Institute Publica-
          tions 40. Chicago.

Luckenbill, D. D.
  1924   *The Annals of Sennacherib*. Oriental Institute Publications 2. Chicago.

  1926   *Ancient Records of Assyria and Babylonia, I: Historical Records of Assyria
          from the Earliest Times to Sargon*. Chicago.

  1927   *Ancient Records of Assyria and Babylonia, II: Historical Records of Assyria
          from Sargon to the End*. Chicago.

Lyon, D. G.
  1883   *Keilschrifttexte Sargon's*. Leipzig.

Madhloom, T.
  1967   "Excavations at Nineveh, 1965–67." *Sumer* 23: 76–79.

  1969   "Nineveh, 1968–69 Campaign." *Sumer* 25: 44–49.

Madhloom, T., and A. M. Mahdi
  1976   *Nineveh*. Historical Monuments in Iraq 4. Baghdad.

Mallowan, M. E. L.
  1966   *Nimrud and Its Remains*. 3 vols. London.

Marcus, M.
  1987   "Geography as an Organizing Principle in the Imperial Art of Shalmane-
          ser III." *Iraq* 49: 77–90.

  1995   "Art and Ideology in Ancient Western Asia." In *Civilizations of the Ancient
          Near East*, ed. Jack M. Sasson, vol. 4, pp. 2487–2505. New York.

Meissner, B., and Rost, P.
  1893   *Die Bauinschriften Sanheribs*. Leipzig.

Meuszynski, J.
  1975   "The Assur-naṣir-apli II Reliefs in the Vorderasiatisches Museum Berlin."
          Études et Travaux 8 (*Travaux du Centre d'Archaéologie Méditerranéenne de
          l'Académie Polonaise des Sciences*, 16) 33–72.

  1975   "The Throne-Room of Assur-nasir-apli II (Room B in the North-West
          Palace at Nimrud)." *Zeitschrift für Assyriologie* 64: 51–73.

  1976   "Neo-Assyrian Reliefs from the Central Area of Nimrud Citadel." *Iraq* 38:
          37–43.

  1979   "La façade de la salle du trône au Palais Nord-Ouest à Nimrud." *Études et
          Travaux* 11: 5–13.

  1981   *Die Rekonstruktion der Reliefdarstellungen und ihrer Anordnung im Nordwest-
          palast von Kalhu (Nimrud)*. Baghdader Forschungen 2. Mainz am Rhein.

Michel, E.
  1955   "Die Assur-Texte Salmanassars III." *Die Welt des Orients* 2, no. 2: 137–56.

  1959   "Die Assur-Texte Salmanassars III. (858–824); Balawat Inschrift." *Die
          Welt des Orients* 2, no. 5/6: 408–17.

1967   "Die Assur-Texte Salmanassars III. (858–824); Balawat Inschrift." *Die Welt des Orients* 4, no. 1: 29–37.

Mohl, J.

1845   *Lettres de M. Botta sur les découvertes à Khorsabad, près de Ninive.* Paris.

1850   *Illustrations of Discoveries at Nineveh.* London.

MR   see Meissner and Rost 1893

Na'aman, N.

1979   "Sennacherib's Campaign to Judah and the Date of the *LMLK* Stamps." *Vetus Testamentum* 29: 61–86.

1991   "Chronology and History in the Late Assyrian Empire (631–619 B.C.)." *Zeitschrift für Assyriologie* 81: 243–67.

Oates, D.

1968   *Studies in the Ancient History of Northern Iraq.* London.

1974   "Balawat (Imgur Enlil): The Site and Its Buildings." *Iraq* 36: 173–78.

Oates, J.

1983   "Balawat: Recent Excavations and a New Gate." In *Essays on Near Eastern Art and Archaeology in Honor of Charles Kyrke Wilkinson,* ed. P. O. Harper and H. Pittman, pp. 40–47. New York.

Olmstead, A. T.

1916   *Assyrian Historiography.* Columbia, Missouri.

Original Drawings

no date   7 folio volumes of drawings of Assyrian antiquities. London, British Museum, Department of Western Asiatic Antiquities, Departmental Archives.

Paley, S.

1976   *King of the World: Ashur-nasir-pal II of Assyria, 883–859 B.C.* Brooklyn.

1989   "The Entranceway Inscriptions of the 'Second House' in the Northwest Palace of Ashurnasirpal II at Nimrūd (Kalhu)." *Journal of the Ancient Near Eastern Society* 19: 135–47.

Paley, S., and R. Sobolewski

1987   *The Reconstruction of the Relief Representations and Their Positions in the Northwest-Palace at Kalhu (Nimrud) II.* Baghdader Forschungen 10. Mainz am Rhein.

1992   *The Reconstruction of the Relief Representations and Their Positions in the Northwest-Palace at Kalhu (Nimrud) III.* Baghdader Forschungen 14. Mainz am Rhein.

Parpola, S.

1970   *Neo-Assyrian Toponyms.* Alter Orient und Altes Testament 6. Neukirchen-Vluyn.

1987   *The Correspondence of Sargon II, Part I: Letters from Assyria and the West.* State Archives of Assyria 1. Helsinki.

Paterson, A.

1915   *Assyrian Sculptures: Palace of Sinacherib.* The Hague.

Piepkorn, A. C.

1933   *Historical Prism Inscriptions of Ashurbanipal. Volume 1: Editions E, B$_{1-5}$, D, and K.* The Oriental Institute of the University of Chicago, Assyriological Studies 5. Chicago.

Pillet, M.

1962   *Un Pionnier de l'Assyriologie: Victor Place.* Paris.

Place, V., and F. Thomas

1867–70   *Ninive et l'Assyrie.* 3 vols. Paris.

Pohl, A.

1942–43   "Le inscrizioni cuneiformi del Museo Vaticano." *Rendiconti della Pontifica Accademia Romana d'Archeologia* 19: 247–54.

1947   "Die neugefundenen assyrischen Relief- und Inschriftbruchstücke der Vatikanischen Museen." *Orientalia* n.s. 16: 459–63, pls. 29–32.

Pongratz-Leisten, B.

1994   *Ina Šulmi Irub: Die Kulttopographische und Ideologische Programmatik der akītu-Prozession in Babylonien und Assyrien im I. Jahrtausend v. Chr.* Baghdader Forschungen 16. Mainz am Rhein.

Porada, E., and S. Hare

1945   *The Great King, King of Assyria: Assyrian Reliefs in the Metropolitan Museum of Art.* New York.

Porter, B. N.

1993   *Images, Power, and Politics: Figurative Aspects of Esarhaddon's Babylonian Policy.* Philadelphia.

Postgate, J. N.

1969   *Neo-Assyrian Royal Grants and Decrees.* Rome.

1973   *The Governor's Palace Archive.* Cuneiform Texts from Nimrud 2. Hertford.

Postgate, J. N., and J. E. Reade

1980   "Kalhu." In *Reallexikon der Assyriologie,* vol. 5, pp. 303–23. Berlin.

Powell, M. A.

1987–90   "Masse und Gewichte." In *Reallexikon der Assyriologie,* vol. 7, pp. 457–517. Berlin.

Preusser, C.

1955   *Die Paläste in Assur.* Wissenschaftliche Veröffentlichung der Deutschen Orient-Gesellschaft 66. Berlin.

Pritchard, J. B.

1969a   *The Ancient Near East in Pictures Relating to the Old Testament.* 2d ed. Princeton (1st ed.: 1954).

1969b   *Ancient Near Eastern Texts Relating to the Old Testament.* 3d ed. Princeton (1st ed.: 1955).

Rassam, H.

1897   *Asshur and the Land of Nimrod.* New York.

1882   "Excavations and Discoveries in Assyria." *Transactions of the Society of Biblical Archaeology* 7: 37–58.

Rawlinson, H. C.

1861   *The Cuneiform Inscriptions of Western Asia, I: A Selection from the Historical Inscriptions of Chaldaea, Assyria, and Babylonia.* London.

1866   *The Cuneiform Inscriptions of Western Asia, II: A Selection from the Miscellaneous Inscriptions of Assyria.* London.

1870   *The Cuneiform Inscriptions of Western Asia, III: A Selection from the Miscellaneous Inscriptions of Assyria.* London.

Reade, J. E.

1963   "A glazed-brick panel from Nimrud." *Iraq* 25: 38–47.

1964   "More Drawings of Ashurbanipal Sculptures." *Iraq* 26: 1–13.

1965   "Twelve Ashurnasirpal Reliefs." *Iraq* 27: 119–34.

1968   "The Palace of Tiglath-pileser III." *Iraq* 30: 69–73.

1970   *The Design and Decoration of Neo-Assyrian Public Buildings.* Ph.D. diss., Cambridge, King's College.

1975   "Assurnasirpal I and the White Obelisk." *Iraq* 37: 129–50

1976   "Sargon's Campaigns of 720, 716, and 715 B.C.: Evidence from the Sculptures." *Journal of Near Eastern Studies* 35: 95–104.

1979a   "Assyrian Architectural Decoration: Techniques and Subject-Matter." *Baghdader Mitteilungen* 10: 17–49.

1979b   "Narrative Composition in Assyrian Sculpture." *Baghdader Mitteilungen* 10: 52–110.

1980a   "Space, Scale, and Significance in Assyrian Art." *Baghdader Mitteilungen* 11: 71–74.

1980b   "The Architectural Context of Assyrian Sculpture." *Baghdader Mitteilungen* 11: 75–87.

1980c   "The Rassam Obelisk." *Iraq* 42: 1–22.

1981   "Neo-Assyrian Monuments in their Historical Context." In *Assyrian Royal Inscriptions: New Horizons in Literary, Ideological, and Historical Analysis,* ed. F. M. Fales, pp. 143–67. Rome.

1982   "Nimrud." In *Fifty Years of Mesopotamian Discovery,* ed. J. Curtis, pp. 99–112. Hertford.

1983   *Assyrian Sculpture.* Cambridge, Mass.

1985   "Texts and Sculptures from the North-West Palace, Nimrud." *Iraq* 47: 203–14.

Renger, J.

1986   "Neuassyrische Königsinschriften als Genre der Keilschriftliteratur: Zum Stil und zur Kompositionstechnik der Inschriften Sargons II. von Assyrien." In *Keilschriftliche Literaturen: Ausgewählte Vorträge der XXXII. Rencontre Assyriologique Internationale, Münster, 8.–12.7.1985,* ed K. Hecker and W. Sommerfeld, pp. 109–28. Berlin.

Rost, P.

1893   *Die Keilschrifttexte Tiglat-pilesers III.* 2 vols. Leipzig.

Russell, J. M.

1985   *Sennacherib's "Palace without Rival": A Programmatic Study of Texts and Images in a Late Assyrian Palace.* Ph.D. diss., University of Pennsylvania, Philadelphia.

1987   "Bulls for the Palace and Order in the Empire: The Sculptural Program of Sennacherib's Court VI at Nineveh." *Art Bulletin* 69: 520–39.

1991   *Sennacherib's "Palace without Rival" at Nineveh.* Chicago.

1998   *The Final Sack of Nineveh.* London.

Safar, F.

1951   "A Further Text of Shalmaneser III, from Assur." *Sumer* 7: 3–21.

Saggs, H. W. F.

1984   *The Might That Was Assyria.* London.

Schneider, T.

1991   *A New Analysis of the Royal Annals of Shalmaneser III.* Ph.D. diss., University of Pennsylvania, Philadelphia.

Schramm, W.

1973   *Einleitung in die assyrischen Königsinschriften. Zweiter Teil: 934–722 v. Chr.* Handbuch der Orientalistik, Abt. 1: Der nahe und der mittlere Osten. Ergänzungsband 5: Keilschrifturkunden, Abschnitt 1, Teil 2. Leiden.

Schroeder, O.

1922   *Keilschrifttexte aus Assur historischen Inhalts,* vol. 2. Wissenschaftliche Veröffentlichungen der Deutschen Orient-Gesellschaft 37. Leipzig.

Scott, M. L., and J. MacGinnis

1990   "Notes on Nineveh." *Iraq* 52: 63–73

Shukri, A.

1956   "Conservation and Restoration of Assyrian Sculpture at Nimrud." *Sumer* 12 (Arabic section) 133–34.

Smith, G.

1875   *Assyrian Discoveries.* London.

1878   *History of Sennacherib.* London.

Smith, S.

1921   *The First Campaign of Sennacherib.* London.

1938   *Assyrian Sculptures in the British Museum from Shalmaneser III to Sennacherib.* London.

Sobolewski, R.

1974–77   "Die Ausgrabungen in Kalhu (Nimrud), 1974–76." *Archiv für Orientforschung* 25: 230–38.

1980   "The Polish Excavations at Nimrud/Kalh, 1974–1976." *Sumer* 36: 151–62.

1982a   "The Polish Work at Nimrud: Ten Years of Excavation and Study." *Zeitschrift für Assyriologie* 71: 248–73.

1982b   "The Shalmaneser III Building in the Central Area of the Nimrud Citadel." *Archiv für Orientforschung Beiheft* 19: 329–40.

1982c   "Beitrag zur theoretischen Rekonstruktion der Architektur des Nordwest-Palastes in Nimrud (Kalhu)." In *Palast und Hütte: Beiträge zum Bauen und*

Wohnen im Altertum von Archäologen, Vor- und Frühgeschichtlern, ed. D. Papenfuss and V. M. Strocka, pp. 237–50. Mainz am Rhein.

Soden, W. von

1965–81   *Akkadisches Handwörterbuch*. 3 vols. Wiesbaden.

Sollberger, E.

1974   "The White Obelisk." *Iraq* 36: 231–38.

Stearns, J. B.

1961   *Reliefs from the Palace of Assurnasirpal II*. Archiv für Orientforschung Beiheft 15. Graz.

Streck, M.

1916   *Assurbanipal und die letzten assyrischen Könige bis zum Untergang Niniveh's*. 3 vols. Leipzig.

Stronach, D.

1990a   "The Garden as a Political Statement: Some Case Studies from the Near East in the First Millennium B.C." *Bulletin of the Asia Institute* n.s. 4: 171–80.

1990b   "Nineveh." In K. Nashef, "Archaeology in Iraq." *American Journal of Archaeology* 96: 280.

1991   "Nineveh." In "Excavations in Iraq, 1989–1990." *Iraq* 53: 178–79.

Stronach, D. and S. Lumsden

1992   "UC Berkeley's Excavations at Nineveh." *Biblical Archaeologist* 55: 227–33.

Suleiman, A.

1971   Excavations at Tarbisu [in Arabic]. *Adab al-Rafidain* 2: 15–49.

Tadmor, H.

1958   "The Campaigns of Sargon II of Assur: A Chronological-Historical Study." *Journal of Cuneiform Studies* 12: 22–40, 77–100.

1968   "Introductory Remarks to a New Edition of the Annals of Tiglath-pileser III." *Proceedings of the Israel Academy of Sciences and Humanities* (English Series) 2: 168–87.

1994   *The Inscriptions of Tiglath-pileser III, King of Assyria*. Jerusalem.

Thompson, R. C.

1934   "The Buildings on Quyunjiq, the Larger Mound of Nineveh." *Iraq* 1: 95–104

Thompson, R. C., and R. W. Hutchinson

1929a   *A Century of Exploration at Nineveh*. London.

1929b   "Excavations on the Temple of Nabu at Nineveh." *Archaeologia* 79: 103–48.

Thureau-Dangin, F.

1912   *Une relation de la huitième campagne de Sargon*. Textes cunéiformes du Louvre 3. Paris.

Thureau-Dangin, F. et al.

1931   *Arslan-Tash*. 2 vols. Paris.

Turner, G.

1970a   "Tell Nebi Yunus: The *Ekal Māšarti* of Nineveh." *Iraq* 32: 68–85.

1970b   "The State Apartments of Late Assyrian Palaces." *Iraq* 32: 177–213.

Unger, E.
    1920   "Die Wiederherstellung des Bronzetores von Balawat." *Archäologisches Institut des Deutschen Reichs, Athenische Zweiganstalt, Mitteilungen* 45: 1–105.
    1926   "Keilschrift." In *Reallexikon der Vorgeschichte*, ed. M. Ebert, vol. 6, 268ff.

Ungnad, A.
    1938   "Eponymen." In *Reallexikon der Assyriologie*, vol. 2, pp. 412–57. Berlin.

Wäfler, M.
    1975   *Nicht-Assyrer neuassyrischer Darstellungen.* Alter Orient und Altes Testament 26. 2 vols. Neukirchen-Vluyn.

el-Wailly, F.
    1965   "Foreward: Nineveh." *Sumer* 21: 4–6.

Waterman, L.
    1930–36   *Royal Correspondence of the Assyrian Empire.* 4 vols. Ann Arbor.

Weidner, E. F.
    1932–33   "Assyrische Beschreibungen der Kriegs-Reliefs Assurbânaplis." *Archiv für Orientforschung* 8: 175–203.

Weidner, E. F. and G. Furlani
    1939   *Die Reliefs der assyrischen Könige.* Archiv für Orientforschung Beiheft 4. Berlin.

Weissbach, F. H.
    1918   "Zu den Inschriften der Säle im Palaste Sargon's II. von Assyrien." *Zeitschrift der Deutschen Morgenländischen Gesellschaft* 72: 161–85.

Wilson, J. V. K.
    1962   "The Kurba'il Statue of Shalmaneser III." *Iraq* 24: 90–115.

Winckler, H.
    1889   *Die Keilschrifttexte Sargon's.* 2 vols. Leipzig.

Winlock, H. E.
    1933   "Assyria: A New Chapter in the Museum's History of Art." *Bulletin of the Metropolitan Museum of Art* 28: 17–24.

Winter, I. J.
    1981   "Royal Rhetoric and the Development of Historical Narrative in Neo-Assyrian Reliefs." *Studies in Visual Communication* 7, no. 2: 2–38.
    1982   "Art as Evidence for Interaction: Relations between the Assyrian Empire and North Syria." In *Mesopotamien und seine Nachbarn*, ed. H. Nissen and J. Renger, pp. 355–82. Berlin.
    1983   "The Program of the Throneroom of Assurnasirpal II." In *Essays on Near Eastern Archaeology in Honor of Charles Kyrle Wilkinson*, ed. P. O. Harper and H. Pittman, pp. 15–31. New York.

Wiseman, D. J.
    1952   "The Nimrud Tablets, 1951." *Iraq* 14: 61–71.
    1964   "Fragments of Historical Texts from Nimrud." *Iraq* 26: 118–24.

Wiseman, D. J., and J. V. K. Wilson
    1951   "The Nimrud Tablets, 1950." *Iraq* 13: 102–22.

Figures Illustrating the Catalogs

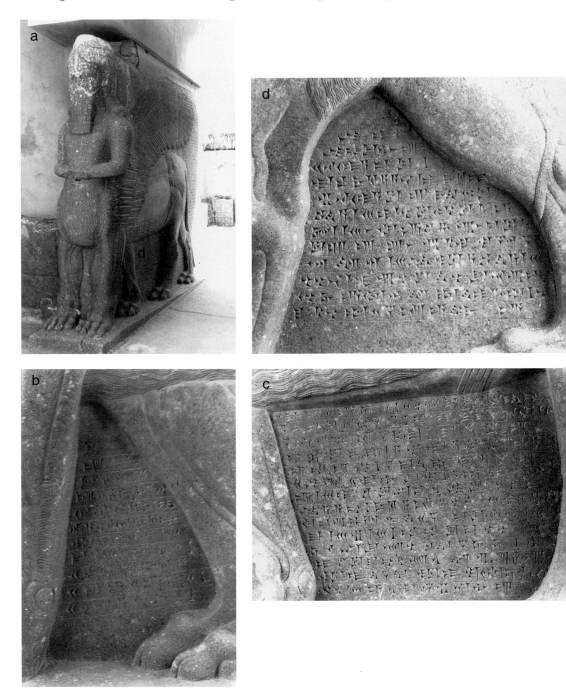

FIG. 83a–e. Kalhu, Northwest Palace of Assurnasirpal II, B-*c*-1 colossus, width 362 cm, in situ (photo: author).

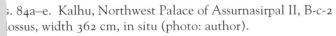

. 84a–e. Kalhu, Northwest Palace of Assurnasirpal II, B-c-2
.ossus, width 362 cm, in situ (photo: author).

FIG. 85a–f. Kalhu, Northwest Palace of Assurnasirpal II, B-*d*-1 colossus, width 370 cm, in situ (photo: author).

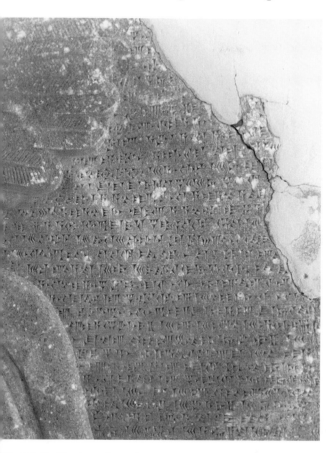

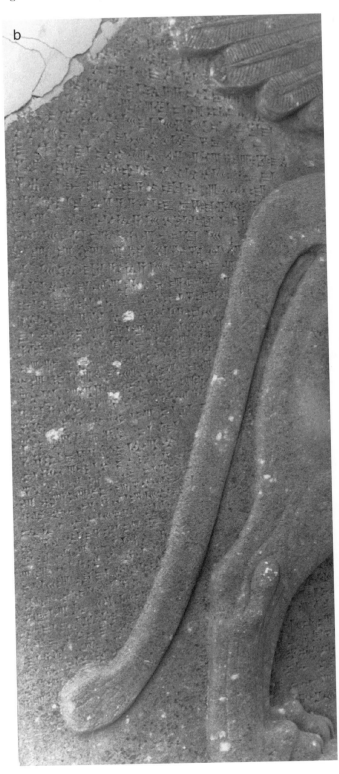

Fig. 86a–e. Kalhu,
Northwest Palace of
Assurnasirpal II, B-*d*-2
colossus, width 371 cm,
in situ (photo: author).

Fig. 87a–b. Kalhu, Northwest Palace of Assurnasirpal II, D-o colossus, width 494 cm, in situ (photo: author).

FIG. 88a–d. Kalhu, Northwest Palace of Assurnasirpal II, E-6 colossus, width 494 cm, in situ (photo: author).

F*IG*. 89a–e. Kalhu, Northwest Palace of Assurnasirpal II, F-*f*-1
colossus, width 358 cm, in situ (photo: author).

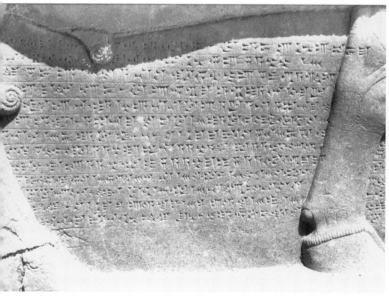

Fig. 90a–e. Kalhu, Northwest Palace of Assurnasirpal F-*f*-2 colossus, width 331 cm, in situ (photo: author).

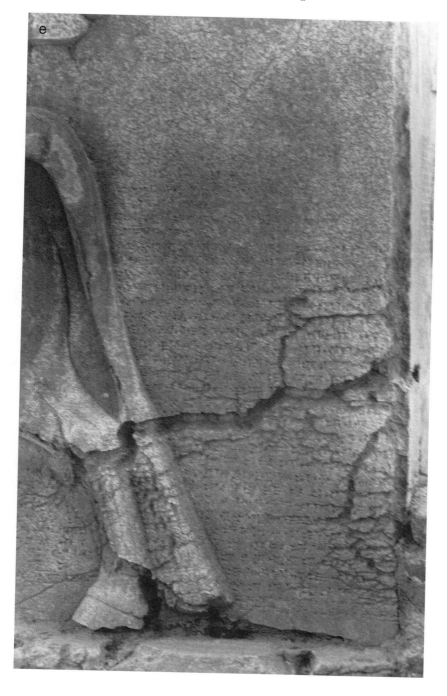

FIG. 91. Kalhu, Northwest Palace of Assurnasirpal II, G-*b*-2 colossus, width 281 cm. British Museum, WA 118873 (photo: author).

FIG. 92. Kalhu, Northwest Palace of Assurnasirpal II, BB-*a*-1 colossus. Original Drawings IV, Misc. 4 (photo: Trustees of the British Museum).

FIG. 93. Kalhu, Northwest Palace of Assurnasirpal II, B-c threshold, part 1, in situ (photo: author).

FIG. 94. Kalhu, Northwest Palace of Assurnasirpal II, B-c threshold, part 2. British Museum, WA 118924 (photo: Trustees of the British Museum).

FIG. 95. Kalhu, Northwest Palace of Assurnasirpal II, B-*d* threshold, in situ (photo: author).

FIG. 96. Kalhu, Northwest Palace of Assurnasirpal II, B-*d* threshold, detail of copper inlay(?), in situ (photo: author).

F<small>IG</small>. 97. Kalhu, Northwest Palace of Assurnasirpal II, F-*f* threshold, in situ (photo: author).

FIG. 98. Kalhu, Northwest Palace of Assurnasirpal II, G-*a* threshold, in situ (photo: author).

FIG. 99. Kalhu, Northwest Palace of Assurnasirpal II, H-*b* threshold, in situ (photo: author).

FIG. 100. Kalhu, Northwest Palace of Assurnasirpal II, M-*a* threshold, in situ (photo: author).

FIG. 101. Kalhu, Northwest Palace of Assurnasirpal II, M-niche pavement, in situ (photo: author).

FIG. 102. Kalhu, Northwest Palace of Assurnasirpal II, N/P threshold, in situ (photo: author).

FIG. 103. Kalhu, Northwest Palace of Assurnasirpal II, R-*a* threshold, in situ (photo: author).

FIG. 104. Kalhu, Northwest Palace of Assurnasirpal II, S-*a* threshold, in situ (photo: author).

FIG. 105. Kalhu, Northwest Palace of Assurnasirpal II, T-*a* threshold, in situ (photo: author).

FIG. 106. Kalhu, Northwest Palace of Assurnasirpal II, unknown threshold (W?-*b*?), in situ (photo: author).

FIG. 107. Nineveh, Southwest Palace of Sennacherib, Court H, Door *c* , width 345 cm, in situ (photo: author).

FIG. 108. Nineveh, Southwest Palace of Sennacherib, Court H, Door *a*, text panels from south bull, width ca. 4.6 m. British Museum, WA 118815a+b, 118821 (photo: author).

FIG. 109. Nineveh, Southwest Palace of Sennacherib, Court H, throne-room façade, Bulls 1 and 3, combined width 12.81 m, in situ (photo: author).

FIG. 110. Nineveh, Southwest Palace of Sennacherib, Court H, throne-room façade, Bulls 10 and 12. Original Drawings I, 33 (photo: Trustees of the British Museum).

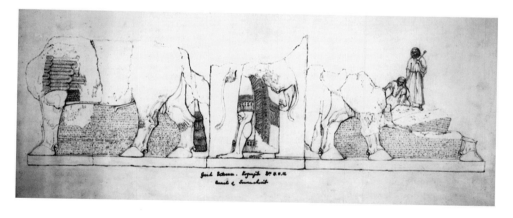

FIG. 111. Nineveh, Southwest Palace of Sennacherib, Room I, Door *d*, Bull 2. L. W. King photograph of colossus in situ, 1903–4 (photo: Trustees of the British Museum).

FIG. 112. Nineveh, Southwest Palace of Sennacherib, Room I, Door e, bull colossi, width 525 cm, in situ (photo: author).

FIG. 113. Nineveh, Southwest Palace of Sennacherib, Court VI, Door *a*, bull colossus, width 420 cm, in situ (photo: author).

FIG. 114. Nineveh, Southwest Palace of Sennacherib, fragment of colossus inscription(?) stored in Room V, width 39 cm (photo: author).

Index